Film Scriptwriting

A Practical Manual

Second Edition

Dwight V. Swain
with
Joye R. Swain

Focal Press
Boston   London

Focal Press is an imprint of Butterworth–Heinemann.

Library of Congress Cataloging-in-Publication Data

Swain, Dwight V.
   Film scriptwriting: a practical manual, 2nd ed.

   Bibliography: p.
   Includes index.
   1. Motion picture authorship.   I. Swain, Joye R.
II. Title.
PN1996.S9   1988   808.2'3   88-7005
ISBN 0-240-51190-5

British Library Cataloguing in Publication Data

Swain, Dwight, V.
   Film scriptwriting: a practical manual, 2nd ed.
   1. Cinema films. Scripts. Composition—Manuals
   I. Title   II. Swain, Joye R.
   808.2'3

   ISBN 0-240-51190-5

Butterworth–Heinemann
80 Montvale Avenue
Stoneham, MA 02180

10

Printed in the United States of America

CONTENTS

Contents

Preface to the Second Edition

The scriptwriting scene has changed since the first edition of this book appeared in 1976. And all nay-saying to the contrary, the change is for the better.

Specifically, the world increasingly is geared to audiovisual presentation. Once virtually a monopoly of the entertainment industry, film today is in major measure the medium of choice for communication in business, in industry, in education, in public relations. The home without a TV set is today a rarity. Add satellite transmission, commercial and cable television, videotape, and the proliferation of VHS and Beta units, and you find viewers in planes in flight, ships at sea, and the most remote villages of India and Brazil.

Technological change also has revolutionized the production end of the business. Faster films, videotape and videodisc recording, more effective and easily transportable lights, and computerized editing equipment have improved quality. And while multi-million dollar budgets still get headlines, the fact is that across the board this improved technology has made it possible to put films on the screen more easily and at lower cost.

That same technology permits inexpensive projection and/or viewing systems to be widely available. Even real estate offices, hospitals, and small country schools have VCR units. And the simplicity of inserting a cassette of videotape versus threading film through a projector means that showing is easier and less liable to the failures which used to plague film showings.

In consequence of all this, the demand for product is approaching the fantastic, to the point that studios producing the traditional theatrical release film no longer hold anything resembling a monopoly on the field. TV movies-of-the-week, series and miniseries, four-walled independent productions, and home and sponsored video have opened the gates of opportunity for an army of talented young people in both the entertainment and informational areas.

The importance of this to the man or woman staking his/her all on creative pencil or pen or typewriter or word processor can hardly be overestimated. For undergirding each project in the onrushing flood lies a script, and someone must of necessity conceive and write it. So while pessimists will tell you how the Writer's Guild registers multi-thousand scripts a year at a time when the industry produces only hundreds, the fact remains that today each of the 50 states (plus a fair number of counties, cities, dependencies, and even the Navajo Nation) maintains some sort of office designed to lure producers. A check of your classified telephone directory will show you that Louisville, KY, lists seven producers, and Little Rock, AR, boasts nine, while Portland, OR, checks in with 42, Kansas City, MO, with 19, and Atlanta, GA, with 54. In the major centers like New York, Los Angeles, and Chicago, the companies run into the hundreds. I myself have helped with scripts and productions in Canada, Mexico, Belize, and Costa Rica. So though chances to script *War and Peace, Apocalypse Now,* or *Gone with the Wind* may be few and far between, there's work to be done, assignments to be had, and money to be made.

The result is that while only a handful of writers in the field will ever achieve fame or riches, ever so many do manage to make an adequate-to-excellent living; and a considerable number even attain the independence and satisfaction of producing features.

It also helps that today it's easier for the would-be scriptwriter to learn how to do his/her job competently than at any time in the past. Courses in both scripting and production are found in well-nigh every state, and chances to break in at the bottom even appear with a fair degree of regularity in metropolitan newspaper employment ads.

Where this book is concerned, I can only say that it's the one I wish I'd had 40 years ago, when I first tackled scripting. Then, just to find a sample script from which to learn format was a major problem. Mastering technique and structure involved an achingly long process of trial and error.

To shorten—though certainly it can't eliminate—such apprenticeship, I've tried to keep *Film Scriptwriting* truly a practical manual, with instruction from men and women whose knowledge of the field is both up to date and grounded in experience. The "Lessons from the Pros" chapter includes excerpts from two Academy Award–winning scripts, as well as from the script of the best-selling non-fiction video tape to date. A new chapter, "The Other Side," offers comments on scripts and scripting from a director of theatrical and network television films, a manager of a major video production facility, a story editor of television series, a producer of home video entertainment films, and a story analyst's report on a novel proposed for film adaptation.

Where the body of the book is concerned, a good many points have been clarified and sharpened in response to questions raised by readers of the first edition. A fair number of new examples, twists, and techniques have also been introduced. In large degree, however, the contents remain the same. Why? Because the principles of drama remain the same. So, by and large, does format; and awareness that production technology is in a constant and continuing state of flux is more to the point than belaboring details of new developments that will be out of date tomorrow.

A note on language, sexist and otherwise: Most of the time, I simply find it convenient to stick with common usage and say "he" when I mean "a human being," or "housewife" rather than "housespouse." I've stood solidly for women's rights where it counted, in terms of equal pay for equal work, for more than half a century, so please don't label me a male chauvinist pig too quickly. Actions, I feel, are more important than deforming or convoluting verbal gender.

A final item: This new edition carries an additional byline. My wife, herself an outstanding scriptwriter of training, documentary, and travel films, has made such insightful contributions to *Film Scriptwriting* this time around that I'd be less than fair and evenhanded if I didn't give her proper credit—even if she'd let me get away with it.

Meanwhile, I'm human enough to take more than a little satisfaction when readers send me copies of scripts they've sold, or credit this book with helping them to job success or solving problems.

I hope this new edition helps you on your way as it has them. Good luck!

*   *   *

As in the first edition, acknowledgements and expressions of appreciation are due to those who have helped with, or granted permission to use their material in, this new version of *Film Scriptwriting*.

To Wes Craven and New Line Cinema for excerpts from *Nightmare on Elm Street;* to Nicolas Noxon and The National Geographic Society for excerpts from *Secrets of the Titanic;* to Oliver Stone and Ixtlan, Inc., for excerpts from *Platoon;* to Benjamin S. Walker and the U.S. Postal Service for excerpts from *Internal Crime Prevention;* to Colin Welland, David Puttnam, and Enigma Productions, Ltd., for excerpts from *Chariots of Fire;* to Charles A. Palmer and Parthenon Pictures for excerpts from *The Gullies;* to Jack Turley for excerpts from *Terror on the Fortieth Floor;* and to Beth Sullivan, Oliver Crawford, and Twentieth Century Fox Film Corporation for story coverage of *The Wednesday Night Killers*.

For interviews, to Judy Burns, Burt Kennedy, Christopher Lewis, Barry Perelman, Richard Thorp, and Dale Launer.

For advice and assistance in ways beyond naming, the Writers' Guild of America, west, Inc.; Mary Nell Clark and the Oklahoma Film Board; Charles Nedwin Hockman, professor of journalism and director of motion picture production, University of Oklahoma; Robert L. and Wanda Duncan and Maureen McGivern, scriptwriters; Gerald Dorey, former commissioning editor, Focal Press; and Gillian Hartnoll, Head of Library Services, British Film Institute.

For help in obtaining permissions, Robert F. Marshall and Jill L. Smith of Greenberg, Glusker, Fields, Clamen, and Machtinger; Carol F. Tilton, Twentieth Century Fox Film Corporation Legal Department; Neil Freedman, Legal Department, New Line Cinema; Michael Lynne, Blumenthal and Lynne; and Joseph M. Blanton, Jr., Permissions Department, National Geographic Society.

Very special thanks go to Arlyn Powell, Karen Speerstra, and Philip Sutherland of Focal Press for their encouragement and support.

And to all my students and participants in the workshops and seminars I've conducted throughout the years for their questions and comments which led to my thinking through problems and how to explain and present them to beginning writers.

Dwight Swain passed away in early 1992, as *Film Scriptwriting: A Practical Manual, Second Edition* neared its fourth printing. The Publisher joins his family in mourning the loss of a gifted writer, teacher, and friend. His creative talents, insights into the writing process, and ability to inspire writers everywhere will be sorely missed.

FOREWORD:

Before We Start

Just what should you expect from a book on film scriptwriting? Answer: Tools.

Let me elaborate. Too many years ago, I took a job as scriptwriter for a producer of informational films despite the fact I'd never seen a film script.

What followed was a groping, nerve-gnawing nightmare. Endlessly, it seemed, I ran pictures back and forth through a battered Bell & Howell projector, trying to figure out what made them tick. On the side, I carried lights, dressed sets, played cable boy, and on occasion swept the editing room floor. When I came upon Vladimir Nilsen's *The Cinema as a Graphic Art* and V. I. Pudovkin's *Film Technique and Film Acting* in the local library, it rated as a major breakthrough. The Calvin Company's annual production workshop in Kansas City had me shaking with excitement, even while I begged scripts from any and all in order to get some idea of proper format.

This is a process called learning the hard way. I don't recommend it.

Eventually, I discovered that writing a successful film script is not one thing, but many; for writing is a process made up of an infinity of sub-processes. "Learning to write" means learning how to go through the steps involved in such sub-processes with facility, and how to relate these various sub-processes to each other and to incorporate them into an integrated whole.

Three elements are involved in such learning: work, luck, and talent.

Why do I give work first place? Because it stands as far and away the most important of the trio. As the old line has it, the way to learn to write is by writing. Given enough time, enough patience, enough practice, even the most inept novice will improve. No amount of talk or theory or study can substitute for it.

Though its role is secondary, luck, too, plays a major role in writing. Call it serendipity, if you will: the faculty for stumbling onto the things you need even when you aren't hunting for them; the blind, unmotivated impulse that leads you to read the right book, talk to the right person, juxtapose the right words or ideas, capture the right insight. And let no one laugh at such a notion who hasn't awakened in the middle of the night with the perfect solution to a problem, then drifted off to sleep again—only to find when he got up that the thought had vanished.

What about talent?

Well, what about it? Obviously, some of us have greater aptitude than others, whether the area involved be auto mechanics or violin playing or bread-baking.

Or writing.

Why this should be so remains open to question, and really doesn't matter anyhow. After all, and regardless of who wins the arguments about heredity versus conditioning, you have to start where you are; work with what you've got. Certainly it's nice to have some sort of built-in facility and/or insight at your fingertips. But I can assure you from a fair amount of experience at both writing and teaching that minimal talent plus work will carry you infinitely farther than maximum aptitude lackadaisically applied.

So where does that leave you—you, beginning scriptwriter?

Not too badly off, really. Mostly, what you need is a willingness to acknowledge that you *are* a beginner: a man or woman essaying a creative task that calls for skills you've never mastered.

That being the case, what you need is less theory and generalization than specific, concrete, step-by-step procedures. Whether the approaches and devices you acquire are the ultimate "best" for their purpose is unimportant, for "best" is a tricky concept—that mode of handling that constitutes perfection for one person may prove awkward to the point of uselessness to another. What counts is discovering some way—any way—of coping with your problems effectively. —The simpler, the better. Later on, as you gain experience, you'll dig out methods optimally suited to your own taste and temperament. Now, what you need is much more basic: down-to-earth tools to help you get your job done.

So. That's what this book is all about: tools, scriptwriting tools and how to use them. And it matters not at all that some old hand takes umbrage and cries, "But that's not the way *I* do it!" or that ten years from now you'll smile wryly at the idea that these procedures once were your standbys, for by then you'll know yourself and your craft a full ten years better.

Meanwhile, day by day and step by step, these techniques will help you turn out solid scripts.

Good luck, friends! It's from the heart.

CHAPTER 1

Film and You

One of the nicest things about film scriptwriting is that it offers not just a living, but a way of life which allows you to make full use of your potential.

In addition, if you're cut out for it, it can prove a tremendous lot of fun.

Next question: What do you need to become a film scriptwriter? Seven things:

1. The kind of rhinoceros hide and iron backbone that won't take "no" for an answer.
2. The ability to become excited about any subject on ten minutes' notice—or no notice at all.
3. Resilience on a level that enables you to take the worst punch in the teeth or knife in the back where your ego is concerned and still come up affable and smiling.
4. Conscience of a brand that keeps you dedicated to making the best of a bad job, even when your every atom churns with resentment/ disappointment.
5. An understanding of how to make the most of your creative talent.
6. A decision as to the area in which you wish to work.
7. A knowledge of the scriptwriter's ground rules and technical devices.

Does this mean that if you have these attributes, success is automatically assured you?

Oh, come, now! Becoming a film scriptwriter is one thing; becoming a *successful* film scriptwriter, a rather different matter.

You see, in this life there's an element known as competition. Certain things loom as desirable—things like high pay, congenial work, ego satisfaction. In consequence, more people want them than can get them.

1

Result: survival of the fittest . . . an unhappy state, for many, in view of the fact that "fittest" may, upon occasion, mean anything from pure genius to possession of an uncle with an inside track. But that's the way of the world, as they say, and the ability to face it and fight it is part of the stubbornness and resilience on which we focused in points 1 and 3 above.

On the other hand, breaks alone can carry you only so far, especially where scriptwriting is concerned. How much success you achieve in the long haul will depend pretty much on your own ability as a writer . . . your ability, plus the seven points listed above, that is.

So, what about those points? Let's consider them one at a time.

1. The kind of rhinoceros hide and iron backbone that won't take "no" for an answer.

If your father is a major movie star, a top director, a seven-figure investor in a film company or a company that buys films, it's quite possible your desire to become a scriptwriter will win a reasonably warm reception. Agents will agree to read your efforts. Producers will chat with you over drinks. A director may even go so far as to take you under his wing; hire you for some minor job so you can observe the process and problems of film making at first hand.

You understand, they still won't buy your scripts or hire you as a writer; not unless said scripts are in and of themselves of top quality, fully up to the level of the competition. Film production is far too expensive a proposition for it to be otherwise. But, you *will* have a built-in "in"—a breach of sorts in the towering walls which otherwise seem to surround the motion picture market.

Most of us, for better or worse, have no such entrée. In consequence, we have no choice but to storm the barricades on our own.

There are easier tasks, believe me. For one thing, scripts submitted by mail ordinarily come back unopened. (I'll explain why in Chapter 16.)

So, you have to shoot angles, start on a different level. Maybe that means doing films on your own, in Super 8 or whatever, in hopes someone will recognize your talent. Or taking film courses in schools that bring in people from the industry to lecture. Or scraping acquaintances with studio personnel, on the theory that sooner or later you'll meet someone with the authority to buy scripts. Or taking jobs as page boy or typist or sweeper, in order to scrape up such acquaintances.

I wish I could pretend that any or all of these approaches held your answer. Unfortunately, they don't. Scriptwriting is a rough field to crack, and for every writer working, there are a dozen struggling to survive with part-time jobs outside the field.

What it comes down to is that *if* you learn the ropes, and *if* you persevere, and *if* you have the writing skill, then maybe—just "maybe," mind you—you'll eventually make the grade.

This doesn't discourage you? Good! Because if you *can* be discouraged, you're better off not to start. Only if the writing of film scripts enthralls you to the point that you can't be stopped do you have any business in this field.

2. The ability to become excited about any subject on ten minutes' notice—or no notice at all.

A friend of mine, half of a husband/wife team long prominent in the ranks of TV and film writers, once told me, "One thing I know. In this business, can you do it in a hurry counts for a lot more than can you do it good." Then he added, "You can't imagine how many jobs we've cinched because we could leave a conference, bounce ideas off each other for five minutes in the reception room, and then walk back in with a fresh angle."

My own experience in the fact-film field echoes that in spades. I have, on numerous occasions, discovered on entering a meeting that someone had billed me as being wild to do a script on quail-hunting, or the acidizing of oil wells, or promotion of a backwoods women's college. Once, even, my phone rang and when I answered I found I was talking to a psychiatrist who wanted a film scripted from a citation in a medical text. On another occasion, a feature producer thrust an abstract painting at me and was shocked when my interpretation of it as a springboard to a film didn't match his.

The point? You'd better be fast on your feet, Jack, and this is no field for negative thinkers.

3. Resilience on a level that enables you to take the worst punch in the teeth or knife in the back where your ego is concerned and still come up affable and smiling.

This is the morning after a week in which you've worked your heart out to build a really spectacular angle for the bright new producer of a science fiction film. He listens while you try to sell it . . . then informs you he isn't interested in "hack work" or "linear thinking" and exercises his right to cut you off the job.

The technical consultant on an industrial relations film accuses you of being a "racist bastard" because you've differentiated two characters in your script by labeling one a Serbian, the other an Italian.

The star of a feature finds your very presence so distasteful that she demands the director bar you from the set. Her stand-in tips you off that the real issue is that Star thinks you've given a bit player better lines than hers in a 30-second exchange.

Yes, you do need resilience!

4. *Conscience of a brand that keeps you dedicated to making the best of a bad job, even while your every atom churns with resentment/disappointment.*

The film is on deer hunting. A conservation man insists that you include a shot of a knife ripping open a doe shot out of season . . . hands lifting out a dead fawn's blood-dripping fetus. You point out it's going to make half the viewers sick, but you get nowhere.

A film on mental retardation for a national agency. A petty bureaucrat, afraid of repercussions, wants to carve the guts out of it for fear of offending one state's medical association.

A feature with a hideously weak director. The male lead continually bollixes plot lines. When you protest, the actor retorts, "George S. Kaufman never made me memorize my sides. Why should you?"

In each of these instances, you have a decision to make. Since you're not in charge, you can't control the situation. So, will you slack off and say, "The hell with it," or will you go on sweating, trying to make the film as good as you can, within the limits of your predicament?

If your answer is, "The hell with it"—please quit before you start. This business has enough eight-balls already. Which is not to say you may not withdraw or demand that your name be taken from the credits, upon occasion. The man I'm objecting to is the one who stays on the job but quits trying.

5. *An understanding of how to make the most of your creative powers.*

It goes without saying that a film scriptwriter must above all be creative. Creativity is one of the major—if not *the* major—tools in his craft-kit.

Some people, obviously, are more creative than others.

It's also a fact, however, that most of us can become infinitely more creative than we are, if we learn how to make the most of our abilities.

The creative person, you see, is one somehow conditioned to make multiple responses to single stimuli. That is, he tends to have a variety of reactions to whatever he perceives. Most often, he's not even conscious that he does this. But—spontaneously, habitually—it's become an integral part of his overall pattern of behavior to operate in this manner.

Thus, consider a candlestick. The non-creative among us see it for what it is and nothing more—as some sort of holder with a socket for a candle.

The creative person, on the other hand, looks beyond this obvious function to see the candlestick's further potentials, based on its size, shape, material, components, relationship to the room and its furnishings, and so on. So if I ask him to devise ten ways to murder someone with a candlestick, odds are that sooner or later he'll come up with something fresh and original, simply because he's formed the habit of envisioning more than one possibility per situation.

You, in turn, can through practice train yourself to apply this same principle to every phase of your writing. If a character seems trite and obvious, *make a list* of half a dozen ways you might increase his individuality via unique goals, background, attitudes, appearance, mannerisms, speech, or what have you. Look at *Tootsie*, with the hero in drag, or the characterization of Sherlock Holmes as a boy in *Young Sherlock Holmes*. *Continental Divide* features an outdoor heroine who dominates woods and mountains, while the man, at home on city streets, is unable to take care of himself in the wilds. *Ruthless People* sees Bette Middler, a kidnap victim, terrorizing her captors. Does a dialogue passage sound dull? Try different lines—a dozen of them! Let the little old lady carry a switchblade in her reticule, or the preacher's wife sleep around. How about a monster of a man who faints at the sight of blood? The bathing beauty who's scared of water? The tycoon who can't read? (Pardon me—better skip that last one; Somerset Maugham built a classic short story around it!)

Similarly, your film's key statement may be dull or it may be spritely (or provocative, or profound, or what have you). Your own taste and judgment will be the deciding factor. Given "What about Susie Schnickelfritz's party?" as a central question, you may come up with answers ranging from "Seven close friends attended" to "Any birthday can be a disaster, if Susie bakes the cake!"

But remember, it takes practice to change habit patterns. Get in the swing of creative thinking *before* crucial need for it arises. To that end, look for faces in clouds. Compare people with animals as to manners or appearance. Devise outrageously appropriate replies to propriety's questions—even if you don't have the nerve to voice them. Leave a movie two-thirds through the picture, set up five possible endings of your own, and then go back for the next performance and see if the scriptwriter resolved the situation as cleverly.

Do keep the fitness of things in mind, however. That is, be sure your characters—whether people, products, or principles—stay in character. Don't throw your picture out of kilter with shock for shock's sake. You'll still have plenty of room to move around, once you learn to devise a variety of fresh handlings—via lists—for every mundane circumstance.

6. A decision as to the area in which you wish to work.

Film production today is a fantastically big field—and all of it needs competent scriptwriters. But you're the one who has to decide which road you want to take.

Thus, there are art films, business films, documentary films, educational films, entertainment films, experimental films, government films, industrial films, medical films, promotional films, religious films, sales films, scientific films, slide films, travel films, and a host of others. Each area offers strengths and weaknesses, advantages and opportunities and headaches.

You need to find out about these various specialties: the demands they make, the rewards they offer. Here, we can strike little more than a glancing blow at an issue that warrants all sorts of study.

Where you're concerned, the important thing is not to fall prey to snap judgments, slap-dash decisions. Above all, recognize that Hollywood represents only the tip of the film world's iceberg. Other types of scriptwriting may, for you, prove far more congenial.

7. *A knowledge of the scriptwriter's ground rules and technical devices.*

By and large, all films fall into one of two categories: fact films, designed primarily to inform; and feature films, whose main purpose is to entertain. And while the degree of overlap between these two fields is great, the differences between them are sufficiently marked as to warrant giving each separate treatment.

Such being the case, I've divided this book into three major segments.

Part 1 concerns how to script fact films.

Part 2 deals with the writing of feature film scripts.

Part 3 is devoted to what I hope are practical suggestions on how to survive and prosper as a writer—especially during that crucial period when you're trying to break in; interviews with people in the script-*buying* end of the business; and examples of film script form and technique, drawn from the scripts of produced films and here presented in their typescript versions, complete with detailed comments.

I recommend that you begin your study by scanning the book in its entirety, in order to get an idea of each chapter's contents. Particularly, do *not* slight the fact film chapters because your main interest lies in features, or vice versa. Otherwise, you'll miss many things you'll need to know.

Bear in mind, too, that I, like any writer, have my own notions as to how my subject matter should be presented. Thus, the traditional approach to scriptwriting tends to act as if all scripts follow a rigid, neatly ordered pattern of development: outline, treatment, screenplay, shooting script. While in general I agree, I also see the picture as a good deal more flexible—even fluid—and so treat it in these pages.

And that's enough and too much of preliminaries. Now, let's get going . . . with a step-by-step look at how to organize a fact film.

PART ONE

THE FACT FILM

CHAPTER 2

The Proposal Outline

Just what is a fact film, anyhow?

In contrast to the theatrical release feature film, the traditional entertainment "movie," the fact film is one designed primarily to inform and/or influence and/or inspire. A "message" picture, it sells ideas in virtually every field of human knowledge. Thousands of such films are made each year, by hundreds of producing units, at a cost that runs high into the millions.

(This is where you come in, of course. Someone has to write a script for each and every one of those thousands of pictures. In consequence, opportunities for the writer are far greater than in the entertainment film field. But more of that later.)

The feature film in most cases is based on a story, fiction. It's produced in the expectation of making money directly, from paid theatre admissions.

The fact film, on the other hand, ordinarily is rooted in life, reality, nonfiction. Most often shown in classrooms, union halls, churches, club meetingrooms, and the like, it's paid for by a client/sponsor whose main object is to communicate knowledge, arouse interest, or induce belief, on topics ranging from how to increase production of telephone components to discouraging suicide to demonstrating improved methods of garbage collection. Titles from one distributor's brochure on my desk include *The California Condor, Stroke, The Wall Street Connection, Learning by Doing, Himalayan Journey,* and *Ways of Dealing with Conflict in Organizations.*

All of which is not to say that some fact films may not entertain to a greater degree than some features. Or that some features may not inform or influence more than some fact films. Or that fact films may not be designed to cash in at the box office or on TV, or that features may not stand first and foremost as propaganda.

Overall, nonetheless, the fact film zeroes in on information/influence/inspiration. To function effectively in this role, it must be properly organized.

Next question: How do you organize a fact film?

You prepare a proposal outline, a film treatment, a sequence outline, and a shooting script.

That is, sometimes you do. But sometimes you don't, for each and every producer—indeed, each and every film—tends to be a law unto himself/itself. Procedures differ from shop to shop, and if there's one item you need in your survival kit, it's flexibility.

The general principles set forth here are sound, however. Adapt them to each specific situation as it arises and you'll have no trouble.

Or at least not too much.

Back to the fact film and how to organize it:

Step 1: the proposal outline.

The idea for a film may originate with a producer, a writer, an advertising agency, within the potential client's operation, or wherever. Eventually, however, Idea has to be cast into some kind of comprehensible form.

That form in most instances is what is termed a *film proposal.*

Heart of the proposal is the *proposal outline.* Often, it's where the writer makes his first appearance, for he's likely to be the man (or woman) called upon to get the key facts down on paper.

The proposal is exactly what it sounds like—a bid to make a film. Ordinarily, it lays out the specifications for the project, and sets forth the basic concept the picture is supposed to communicate. In so doing, it establishes a foundation of agreement between client and producer . . . tells the potential sponsor what he may expect for his money, and lets the filmmaker know what he'll be called on to deliver. The document involved—that is, the proposal—may be short or long, simple or elaborate. (The trend is to the short and simple.) All points are subject to negotiation.

For you, the writer, all this probably will first come into focus at a preliminary conference, to which you've been invited by producer/agency/client. (How you get that invitation is something we'll take up in a later chapter. Same for financial arrangements and how you get your money.)

On to the conference!

Hopefully, it will be small—six or eight people at most. Big conferences tend to spell trouble. It's just too hard to work things out or get agreement when 20 or 30 participants are involved.

So: Here you are, sitting down with Client and an aide or two . . .

producer and partner . . . ad agency account executive . . . maybe a couple of other intermediaries or abettors of uncertain status.

The business of conference strategy is another item we'll take up later. Right now, for you, the issue is one of digging out certain critical information. Simply put, you need to learn three things: the topic of the proposed picture, its purpose, and who will comprise its audience. But like most things that are simply put, that tends to end up just a bit *too* simple. So let's go a step further and focus your probings into ten specific questions:

1. What's Client's purpose in making the proposed film?
2. What's the film's topic, and what does Client want to say about it?
3. Whom does he want to say it to?
4. How much does that audience already know about the topic?
5. What does Client want Audience to do when the lights come on?
6. What are the film's technical specifications, including conditions of use?
7. What's the budget?
8. Are there any particular cost factors on which Client has his heart set?
9. Who's to be your technical advisor?
10. Who has the power, the muscle, the final say?

At first glance, it would appear that some of these matters are primarily problems of the producer, rather than the writer; and first glance would be right. But experience also says Writer too had better bear them firmly in mind, lest later his neglect of matters apparently outside his bailiwick should box him into unanticipated—and uncomfortable—corners.

Now, what is there to say about each question?

1. What's Client's purpose in making the proposed film?

Shall we be blunt? There is only one reason anyone makes a fact film, and that reason is dissatisfaction. That is to say, Client wouldn't be spending his money on a picture if he were happy with the way things are, the *status quo*. Always, he seeks change . . . change in somebody's state of affairs and/or state of mind, even if the issue is only to bring new awareness of the nesting habits of the rosy-breasted pushover. To that end, he proposes to produce a picture.

This is a matter of vital concern to you, because it poses one of your major tasks: to discover what it is your client is dissatisfied with in his present situation and how he'd like to see it changed.

Unfortunately, this isn't always easy. A good place to start, however, is with the question of purpose.

Said question is one you should raise early in the meeting, pinning down what the film is supposed to achieve in the most practical terms possible: "Who do you want to do what?" "Why is this film being made?" "What are you trying to prove?" Then, listen with all three ears—and not just to Client's words.

Your answer, you see, if you're properly perceptive, will come through on at least two levels. The first will be the film's *ostensible* purpose; the other, its *true* purpose.

Ostensible purposes will be obvious indeed, and frankly stated: "We want to improve our company image." "We want to sell more widgets." "We want to help kids understand ionization." "We want to reduce crime in the streets." "We want to teach doctors how to cope with staph infections."

True purposes may prove more difficult to zero in on: "We want to make the competition look like small potatoes." "We want to do a little empire-building—corner a bigger share of next year's appropriation." "We want to take the edge off those things that damn' Congressional committee said about us." "I want to register as a comer—improve my chances for that promotion." "I want to make time with that cute doll in Department 7 by getting her a part in this picture."

Obviously, you won't always be able to pin down the true issues behind production of a film. Indeed, upon occasion you'll find situations where everything is out in the open, sans guile. But it's still important that you have your antennae up and quivering for any clues Client or his colleagues may drop as to their motives. After all, making the competition look like small potatoes may involve trying to buy $100,000 worth of cinematic flash and glamor for $30,000. Empire building or over-ambition may rouse antagonism in people in a position to sabotage the project. That cute doll in Department 7, on film, may prove an utter disaster.

Being aware of such, it's possible you can walk wide around the traps these gambits represent . . . not to mention improving your chances of preparing a script that satisfies *both* Client goals.

2. *What's the film's topic, and what does Client want to say about it?*

Every film's pattern of organization is built on the same two underpinnings: a topic and a point of view.

The topic element is simple enough. It's the answer you get when you ask, "What's this film to be about?"

Back comes the answer: "Ulcers." "Wire rope." "Executive aircraft." "Cockroaches." And there's your topic.

Point of view is something else again. Assuming there's a client/

sponsor, it's his *subjective attitude* towards the topic. You uncover it by asking, "But what *about* ulcers/wire rope/executive aircraft/cockroaches?"

Now quite obviously there are a number of possible answers to these questions. Take cockroaches, for example. Is Client for them or against them? Does he look on them as pests, or playmates, or the firm foundation on which he's built his extermination business, or potential laboratory livestock for cancer research?

Your goal as writer is to sift through all such possibilities until, ultimately, you come up with a *core assertion:* a clear, concise statement of precisely what point the film is to sell to the audience.

Again, this will not necessarily be an easy task. Client and colleagues may themselves disagree, for instance—I once ached through a college chemistry faculty's eight-hour debate as to precisely how to define the pH system for measurement of acidity and basicity of aqueous solutions. Or, no one may have thought the matter through beyond the "Let's make a movie about our new framistan" level. It's entirely possible two or three sessions may pass before you arrive at the right answer.

But then, who said writing film scripts would be easy? The big thing is that if you know what you're after and you keep plugging, sooner or later you'll come up with the right core assertion, the key point your client really wants to make: "Modern farm equipment gives you extra hours—and time is money." "Those happy, happy college days. I grew up here. I found the real me." "Get more fencerows for bobwhite. Help our quail to find an Oklahoma home."

I can't overemphasize the importance of this phase of your work. Pinning down the right core assertion takes you a giant step along the road to building a solid script, an effective film. Failing to do so is a virtual guarantee of later headaches.

Two hints: It will be to your advantage if you research your film's topic thoroughly at your earliest opportunity, both on your own and in company with your technical advisor. Only as you know your subject can you hope to capture its essence in a razor-sharp core assertion.

Also, often, it will help if you throw out hypotheses as to what Client seeks vainly to put into words: "You mean, then, that when an Indian wears one of these ceremonial masks, he feels that he and the god are one?" "So the big edge Angus have over other cattle is that they're natural polls?" "In other words, it's the man and not the gun that does the killing?"

You'll miss the target more often than not, of course. But the very fact that you've injected a fresh viewpoint has a tendency to jar Client loose from dead center. That helps him—and you—to come up with an intelligent statement that captures the heart of what your picture's all about.

3. Whom does he want to say it to?

Implicitly or explicitly, every film has a target audience—a particular group Client seeks to inform or influence or inspire, whether it be eighth grade science students, suburban Parent-Teacher Associations, potential polar bear hunters, or oil field drilling contractors.

Quite possibly you'll have trouble finding just what group this is, because Client, lost in ego inflation, will claim that "everyone" or "the general public" or "the whole Yew-nited States" is his bull's-eye.

This just won't do. You *must* narrow the field. Why? Because you'll need one mode of attack for salesmen, another for engineers, yet a third for consumers.

Further, what fascinates a network TV audience may very well drive surgeons (or artists, or numismatists, or pro football players) to snorts of disgust.

In general, the broader the audience, the harder it will be to hit it with anything meaningful. A mass audience is infinitely more interested in dramatic action than it is in content.

The narrower your audience, in turn, the greater your chances of really striking home. Tailoring your presentation to viewer interests, attitudes, and feelings, you can maximize appeal and impact.

One final point: Be sure the audience your client says he's seeking is actually the one to shoot for. Why? Because Client won't accept blame for steering you wrong if you miss the target. He'll just say the film's a failure.

Thus, once upon a time, I took on the scripting of a film for an expensive summer resort. The audience? Young swingers, the way the owner told it.

Prowling the grounds, however, I soon discovered that the clientele was middle-aged at least.

Had Client been lying to me, then?

Not really. It was just that, aging himself, he zeroed in on the younger patrons to the point that, in his mind's eye, the older majority faded to minor significance.

4. How much does the target audience already know about the topic?

The greater the prior interest of an audience in your subject, the less your need to fancy up the presentation.

Embellishing a film that's intended for an audience of experts frequently will alienate that audience. If you're writing for surgeons about a new operative technique, dragging in Dr. Kildare will outrage them.

If viewers know and/or care nothing about your topic, on the other hand, you'd better scratch around till you find a way to hook their interest. Then, *Symptomatology of Undetected Diabetes* becomes *Diabetes and You Too,* complete with a high-school girl who tires too easily to make the swimming team and a fat widowed mother looking for a husband.

Don't take it for granted that your client is correct in his assumptions about audience knowledge. He may assume too much or too little.

How does a scriptwriter learn whether his potential viewers are interested in a subject, or know about it?

He puts on his hat and goes out and asks questions of said viewers. He does *not* take it for granted that their tastes and level of information are the same as his—or his client's.

Neither does he kid himself that giving heed to audience consists merely of eliminating polysyllables from narration about how to operate a new-type manure spreader.

5. What does Client want Audience to do when the lights come on?

Action—*audience* action—is ever and always your ultimate goal when you script a fact film. So it makes good sense to try to decide just *what* action will best relieve your client's dissatisfaction with the World That Is.

Perhaps Client's dream of paradise is to see Audience head en masse for a mobile chest x-ray clinic. Or to watch brain surgeons step into the operating theatre tomorrow morning with total confidence in their mastery of a new technique. Or a sales staff move to the attack selling boxer shorts. Or customers clutch pens in frantic haste to sign insurance policy applications.

Isn't this all the same as film purpose? No, not quite. Purpose tends to drift up into generality and abstraction on occasion. "What do you want the audience to do when the lights come on?" yanks goals back down to earth.

6. What are the film's technical specifications, including conditions of use?

Is this picture to be sound or silent? Narrated or lip sync? Color or b&w? Live action or animation? 8mm, Super 8, 16mm, 35mm, 70mm? What length? Under what conditions will the film be shown? Do facilities exist to bring it to the target audience?

Yes, you do need to know these things. They'll have an influence on the kind of script you write.

Thus, shooting lip-synchronized sound involves an infinity of problems absent in the narrated film. For one, you the writer have to come up with acceptable dialogue! A five-minute picture can be highly effective for some topics; impossible for others. Color can make some pictures—yet spoil a mood piece. Sound seldom is the best when a 16mm print is shown in theatre-size facilities. The list goes on and on.

7. *What's the budget?*

Here the main part of your function will be to keep quiet while Client and Producer wrestle this weighty question. But you do need to pay attention, because the size of the budget will play a large role indeed in determining what you can or can't include in your script for the forthcoming epic. Awareness now will help you to avoid shocks later. But more of that elsewhere.

8. *Are there any particular cost factors on which Client has his heart set?*

In general, this too is a matter which you can leave to the producer. But you do need to keep your ears open.

Consider, for example, the client who stands fast in his determination to have key scenes shot at his cabin in the woods, where the sun and a Coleman lantern are the only sources of light. But that's all right, because Client wants this to be a historical sequence, featuring Abe Lincoln's boyhood and starring Bob Hope as the friendly neighbor—you know how name talent adds audience interest! And then, of course, Client really wouldn't mind if you included *him* in a few brief bridging scenes; after all, his stutter isn't *that* bad. . . .

Well, you get the idea.

9. *Who's to be your technical advisor?*

Now hear this: *There's no such thing as a film on which you don't need a technical advisor.*

That is to say, some people have more expertise in a given area than do others.

Expertise is a thing you need, even if the film you're scripting is a saga of a freshman's college year, *A Trip to the Zoo with Jen and Jerry,* or the doings of a housewife in her native habitat. So insist that your client assign you an appropriate technical advisor—a man or woman who knows the film's topic intimately and has the ability and willingness to talk about it freely.

How can a good technical advisor help you?

Well, he can save you endless hours of research, for one thing. He can catch slips which otherwise would make you look like a fool and maybe cost you future assignments. He can clue you in on company/organization/agency personalities, policies, problem areas. He can brief you on specialized terms, help you brighten narration or dialogue with "insider" touches. Oh, there are so many things he can do!

To manage all these chores, however, he's going to have to be the right person—one who's interested enough in your project to want to help.

Your client, in turn, must be willing to make this paragon available to you, so that you can reach him when you need him. An international authority is worthless if it takes you three days to get an appointment, or if he never seems able to spare you more than five minutes.

Public relations types may prove splendid technical aides, or they may be a total waste of time. It all depends on whether they really know the operation. My own all-time favorite tech advisor was a metallurgical engineer who'd transferred to Sales.

Have your technical advisor assigned before you leave Meeting No. 1. It can make all the difference between a good, pleasant, profitable job of which you can be proud, and a financial disaster on which you want to slash your wrists.

10. Who has the power, the muscle, the final say?

Whether your client be a business, an industry, a governmental unit, an association, or what have you, know in advance that a pecking order exists within it.

It's important to you to determine precisely who speaks with the voice of authority where your script is concerned. Failure to do so can have horrifying results, in terms of your doing your work under the impression that one man is in command, when actually another has the final say. As a case in point, I once worked up an entire treatment for a group I falsely assumed represented an organization, only to have the treasurer, who viewed them as dissidents, refuse to pay a nickel for it.

Along this line, it should be mentioned that at all stages of any script work, it is highly desirable—indeed essential—to get approval signatures from the client; and to make it clear in your contract or letter of agreement that later deviations from such approved handling will result in increased charges.

*   *   *

At last the preliminary conference is over. You go away and do some thinking; some checking with your technical advisor.

Part of your cogitations should be devoted to a question too often slighted: Is this material best presented on film?

It would be nice, you see, if film were the answer to everybody's problems. Regrettably, sometimes it doesn't work that way. If you, the writer, are to keep out of hot water and impossible assignments, you need to know the factors to consider.

Thus, film has these advantages:

a. Film shows motion.

A horse running, a machine operating, a fight in progress—all come through vividly on the screen.

b. Film reveals what the eye can't see.

With time-lapse photography, you can watch a year of plant growth in a minute. Slow motion reveals how the magician performs his sleight. Animation lets you see the moving parts within an engine.

c. Film transcends time and space.

It enables you to stretch a minute to ten or reduce it to nothing . . . to jump from the North Pole to the South, from New York to London to Moscow to Peking.

d. Film enables you to pinpoint the exact audience you want.

If you prefer that only psychiatrists or coffee shop managers or demolitions experts view a picture, you can so stipulate. Many films have been made whose sole audience was to be a seven-man board of directors or the president of a company.

e. Film is reusable.

Which same is why live TV drama went down the drain. Once a play's filmed, you can run it over and over, not to mention selling or renting prints to each new station as it opens. Similarly, fact films can be shown to generation after generation of school children, to each new group of employees, and so on.

f. Film repeats accurately.

This obviously is a tremendous advantage. Memory is fallible, and no speaker does precisely the same job every time. So, if you're a college football coach, you don't need to rely on your recollections of last week's game. Good and bad plays, filmed and shown in slow motion, can help you pinpoint errors and devise more effective strategy.

g. Film is visual.

The importance of this comes into focus when you realize that assorted studies indicate human beings learn at least 75 per cent by sight.

h. Film may have color or sound.

Color isn't always an unmixed blessing, but there certainly are some things you can't show properly without it—the look of growing grain, for instance; or diseased tissue vs. normal; or paintings, fashions, hair colors, etc.

Sound, in turn, may change the whole world film reveals, as well as our reactions to it—witness the horrors perpetrated via TV laugh tracks.

i. Film emphasizes, emotionalizes.

By filling the screen with the right details, you can create virtually any feeling you want in an audience. Consider the World War 2 German newsreels used to soften up countries soon to be invaded: Their graphic portrayal of the destruction wrought by Panzer divisions and Stuka dive-bombers so terrified viewers that they fled at the first rumor of attack.

j. Film may offer extra attention value.

A good case in point is film or video tape in suitcase units that include both projector/player and screen/CRT. "I want to show you a film," says the salesman who brings it. "The time involved will be precisely ten minutes. If you're not interested in my proposition after you see the picture, I'll leave without a word." An incredibly high proportion of the time, the prospect will agree . . . which clears the way for a 10-minute presentation put together by master sales psychologists and seen sans interruptions by secretaries or phone calls.

So much for film's advantages. Now, what about the disadvantages?

These break down into three categories: subject factors, production factors, and use factors.

a. Subject factors.

(1) STATICITY. . . . which is just a fancy way of saying the subject doesn't move. Consequently, film's wasted on it, even though *camera* movement may lend it some air of vitality. An example? Consider the film which shows a painting. True, you can zoom in on specific details or pan across it while a narrator comments, voice over. But the subject is still static, still poorly adapted to filmic treatment.

(2) COMPLEXITY. Your topic is *The Causes of Poverty.* Granted, you can make a film about it. But the problem itself is so complex, so subject to controversy, that you can deal with it only by resorting to a simplistic treatment that does it less than justice or even distorts the facts. There's just too much ground to cover in one picture. So, either break it down into smaller bites or leave it alone.

(3) SIMULTANEITY. Remember *The Thomas Crown Affair,* or the *Mannix* titles? Using split screen techniques, several pictures are shown to the viewer at the same time. While gimmicky and often fascinating for the moment, such tends to confuse more than to enlighten in many cases. If you can break the simultaneous element down into a series of *sequential* developments ("This happens . . . and, meanwhile, this is hap-pening . . . and this . . . and this . . ."), fine. But if you have to show 17 things happening at once and there's no way of separating or cate-gorizing them, forget it.

(4) LENGTH. Much as in the case of complex subjects, you some-

times are confronted with topics which demand such a length of film (and running time) as to make them impractical—and this in spite of the fact that, upon occasion, the entire history of the United States has been compressed into a three-minute montage.

Consider, for example, various psychological/psychiatric case studies. Months—perhaps years—of psychotherapy are involved, with little clear-cut progress at any given moment. Any film you make of such will either have to oversimplify, or to deteriorate into an Andy Warhol sleeping-the-happy-hours-away movie.

(5) ABSTRACTION. Art has a concept called "negative space." But I'd hate to have to film it. Same for the philosophy of Zen or statistical analysis.

Understand, films can—and probably have—been made in defiance of virtually every one of these factors. But they do complicate the writer's life by forcing him to oversimplify or to make use of strained parallels or false analogies.

b. Production factors.

(1) COST. No doubt about it, movie-making costs money. But more important than cost itself, by far, is the ratio of expense to return. In other words, it doesn't matter if a neo-*Cleopatra* costs $50 million, if the box office returns total $250 million. On the other hand, a $15,000 industrial film may prove a disaster for a small company's public relations man if the firm's president secretly views the whole project as a needless frill and is anticipating a bill for $5,000.

(2) TECHNICAL DIFFICULTIES. Closely related to cost is the fact that virtually anything in this world can be filmed if you're willing to spend enough money. But entirely apart from expense, if a crane shot is essential in a factory sequence and you haven't got a crane, you're in trouble. Even a baby elephant that refuses to behave can throw your budget—and story line—out of kilter, as I once witnessed during the filming of an episode of Ziv's old *Science Fiction Theatre*.

(3) TIME PROBLEMS. A friend of mine was forced out of the film business because he hadn't given proper weight to the fact that the writer of a picture he'd contracted to produce had set sequences in each of the four seasons—which meant production was going to have to extend over an entire year.

Similarly, it may prove impractical to schedule filming of a particular rock festival, to obtain the services of a particular actor for a particular time, or to push through the editing or processing of a film to meet a deadline.

Any number of producers have bucked these odds, you understand. But you do need to consider them before you sign on to do a script.

c. Use factors.

(1) LACK OF VIEWING FACILITIES. Most of us take screens and projectors for granted. It's a mistake. The sheepherder or pipeline walker your film is designed to influence may never get to see it, simply because there's no place to show it. In the same way, many educational films win few viewings because teachers don't want to bother with requisitioning, setting up, learning to operate, and operating projectors.

Or how about the picture shown in a packed union hall, with the air conditioning turned off because it interferes with the sound? And that's not even mentioning lack of competent projectionists, erratic power sources, broken film stuck together with cellulose tape, and a dozen other potential disaster areas.

When VHS units are available, problems may arise involving screens too small for the entire viewing audience to see easily, poor light and sound quality, poor lighting in the viewing area, inadequate sound for large viewing areas, and small, indistinct images on the screens.

(2) LACK OF PRINTS. You know about a good film on some phase of chemistry, or algebra, or history. You'd like to show it to your pupils. But can you get a print when you need it, or will you have to wait till the class is seven weeks past the topic? For my own part, when I was teaching scriptwriting at the University of Oklahoma, at least half the pictures I wanted to show students as classic examples of particular techniques had been withdrawn from circulation. (Today, however, this is less of a headache, simply because video tapes are so accessible, inexpensive to purchase or rent, and easy to store.)

(3) PROBLEM AUDIENCES. How do you show a film—effectively, that is—to an audience that doesn't speak the narrator's language? How do you show it to primitives in New Guinea who haven't yet learned to see in two dimensions and so view the images on the screen as mere flickering shadows? How do you show it to Kurd tribesmen who've never seen or heard of a refrigerator and so don't know what the one in the film is for? How do you show it to guerrilla-indoctrinated *campesinos* who think the film is part of an imperialist plot against them?

Summing up, then, film is a great thing—but not at all times nor in all situations. Sometimes the smartest thing you can do when someone comes to you with a great idea—and yes, he *does* have money and *is* prepared to pay you—is to forget film in favor of still pix, slides, a brochure, or even just a simple sheet of printed instructions.

Now, three frequently raised questions:

1. Is it really necessary to organize a film completely before the shooting starts?

Or, to put it more bluntly, why bother to write a script at all? Why not just go out and shoot whatever footage comes handy and worry about organization later?

No, this is not a rhetorical issue. The world is full of would-be filmmakers eager to plunge into production with no time wasted on pre-planning.

Trouble is, any writer could retire on the money spent by befuddled clients on "shot-off-the-cuff" films that never reached the screen. For there's more—much more—to making any film than simply shooting pictures. Both time and money enter, and the question that always arises is what shots to shoot, how to shoot them, and in what order to arrange them *in order to end up with an effective film.*

There, of course, is the issue. It's easy enough to make a fact film. But to make an *effective* one—in terms of audience, purpose, and client satisfaction—is something else again.

The shot-off-the-cuff film begins by being wasteful. Instead of tying up the time of one man—the writer—it ties up the time of an entire crew. Then, lacking a carefully laid-out script—which is to say, lacking adequate pre-planning—it racks up fantastic bills for raw stock and processing.

Later, when editing time comes, this waste grows even greater because, lacking a clear-cut concept and chain of logic, it's hard to put the thing together. In addition, many vital shots are bound to turn up missing, simply because no one realized that this closeup would prove essential, or that jump cut would require a covering cutaway.

Finally, like a joke told by an inept comic, all too often the whole thing somehow ends up both looking like amateur night and missing the point the client wanted to make.

Yes, it *is* important to organize a film as completely as possible before the shooting starts!

2. Doesn't this kind of pre-planning limit the director's creativity— his opportunities for improvisation, capturing the insights and inspirations of the moment?

Alfred Hitchcock speaking: "When I hear of a man shooting a film off the cuff, making it up as he goes along, I think it's like a composer composing a symphony before a full orchestra. I like to improvise in an office, not on a stage in front of a hundred technicians."

Actually, of course, having a well-planned script is a help rather than a hindrance to a competent director. In the first place, in all like-lihood he'll have worked with the writer and/or studied the script in detail, incorporating his own pet notions in the process. In the second, he'll still be able to improvise within the framework of the script, should something that develops on the set or location give him a fresh idea.

The only thing he's really barred from doing is based on the ethics of his relationship to the client. That is, he shouldn't abandon the script's plan of action, its line of development. That plan, that line, has been worked out with painstaking care so that it makes the client's point. To throw it out the window during filming is to betray the trust the client has placed in him.

3. *What do you as a scriptwriter do when you find yourself stuck with a pre-shot film?*

A film shot without a script, that is; and yes, it *does* happen, and writers *are* called in to help cope with the problem. In fact, often it's an entirely legitimate situation: The circumstances were such that it simply wasn't possible to plan things in advance, as in the case of some friends of mine who spent six weeks with the Lacandon Indians of Chiapas, four days on foot from the nearest road. They had no real idea of what they'd find when they arrived, so they flew by the seat of their pants, as it were—shot footage of everything that looked interesting and hoped it could be cut into some kind of meaningful pattern later.

Similarly, you some day may find yourself confronted with 9,000 feet—four hours plus—of 16mm film taken by Joe Bigbux on his African safari, or a mile or two of catch-as-catch-can shots of Guatemalan guerrillas in action, or reel after reel of coverage of the various steps in the construction of a new housing development.

You meet such challenges in much the same way you'd attack any other picture topic. That is to say, you hunt for a point of view, an angle: some kind of core assertion that makes sense and captures the idea. *But you do it within the limitations of the footage at hand.*

Thus, in the Lacandon Indian epic cited above, I ended up with the core assertion, "The Lacandones are a people trapped between two worlds." The unifying concept behind endless footage of kindergarten children was finally sifted down to "Play is children's work, a tool for growth." A mass of ill-assorted campus shots gave birth to "A school's spirit is what shapes its students' futures."

What—? You lack essential footage? Well, I agree that can be a problem. But sometimes there are ways around it. We'll take them up in a later chapter.

$$* \qquad * \qquad *$$

And so, at long last, this first phase of your thinking's done; your questions answered, your concepts organized. It's time to put your proposal down on paper.

How to go about it? A system that's worked well for me is simply to ask the producer for a copy of his favorite presentation. Then, I follow that pattern.

Make it a rule to keep your writing style as clear and simple as possible. Also, incorporate your core assertion, if you've developed one that satisfies you. (If you haven't, it's no sin to hold off on it till you write your film treatment.)

At this point, just in case you haven't found another model, a format may prove useful—not the only possible format, you understand, nor even necessarily the best. Indeed, many presentations will be much more elaborate. But a handling such as this one is acceptable in most situations.

Among items often (but not always) included are:

Heading: designation of your presentation as a proposal . . . work-
    ing title, so labeled.

Content outline: purpose of film, audience, summary of key data to
    be included.

Specifications: length, color, sound, animation or major special ef-
    fects (if any).

Shooting schedule: where and when the picture will be shot.

Production schedule: any and all deadlines, up to and including de-
    livery date for the finished film.

Budget: details as required.

Approvals: producer, client, dates.

What does an actual proposal look like? Here's an example:

Film Proposal

WHAT THE TEACHER SEES

(Working Title)

This 16mm film is intended for teachers in the elementary schools
--primarily those teachers with relatively limited experience.
Its purpose is to give them an approach to the problem of pupil
health appraisal, and to provide them with key data needed in
order to make such appraisals intelligently.

The film will be approximately 20 minutes in length, and will
be shot in sound and color. Both voice-over narration and lip-
synchronized dialogue will be used.

On the assumption that client will provide technical advisor
and all players without cost to producer, budget is estimated
at $27,500. This estimate is subject to revision upwards if
animation is required. Additional charges for travel will also
be made if filming outside the Oklahoma City area becomes
necessary.

Revised version prepared for

OKLAHOMA STATE DEPARTMENT OF HEALTH

Approved:

For the Producer _____Date _____

For Department of Health _____Date _____

So there's your proposal, signed and sealed. What comes next? Why, obviously, you proceed to your film treatment.

CHAPTER 3

The Film Treatment

The film treatment (or "treatment outline") is a succinct, third-person, present tense summary of your proposed film. Its purpose is to flesh out your proposal outline into a more detailed presentation of material and approach, so dramatized—that is, made vividly expressive—as to excite your client in regard to the picture-to-be, as well as to inform him. It also serves as a preliminary check on weaknesses and/or disagreements before you proceed to the even more comprehensive development known as the sequence outline.

To these ends, the treatment should block in approach and handling, specify (at least in broad outline) the information to be included, and otherwise capture the essence of your thinking. It may be of almost any length, from two or three to 40 or 50 pages—the briefer, the better, in most cases.

I like to divide the building of an effective film treatment into two phases: a *thinking through* phase and a *writing* phase.

THINKING THROUGH YOUR TREATMENT

I hope no one who reads this book thinks writing a filmscript is just a matter of putting words on paper, for such a belief could hardly be farther from the truth.

Actually, most "writing" is essentially complete before a typewriter or word processor key is struck. It takes place in the writer's head as he figures out how to attack his topic.

I can't overemphasize how important this is. Please, please, if you have any desire at all to succeed in this field, do think things through! Or, as the old gag has it, don't put typewriter in motion until brain is in gear.

My own approach to this thinking-through process tends to involve three elements: an *information line,* an *interest line,* and a *presentation structure.*

This is not to say that these constitutents are treated in that particular order. Rather, the trick is to catch any passing thought in notes as it flashes by, weaving it into an integrated pattern later. But just knowing you do have an information line and interest line and presentation structure helps keep you from forgetting or leaving out some vital factor. Also, it gives you solid answers when Client or Producer asks why you're handling this or that in some particular way.

So. Let's take a look at

1. The information line

The purpose of the information line is to insure inclusion and effective arrangement of your film's key data. To this end,

    a. You research your film's topic and point of view.
    b. You frame a core assertion for your film to make.
    c. You back up this core assertion with subassertions, proof points.
    d. You prove each of these points visually.

Shall we consider these issues one by one?

a. You research your film's topic and point of view.

As pointed out in the preceding chapter, the primary goal of the fact film is to inform and/or influence and/or inspire a specified target audience; to sell its viewers a particular attitude on a given topic.

It's an axiom of successful salesmanship that you first must know your product. Similarly, in scripting successful fact films, you first must know as much as possible about your topic/attitude package.

Sound research attacks this issue on three fronts, digging up information via print, interview, and field investigation. Slight any one of these and you're tempting disaster.

Print research means reading books, brochures, catalogues, trade journals, company reports—anything whatever about your topic on which you can lay your hands. Not too much at first, however, and not in too great depth. There's a mass of data available on almost every subject. Much of it is bound to be outdated, or unrelated, or inapplicable. What you need at the beginning is less true expertise than a sort of scanning knowledge, designed to fill in on the big picture, the broad panorama, *to a point where you can ask at least semi-intelligent questions.*

Now, enter *interview research:* specifically, talk with your technical advisor.

This is where your preliminary print research will pay off. Experts often tend to be short of patience. If they feel they're dealing with a total idiot, they give said idiot short shrift.

If, on the other hand, you've already briefed yourself in private to a point where you know the difference between a walking beam and a Christmas tree, an id and an ego, a Doppler shift and a *doppelganger,* Advisor may conclude it's worth his while to fill in your blind spots, bring you up to date, and explain confusing details.

The value of this just can't be overstated. Ever so much rule-of-thumb procedure in any field simply never gets into print. Slang, trade jargon, specialized terminology can leave you staring slack-jawed. New developments render whole textbooks obsolete. But with the right technical advisor on call, you'll weather such perils with minimal damage.

Too, a good t.a. often can and will refer you to other, associated experts. Before you know it, you'll find the impossibly complex come clear; the inscrutable unscrewed.

Somewhere along the line, hopefully, you'll also find yourself involved in *field research,* a term which means simply that you go forth and examine your topic in its natural habitat, alive and breathing. This may involve anything from running an obstacle course to observing a swimming class; invading a steel plant to peering through a microscope. The important thing is: If at all possible, *do it.* Realistic writing demands experience, not just talk and reading. Good copy is built on feelings, sensory perceptions—sights, sounds, smells, tastes, touches; how hot, how cold, how frightening, how overwhelming, how pitiful, how stirring. The rebelliousness of young people in the '60s will mean more to you if you've been moved off Venice Beach by the Los Angeles Police Department's Tactical Squads, along with 20,000 other rock fans. You'll understand mental illness better if you, too, have heard the clang of iron doors closing.

It also should be mentioned that research is seldom a thing once done, then over. Throughout your work on any given script, you'll find yourself stumbling or hung up for lack of some fragment of information. When that time comes, don't stall and don't fake. Just plunge back into further research, digging until you find your answers.

Remember, too, that things are not always what they seem. Thus, in preparing the script for a film designed to sell executive aircraft, I kept running into endless nit-picking hassles that at first glance seemed totally without meaning. Only after hours of digging did it finally come out that certain key personnel felt their product's strongest selling point was its potential for use by buyers to transport young ladies other than their wives to resort areas with minimal risk of discovery.

Resolution of the problem consisted of including footage that showed mountains, beaches, luxury hotels, and the like, plus an assortment of alleged secretaries boarding the featured plane for duty at conferences. If anyone wanted to draw conclusions from same, that was his business.

As pointed out earlier, research *can* help!

b. You frame a core assertion for your film to make.

This is an issue we've already dealt with in some detail, in the preceding chapter. I mention it here only to reemphasize (1) its importance and (2) the fact that it's not always easily managed. You definitely should have it worked out to everyone's satisfaction by the time you write your treatment, however. Otherwise, your film's line of development will almost certainly prove weak and wandering.

c. You back up this core assertion with subassertions, proof points.

Every core assertion, of necessity, rests on an undergirding of subassertions—sound reasons why the core assertion is true.

Thus, a core assertion that "Colorado is a wonderful place to vacation" may rest on such subassertions as "The Rockies are spectacular in their beauty," "Swimming in Colorado lakes is fun," "Is fishing your thing? You'll catch the big ones here," "Ghost towns are fascinating to explore," "Comfortable tourist facilities are available throughout the state on every budget level," and so on.

Apply this pattern to your own script jobs.

First, list all the reasons your core assertion is true.

Second, arrange these reasons in some sort of order that is (1) logical, and (2) of increasing interest, with the most impressive reasons at the climax. Your goal should be to make it as clear as possible how, individually and/or in sequence, the subassertions lead to the conclusion that is your core assertion.

It may help if you simply type out everything you can recall which seems at all pertinent to your topic/assertion, paying no attention whatever to arrangement beyond placing each thought, each idea, each unit of information in a separate paragraph.

Finally, you'll run out of things to say. When that happens, snip apart the paragraphs and group like with like, until the key points stand out sharp and clear. Or, if you work with a word processor, its capacity for juggling bits and pieces will really speed things up.

Arranging these key points logically will vary from script to script. A historical subject, for example, might best be presented *chronologically*, in the order in which the events took place. If a number of locations are involved, it may seem preferable to attack *spatially*, moving from one setting to another. Other common approaches are *simple to complex, specific to general, familiar to unfamiliar, problem to solution, cause to effect,* or what have you. Or, you may choose to combine various of these patterns—*chronological* with *spatial* with *problem to solution,* for example, in the case of how a company with plants in seven states dealt with a pollution hazard first discovered in 1969.

Often, too, logic will prove to be something you invent; and the same for the matter of increasing interest. That is, no one line of attack is necessarily right, let alone the only one possible.

Thus, what is the reasoning behind my attack on the Colorado vacation issue? Let's reduce it to the sketchiest of outlines.

First, I wanted something to catch the eye—and what's more eye-catching than the Rockies?

But mountains are remote and lack the human factor, so I visualized turning next to crowds of happy swimmers . . . then closing in to the isolated individual, fishing.

Finally, what's most important to most people in planning a vacation? Answer: Money. So we conclude with a brief montage of footage emphasizing the attractive facilities and comfort available "on every budget level."

Is this the only way to approach the issue? Of course not. The elements available may be arranged in almost any pattern, *provided you develop some sort of order of presentation and emphasis that makes sense*—first to you; then, through you, to your film's ultimate viewers.

Working out this kind of thing won't necessarily be quick or easy, of course. Count on it, you'll find yourself repeatedly bogged down by false starts, holes in your thinking, inadequate information. Don't let such discourage you. The difference between the amateur and the professional, often, is that the amateur gives up. The old pro, in contrast, knows that if he keeps banging his square Dutch head against the apparently insurmountable stone wall of his current stumbling block, sooner or later that wall will fall down. The issue is merely to pinpoint the problem and then work out a solution—with additional research, with rethinking, with rearrangement of ideas.

d. You prove each of these points visually.

Back to the statements that back our Colorado core assertion: "The Rockies are spectacular," "Swimming is fun," "You'll catch the big ones," and so on. Note that each of these subassertions (that is, proof points) is subject to cinematic demonstration. A camera crew can take appropriate footage to make every point visual.

These filmed fragments, in turn, convince your audience, because *seeing is believing.* It forces automatic agreement.

A point *without* such visual backup, on the other hand, offers no conclusive end to the argument; in the last analysis, it rests on opinion. "This is a film" is instantly and demonstrably true. "This is a *good* film" introduces an element subject to endless debate.

It's also wise to remember that the true basis for any "proof" or "reason" always comes down to the individual case, the illustrative instance. That's why the "case study" approach is so common: By following one person as he experiences a situation, the writer acquires a built-in story line. Indeed, there are worse rules of thumb to follow than that of thinking first in terms of translating your data into terms of people doing things.

Whatever road you take, the trick always is to figure out specific action/incidents which will *show* your assertion is true. *Telling* just isn't good enough.

Thus, if I *tell* you I have the power to levitate myself, to float through the air without support, you may or may not believe me—with the odds strongly on the "not" side.

If, on the other hand, I simply say, "Look, I want to show you something," and then, before your very eyes, still in a sitting position, rise slowly from my chair into the air, drifting here and there about the room above your head, you may be tempted to refuse to believe me. Yet you dare not, for how can you deny the evidence of your own senses? I shall have proved my point in spite of you.

Where you the writer are concerned, this means you must train yourself to translate glib generalities into photographable specifics ("spiritual forces" become churches and religious rites of every faith), and to draw generalities *from* specifics (ghetto shacks and ragged children become "the blight of poverty"). You must devise ways to put abstractions like *fun* and *love* and *culture* on the screen . . . figure out how to *show* a girl as sloppy, a man conniving, a child evil-minded. Only as you learn to combine clips of film to establish a firm's reliability, a city's corruption, a party's dedication to the people's welfare can you say you've mastered your craft.

The road to such mastery lies in practice, endless practice; plus the nerve and experimental turn of mind that sees you eager to try something new.

Nor will it hurt you any to study others' films, just in case they in their turn have come up with something new and different.

So much for your factual content, your information line; an organized, unified, effective pattern for presenting the ideas and data necessary to bring alive your client's core assertion, the things he wants the film to say.

Your next step is to devise a plan of action to hold your viewers' attention—what I choose to call

2. The interest line.

The purpose of the interest line is to capture and hold your viewers' attention.

Obviously, there are a host of ways to do this. Self-interest, spectacle, shock, contrast, the impossible, the unattainable, the forbidden, the disastrous, the incongruous, the logical yet unanticipated—all have their devotees, their demonstrated values.

The most consistently useful device, in my own experience, is injection of a conflict element, a struggle between two opposing forces. Why? Because conflict, on whatever level, automatically raises a question as to which side will win. In so doing, it also creates tension in an audience.

Tension is the basis of *attention*. It's what keeps your viewers awake—maybe on the edge of their seats.

If they're awake and excited, they may even catch the message your client is trying to put across. Which same will prove a star in your crown, not to mention getting you new assignments.

Next question: How do you put this principle to practical use in your film script?

    a. You develop a character (or characters) with whom viewers can empathize.
    b. You face this character with danger.
    c. You draw a conclusion, make a point from the conflict.

Again, we'll take the process a step at a time.

a. You develop a character (or characters) with whom viewers can empathize.

In any filmed conflict, it helps if you can involve your audience in the struggle. How? By means of what the psychologists call *empathy*—the tendency of people to share the feelings and experiences of others. "To see with the eyes of another, to hear with the ears of another, to feel with the heart of another," as someone has said. It's the thing that makes you yawn when the man beside you yawns; flush or clench your fists at the humiliation of another; cringe back when a passing car splashes water on someone else.

To achieve empathy with an audience, you introduce some character who, in effect, is on the audience's side. That is, he shares your viewers' desires and attitudes and feelings. Thus, *Love That Car,* a hilarious yet effective five-minute short from Parthenon Pictures, featured vignettes of eight motorists whose carelessness regarding car care got them into trouble. Viewers laughed and empathized—because they too were motorists and had had car trouble brought on by such neglect.

In planning conflict situations, bear in mind that your audience can empathize with anything, animate or inanimate. So characters may be individuals, groups, objects, phenomena: witness Pare Lorentz's famed *The River,* with the Mississippi as star. A germ or an elephant or a tractor, skillfully handled, can play hero or villain just as well as a man.

In each case, however, you must be able to impute a goal, a desire, to the "character." Why? Because that which can desire and strive has in it the potential for success or failure and, therefore, for an implied "story question": "Will this striver succeed or fail in its strivings?" Viewers then become involved as they do with one or the other of the opposing teams at a football game.

Without desire, on the other hand, there can be no conflict—and no conflict, no interest.

Which is not to say that goals necessarily have to be spelled out. The fact that a given character is driving to work or cooking dinner or running a milling machine *implies* a goal and/or direction, even if it isn't stated.

Handling, in turn, can be on any level, from cool understatement to slapstick, so long as it fulfills your client's needs effectively.

Once you've built your empathetic character or characters (Chapter 8 will give you additional help), you're ready to add interest line component number two:

b. You face your character with danger.

Conflict is a man trying to walk through a locked door. It's attempting to attain goals in the face of opposition, obstacles.

This being the case, you not only give your empathetic character something to strive for, you also confront him with something to *struggle against*. Whether he's a man or a carburetor or a theory, you make it hard for him. You emphasize the obstacle, the irritation, the pain in the neck.

This opposing element, this factor which threatens your character's chances to attain his goal, I label *danger*. It comes in three categories.

First, there's that old reliable of melodrama, the *threat to life itself*. In film, you see it on levels ranging from the mad killer with the axe to the Anopheles mosquito; from the car roaring out of control to the improperly packed parachute or the crumbling cement at the dam base.

Second, there's drama's standby, the *threat to happiness:* the boy whose girl says no, the aging executive whose company folds, the family whose home is to be sacrificed for a freeway.

Third, comedy chuckles at the *threat to dignity*. Here stands the lonely bachelor whose brags about a non-existent sweetheart are about to be unmasked; the male chauvinist pig whose new boss turns out to be a female; the woman who discovers that her husband has invited in his Dirty Old Men's Club for the same night she's entertaining the Temperance Circle.

Why do I belabor this breakdown of danger in such detail? I do so because too many writers—and not just beginners, either—see danger only in terms of blood-and-thunder, threat to life . . . when, actually, for most of us, threat to happiness or to dignity are infinitely more useful working tools.

At any rate, and one way or another, it helps to hold viewer interest if your script incorporates struggles between desire and danger.

This conflict element may run through an entire picture, or it may be limited to bits or a sequence or two, depending on your needs. Thus, a typical college recruitment film invariably includes a tour of the campus. Equally invariably, said tour proves a drag and a bore where the audience is concerned.

Suppose, however, that we incorporate a pretty blonde freshman taking such a tour. Then, give Blonde a pair of brand new, too-tight shoes so that her feet are killing her.

Result: humorous conflict, girl versus shoes. The curse is taken off the tour sequence, and there's even a payoff when another girl loans Blonde more comfortable footgear, thus demonstrating what a friendly campus this really is.

Conflict to run throughout a film? My *Retire to Life* dealt with retirement problems . . . the conflict, with a man versus old age.

Non-human conflict? How about a grain of sand versus a pump valve? Acid battling oil-bearing rock strata? Wind and water against topsoil? In each case, danger battles desire—and viewers pay attention.

c. You draw a conclusion, make a point from the conflict.

This is what's known as stitching your interest line and your information line together. It's based on the rule-of-thumb that any conflicts you introduce into a script should be indigenous to your topic, born of it, rather than grafted on outside.

Thus, a tour of the campus is pretty much indigenous to college recruitment, and so are new freshmen. Q.E.D.: A blonde heroine with aching feet fits in. And the payoff, the friendly campus bit, makes a point that helps to prove the core assertion—that this is a good place to go to school.

Similarly, there's nothing alien about sand and pump valves. Reality sees them fight it out with devastating regularity. Their conflict is part and parcel of the topic. Same for erosion and conservation, man and old age, careless motorists and car problems.

In contrast, the phoniness of talking clocks, "investigations" of the facilities of luxury resorts by private detectives, ghosts who fight or try to force change, and the like, can prove disastrous, simply because they're so obviously hokey as to turn audiences off.

A final question: How much of an interest line do you need?

If any.

This is no idle matter. There's a tendency in the fact film business, too often, to assume that some kind of story line, some sort of interest hook, is ever and always an essential.

Such isn't necessarily true. For as mentioned in the preceding chapter, too great a preoccupation with noninformational elements may irritate or distract rather than enhance.

It's wise, therefore, to consider three points before you plunge headlong into development of an all-out interest line:

1. *What is this film's job?* Specifically, what does Client seek to accomplish? Is his goal to inform, to influence, or to inspire? Does he want to show workers how to tie a bowline knot, persuade citizens to pledge to the United Fund, or convince unbelievers that God is love?

2. *Why are the viewers watching this film?* Are they already interested in the topic? Is knowledge of the picture's contents important to them? Are they killing time, seeking entertainment, fighting boredom?

3. *Under what conditions are they viewing it?* Is viewing a voluntary act, or do we have a captive audience? Of individuals, small groups, large groups? Are they at home, at work, among friends, in a social or business situation?

There is no "right" answer to these questions. All they give you are raw materials of varying weight on which to base a private judgment—and yes, you *can* guess wrong.

In general, though, straight-out instruction—the bowline knot bit, for example—requires no "interest" dressing. Neither does the documentary of events at the top of the news, or the film whose contents have a built-in importance to Audience.

(I still remember the outburst of a technical consultant on *Microscopic Studies of Fluids in Porous Matrices:* "I don't give a damn if the audience *doesn't* understand this film the first time round. These men are engineers. They'll keep on running it till it *does* make sense; their jobs depend on it!")

On the other hand, dramatized "most needy" incidents within a fact film framework may go miles in coaxing charity contributions; and there's a sound reason the popular *Insight* TV program uses fully dramatized, professionally written and acted stories, rather than pulpiteering, to get across its ideological messages.

It's also important to consider the competition. If your public service film on psychological factors in home accidents is to run in the time slot in which another TV channel has a John Wayne western on deck, you'd better come out swinging with a strong, clever interest line. And double that in spades for the training film scheduled for showing after lunch to troops already worn down by a morning's hard-at-it physical activity.

3. *The presentation structure.*

The purpose of setting up a presentation structure is to insure that the materials incorporated in interest and information lines reach the audience in the most effective order.

The simplest fact film organization formula I know to achieve this goal is the old familiar "Hey!—You—See?—So . . ." I like it because it's so loose it accommodates almost anything you can think of, rather than restricting your creativity; yet applied with a little imagination, it gets the job done.

The formula works this way:

Hey!   = some element of your film's topic that strikes you as holding potential for capturing your audience's attention—an intriguing situation, a change in that situation, a bit of action, an interesting character, you name it.

You   = something to involve the viewer subjectively . . . draw him into the topic on a personal level. A starting place? Try striking for known target audience attitudes. Or ringing changes on sociologist W.I. Thomas's famed "four wishes": adventure, security, response, recognition. Or the Gypsy fortune teller's love, health, wealth, trouble.

See?   = the evidence you introduce to develop your subject, prove your point.

So . . . = the conclusion you draw, the point you make, the residual impression you leave.

Beyond this, and like any other "linear" literary form, a well-constructed film treatment is laid out in terms of beginning, middle, and end.

a. The beginning.

The good beginning does two things:

1. It sets forth an audiovisual "hook" with which to catch the viewer's interest.
2. It establishes the core assertion, the point the client wants to make and around which the film is to be built.

There are, at a conservative estimate, an infinity of ways to accomplish these worthy ends. You learn them by viewing films without number—viewing them critically, with an eye to their strengths and weaknesses—and then experimenting with your own film topic plus imagination.

Thus, by way of yelling "Hey!" a good beginning may fade in on an ambulance racing down the street, siren screaming; or on the house at which said ambulance eventually will stop; or on the patient within the house; or on the operating room to which he will be taken. But it can equally well open on bacteria on a slide viewed through a microscope, or on a clinician on his way to work, or on Patient-to-be eating a picnic dinner, or on his wife calling the hospital, or any number of other ways.

You see, the good opening's "Hey!" isn't necessarily shouted in a loud voice. Bomb-bursts or rifle shots are seldom vital.

What, then, does it take to make a good beginning?

Three elements: *curiosity, change,* and *consequences.*

The curiosity factor is more or less self-explanatory. Open with the ambulance, and Viewer wonders where it's going and why. Show him the house, and he puzzles over what's happening there, that we should focus on it. Zero in on the patient, and people ponder the poor man's fate: What's wrong with him? Will he live or die? Why?

But curiosity will carry a film only so far. In an appallingly short time, Audience will begin to grunt, "Get on with it!"

In other words, "Why did you show us that first shot? What's its purpose? Where's it leading?"

And believe me, it had better be leading somewhere, if you hope to hold your viewers!

The best place for it to lead—directly or indirectly, swiftly or slowly, subtly or without ceremony—is to a *change* of some sort, or at least the promise of change.

What's change? Let's define it as some aspect of reality becoming different in some way.

Change is, of course, the source of every news story: Something has happened, is happening, will happen. Or here's something we want to happen.

Change is also an aspect of life that intrigues us immeasurably. For the best of reasons, too. Change almost invariably has *consequences . . .* consequences which very well may warp our lives or shape our destinies on any and all levels.

Let a film rouse our curiosity with its opening shots, then springboard from them into some change that has consequences which, via empathy, hold our interest, and that film is off to a good start.

Thus, the folksy, familiar pleasure of Patient-to-be eating a picnic dinner builds from mild curiosity to a deeper involvement as we cut to his home that night and watch him writhing in pain, then see him—in consequence of this anguish—rushed to the hospital for diagnosis and treatment.

Especially if his ailment is such that *you* might very well be in his place!

This principle is equally valid for the most pedestrian of instructional films, if it's handled rightly. Topic: the life of the spider. The opening shot centers on the mass of eggs, rousing curiosity by the very fact that only the experienced eye can identify them for what they are. Then—change—the eggs begin to hatch and—consequence—tiny spiders in motion fill the frame.

Is this curiosity-change-consequence the only way to start a picture? Of course not. But I like it because it does have the advantage of forcing you to think of your topic as a dynamic, developing entity rather than a static thing.

On to *core assertion*.

Though in and of itself a statement about your topic, often the core assertion is best presented in question form: "Is there really hope for Man, then? Is there really a chance to build a better world?" "Just what *can* a public health nurse do for the mentally retarded child?" ". . . so now, let's take a closer look at scientific occupations. Is there really room for your kind of gal or guy within the field?"

The important thing is to get that point you want to make in early. For until it—your core assertion—is established, your picture hasn't really started.

In turn, where your interest line's concerned, the beginning's the place to introduce your empathetic element—your central character, animate or otherwise—and plunge said element into the conflict with the opposition.

b. The middle.

A film's middle sequences constitute the "See?" element of our formula. The "See?" in turn is made up of the subassertions on which your core assertion is based, linking them into a chain of logic designed to prove the assertion.

The main thing to bear in mind when doing this is that it's of more than passing importance to set up your major points in ascending order of importance/intensity/interest. For as it has been noted since Aristotle, anything that follows a climax must be either a greater climax or an anti-climax, and tension—and attention—diminishes if you allow anti-climax to take over.

This being the case, the middle sees the clash between the interest line's "character(s)" and opposition build to a peak.

c. The end.

The "So . . ." of our formula is the conclusion our film draws . . . a reiteration of the core assertion. It comes at the film's end, and preferably should hammer home the assertion in a summarizing "key phrase" which nails down the residual impression with which you hope to leave the audience.

Here, too, you resolve any remaining conflicts your interest line has developed. If you can do so in appropriately clever and pertinent fashion, so much the better. In *Love That Car,* the twist was the garage's tow truck running out of gas—a neat reversal that brought yet another laugh even while it wiped out any chance viewers might feel they were being lectured to by some authority figure who was never himself careless or neglectful.

d. Special tools.

So far, I've tried to avoid mention of anything too specifically cinematic. But now, the time has come.

Why? Because occasionally, in preparing a treatment, you're going to encounter a situation where nothing you can think of seems to solve the problems. When that moment arrives you may find your answer in *special effects* or *animation.*

Special effects—that is, footage unobtainable by ordinary routine shooting techniques—makes it possible for the filmmaker to freeze action, slow it down, allow time to pass between frames, modify or obstruct light, put foreground action against different backgrounds, superimpose one shot upon another, split frames, and perform a host of other visual miracles.

Animation is a cinematic procedure for giving apparent life and movement to inanimate objects. By means of photographed drawings, it enables you to minimize, maximize, go inside the human body, or capture both the history and spirit of science in a 15-minute film.

The problem with both animation and special effects is that all too often they prove fantastically expensive. But they're such valuable tools you can't afford not to be aware of their potential.

Because they're too complex to discuss in detail here, I suggest you investigate them by means of the various books on the subject listed in Appendix C, "For Further Reading."

WRITING YOUR TREATMENT

Planning's one thing, writing another. The initial thinking through of how best to handle your topic is vital, to say the least. But once that's out of the way, the less attention you pay to mechanics when you sit down at the typewriter to hammer our your first draft treatment, the better. Write from the moment's impulse, rather, getting down everything in the wildest rush of enthusiasm you can muster. Hunt for the aspects that intrigue you, excite you, turn you on.

Rules? Patterning? Structure? Use them as checklists later, not as guidelines to creation. That is, get the picture you visualize down on paper and *then* go back and see if you've left out anything essential.

Where your information line and interest line are concerned, neither *as such* goes into the treatment. What you describe is an integration of them, a presentation drawn from them. Or, to put it in another way, they exist only as part of your planning. Writing, you incorporate their essence, not their form.

The cardinal sin in the treatment is to reduce it to a dry-as-dust outline. You *must* dramatize to some degree, in all but the most technical of cases, if you hope to prove effective. To that end, present your ideas in descriptions that enable producer and client to *experience* with the audience . . . *understand and empathize* with the characters. Tell your man the conclusions you want him to draw, the way you seek to have him react. If that takes occasional brief passages of dialogue, or dramatic descriptions of action, or inclusion of emotionally pertinent detail—fine! The important thing is to get your concepts across, with pictorial nouns and action verbs and short, simple declarative sentences.

What about format? Actually, there's no such thing as *a* treatment format. There are only the formats for specific treatments.

Herewith, a sample of one I like, one that also shows how a preliminary outline or proposal expands as it reaches the treatment stage. Accept it as that and nothing more, and then go on to develop the private pattern *you* prefer.

Proposed

Film Treatment Outline

WHAT THE TEACHER SEES

(Working Title)

Opening titles will be (1) sponsoring organization's name, (2) main titles, and (3) production credit titles. These titles will appear over shots of children (ages 5 to 12) at play on school playground.

The titles fade as school bell rings and the children enter the school. Our central character, an attractive young teacher, monitors them as they push through the doorway. Narrator raises the central question which the film proposes to answer: Miss Jackson wants to be a good teacher. She knows that to be taught effectively, children must be in good health. But inexperienced as she is, what standard should she use to judge her pupils? Are there danger signals she should watch for? Above all, how can she recognize the signs of health?

The main body of the film demonstrates that careful,

continuing observation is the key to success. Or, as a
friendly older teacher (portrayed as a model well worthy of
emulation) explains it to Miss Jackson: "Just remember one
thing, my dear. A good teacher doesn't teach just subjects;
she teaches children."

Under this teacher's tutelage, Miss Jackson considers
a variety of typical children...learns how to use the youngsters
themselves as the basis for a norm by which to judge health.
Included are children who show (1) good body development, (2)
good nurture, (3) good posture, (4) good motor coordination,
(5) good respiration, (6) good skin, (7) good vision, (8) good
hearing, (9) good speech, (10) good emotional health, (11)
freedom from disease, and (12) freedom from injury. Children
who deviate from this norm also are shown, by way of contrast,
but the dominant emphasis remains strongly on the side of
normality. As Miss Jackson observes the signs of health or
deviation, she makes written notes of her observations of
significant health and behavioral problems, consults with the
school nurse, talks with parents, etc. However, it is stressed
throughout that the teacher's role is not and should not be
that of diagnostician. Her function is only to observe the
norm and deviations from the norm.

Concluding scenes show children leaving Miss Jackson's
class for recess. Miss Jackson joins Mrs. Carter, the older
teacher. "How best can you make sure you're doing right by
your class?" narrator asks the audience, recapitulating. "It's
simple, really. Just use your eyes and ears, your senses.
Watch for the signs of health. Get to know each and every
pupil as an individual. As Mrs. Carter says--a really good
teacher doesn't just teach subjects; she teaches children!"

Laughing and talking (and with Miss Jackson's
admiration for Mrs. Carter plainly showing) the two teachers

cross to a window and look out. They see the children at
play on the playground, in a shot which roughly matches the
one on which the film opened. Concluding narration emphasizes
Miss Jackson's growth and development, and the emotional
satisfaction it gives her.

End titles come on over.

<u>The End</u>

Revised version prepared for
OKLAHOMA STATE DEPARTMENT OF HEALTH

Approved:
For the Producer_____Date_____
For Department of Health_____Date_____

So much for the film treatment. With practice, you too can learn
to write it.

But you can't stop there. Not when you still have to learn about
the sequence outline.

CHAPTER 4

The Sequence Outline

Seq. 7: In his lab, Dr. Smith
works on his immunology
project. Narrator
emphasizes that entirely
apart from the project's
importance, Smith gains
tremendous satisfaction
from the work itself.
But work's only one part
of his life. Outside the
lab lie a host of other
interests.

DISSOLVE TO:

Seq. 8: Dr. Smith and family at
symphony concert.
Narrator's comments
enlarge on the normal life
angle.

DISSOLVE TO:

Seq. 9: The Smith kids romp with
         their parents in bed on
         Saturday morning.
         Appropriate comments.

DISSOLVE TO:

Seq. 10: Dr. Smith and friends
         play golf. Appropriate
         comments.

DISSOLVE TO:

Seq. 11: Dr. Smith and family
         watch Sunday night TV.
         Appropriate comments.

DISSOLVE TO:

What you see above is an excerpt from what's known as a *sequence outline,* the phase in script preparation that ordinarily follows writing of the treatment.

Next question: Just what is a sequence?

A motion picture is made up of a series of still pictures (each termed a *frame*) taken at the rate of 24 pictures per second.* The illusion of movement is the result of a physiological phenomenon known as *persistence of vision*—the fact that the image of Picture 1 lingers long enough in the eye to overlap Picture 2, thus making it seem to the viewer that he is observing continuous action rather than a series of separate photographs.

The piece of film resulting from a single camera run—that is, the series of still pictures taken between the moment a motion picture camera starts and the moment it stops—is called a *shot.*

A *sequence* is a related series of shots—a group of individual film cuts tied together by some element they hold in common. A *sequence outline* is a succinct list/description of the sequences to be included in a film.

*This is the rate for sound film. Silent film ordinarily is shot at 16 frames per second. Film shot at speeds slower than 16 frames gives the impression of flickering when projected.

Just as the film treatment fleshes out the proposal outline, so the sequence outline elaborates on the treatment. It translates the points the picture is to make into units of thought and/or action by forcing you to visualize how you're going to present your material on film. It "sells" your basic idea/core assertion step by step, instead of just rehashing generalities on a "Gee, this is great!" plane.

This means that, to write a sequence outline, you must learn to think of your subject matter in terms of related groups of shots—more specifically, related groups of shots each group of which makes a point.

Thus, in the fragment of sequence outline at the beginning of this chapter, the point of sequence 7 is that Dr. Smith is doing valuable work which he enjoys. Sequences 8, 9, 10, and 11, in turn, show—that is, prove by visual demonstration—that Dr. Smith (and, by implication, all research scientists) remains an eminently normal human being who enjoys the same kind of things other men do—home, family, sports, music, TV.

Each sequence does this in a related series of shots.

But that's just a beginning. Actually, to build an effective sequence outline, you need to understand not only how shots are related, the types of sequences, but how to outline a sequence, and how to break a treatment into sequences.

1. How shots are related.

In the fact film, shots may be related—that is, tied together—by such unifying elements as

a. Concept, idea, thought.

A sequence has sphericity as its topic. Footage of such divergent items as basketballs, marbles, world globes, and fortune-tellers' crystals is incorporated into it. These dissimilar objects are tied together by narration which calls attention to the fact that all the articles filmed have the state of being spherical in common.

b. Action.

Last round of a prize fight. Champion comes out of his corner fast, hammering Contender into the ropes. Clinching, Contender heaves himself to one side. The maneuver momentarily frees his right arm, just enough for him to explode a short, jarring uppercut to Champion's jaw. Then—

Film coverage of this action may involve two or three cameras; half a dozen or more shots. Cut together in proper order, these shots form a sequence, unified by continuity of action.

(In all likelihood, sequences 7, 8, 9, 10, and 11 in our opening example will each be developed in terms of such continuous action.)

c. Setting.

The scene is a park. It unites shots of strollers, old men on benches, gnarled trees, a fountain, children swarming over playground equipment, riders cantering along a bridle path. The thing they have in common, the element which makes them a sequence, is setting.

d. Character.

A backpacker strides briskly down a grassy slope, clambers up rocky outcroppings, plods through loose shale, drinks at a spring, pauses and wipes his brow as he crests a rise and gazes out across a broad valley. The idea behind the action isn't revealed, the action itself is far from continuous, the settings are divergent. But the focusing of attention on one character (it might equally well be a group) unifies the sequence.

e. Mood.

Slum streets around the world. Shots of sagging buildings, gutter filth, slumped shoulders, ravaged faces combine to create a mood that, simultaneously, ties together a sequence.

Obviously, there may be wide overlapping areas between these or other categories. An idea, a continuing flow of action, a setting, a character, and a mood all may join in one sequence. The proper label is a matter of context and decision, with no two writers or filmmakers necessarily agreeing.

Internal development of sequences may be chronological, spatial, familiar to unfamiliar, cause to effect, or any of the other patterns for building an entire film which we listed in the preceding chapter. Additional useful tools include

Dramatization: The film deals with marriage counseling. Here is a sequence in which a man and a woman, playing husband and wife, lash out at each other in simulated fury.

Analogy: Same film. A sequence features a snarling dog circling a bristling cat. The analogy to the angry couple previously cited is clear.

Example: An actual couple—the wife with a black eye, perhaps—discuss their problem with a counselor, while a hidden camera captures the moment on film.

Comparison: Here alternating sequences show two couples, one happy and one unhappy, or one unhappy in one way, the other in another.

Yes, there are a host of additional ways to develop sequences. Use your imagination.

2. Types of sequences.

Whatever your material, whatever your handling, each sequence you build will fall into one of two categories: *continuity* or *compilation*. An understanding of how these types differ will go a long way towards simplifying the issues involved in creating a solid sequence outline.

a. The continuity sequence.

A unit of *continuing action,* the continuity sequence may include a host of shots, but ends when there is a break in time. Traditionally (but not always, these days, by any means!) its conclusion is marked by an optical effect—a DISSOLVE, a FADE, a WIPE, or such. Casual reference to a given continuity sequence quite possibly may term it "the fight sequence," "the wedding sequence," "the dinner sequence," or such, thus tacitly acknowledging the fact of continuing action; the lack of break in continuity.

b. The compilation sequence.

A unit of *information* or *thought,* and sometimes called a newsreel sequence, the compilation sequence is particularly common in fact films. Often you'll see it in coverage of a flood, a tornado, a travelogue, a tour of a factory, or the like. This is because it enables the filmmaker to use narration to tie together a wide range of divergent individual shots taken with no regard for continuing action. References to such a sequence frequently focus on topic, rather than continuity: "the manufacturing sequence," "the growth sequence," "the hospital sequence," etc. Just as in the case of the continuity sequence, an optical effect frequently marks the conclusion of the compilation sequence. *Unlike* the continuity sequence, however, and because the compilation sequence's scope ordinarily is too broad to be encompassed by continuous, no-break action, opticals may be used within it, to link the divergent times and places involved. It ends when discussion of the topic itself ends.

c. The combining of sequences.

Both types of sequence—continuity and compilation—often are used in the same film. Thus, a picture may begin with a continuity sequence of dramatized action designed to hook audience interest . . . follow it with a compilation sequence which introduces the film's topic and emphasizes its scope . . . go to a second compilation sequence which establishes the broad outlines of a particular locale . . . move on to a continuity sequence which pinpoints a bit of dramatic action in that locale . . . and so on.

This technique is particularly useful in the fact film, since it makes practical the introduction of a heavy load of information, on the one hand, while permitting the building of viewer interest, on the other.

3. How to outline a sequence.

As in so many areas in film, there's no set format for outlining a sequence. But a good many writers find it useful to follow a three-pronged plan of attack. For each sequence, they make sure to include:

a. *Point to be made.*
b. *What's seen.*
c. *What's heard.*

Items *b* and *c* are clear enough on the face of it. The main thing to bear in mind in their regard is that a sequence outline is, indeed, an *outline*—that is to say, it should be kept as terse and concise as possible.

Item *a*, however, is a frequent source of problems. Why? Because too often, a writer or filmmaker caught up in an intriguing bit of action tries to incorporate it even though it has no particular bearing on the issue at hand. (On one occasion, indeed, I recall an eager-beaver director on a tight budget burning nearly a thousand feet of 16mm film on the cavortings of a couple of stray dogs. Allegedly, they were going to provide "atmosphere." Actually, they only wasted time and money and ended up on the cutting room floor.)

Let us state the issue loud and clear, then: *A sequence should always make a point.* If it has no point to make, it's pure waste motion. If it has a point but doesn't make it, it's a bad sequence.

This should come as no surprise. As previously reiterated so tediously often, your film itself is designed to prove a point, establish the truth of a core assertion. To this end, you build in subassertions, proof points supporting your main point.

That proof must be set forth visually in a sequence. And if the subassertion is so complex as to require development in sub-subassertions, then each of them, in turn, should be presented in a sequence of its own.

So: Step 1 in outlining a given sequence is to decide what point it is to make . . . after which, you go on to the matter of what's seen and what's heard.

Beyond this, some writers and some producers like to have transitions between sequences indicated in the outline. It's a matter of personal preference.

Here's how all this works, where the outline of a *compilation* sequence is concerned:

```
     Now we show that a Lakewood vacation

   offers fun for every taste.  Mixed shots of

   young and old alike (including plenty of
```

```
closeups of happy faces) pinpoint the

pleasures of fishing, swimming, golfing,

skeet shooting, indoor games, sunning, girl-

watching, etc.

    Narrator offers appropriate comments

that emphasize (with sensory words in profusion)

the pleasures of each activity, plus the release

from nervous tension that freedom from care

brings.                          DISSOLVE TO:
```

Do you see the pattern? The very first sentence makes clear the point the sequence is to make: . . . *a Lakewood vacation offers fun for every taste.*

The remainder of the paragraph summarizes what viewers will see when the film's completed. The description of the footage to be included makes it clear that the camera is going to be jumping all over the place, catching a flash of this, a few frames of that, a cut or two or three of the other thing. But all the shots are related, in that they deal with the same topic: a Lakewood vacation; and paragraph 2 sees the narrator pinpoint this in terms of what the audience will hear from the soundtrack.

Finally, the DISSOLVE TO: nails down the transition device designed to move the action from this sequence to the next.

Note also that while the writer covers the ground involved adequately, he keeps his presentation brief.

What happens in a *continuity* sequence?

```
    Back to Bob and Jill.  In the dining room

now, they help their plates at the evening buffet

...eat at a properly appointed table, complete

with snowy linen, shining silver, flowers, and

maybe even candlelight.  Both of them (or

narrator, if it's decided to handle this

sequence voice over) comment ecstatically on

the wonderful variety and gourmet preparation

of the food.

                          DISSOLVE TO:
```

There's no jumping here, please observe. The flow of action is continuous, beginning to end—even though quite possibly the director will cheat a bit by compressing time, via one of the devices we'll explore in the next chapter, when we deal with the shooting script.

The *point?* Here it doesn't appear until the very end, where the characters "comment ecstatically on *the wonderful variety and gourmet preparation of the food.*" What's seen and what's heard *proves* it visually—seeing is believing—and we exit to the next sequence via a DISSOLVE TO:

But outlining a sequence isn't all there is to building a sequence outline. Equally important is the matter of

4. How to break a treatment into sequences.

Allegedly, by the time you've finished your treatment, you have your film's action clearly in mind.

Allegedly.

Yet more often than not, when the time comes for you to prepare a sequence outline, problems arise. In spite of all your previous work, you find yourself floundering through gaps, miring down in confusion, wandering off into a maze of false paths and dead ends.

Why? Frequently, because your original concept and line of development just don't work out well in visual terms.

Solution: Go back over your treatment, and make a list of all the major and minor points to be made.

Then, devise a way of putting each across on film—that is, visually—via either continuity or compilation sequences.

I hate to tell you how much hard work this is going to take. Or how much additional research. Or—especially—how much creative imagination.

The reason is that it's not going to be enough merely to come up with a disjointed series of fragments. What you're after is a picture that's a unified whole, with each sequence integrated smoothly into the film's overall line of development.

This is why it's greatly to your advantage to have worked out a strong information line and an equally muscular interest line back when you prepared your treatment. Now, out of the research that went into them, you can draw incidents, units of data or thought or action to plug holes, illustrate abstractions, drive home principles, or perform whatever other creative miracles you need.

On the other hand, I'd be kidding you if I pretended that the building of a sequence outline—or any other phase of a film script, for that matter—is entirely neat and logical and by the rules. More frequently, in truth, it's a matter of flying by the seat of your pants, catch-as-catch-can, and then developing these ideas via continuing elaboration. Here's an intriguing bit, there a block of solid information. Then along comes an incident or two; a colorful setting; a brisk exchange. Finally, you gather them all together, and somehow tie them into a package.

I still remember one such instance. The man was a former state politico, a powerful figure of yesteryear. Now his son had attained high office and officials of one governmental subdivision in particular were fearful that reprisals for past affronts might be meted out.

A short film honoring Politico for his place in history might help calm the storm-tossed waters, it was decided. The task of scripting the picture fell on me. All I had to work from was a back-of-envelope list of high points in Politico's career.

Each note, clearly, was basis for an effective sequence. Trouble was, the footage available on Politico was strictly limited, to the point where it seemed impossible to make anything of it.

For days I paced the floor. Still no answer.

Then, one afternoon, someone's private angel led him to thread up a reel of stock footage on the projector.

You couldn't have found anything much more remote to politics. All it offered was a few hundred feet of color film shot from the front bumper of a pickup truck as it bounced and jounced down a narrow woods road. Lord only knows why anyone had taken it.

Yet there it was, the living, breathing answer to our problem: "It was a long, hard road old Sam Smith"—not his name, of course—"traveled on his way to state leadership and a place in history. . . ."

Well, after that, the rest was easy. We did it with stock footage of hands, mostly: hands chopping wood, hands laying brick, hands holding law books, hands pounding gavels. Each bit made a point as we traced Politico's career. Where footage of the old man was available, we used it, along with shots of houses, roads, state buildings, and the like that fit in. Where we had nothing that would fit, we fell back on our bouncy woods road color, with appropriate comment about Old Sam's climb to glory.

The result was hardly a prize picture. But it did solve the immediate problem. And, to my amazement, not long ago I discovered that it's still in circulation.

So what's the lesson to be drawn from this epochal incident?

Would you believe "It's easier to make an acceptable picture when you have points to make but no footage than when you have all sorts of footage but no points"?

Finally, a word of warning: Sometimes a rushed or sloppy producer won't ask you to prepare a sequence outline. Do so anyhow; you'll find it helps you build a solid script far beyond any time or trouble it may take.

Particularly, it's vital when you come to the next stage of your job: preparation of a shooting script.

CHAPTER 5

The Shooting Script

A shooting script is the detailed plan for a proposed film. Sometimes called a "shot list," it consists of a description of each shot to be incorporated into the picture.

Though largely supplanted by the master scene script (see Chapter 13) where the writing of feature films is concerned, the shooting script remains more or less standard in the fact film field. In effect an instruction sheet for technical people and talent, it tells the actors what to say and do; the crew, what to take pictures of. In major measure, it determines what the audience will see when they view the finished film.

Because these things are so, the shooting script should at all costs avoid (a) pictures which confuse the audience, and (b) instructions which confuse cast and/or crew.

To this end, you need to learn how to break down action, how to describe shots, and how to set up a shooting script in proper format.

1. How to break down action.

The first step in writing a shooting script is to break down each sequence from your sequence outline into its component individual shots.

The trick here is to get in the habit of projecting the finished film in your head as you write it. Visualize each scene in careful detail as it develops. Watch the flow of action in your imagination.

Simultaneously, break down said action into shots: single runs of the camera.

This is a knack, believe me. The simplest way to master it, in my own experience, is to make contact with some amateur or professional worker in the field who will grant you the loan of some reels of edited film, a couple of film winds, and a tabletop rear screen projection device called a viewer. You then wind the film back and forth through the viewer, as slowly as need be, until you're aware of shots as shots, not just a flow of action. Or, in a pinch, you can rent a couple of videotapes and play small segments over and over and achieve much the same effect.

Indeed, there are worse ways to learn to write a shooting script than to maneuver yourself into involvement in the process of film editing, whether as participant or as observer. Watching, watching, watching over some old hand's shoulder as he labors at editing bench or Moviola, asking as many questions as you can get away with as to where and why he's cutting, can prove a major step in your education as a scriptwriter.

Another possible though tedious procedure is to sit through the screening of a feature half a dozen or more times, till you're so totally bored with the story that you can see the cuts—that is, the individual shots.

In any event, and whatever route you take: Do learn to see not-yet-filmed action in your mind's eye.

Simultaneously, keep asking yourself, *"What do I need to have the audience look at next?"*

Your primary guideline in answering this question is of course the point you're trying to make in the particular sequence: the subassertion it's designed to prove. This is why it's so devastatingly important that you write a sequence outline before you start your shooting script, whether anyone demands such of you or not. Without it, you can wander in endless circles, getting nowhere. It's a major reason for films that drag and jerk and ramble.

So: What do you need to have the audience look at next? A tight closeup that will call some crucial detail to their attention? An establishing or reestablishing shot, far enough back to orient them to the broader action? A reaction shot, to help shape their attitudes?

And always, the issue will be the subassertion you're trying to back with visual proof.

Break the question down, if need be. Consider such matters as

—What point am I trying to make *in this shot?*
—How does said shot tie in or relate to the point I'm trying to make in the sequence? In the film as whole?
—What should the action be, in order to make the point most convincingly?
—Am I forgetting anything, leaving something out that needs to be included?

Again, a guideline: The answer, in one word, is always *pertinence* . . . logical fitness, applicability, relevance. Every shot should be designed to intensify the effect you seek.

Pertinence is of two types:

Visual pertinence . . . shots that sustain the flow of action or impression.

Emotional pertinence . . . shots which create the audience reaction you seek.

Naturally, in a host of instances—perhaps most—these tend to overlap. But both are elements you create with malice aforethought . . . products of thinking, pre-planning, floor-pacing, organization . . . calculated selection and arrangement of action/footage. And while a large part of the responsibility for the finished product of necessity falls on director and/or editor, the fact remains that the writer plays a major role just by the way he blocks things in. The better he understands film principles, the more likely he is to come up with a script that offers the other people involved ways to put an effective presentation on the screen.

a. Problems of visual pertinence.

Visual pertinence consists of visual flow honed razor-sharp with applicability to the point you're trying to make.

In the continuity sequence, the issue will be to maintain the flow of action. To this end,

1. *Coverage must be functional.* That is, image size and angle must fit the needs of viewers where the particular situation is concerned. Thus, at certain times, it's essential to orient your audience by establishing the relationship of characters to the background and to each other. At others, the action and/or appearance of characters and/or objects are what's important. Or, the issue may be attention to certain key details.

The writer must anticipate these needs, this functional aspect of visual continuity, and provide for them in the script.

2. *Coverage must be logical.* Here the issue is less viewer needs than viewer desires, anticipations. If a character gives sudden, intent attention to his watch, Viewer is going to want to see the watch face. If murky shadows stir, Viewer will want to see what's stirring; or, perhaps, Character's reaction to it. If Character races down the street, Viewer will want to see what he's pursuing, what's pursuing him, or what hazards lie ahead.

3. *Coverage must give the illusion of continuity.* Confusion is a grave sin indeed in the continuity sequence. Change of angle, image size, or the like must be motivated, as when the camera jumps from a position aside and behind a running character to aside and ahead, in order to prepare for his sudden veering into an alley. It must also be substantial enough not to appear accidental. Yet on the other hand, it must not take so great a leap as to leave the audience groping as to where the action is taking place, who's who, or what's going on.

The shots must also be so smoothly joined that no break in the action is apparent.

To this end, continuity sequences are developed in terms of *match cuts* and *cutaways*.

A match cut is one in which the second of two shots of continuing action includes part of the action in the first shot. The shots are cut together where the action overlaps in a manner to insure smooth transition from shot to shot.

The cutaway, in contrast, does not include any part of the preceding shot.

Thus, we might open with a shot of an office, complete with desks, chairs, filing cabinets, and the like, but devoid of people. A door opens. A man and woman enter.

A second shot gives us a closer view of the pair. Woman moves a few steps further into the room. Shot 3 concentrates on Man as he closes door. Shot 4 sees Man cross to Woman. They embrace. Man unbuttons top button of Woman's blouse. A fifth shot zeroes in on the doorknob, out of frame in shot 4. Knob turns slowly.

Since shot 2 includes part of what was seen in shot 1, it's a match cut. Shot 3 includes part of what was seen in shot 2—again, a match cut. Shot 4? Another match cut.

Shot 5, however, was *not* included in shot 4. In consequence, it's a cutaway.

The value of the cutaway in maintaining the illusion of continuity is beyond measure. Among other things, cutaways can successfully mask spots where the flow of action in two shots doesn't quite mesh together properly. They can introduce parallel lines of action. They can clarify situations. They can break up an otherwise static scene. They can add suspense. They can speed up time passage.

Take our example. The cutaway of the doorknob introduces a parallel line of action, breaks up what might otherwise be a static scene, adds suspense. Perhaps, if we have been wondering what's become of some other character, it clarifies the situation. If, after the cutaway, we cut back to Man and Woman and discover that three of Woman's blouse buttons are now unbuttoned, we've speeded up time passage. And if this new shot reveals that Man is doing the unbuttoning with his left hand, when he was using his right in shot 4, we've also masked a break where two shots don't cut together properly.

Visual pertinence operates a little differently where the compilation sequence is concerned—for in such, unity is provided by *topic* and *narration*.

In consequence, the goal in cutting often is to *avoid* the impression of continuity, continuing flow of action. Shots very well may be chosen for contrast, with emphasis on dissimilar colors, dissimilar sizes, dissimilar objects or action. Extreme closeups may be juxtaposed with extreme long shots, high angles with low, books with bursting bombs, people with machines or monsters.

So much for visual pertinence. In and of itself a fascinating subject, it rates intensive study on the part of every would-be screenwriter. The best place to carry out said study is in the cutting room, under the tutelage of an experienced film editor. Lacking the opportunity for that, much can be learned from the books in Appendix C.

b. Building emotional pertinence.

Emotional pertinence—shots which create the audience reaction you seek—is at least equally vital to visual, in that it has in it the power to make interesting what might otherwise be dull footage. Indeed, when someone tells you that you need to "build" a particular sequence, what he often means is that you need to add shots that will give it greater emotional pertinence.

You give a sequence emotional pertinence through your control of (1) *time*, (2) *emphasis*, and (3) *reaction*.

Take *time*. In a typical factory tour—live, not filmed—90 per cent of the actual, chronological time may be waste motion devoted to chit-chat, bad jokes, walking from department to department, and so on. To include it in a film is to reduce effectiveness via boredom. Therefore, in building the tour from sequence outline to shooting script, you eliminate such immaterialities, leaving only essentials to be filmed—a montage that catches the key action in each unit, perhaps.

Emphasis may be the issue where a new widget-stamping machine is concerned. Though each step in its operation occupies only a fraction of a second, one particular meshing of gears or junction of parts is tremendously important. Made aware of this by your research, you break the overall process down, filling the screen with strong, pertinent extreme closeups which *emphasize* the details to which you want to draw attention. The split second involved in the actual stamping thus may end up stretching to a minute or more on the screen.

Or consider a continuity sequence in a home accident film. Our hero, disgruntled after a fight with his wife, goes out to move a heavy trunk from the garage to the basement via an old-fashioned outside stairwell. A broom lies across the threshold. Tossing it into the basement, and more irked than ever, Hero begins backing down the steps, bracing himself against the trunk's weight. Past him, as we watch from above, we can see the broom, now caught crosswise across the stairs close to the bottom.

Cutting back and forth between man and broom, emphasizing each in turn, we can prolong Hero's descent to an endless agony of suspense: Will he trip? Will he fall? Will the trunk crush him? Witness Alfred Hitchcock's famous *Psycho* scene of Tony Perkins stabbing Janet Leigh in the shower; it built through 78 shots!

Reaction? In a compilation sequence, it quite possibly will be provided by a narrator, who in effect tells the audience what to think, how to interpret the mixed shots on the screen. Or, perhaps a dialogue interchange between actors calls attention to the emotionally pertinent points.

In the same way, a reaction factor can be injected into a continuity sequence on squirrel hunting by appropriate interpretation via narrator. Or, the reaction—and emotional pertinence—may be supplied by the enthusiastic behavior of the hunters themselves.

So much for the principles and procedures by which you build a shooting script. Now, on to mechanics:

2. How to describe a shot.

For clarity's sake, let's work from a sample, checking it against eight points:

Now, our checklist:

a. How do you get into the shot?

That is, does the shot come onto the screen by means of a FADE (the screen black at first . . . then the picture appearing, brighter and brighter) . . . a DISSOLVE (one picture gradually fading out while another fades in) . . . a WIPE (one picture pushing another off the screen in any one of a wild variety of ways, from straight vertical or horizontal to explosion), or what have you?

(If one shot follows another instantaneously, with no transition device specified, a CUT—the end of one piece of film simply pasted to the next—is taken for granted. Ordinarily, it isn't mentioned in the script, unless perhaps used for shock effect.)

In our example, we FADE IN—all caps, note—because *every* shooting script so begins.

b. What are the conditions of work?

Three items are included here. All go on one line of the script, all are typed all caps, and all always go in the same order. They're omitted if no change in conditions from the previous shot has taken place.

The three items, all essential information for the crew, are:

1. Interior (INT.) or exterior (EXT.).
2. Place (MACHINE SHOP, BEDROOM, STREET, RIVER BANK, etc.).
3. Time (DAY or NIGHT).

c. What's the numerical designation?

Shots are numbered in sequence from a film's beginning to its end. In production, before the action of a given shot starts, the shot itself is "slated." That is, its number and other identifying data are chalked on a slate and filmed. This enables the director to avoid confusing the editor when he shoots out of sequence—as he almost certainly will, at one point or another.

d. What's the image size and subject?

Both size and subject *must* be included. There's no such thing as a "medium shot," or whatever, in and of itself. But more of that later.

e. What's the camera position?

This is the kind of thing you mention only if a particular position is essential to the point to be made—"high angle," "low angle," "shooting from back window," etc. Fool around with such too much, or try to get fancy, and the director will both hate you and ignore your instructions.

f. What action is seen?

What—if anything—happens? Does an actor move? Does a machine function? And remember, the closeup of a knife on a table may be vital and highly dramatic, yet involve no action.

g. What sound is heard?

The thing to bear in mind here is that sound includes *effects* (motors roaring, hooves pounding, bells ringing) and *music* (which may or may not be designated according to type—BACKGROUND-PASTORAL, MYSTERIOSO, FANFARE, BACKGROUND-INDUSTRIAL, etc.) as well as *narration* and *dialogue*.

Any sound element you specify should be labeled, ALL CAPS, each time there's a change—as from narrator to actor, actor to actor, sound effects to music, music to narrator/actor, etc.

h. How do you get out of the shot?

The issue here is precisely as in item *a*, above. Since no technical effect is mentioned, we assume that the shot closes with a cut.

So much for how you describe a shot. Beyond this, however, in item *d*, above, we made mention of image size. This is such an important—and potentially confusing—subject as to be worth particularly detailed treatment.

IMAGE SIZE DESIGNATION

How large should a given object and/or action appear on the screen at a given time—and how do you label it in your script so it will come out within gunshot of the way you want it?

Your three basic image sizes are *long shot, medium shot,* and *closeup.* More often than not, scripts abbreviate these to LS, MS, and CU . . . or to such variations as ELS (extreme long shot), MLS (medium long shot), MCU (medium closeup), ECU (extreme closeup), and so on.

The key principle to bear in mind in using these various shots is *relativism.* That is, a long shot of a man may very well be a medium shot of the car he's driving—and a closeup of the spotlight in the foreground.

In essence, each type of shot has its special function. You don't use it just as a matter of whim, but because you have a particular job that needs doing.

Thus, a *long shot* is an orientation shot, an establishing shot. It relates a particular object and/or action to its surroundings, its background. In consequence, there's no such thing as a "long shot," *per se* . . . only "LS, Susie. Wearily, head down, rain hat pulled about her face, she plods up the walk."

A *medium shot* is a subject shot . . . the object and/or action in and of itself, with a minimum of distracting background. "MS, Susie. She reaches the porch steps," probably will include Susie, head to toe, but very little else save perhaps enough of the steps to make them identifiable.

A *closeup* is an emphasis shot—one which calls attention to the specific detail of the subject which makes the factual or emotional point you seek. Thus, in our imaginary sequence, we might very well follow the two shots above with "CU, Susie's head. She raises it full face to camera. Her right eye is blackened, her cheek scraped and bruised. Tears stream down her face."

And there you have it. No matter what story you seek to tell, what information you want to convey, you forever work with LS-MS-CU and their variations, even though for effect you choose to combine them in all sorts of outlandish orders.

Remember, however, that too great a jump—from ECU to ELS, for example—quite possibly may confuse your viewers; that too many closeups in a row may disorient your audience: frequent reestablishment of characters or whatever in relation to background is a must; and that your inspired dream of a shot that zooms in on Earth from outer space to a closeup of a gnat's eyebrow may of necessity have to be tempered a bit in view of technical limitations.

Remember also that a given director or cameraman may not see a given image size as you do. Your "long shot" of a dining table may, in his eyes, be a "medium long shot"—or even a "medium shot" or "medium closeup." Your only defense is clarity and precision of description every step of the way. If you want someone's eyeball to fill the frame, say so!

And yes, there *are* other terms in use, almost unto infinity. A *full shot* takes in a person, head to toe; a *knee shot* chops him off at the knees; a *waist shot,* at the waist and so on. A *close shot* is a sloppy designation which indicates only that the camera is near the subject. In Britain, you'll run into the BCU (big closeup)—we'd probably call it an ECU. But don't worry about such; you'll pick up the terms you really need as you go along. (I've listed some in Appendix D, the *Terms You'll Use* section.)

3. Shooting script format.

The fact film shooting script ordinarily utilizes a two-column format, as per the sample in the following pages. Shot descriptions are in the left-hand column. Sound (a term which here includes dialogue, narration, music, and effects, remember) is on the right.

Set up with your paper's left edge at zero in your typewriter. Assuming your machine has pica type (and industry practice says it should have), the following horizontal spacing will ordinarily be observed:

10—shot numbers
15—shot descriptions—40
30—transitions
45—sound descriptions—70
75—page numbers

Vertical spacing:
    Page number—two spaces below top of page
    First line—four spaces below page number
    Conditions of work, shot descriptions—four spaces below preceding copy
    Transitions—two spaces below preceding copy

Note that while directions, speeches, etc., are *single* spaced in the master scene script (see Chapter 13), the tendency in most fact film shooting scripts is to *double* space both shot descriptions and speeches. This will vary from shop to shop, however, so it's always wise to try to check a sample.

Note also that sometimes the fact film will use master scene format.

Where capitalization is concerned, the following should be typed ALL CAPS:

Character names (often on first appearance only)
Conditions of work

Image size
Camera movement
Transitions

The pages which follow are designed to give you an idea of how a typical two-column fact film shooting script looks. Probably it spells things out more than is necessary. But the director can always adapt to his own taste and style, whereas too sparse a presentation may give him too little to work with.

BOOKS AFIELD

(Shooting Script)

FADE IN:

EXT. - CHURCH - DAY

1	MLS, church, head on from Jardin. A group of TOURISTS straggle out the main door.	SOUND: Church bells ringing.
2	MS, church's main door. Last of the tourist group is ED CRAWFORD (40s, good-natured, non-handsome, tired). He pauses on the threshold.	
3	MCU, Ed. Wearily, he looks this way and that...starts forward.	
4	TAIL-AWAY SHOT, Ed. He plods towards the Jardin.	SOUND: Bells down. Segue to MUSIC: In and up.

EXT. - JARDIN - DAY

5-10	Mixed shots, Jardin, from church angle--men and women of all ages reading papers or chatting...girls	

and boys flirting...kids
playing around bandstand,
etc.

11   MLS, Ed. He enters Jardin.
Camera (in Jardin and
slightly to Mojica side)
PANS to hold him center
frame. He turns in the
direction of Colibri.

12   MS to MCU, Ed. Camera is
in front and slightly to
one side of him now. He
plods towards Colibri.

13   CU, Ed's face. He frowns
slightly and sighs.

14   MCU, Ed. Camera is at
Jardin corner, across
street from Colibri. Still
frowning, Ed pauses...
glances up at Colibri sign.

15   MLS-MS, Colibri sign (Ed's
POV). Camera ZOOMS in to
MCU-CU of sign.

16   **CU, Ed. His frown fades,
replaced by interest. He
starts forward.**

17   **MS, Colibri entrance,
perhaps from angle to
include Ed or over his
shoulder.**

INT. - COLIBRI-- DAY

18   MS, store interior, from   MUSIC: Down to BG.
doorway. LUPE (30s, eager
to please, Mexican) stands
back to camera on ladder,
hanging up picture frame
or the like. MARJ (40s,
volatile, American),
smoking cigarette, works
on book display wall.

19   MS, Colibri doorway from
inside store, to favor Ed
as he pauses at threshold,
glancing about.

20   MS, Lupe (Ed's POV).
She still hasn't noticed
him.

21   MS, Marj (Ed's POV). She
doesn't see him either.

                                       MUSIC: Out.

22   MCU, Ed. Looking a bit
helpless, he advances a
step or two...speaks.   ED: Uh...

23   MS, store interior, to
favor Lupe and Ed. She
turns...sees him...looks   LUPE (GETTING DOWN FROM HER
slightly nonplussed.   PERCH): Oh...lo siento;

24   MS to MCU, as Ed   I'm sorry. May I help you?
approaches Lupe.
                                        ED (WRY GRIN): I guess I

just can't take any more
churches. What have you
got to read?

LUPE (LAUGH AND SMALL
HELPLESS GESTURE): Well...

MARJ (O.S., INCREDULOUSLY):
What have we got to read--?

25   MS three-shot, to favor
      Ed. He's obviously
      startled. Marj now
      faces him.

26   MCU, Marj (Ed's POV).
      Smoke curls about her
      face.   --Man, are you <u>crazy</u>?
                                         (GESTURING TO SHELVES,
                                         RACKS) I mean, here you
                                         stand in the big fat middle
                                         of the biggest bookstore
                                         north of Mexico City and
27   CU-MCU, Ed. He bursts out   ask us what have we got
      laughing.   to read--?

28   MCU, Ed and Lupe. Their
      eyes meet. She laughs with
      him.

29   MS three-shot, to favor
      Marj. Laughing, she
      crosses to join the others.
      Camera ZOOMS back to
      entrance.

                    DISSOLVE TO:

EXT. - COLIBRI - DAY

30   MLS, Colibri, from Jardin   MUSIC: In and up.

corner...normal foot and

vehicular traffic. Shot

holds as

TITLES COME ON OVER:

     The

  Book Publishers

International Council

    presents

BOOKS AFIELD

(OTHER TITLES AS DESIRED)   MUSIC: Down and out.

        FADE OUT

    FADE IN:

    EXT. - CHURCH - DAY

31   REPEAT OF SHOT 1.   NAR. (CHUCKLING): Yes,

         DISSOLVE TO: sooner or later we <u>do</u> get

                       tired of churches--even if

                       that's what we came abroad

                       to see...

    EXT. - MARKET - DAY

32   MCU, American COUPLE and   We get tired of shopping,

appropriate foreign   too.

MERCHANT. They bargain,

merchant displaying some

native craft work.

         DISSOLVE TO:

```
        EXT. - FIESTA - DAY
33-     Mixed shots, fiesta.            Fiestas.
38
                    DISSOLVE TO:


        EXT. - DESERT - DAY
39      MS-MCU, spinsterish WOMAN       Even travel itself.

        on camel or burro.  Her face

        mirrors comic anguish with

        the animal's every step.


40      CU, woman's anguished face.
                    DISSOLVE TO:


        INT. - HOTEL ROOM - NIGHT
41      MS-MCU, fat MAN (nice guy       When that time comes...

        type) in pajamas.  Wearily,     well, what better answer

        he gets into bed.  A table      is there than a good book?

        with lamp and book stand

        beside him.


42      CU, man.  He sighs with

        relief...takes the book

        from the stand.


43      INSERT:  CU (man's POV),

        appropriate book jacket.
```

. . . and so, onward and upward, through 10 to 20 minutes of script.

But we can't take time right now for all that. It's more urgent that we move on to the next chapter and learn a bit about how to write narration.

CHAPTER 6

Writing Narration

CYNTHIA

4-1 CMU, C rubs bottom   Learning to ride really wears

you down...especially in some

places!

2   MS, A at C's door, Atascadero But the setting helps you

to recover. I can't imagine

a lovelier spot than the

                                            6500
Atascadero...~~six thousand~~

feet...so cool, so comfortable.

                                            Adrian around to
4   Especially with ~~Bill to help~~
                                show me the town.
                                ~~me to enjoy it.~~

6   LS, town   ~~The town, too~~...San Miguel de

Allende. ~~It's~~ A storybook

town, straight out of Colonial

days...a place to see for

yourself what the ~~really~~

                                true
~~truly~~ Mexico is like.

9   MS, C&A entering Instituto The Instituto was another plus

...a center for all the arts,

from ~arts & crafts to writing...
~~credit on a master's in your~~
~~free time if that's your thing.~~

17 MS, C&A walking to corral
   MS, colts playing

Is there anything more
beautiful than young colts
playing?

19 MS, tennis serve

Tennis ~~got a big play from~~ is big with most
horsemen.
~~a lot of our friends.~~

24 MCU, C watching dive

But
~I liked swimming best~~, though.~

26 MS, water skiing

Where else can you water-ski
a submerged steeple
past ~~towers of villages~~
~~submerged~~ in a mountain lake?

29a MS, setting sun

Then, ~~the~~ end ~~of~~ the day ~~, a~~ with
~~the~~ parties. ~~Your~~ My kind of
talk...~~your kind of friends.~~

36 CU, C&A drinking

~~Your~~ My kind of drinks, too--
~~oh,~~ how I loved those
margaritas! ...Or maybe
I should just say, oh, how
I love San Miguel!
JONATHAN

5-1 LS, pan three rings
  2 MLS, J laffing

Play's fine, all right. But
that girl's here to learn to
ride. I'm going to see she
does it.

8 MLS, students going over
  cavelette bars

I like to watch the students
working out on the cavaletti
~~bars.~~ ~~It's~~ Good training ~~for~~

~~The~~ horse and ~~the student~~ *rider.*
~~Learn together.~~ *,* The bars
& elevation
give cadence‸to the horse's
action. Elevation, too.
As the bars go up, the horse
gears himself to accommodate

Shorten

to them... ~~learns to plant his~~
~~hind feet right, too. If~~
~~he doesn't, he trips.~~

15   MS, students over a low
      jump

switch shots

You space the bars to match
the gait you want...walk, trot,
canter, ~~gallop~~ ...A few
days' practice, pretty soon
last week's beginners are
taking low jumps off a trot
from the cavalett‸es.

Narration is the sound-track commentary that sometimes accompanies a fact film's visual images. Most often it's "voice over"—that is, spoken by one or more off-screen commentators. Thus, the sample from the final narration script polish job of *Riding Holiday in Mexico* on which we opened features two alternating speakers, a girl, Cynthia, and—so help me—Jonathan, a talking ram.

The writing of narration ordinarily goes through two phases. First, while writing the shooting script, you block in tentative lines to go with it, so that client, producers, director, and whoever can follow your thinking. Second, you prepare a revised track to go with the film itself, as shot and edited. Polishing on it continues straight through to final recording, as witness the penciled changes on our sample.

Before any of this can take place, however, you have decisions to make. Grouped together, they constitute what has been called

THE PROBLEM OF APPROACH

Your film has been conceived with a particular slant and mood in mind. Now, it's important to be sure the narration matches that tone.

Sometimes that's easier said than done.

Excerpts from *Riding Holiday in Mexico* © 1975 Allende Productions.

Should the lines, for example, be formal, casual, folksy, or what? With vocabulary reflecting the classroom, the office, the laboratory, or the street? In first person, second, third? Sober or slangy, light or authoritative, cool or warm? Heavy on the information, or letting the pictures tell the story?

The best solution quite possibly may be to try out several styles till you find one that seems to fit. Then, having found it, hang onto it! This is an area where unity's especially important.

Naturally enough, this search for the right narrational approach won't be a separate enterprise, but one you feel your way through as the shooting script takes form. For even if you thought you had the problem solved 'way back when you were writing your treatment, you now may discover that subtle changes in your concept have taken place, forcing you to revise your approach appropriately.

GETTING IT DOWN ON PAPER

The best way to learn to write narration is to write narration. In quantity. In all sorts of styles and on all sorts of subjects. It helps, too, if you study the sound tracks of a host of films for narration devices and techniques, good and bad.

Procedure in writing narration is pretty much a catch-as-catch-can matter, in most cases. Ideas for phrases, lines, modes of attack, frequently begin to take form early, as you develop your core assertion and organize your approach to proving points and sub-points.

The trick is to jot down such bits and pieces, setting them aside for future reference. With luck, by the time you're ready to block in your shooting script, you'll have at least the broad outlines of your narration in mind also.

The two things *not* to do with these preliminary fragments are (a) to ignore and forget them, thus losing them forever, and (b) to try to develop them too rapidly or too completely, ignoring the script's visual aspects.

Assume, now, that you're ready to write your shooting script. What happens where the narration is concerned?

With most of us, I suspect, the rough draft of both picture and sound columns of the script go down on paper pretty much simultaneously—sometimes with the action momentarily leading the narration, sometimes vice versa.

There will also, of course, be those stubborn blank spots where nothing takes form in either area and you have no choice but to grope and fumble your way through. Ordinarily, it's not desirable to let these roadblocks hold you back too long. Better to skip ahead, and then return later. Most such problems tend to solve themselves once you've slept on them.

The key fact to remember where your first rough draft is concerned is, let it be rough. From your sequence outline, you know the points you need to make, and how you plan to make them. Beyond that, better to slop down half a page where a line is needed, scraping every last sliver of idea from your brain, rather than limiting yourself to neatly developed, pre-packaged concepts. Only thus can you hope to capture the right words, the right phrases, the alliterations, euphonies, images, rhythms, and twists of language that go to make up truly effective narration copy.

Once that first awful rough is done, it's time to start cutting, chopping out the deadwood.

Herewith, a few points and principles to guide you:

1. Good narration sets the stage.

That means narration should *establish* a number of things as needed—the subject, the setting, the mood, the core assertion; whatever.

Which is *not* to say that narration should try to take over the whole show. If your film starts with breathtaking footage of the Cornish coastline, for heaven's sake let your viewers enjoy it in peace. Narrator can always name the locale later, as a shot zooms in on a crumbling fishing village.

2. Good narration keeps your audience on the right track.

Are there things your viewers need or want to know that can't be communicated visually? Do you need to call attention to something? Set limits? Lead the way through tricky transitions? Recapitulate? Tie up the package when the film ends? The right narration very well may be the answer.

In the same way, nail down the subject and/or setting of each new sequence as soon as possible in said sequence. That means getting in the key word ("cue word") of your commentary early. Don't hold it back till the end of the sequence or other unit—by then, the footage to which it applies may already have gone by.

Also, unless you're using it as a planned transition device, do *not* let the commentary for one sequence "bleed over" into the footage for another.

3. Good narration stays with the subject.

This is another way of saying you shouldn't talk about things not on the screen. On the other hand, neither should you describe things that *are* on the screen and therefore obvious. The solution? Good narration *interprets* the subject. To that end, often the best trick is to generalize when the film shows specifics . . . talk in specifics when the footage is general. Always bearing in mind, however, that specifics *may* require specific comment; general footage, general.

4. Good narration involves the viewer.

Second person and *active voice* are two of your most useful tools in writing fact film narration. "You go right at the crossroads . . . across the moors, all the way to the sea" comes through infinitely stronger and clearer than "A path will be seen to veer right by the observant traveler."

5. Good narration is clear and to the point.

Terse, conversational copy helps. So does a preponderance of simple declarative sentences. Wherever practical, use complete sentences. Don't fall prey to long, bridging pauses in which the audience has to hold the first part of a sentence in mind for six seconds before you let them hear the rest.

A particularly deadly trap is the *list,* in which single words are tied to individual shots. The timing never quite matches the footage, with the result that the whole sequence comes out jerky, disjointed, and awkward.

Specialized terminology is another pitfall. Just because *you* know what a megalith or a macule or a kelp skeg or a lych gate or a roach clip is, don't assume your audience does.

6. Good narration is uncrowded.

A foot of 16mm film can carry about four words of narration. But the fewer feet you ask to do it, the better. Few things wear down an audience more than an overloaded narration track and a narrator who ends up panting. Many writers limit themselves to 100 words per minute (36 feet) of 16mm film, and even that can prove too many.

The remedy for too tight a track? Cut back and space out. Eliminate all the words you can. Then group those that remain into units: one sentence here, three there, two the other place.

Remember, too, that silence, music, and sound effects all have their value. After all, the audience deserves *some* time just to look at the pictures!

7. Good narration is imaginative.

Narration is an area in which to be creative. Don't hesitate to experiment with contrasting narrators, one-man dialogue (rhetorical questions and answers, etc.), sound effects as personalities (remember Alec Guinness in *The Man in the White Suit?*), and the like. It can not only prove effective, but fun—as witness a picture I once scripted with a pseudo-folksong for narration. The junior high audience towards which it was aimed loved it.

Now, four negative points to balance off the positive:

1. Avoid statistics.

True, you can fit in a few figures, if they're essential. But a narrator reading a long list of such onto the sound track is deadly. If figures must be used, try integrating them with filmed charts and graphs.

2. Soft-pedal "commercial copy."

All too often, over-eager clients will want to work in the name of the company or product every other sentence. Result: an alienated audience.

It will help, sometimes, if you point out to such clients that this injection of what amounts to advertising is about the quickest way possible to kill their chances of seeing the film win free public service TV time.

3. Nobody likes a phoney.

Pomposity, grandiloquence, pseudo-intellectualism, forced humor, oversold gimmicks, kettle-drum finales, and the like will win few friends for your client.

4. Don't play it again, Sam.

A cliché is a word or phrase that has worn out its welcome; an expression so trite and hackneyed as to have lost its impact. Most of the time, when you say something's *neat* or *cool* or *sharp as a knife* or *black as night,* you're talking to yourself, not to your audience.

The same principle applies to other forms of repetitiousness. Singing a reprise of your paean of praise to the triple-scragged framistan is more likely to induce snores than conviction. What you need, rather, is a new twist, a fresh angle.

AFTER THE STORM

So far, remember, you're just writing the script.

Finally, it's finished and approved.

Time out while the camera crew gets busy. Eventually, they and the editors will have had their way with your epic. You get a call to come back and do a polish job on the narration.

Know in advance that you're in for a shock. Almost always, expedience will have taken over, lock, stock, and barrel, changing—it will seem to you—virtually every scene you wrote. In consequence, your original narration no longer fits either time or footage.

This is hardly the best of moments for any writer. But you have little choice but to grin and bear it.

While you're grinning and bearing, you can pass the time by running the picture again. Said picture, at this stage, will be an edited workprint—a special print of the film used for preliminary cutting and juggling in order not to damage the original. It will be much scratched and patched, and minus optical effects and sound track.

Forget the lack of sound and opticals; the scratches, the patches. Just how does the film, as a film, look? Does it make visual sense? Is there a clear-cut, well-balanced beginning, middle, and end? Are the sets and locations well lit, realistic? Do the actors look human, or are they forever falling over each others' feet and staring into the camera? Do the continuity sequences follow the flow of action; the compilation, the developing idea? Is the cutting smooth, shots fitting together with a minimum of jerking and confusion? Are there well-planned cutaways to cover bobbles?

This is a list of questions without an end. Further, the first few films you script, your impulse will be to slash your wrists on the spot. Looking at a workprint and seeing the potentialities for a decent finished product that lie in it is a skill that takes learning. But count on it, given perseverance and a strong nervous system, you'll eventually get there.

The real issue is whether the footage constitutes a good silent picture. If it does, quit worrying and settle down to your polish job.

Narration polish jobs are done in one of two ways: You can write to the footage, by measure, using the four-words-per-foot rule. Or, you can read against the projected picture.

A combination quite possibly will prove your most satisfactory solution. Thus, a long strip of film may best be run through the footage counter to give you an idea of how many words maximum you have room for. Later, you can read your first efforts against the projected picture, for precise timing and smoothing of details.

It will help considerably if you make it a practice to read your copy alone, unit by unit, as you work it over. Nothing will go further towards unmasking strings of sibilants, difficult words, tongue-twisting phrases, inadvertent double entendres, deadwood sentences, and the like. Even at the recording session, you'll probably have to make last-minute changes to accommodate the verbal patterns and idiosyncrasies of the narrator.

A tedious task? It indeed can be. But though it takes all night upon occasion, there's simply no other way you can trim and hone and insert and rearrange till the finished product is just right.

Finally, the job's done; and with it, in all likelihood, your contribution to the picture. Now there's nothing left for you but to wait out the laboratory till at last the day arrives when you and your fellow workers/craftsmen/artists sit down to view the answer print, the first copy of the picture in release form, complete with sound and opticals.

How does it come off? Like a dream, of course? A rhapsody of pure perfection?

If it does, you're luckier than most. All too often, the print's a bit on the green side, the music track fights the narration, two crucial shots are juxtaposed, your best twist's bombed, and someone's forgotten to include your credit.

Don't panic, though. These are details that can and will be fixed. Besides, a film always looks worse to those who've worked on it than to anyone else.

The big thing is, the picture's finished; your first picture. But don't take too much time out for self-congratulation. You need, instead, to be scrambling around for Contract Number Two—another script to write; and this one, you promise yourself, is going to be better.

Or, if your interests lie in that direction, you might move on to consideration of the feature filmscript, which is the topic of Part 2. It begins with Chapter 7, an appraisal of how a film story's put together.

PART TWO

THE FEATURE FILM

CHAPTER 7

The Film Story

A story is the record of how some imaginary person copes with life.

(No, don't tell me that stories may very well concern actual people. Any person in a story is fabricated. Though I write of Charlemagne or Catherine the Great or my 11-year-old daughter, I am none of these people, for I cannot get inside their skins. No matter how faithfully I record their actions, my interpretation of their dreams and thoughts and motives, their inner worlds, must of necessity remain my own. This being the case, these characters are in truth as imaginary as if I had created them from whole cloth.)

So: A story is the record of how some imaginary person copes with life. It satisfies a need in us by the way it gives a sense of form and order to our chaotic world.

A *film* story is a work of fiction, designed for presentation in motion picture form.

An *effective* film story is one that, when produced and released, pulls audiences into theaters. Often it achieves this feat in the face of competition that headlines bigger stars, a higher budget, greater "production values," and more promotion.

The effective story does this by its use of desire and danger to manipulate tension in viewers. That is to say, it poises them for action, then relaxes them, according to a preplanned pattern. People attend films because they find this ebb and flow of tension stimulating and pleasurable.

How do you learn to manage these so-vital tensions?

A first step is to come to grips with precisely what constitutes desire and danger.

Desire is Humankind's yearning for happiness, the one objective we all seek. But different things symbolize happiness to different people. One man dreams of eagerly wanton females. Another aches for the luxury wealth buys. A third pursues the power to make others fawn and grovel. And yes, you find desire at work in a suicide, too, or a misanthrope, or a failure.

Danger, in turn, is something, anything, which threatens our present or future happiness to the point where we're forced to feel an unpleasant emotion: loneliness, loss, anger, inferiority, fear, hatred, or what have you.

Emotion is another name for inner tension; and tension is the driving force that powers all action.

Whatever fails to evoke emotion is worthless in any form of fiction. Anything that *does* involve a character, so deeply and disturbingly he'll fight dragons to change the precipitating situation, will unfailingly involve viewers also. Why? Because the people, the mass audience, pay little heed to anything they view objectively. They *want* to be hooked on tension, drawn taut by feeling. They yearn to see a hero win, a villain lose: a human struggle against odds.

Thus, the drive of desire is the life's blood of every film. And danger is its heartbeat.

"We go to the theatre to worry," observed the late Kenneth Macgowan, outstanding Hollywood producer and long-time chairman of the University of Southern California's Department of Theatre Arts. "Whether we see a tragedy, a serious drama, or a comedy, we enjoy it fully only if we are made to worry about the outcome of individual scenes and of the play as a whole."

A writer's plan of action for thus manipulating tension, evoking worry, is called a plot.

So, how do you plot a film story?

One of the easiest ways to start is with the old Hollywood springboard, "Who wants to do what, and why can't he?" In other words, you pick someone who aches with desire. (No one else is worth a hoot, remember. Unless Character aches, he won't strive; nor can he be defeated.) Another way of putting this is that when we say someone "aches with desire," what we really mean is that Character *wants to change something,* and he wants it so desperately that he stands ready to take whatever action is necessary in order to make that change. Maybe, trapped in a low-pay job, he wants a raise so badly he's willing to brace the boss for a raise even though it may get him fired. Or he applies for a job elsewhere. Or he sets about seducing Boss's daughter so that Boss will see him as a prospective son-in-law and so be inclined to promote him. Or he devises a scheme to maneuver Boss into a situation so compromising that Management will replace Boss.

The list can go on endlessly. What counts is that Character sets his—or her—sights on change: Woman wants Married Man, so she seeks to change his status by somehow eliminating Wife. Impoverished Nephew wants to become Rich Heir—a change!—and if that means offing Aged Aunt, so be it. Priest's dream is to win favor in God's eyes by—change!—refurbishing his run-down church.

In each case, the trick is to commit Character to change. Then, threaten his hopes of attaining said change via dynamic opposition—a man or a task or a world that fights back.

But we're getting ahead of ourselves, for a film story doesn't spring into being full blown. Rather, it's developed through a process of continuing elaboration, in a series of five phases: premise, outline/synopsis, treatment, step outline, and master scene script.

We'll deal with it that way, then. In steps, phase by phase. Building from nothing to something.

Where do you start?

You begin by tracking down a premise.

FINDING THE PREMISE

A premise is the basic idea or concept behind a feature film.

It's not an outline of the story itself, you understand; not even an explicit statement of the situation.

Indeed, it's a most peculiar entity. All sorts of people get confused about it.

Why do they become thus confused? Mostly, because in the motion picture industry premise tends to be lumped with what I like to term a presentation.

Now a presentation *is* a sort of outline—a selling outline, as it were. If you try to include it with the premise, or attempt to pretend it's the same thing, you end up with a mishmash that makes little sense to anybody.

Here, then, let us separate the two, disregarding any screams of outrage that may arise.

Also, let us reiterate the point we first made: A premise is the basic idea behind a film; the bedrock from which your story springs. It is *not* an outline.

Think of it, rather, as a hypothetical question—one that lays the foundation upon which your story situation is to be built.

How does a solid premise come into being?

1. *You find a topic that intrigues you.*
2. *You discover/develop a unique angle from which to view said topic.*
3. *You cast this idea within the framework of a hypothetical question.*

Like the fact film, you see, the feature is undergirded by *topic* and *point of view*. The difference between them lies only in the way they focus.

In the feature, they combine to create a central "What if—?" question: the premise from which the feature's story springs.

Do these events take place in neat 1-2-3 order: topic—angle—premise?

Well, hardly. Indeed, you often may find yourself with little control over how, when, or even if, they take form.

The situation is somewhat like that of a woman walking down the street. She remains just a woman—until someone, looking at her, suddenly sees her as a potential subject of seduction.

Similarly, a bank is just a bank, until someone views it as a potential source of loot, rather than a business institution. Or a wardrobe is just a piece of furniture until mental lightning strikes and, in some mind's eye, it becomes a place to hide a body.

Now obviously this is nothing new. Your point of view is simply your subjective attitude towards a topic: the potentialities you see in it as foundation for a fictional situation. Its basis is your own heredity and conditioning, and no two people see any topic exactly the same.

The "good" topic is the one that stimulates your imagination to come forth with a "good" angle.

The "good" angle? It's one that excites you, preoccupies you, sends your imagination soaring off on flight after flight of story-focused inspiration.

And yes, this *is* important. Tricks, techniques, mechanics, facility with language—all are vital to the scriptwriter. But they can never hope to substitute for the surge and drive born of your own very personal excitement.

But back to premise proper. Consider the picture of a few years ago, *Guess Who's Coming to Dinner*. Undergirding the plot lies one simple yet provocative thought: *What if an upper class white woman fell in love with a black man?*

That question is the story's premise. It sets forth an idea that hooks your interest, needles your imagination. What you do with it, how you develop it, depends on your own taste and talent. You may produce a work of genius, or pure garbage, or copy at any level in between. But without the premise, you have nothing, even at the garbage level. Premise remains the writer's firm foundation. All else is superstructure.

Consider the Disney hit, *The Apple Dumpling Gang*. Behind it, too, lies a simple premise: *"What if a footloose gambler in the pioneer West suddenly found himself saddled with a brood of children?"* That delightfully offbeat picture, *The Gods Must be Crazy*, takes off from *"What if a Coke bottle dropped from an airplane were to totally disrupt life in a primitive African tribe?"*

Space Camp springs from *"What if an accident during a routine engine check sends a diverse group of teenagers into orbit?"*

Or, suppose we here devise a premise of our very own.

Let's begin with a topic: in this case an object, a Brinks-type armored truck.

Why an armored truck? Because a few years ago I reviewed a top-notch suspense novel, *The Kidnapping of The President,* by Charles Templeton. The author made excellent—and unique—use of an armored truck in his story. Couple that with another intriguing volume from my shelf, John A. Minnery's *The Trapping and Destruction of Executive Armored Cars,* and I found myself preoccupied with the challenge of finding a different yet interest-hooking point of view on armored trucks to play with. What shall it be? Robbery? A hiding place? A mobile fort? Some sort of red herring?

Well, robbery's out, of course; too commonplace. And neither the hiding place nor mobile fort bits strike any sparks in my imagination. As for the red herring gimmick . . .

But wait—! Suppose we use robbery, after all, only the robbery's not really a robbery, but a cover-up, a red herring! Maybe, for instance, someone wants to conceal an embezzlement with a fake robbery. Or to distract attention from a bank heist with a noisy, flamboyant attack on an armored truck. Or to launder hot Mafia money by switching it for the truck's load—

Hey, that's it! A switch! But not the Mafia thing; that's old hat and besides, if Mafia types are going to the trouble of knocking off an armored truck, they're going to hang onto *all* the money, not just part.

No, we need something much more human; much less routine. But we'll find that, given a little time. Meanwhile, what's important is that we've found our angle—an angle we can frame neatly in an appropriate, intriguing "What if—?" question: *What if someone robbed an armored truck just in order to switch hot money for that aboard the vehicle?*

The important thing about working from a premise thus is that it forces you to razor-sharp awareness of your story's basic concept.

Every story has such a core idea, you see. The only issue is, is said idea strong or weak? Unless you zero in on it, in its simplest, starkest form, you may discover too late that it holds fatal flaws that point you straight down the track to disaster before you ever set a line on paper.

Given a clear, incisive premise, on the other hand, your story is stripped of many of the ills that might otherwise beset it. In writing, you're able to avoid the extraneous . . . shear away fuzziness and sharpen focus. You present a concise, tightly organized product, geared to maximum impact and effectiveness.

Producers and story editors like that kind of work. They find a place in their hearts and checkbooks for the writer who writes it.

How do you create a solid premise?

1. As already described, you frame the basic idea of your story, the concept on which it rests, in terms of a "What if—?" question.
2. You check this question for
   a. Freshness.
   b. Relevance.
   c. Dramatic implications.
   d. Practicality.
3. You sharpen and strengthen the idea at any point where weakness becomes apparent.

Point 1 is, I trust, already clear. But what about point 2a, and *freshness?*

Your goal, in premise, is to catch attention, arouse interest. The trite or familiar just won't do this. Clichés in speech constitute a reasonably apt parallel: The first time you heard someone speak of something as "smooth as glass" or "cold as ice" or "sharp as a knife," it probably caught your ear . . . created a vivid image in your mind.

Today, as we observed in our chapter on narration, those same phrases no longer touch you. Overuse has worn away the edge of each to where you're hardly aware the words are spoken.

It's the same with stories. *Freshness,* the unique twist, stands all-important. Tell someone your tale concerns boy meets girl and his mind switches off—until you add, "and the girl is a Siamese twin!" A story set in a florist's shop seems too routine to hold interest on the screen. But, if the prize plant eats people—well, remember *Little Shop of Horrors?*

It's also worth bearing in mind that ideas often come from the most unlikely places and by the least likely routes. That hilariously refreshing comedy, *Ruthless People,* offers a case in point. It's about a couple who abduct a woman who's such a harridan that her husband doesn't want her back. When he stalls on paying for her release, it enrages her so much that she joins forces with her kidnappers.

I took it for granted scriptwriter Dale Launer's inspiration had been the old O. Henry short story, "The Ransom of Red Chief," in which a super-brat seized by an inept pair of crooks drives them up the wall. But when I talked to Launer, I learned that I was wrong. Although he was familiar with "Red Chief," his springboard to *Ruthless People* actually had been Patty Hearst's kidnapping by the Symbionese Liberation Army terrorists.

"They asked for a big ransom. When they didn't get it, they somehow convinced her that her parents didn't want her back," he explained. "They did such a good job that she joined them, and I thought that was actually kind of funny."

Relevance? That's simply another way of saying your story must make emotional sense to your viewers. To that end, it needs to catch them up in the kind of feelings they themselves have felt and so understand, all projected in terms pertinent to life today. Thus, the success of *Under Fire* and *Silkwood* lay in their use of color and today's political realities to evoke fears that lurk in all of us; recent Vietnam pictures offer such disturbing insights and conjectures regarding that bloody conflict as to rouse fears, and so become relevant to us. *Half Moon Street* portrays a liberated, highly educated, politically sophisticated woman turning to prostitution to increase her income.

For a premise to have *dramatic implications,* in turn, means that it must show the possibility of plunging people into conflict. Preferably, this conflict should be visible and involve other people. For while the story rooted in a monk's inner struggle as he kneels in his cell will fascinate a certain number of viewers, far more will be caught up in clashes that match man against man. (Or against woman—conflict exists wherever will battles will, of course, and this holds as true in a seduction as in a fist-fight.)

Practicality becomes an issue on two levels: First, technical difficulties involved in filming can stop a project cold. A premise of "What if the world came to an end and our hero alone, surviving, had to reassemble Earth from atoms?" involves complications few producers would care to tackle.

Level Two is cost. If you're trying to connect with a shoestring independent who lacks even set rent, it seems unlikely he'll be interested in a script based on the premise, "What if Napoleon, rising from the dead, led France's legions through a new conquest of Europe?"

On to point 3: Is it easy to sharpen and strengthen a premise?

Here the answer is, "Sometimes yes, sometimes no." Despite your best efforts, on occasion, your premise will remain tired and trite. You'll find yourself unable to give it appeal to a sufficiently wide audience. Or you'll recognize intuitively that the public will feel it irrelevant or view the conflicts it offers as too shallow or trivial. Or you'll be forced to acknowledge that practical problems or costs will simply prove too great to warrant producer interest.

When such happens, the answer is to move on to another, stronger project, rather than to waste time and energy beating the dead horse of an idea gone sour.

But more often than not, things will fall into place far better than you anticipated. The secret of success is to use the principles we dipped into in Chapter 1, in discussing how to make the most of your creative powers. Get in there and juggle pieces! Inject new elements! Work till you hit a combination that captures your own imagination! A couple of young fellows traveling cross-country by cycle is mildly intriguing—who hasn't had a yen to do so? But make the pair hippies and you add whole new dimensions of freshness and relevance and conflict. A producer seeking a hit is old hat; one striving to fail comes off as new, different, funny.

So keep analyzing; keep rearranging; keep striving. Even though your first efforts seem incredibly clumsy, totally fruitless, the very effort of trying to set up a clear, sharp premise can't help but whet your own skills at thinking and at writing. And such keen-edged tools are a first step towards success in this scripting business, believe me!

Bear in mind, however, that not every idea, not every premise which you develop, is going to strike sparks in others also. A good many times, you'll discover someone else has already made use of the same concept, as I did once some years ago when Jack Emanuel at Warner Brothers blasted one of my pet ideas by citing chapter and verse of at least three times it had been used previously.

In other instances, prior producer/director/actor commitments, technical difficulties, financial involvements, or just plain ineptitude on your own part will shoot you down. You'll find you're lucky indeed if you hit with one "What if—?" out of five or ten.

Further, a gleam of interest in regard to the presentation you build from a given premise is no assurance said interest will continue. Quite possibly you'll be cut off at the next stage, or the next. I still can bleed when I think back. . . .

But that's enough on the negative side. Right now, let's assume you've found a truly satisfying premise.

Next question: What do you do with it? Whom do you show it to?

If you take my advice, in all likelihood you won't show it to anyone. Why not? Because a premise, in and of itself, is a poor calling card.

Instead of charging off in all directions the moment you come up with a premise, therefore, consider your idea as a seed only—a seed which may or may not sprout. You, because you know it so well, can already envision the lovely plant which—potentially—will spring from it.

It's unlikely, however, that anyone else will be able to appreciate it fully. So it follows that it's wisest not to show your treasure around at this stage. Rather, be patient. Cultivate and nurture your prize in private. Work on it till you have it developed into a fuller form; one more likely to excite others.

This form is one that goes by many names—synopsis, outline, story line, synopsized theme. The term I prefer, the one we'll use here, is the *presentation.*

PREPARING THE PRESENTATION

A presentation is a sort of sales-pitch for a premise. Indeed, script-writers ordinarily use the term *pitch* when they speak of making a presentation.

The purpose of a pitch, a presentation, is to hook a producer's attention. It's designed to give you a chance to set forth your basic idea. You can do this with a hook, a gimmick, a character, a scene, or the abovementioned basic idea itself. If you catch the interest of producer or story editor or whomever, you then can sketch in your story's broadest outlines—and do so in such terms as to develop the contact further.

What persuades a producer to o.k. an idea?

First, a belief that the premise itself has strong audience appeal.

Second, a demonstration of the premise's dramatic potential.

How do you give such a demonstration? Every writer has his own system—and every one of them that works is right.

You, too, eventually will develop private notions on the subject. Meanwhile, however, it may help to have some sort of rule-of-thumb procedure to fall back on while your own ideas are jelling.

Remember what we said about desire and danger, back in our section on the film story? About the necessity of building our attack around a someone who wants something desperately, but whose chances of getting it are somehow jeopardized?

Well, there are worse places than that to start, when you set about laying out your project.

It will also improve the odds, I suspect, if you'll plan your epic work in terms of an old-fashioned, Aristotelian beginning, middle, and end.

Above all, you'll chalk up brownie points if you work from a thing I call a *starting lineup*. For while many will snort, and while it certainly isn't the only approach to building a story, it does offer a simple, practical procedure for the beginner to use as springboard.

The lineup is a sort of checklist designed to focus story elements into a pattern which allows appraisal of their dramatic potential. To that end, it zeroes in on five factors:

1. A character.

The central character in your story, that is.

Actually, a character isn't just a person; he—or she—is a point of view. An individual with a strong attitude towards your topic, he's someone you can involve in the "What if—?" of your premise with full faith that he'll react.

2. A predicament.

A predicament is a premise-related state of affairs somehow sufficiently uncomfortable as to arouse emotion—that is, tension—in Character; and so, hopefully, to arouse emotion and create tension in viewers also. The issue is empathy, as we observed in Chapter 3.

3. An objective.

An objective is a prize for Character to fight for . . . a new and different state of affairs, happier than that revealed in Predicament, which Character hopes to attain.

4. An opponent.

An opponent is someone or something for Character to fight against. He, like Character, is a point of view—but one in such contrast to that of Character as to insure conflict within the situational framework arising from the premise.

5. A disaster.

A disaster, as I use the word here, is the potential terrible fate with which you confront Character at climax as his penalty should he lose. It also provides the ultimate focal point for audience tension.

So much for the ingredients of our lineup. Obviously, they're designed to provide broad outlines only. But don't worry about holes; we'll plug them later.

Next step: Group the five ingredients into two sentences—the first a statement, the second a question.

> *Sentence 1:* A statement of story situation in terms of character, predicament, objective.
>
> *Sentence 2:* A "will or won't Character succeed?" story question, compounded of Sentence 1 ingredients plus opponent and disaster, and all designed to keep your viewers panting with excitement.

Together, these two sentences will go a long way towards keeping your script soundly structured, on the one hand, yet tautly gripping, on the other. For the pattern they provide does work.

Let's take the sample premise we built earlier . . . develop it as a case in point.

Remember the premise? *"What if someone robbed an armored truck just in order to switch hot money for that aboard the vehicle?"* Where do we begin, in turning this into a starting lineup?

Well, why not start with the "someone"? Arbitrarily, we'll assign him the name of Earl Parrish. Age 30, in order to appeal to a young audience. And since robbing an armored truck may prove on the strenuous side and call for appropriate skill with weapons, we'll make him a former Marine, survivor of the disastrous 1983 barracks bombing in Lebanon. After all, if any part of this doesn't work, we can always change it later.

Next question: Why has Earl decided to go into the armed robbery business? Is he vengeful, money-hungry, criminal psychopath, or what?

Somehow, none of those angles turn me on. For even though I've barely met Earl, I find myself liking him. I doubt he's just a common thug.

So what would turn a non-thug to robbery? Duty? Blackmail? Altruism?

Duty, in these circumstances, strikes me as a little too James Bond-ish. Blackmail? Well, maybe. Altruism? Hmm . . .

Then, while I brood, the right word comes. It's *loyalty,* a trait admirable in and of itself, yet in whose name all sorts of crimes have been committed.

Shall we try it for size? To whom or what is Earl loyal? A relative? A friend? A sweetheart? A Service buddy?

But no. All such are too routine, too predictable. Let's reach farther out . . . try to find some figure who'll give our plot-to-be a logical yet unanticipated twist.

Like one of Earl's former school teachers, for instance.

And there we have it—we hope: One of Earl's old school teachers is in trouble. Maybe, for an added touch, she doesn't even know it. Innocently enough, she's bumbled into a situation where she's in possession of a suitcase full of demonstrably stolen money. The only way to get her off the hook is to switch the hot cash for cold. One thing leads to another, and the next thing Earl knows, he's committed to making the exchange via an armored truck robbery.

Fine! But that's only the first unit of our lineup, the statement of the story situation. Now, what about the second, the vital, suspense-building story question?

Well, for one thing, we need an *opponent,* an adversary for Earl to battle. Not to mention a *disaster,* a startling—and devastating—twist around which to build our climax.

For now, let's take the easy road where Opponent is concerned: We'll keep his identity a secret from Earl.

As for the disaster, there's an old rule of thumb about such that says make it the most appalling thing that can possibly happen.

What might that be, in Earl's situation?

A possibility: Earl robs the truck, gets the clean cash—and then Villain not only steals it from him, but frames him for the theft!

Here are how these points look, set up within the framework of a starting lineup:

Predicament:	Too loyal to abandon a former teacher,	
Character:	Earl Parrish, 30, footloose Marine survivor of the 1983 Lebanon bombing	Statement of Situation
Objective:	sets out to rob an armored truck in order to switch hot bills for clean, to save Teacher's funds and reputation.	

Opponent: But can he succeed, when an unknown ⎫ Story
Disaster: adversary heists the clean cash and lays ⎬ Question
                the robbery at his doorstep?   ⎭

Please note that the lineup offers basic story elements only. Starkly skeletal, it makes no pretext of revealing the entire picture. Like the premise, it's more a writer's working tool than something to pass on to others. Its greatest value is that it forces you to think in fundamentals. Yet because it lays out a dynamic plan of action, certain elements to look for and decide on, it blasts you off dead center. Do learn to use it!

Clearly, this kind of thing takes practice. Go see three or four or five feature films, entertainment movies. Then, write out a two-sentence starting lineup for each, as outlined above.

Once you begin to get the knack, frame up potential film stories of your own. To acquire facility, work out one each night before you go to bed. You won't believe how much you'll improve in a month. Besides, it's not that much work . . . only two little sentences per night . . . just the kind of preparation you need for your next step, the sketching in of

BEGINNING, MIDDLE, END

Lay out a story based on one of your starting lineups in whatever manner best suits your tastes. Then, break it down into beginning, middle, end. Develop each in a paragraph or two, not more—the idea, remember, is to frame up broad outlines only.

The *beginning* establishes your character within the framework of his predicament, nails down his objective, and carries the story forward to that point where Character commits himself to fight to the bitter end to attain his desire.

The *middle* reveals the various steps of Character's struggle to defeat the danger which threatens him. And if you want your viewers to sit through it, you'd better cram it with fresh ideas, intriguing twists, and intensity of feeling.

The *end* sees Character win or lose his battle. Remember, in this regard, the story doesn't truly end until the struggle between desire and danger is resolved, with some kind of clear-cut triumph of desire over danger, or vice versa.

Applying this breakdown to our money truck caper story, we might end up with something like this:

Beginning: What if someone robbed an armored money truck just in order to switch hot money for that aboard the vehicle? This is the situation we confront in this different caper story.

Our setting is Appalachian Chicago—the decaying Uptown neighborhoods along Kenmore, Wilson, Argyle . . . our central figure, 30-year-old Marine vet Earl Parrish, currently footloose but in all likelihood en route to a mercenary's job training troops in Latin America. Now he learns that the safety deposit box of a dying hillbilly schoolteacher who helped shape his life when he was a boy back in West Virginia contains $60,000 in sequentially numbered bills, hot currency from a bank robbery. If the authorities discover it, it will not only destroy Teacher, but put an end to her dream of a small private program to help disadvantaged hill country kids from her home county.

At present, Teacher knows nothing of all this. It's unthinkable that she could be involved. So the only way out is to switch the stolen money for clean bills. To that end, and despite the fact he's an ex-deputy sheriff, Earl agrees to head up the robbery of an armored truck.

Middle: Gathering together a weird assortment of Teacher's other ex-pupils to help him, Earl plans and carries out the switch . . . halting the truck by spray-painting all windows, forcing crew to open it by pumping tear-gas through the ventilating system, etc. His task is made immeasurably more difficult by the divergent personalities and motives of his aides.

End: The time to put the switched cash into Teacher's safe deposit box arrives. Only now Earl discovers that the money's missing; the only likely suspect, dead. But the very fact of Suspect's death clears all members of the heist group . . . lays guilt in the lap of an ex-hillbilly minor bank official who had access to Teacher's box.

When Earl goes to confront Official, he himself is trapped. Though he kills the bank man and recovers the cash, he now has no way to get it back into Teacher's box. The cops are hot on his trail, too. He has no choice but to run. His girl, a social worker who first discovered the hot money in Teacher's box and then conceived the robbery scheme, asks to go along. Earl refuses; he must take the mercenary job. Her assignment, in turn, is to deliver the suitcase of cash to a small-town West Virginia bank. Banker, Earl's friend, will see that it's used to carry out Teacher's plan.

Earl leaves. Girl watches him go . . . sets off down street with suitcase . . . pauses to greet a pre-planted Mexican or Puerto Rican vendor: *"Buenas noches,* Ramon." And then: "Tell me, *amigo,* how long will it take me to learn Spanish?"

Note, please that our story is growing as we go along. Just as premise expanded into lineup, so lineup now has been fleshed out into a more coherent story.

This is as it should be. If there is one principle that underlies every form of writing—and, especially, of film scriptwriting—it's this concept of continuing elaboration, building from seed idea through step after step to finished form.

Thus, Earl Parrish is taking on stature almost by the minute . . . becoming less a name and more a person, complete with past and future as well as present. "Plus" elements—colorful people, striking settings, unusual scenes, unique mood material, and the like—also are beginning to appear: Note the incorporation of the "Appalachian Chicago" background; the assembling of transplanted hillbillies to pull a metropolitan caper; the halting of the armored truck by spray-painting the windows, and so on.

These bits are still in embryonic form, of course; only just beginning to develop. But that's all right. It takes time to build a solid film script.

Finally, there's the matter of a working title. Make it as intriguing as you can, naturally. But even a bad title is better than none at all. It at least gives people some sort of label by which to designate your opus.

What shall we call Earl Parrish's saga? Tentatively—and with apologies to all concerned with that thrill-packed epic, *The Taking of Pelham One Two Three*—let's title it *The Heisting of Money Truck Four Five Six*.

HOW ABOUT FORMAT?

As you'll see from the sample that follows, and those in Chapter 18, there are few rules as to how to set up a presentation. Striking content, plus enthusiastic dramatization, are what count. Just be sure to include— in whatever form or order—premise, starting lineup elements, beginning-middle-end, "plus" factors, and title, and you're not likely to go too far wrong.

Film Outline

The Heisting of

M O N E Y   T R U C K   4 5 6

(Tentative Title)

Earl Parrish is a man cool and tough enough to rob an armored money truck, but he has principles. Indeed, it's precisely <u>because</u> he has principles--especially a sense of loyalty--that he agrees to stage the robbery.

Our setting is Appalachian Chicago--the decaying
neighborhoods along Kenmore and Wilson and Argyle. Thirty-year-
old Earl, our central character, is the coolly dangerous
product of a West Virginia mining county, an ex-Marine now
jobless and footloose like thousands of other veterans, Chicago
is a last fling for him before he signs on as a mercenary to
train troops in Latin America.

Quite possibly we first meet Earl as he tramps
purposefully along a drab Chicago street. Then an armored
money truck pulls up across the walk and blocks him off.
Guards get out and take posts while money is loaded or unloaded.
Earl scowls at the car. We follow his glance, zoom in to a
frame-filling closeup of its number, 4-5-6, and then cut back
as titles come on over.

Earl has a problem. One of the most important people
in his life has been a hillbilly schoolteacher who helped
shape him when he was a boy back in West Virginia. Now that
teacher lies dying here in Chicago. Her life savings of
$60,000, which she wants to see devoted to helping disadvantaged
hill country kids from her home county, are in a safe deposit
box in a neighborhood bank. The only catch is that a girl
social worker has discovered that said savings have been replaced
with sequentially numbered bills, hot currency from a bank
robbery. If the authorities discover it, Teacher's dream will
be shattered, her heart broken, and her good name besmirched.
The only way out, as Girl sees it, is somehow to switch the
stolen money for clean bills. To that end, she wants Earl to
direct the robbery of an armored money truck.

Loyalty to Teacher overrides good sense, for Earl.
He agrees...recruits a weird assortment of other ex-pupils of
Teacher now in Chicago.

Planning and carrying out the robbery is made immeasurably more difficult by the divergent personalities and motives of these aides. But Earl finally succeeds in bringing off the heist by spray-painting the truck's windows so it has to stop, then pumping tear-gas through the ventilating system to force the crew to open the doors.

When the time comes to put the clean cash into Teacher's safe deposit box arrives, however, Earl finds the armored truck money is missing; the only likely suspect in the theft dead. But the very fact of Suspect's death clears all members of the heist group...lays guilt in the lap of an ex-hillbilly minor bank official who had access to Teacher's box. Confronting him, Earl himself is trapped. But though he survives to kill the bank man and recover the cash, he now has no way to get it back into Teacher's box. The cops are hot on his trail, too. He has no choice but to run.

First, though, he takes the money to the social worker. Unhappily, she reveals that it makes no difference now, for in the interim, Teacher has died. As for Earl's running, she wants to go along.

Earl refuses; he's off to take the mercenary job. Girl's assignment, in turn, is to deliver the suitcase of cash to a hill-country West Virginia bank. Banker, Earl's friend, will see that it's used to carry out Teacher's plan.

Earl leaves. Girl watches him go...herself sets off down the street with the suitcase...pauses to greet a pre-planted Mexican or Puerto Rican vendor: "Buenas noches, Ramon." And then: "Tell me, amigo, how long will it take a girl like me to learn Spanish?"

THE END

A final question: What about the validity of the pattern I've outlined?

Have no illusions. Jean-Luc Godard won't approve, and neither will Jonas Mekas. But the approach *does* work—most successful feature films fit in—and it *is* the pattern of life . . . which is to say, the pattern of People with Problems. You can see this even in your own conversation: "Mrs. May left for church at 10:15 today" interests no one. "Mrs. May left for church at 10:15 today—and no one's seen her since," captures instant attention.

This isn't to say that chronological order is always the best way to present your material. Quite possibly you'll find good reasons to depart such in order to start from some more dramatic or more mood-inspiring or more emotionally meaningful moment. The issue is simply to think through basic story first, then pick the most effective way to present it.

Also, in any particular picture, story may be subordinated to other elements. Thus, fantasy dominated in Woody Allen's *The Purple Rose of Cairo* . . . violence and special effects in *Aliens* . . . sex and horror in *The Fly*.

So it is with your presentation. Its goal is simply to cast whatever raw material you choose to use into some sort of interest-catching form, with a central character set up to move in a particular direction. Then, because the human animal likes life to show at least a semblance of meaning, order, you make sure to include an ending that rounds things out by postulating the victory or defeat of Character in his efforts.

Observe how free this approach leaves you. Though I've here developed *Money Truck 456* as straight melodrama, it could equally well be shaped for dramatic comedy on the *Tough Guys* order, or *Prizzi's Honor* brand tragedy, or almost anything else you might choose.

*   *   *

So much for the film story. Now, let's take a closer look at its most vital ingredient: the film character.

CHAPTER 8

The Film Character

Three guests dropped by last night. One was a gaunt, fragile man in his middle 70s, the second a sexy widow approaching 60, the third a proper Englishwoman of 32.

Our visitors' chief topic of the evening was Sexy Widow's impending marriage to an older man several states away. Sexy Widow's approach to the subject was one of wholehearted enthusiasm. As she somewhat tritely phrased it, "A woman needs a man."

"You should know," Male Guest muttered dourly. "At your age, though, you're right. You need to get settled into another marriage."

"No, no!" Proper Englishwoman protested. "She's only buying trouble. An older chap especially—he'll be forever fussing."

"Let me worry about that," Sexy Widow retorted. "I can be quite persuasive in the dark."

Male Guest snorted. "That may not count for as much as you think. Not if this fellow's really ten years older than you are."

"Old or young, what does it matter?" Proper Englishwoman shrugged. "I played nanny to one husband for seven years. I've no desire to take on another." A sidewise glance. "I do wonder, though: How will this chap react if he finds out about your affairs?"

Sexy Widow shivered. "Please, don't talk about it!—Oh, I don't know what I'd do!"

I bring up this episode because it constitutes an excellent lesson in the basics of film characterization.

Thus, the broad externals of character can be reduced to three elements: sex, age, dominant impression: man, middle 70s, gaunt and fragile; sexy widow, approaching 60; proper Englishwoman, 32.

Do you see how simple it is to draw the picture? And how effective? Actors and casting directors alike will love you for it!

Character's inner aspects? Again, they can be approached in terms of three elements: point of view, dominant attitude, interests.

Point of view, you'll recall, is a character's subjective outlook on a given topic. Take Sexy Widow. She viewed marriage enthusiastically, and strongly in terms of the man-woman relationship involved. Male Guest went along with the idea, too, but with emphasis on the security angle. Proper Englishwoman, in contrast, disapproved: In a flash, she could see potentialities for disaster.

These reactions to the specific situation were only a reflection of the trio's broader attitudes; their total approach to life.

Thus, Sexy Widow is a woman who views bed as a solution to all problems. With advancing years, Male Guest's preoccupation is with old age and the fear of inadequacy, insecurity. Proper Englishwoman sees close involvements of any kind as fraught with peril.

Interests, in turn, flesh out the picture. This became particularly apparent as the evening wore on. Sexy Widow had trained in interior decorating. Already, she was visualizing the things she'd do with her new home. Proper Englishwoman, who was into sculpture, tended to sniff at that as dreadfully middle-class. Male Guest, a retired oil company accountant, found all such artsy-craftsy stuff wryly amusing in comparison with the man's world of business through which he'd moved.

For my part, as a writer, I found myself involuntarily considering each of my visitors as possible hero/heroine in a film. To that end, I measured by the two standards—goal, and what I term climax potential—which habit leads me to apply.

Where goal was concerned, Sexy Widow came in first by a country mile. She wanted to get married, and she had no intention of letting anything stop her.

Male Guest and Proper Englishwoman, on the other hand, were bystanders, spectators—at least, insofar as the evening's situation went. On the surface, they were interested, but they weren't deeply enough involved to really strive. In consequence, they had drift, rather than direction.

Climax potential, in turn, in my view, centers on a goal-motivated character's capacity for harboring two strong emotions at once.

I say this because I feel the peril at the climax of any story, whether for print or screen, should be emotional as well as physical. It's not enough that hero or heroine should simply kill or otherwise defeat the villain. In addition he/she should also have to win a battle within, in which desire is ranged against duty, honor, integrity, principle, uprightness, spirit, or what have you. If you want a brilliant example of such, think back on that classic, *The Maltese Falcon,* in which honor is enough more important to Humphrey Bogart than is his love of Mary Astor that he sends her off to prison at the climax.

It's this inner clash, coupled with the outer, that gives real depth and interest to a story. And you get it by choosing a central character who has climax potential—that is, a character who, though driven well-nigh compulsively by desire, still can feel the pull of another, contradictory emotion.

How does Sexy Widow meet this test? Pretty well, I think: for even now, before the fact, she shudders and whispers, "Oh, I don't know what I'd do!" Clearly, the right circumstances could set up a strong state of conflict in her. Desire might very well have to battle it out with some other emotion—honor, for example, or pride, or love.

And there you are: characterization basics, alive and breathing, as exemplified in one evening and three visitors.

Have I oversimplified the issues? Of course; and that's as it should be, for it brings us down to the key principle of film character development: *A film character is a simulation and simplification of a person. Though played by a living actor, he is not an actual human being.*

A person, a human being, is a creature of infinite depth and subtlety, infinitely complex; and this whether you label him the product of Deity or evolution.

A person is also infinitely confusing. Philosophers and savants have spent centuries probing for personality's essence. Psychotherapists without number have grown wealthy delving for the source of the troubleds' troubles. Generations of husbands have striven—and failed—to understand their wives; and vice versa.

Film scriptwriters find all this cold comfort. Nor do motion picture audiences show much desire to share in such confusion. They prefer, instead, to be entertained.

That is, they like film characters who *appear* to be living, breathing human beings, but who have been simplified to the point that they are understandable. Indeed, it may be said with little fear of contradiction that far more film characters fail through being too complex than being too simple.

Which is not to say that a film character cannot come to exist with perhaps even greater reality than a person. Witness Clark Gable *(Gone With the Wind),* Judy Garland *(The Wizard of Oz),* Marlon Brando *(The Godfather),* the little alien *(E.T.),* Humphrey Bogart *(Casablanca),* Rita Hayworth *(Gilda),* Gary Cooper *(High Noon),* Marlene Dietrich *(The Blue Angel),* and a hundred—a thousand—others.

It would, in fact, not be too far amiss to title this chapter "An Ode to Actors," on grounds that all we writers give players to work with, on the face of it, are things to do and things to say . . . after which, it is they who translate the dead words from our pages into vibrant, dynamic individuals, on the screen and in the hearts of viewers.

Yet beyond all our debts to actors—directors, too—there are at least two crucial aspects of film character manufacture that rest squarely on the writer's shoulders: the original *conception* of the character; and the *presentation* of said character, as conceptualized, within the framework of the script.

Both these phases of the writer's work are superskilled; inventive to the *n*th degree. And it is here, in carrying out these master services through creative application of a few basic principles, that the writer earns his pay.

(It is also, incidentally, at this point that the whole ridiculous theory of the director as *auteur* collapses. Film characters, film stories, are born in the brains of writers. The director only interprets. If the original conception is his, it is only because, at that moment, he is wearing the writer's hat. Or, as one irate scriptwriter is reputed to have bellowed, throwing a swatch of blank paper at a director, "Here, damn you! Give *this* your famous touch!"

How do you *conceive* a character, then?

The best procedure, always, is first to let your fancy run completely free, in any direction and as far as it will go. Let it catch a flash of today's friend here, a bit from yesterday's foe there, an overheard fragment of conversation after that.

As you build on and develop these bits, pay particular attention to what each character cares about. For if your characters do not care, your reader/viewer cannot.

Bear down especially hard on this where your central character is concerned. Why? Because what you care about is what you are. *To care about* something means that you believe or feel it to be important, as in "It's important to Sue to protect her ego," "to have her mother's blessing," "to escape marriage/Mafia vengeance/the police." Goal and purpose spring from caring. For story purposes, the character who doesn't care about anything is useless.

(*Why* does he/she care? Don't worry about that at this time. It's something you can figure out later.)

So, what does Character care about? A man? A child? A million dollars? A line of cocaine? The super's letter of commendation?

Note, please, that each of these targets is a *symbol* of caring—specific, concrete, immediate, visual; something Character can take action to attain *now*. It's not enough that Character yearns for love. Audiences will find "getting Gretchen into bed" more meaningful. "Fame?" "Making an appointment for an audition" will take a better picture. "Revenge?" Try "seeing rival marched away in handcuffs."

Remember, too, that we all care about *many* things, which means that you must pick and choose between those your character feels to be important . . . select the one (or ones) which, for him, is predominant at this moment.

Further, everything in your story must, one way or another, relate to your central character's caring. All else is extraneous. Incorporate too many other elements and your film will prove diffuse.

Beyond this, the key principle to bear in mind at this point is that it's essential that you cast your script for contrast.

That is, you decide just what characters should be in your story, and—roughly—what kind of people they are.

To this end, you balance necessary characters one against the other.

As a general rule, each character should be different from his fellows. Different physically. Different in point of view. Different in the impression he makes. Different in attitudes. Different in interests. Different in goals. Different in tags. Different in potentialities and background.

Because they're all so different, these characters will have different relationships to each other. Character A will like Character B, love Character C, hate Character D, distrust Character E, think Character F a fool, and so on.

This is important. Failure to contrast characters and to develop meaningful relationships between them is one of the commonest causes of shallow pictures.

Consider the people in our money truck epic. Earl Parrish, the central figure, is a 30-year-old Marine veteran, originally a deputy sheriff from a West Virginia mountain county, but now discharged from the service and roving the streets of Chicago.

Selection of these first rough characterizing details for Parrish is a purely arbitrary matter. Young enough to appeal to youthful movie-goers, he also has enough years and experience to come through with a more mature audience. His service as a deputy sheriff and in the Marines not only gives him a certain color, but provides him with the potentialities called for by his role—a matter we'll take up in more detail later. His years in West Virginia offer sharp contrast to his present presence in Chicago—yet is entirely believable, in view of the heavy influx of Appalachians into midwest metropolitan areas.

Please note, incidentally, that we've given Parrish no physical description. This is with malice aforethought. Beyond the broadest generalities ("burly, bull-necked," "sex symbol," "ribbon clerk," "roughneck," "sickly looking"), most such is a waste of time. Picking people to play roles is the assignment of the casting director. To limit him by picturing a character as "six feet tall, 140 pounds, stoop-shouldered and with crossed eyes" is to make his job unconscionably difficult. Or it would, if he paid any attention to what you say, which in such circumstances he won't. So, hold back on all such, unless physical detail has a definite bearing on the story—as in the case of a plot that makes essential a girl with one hand, a man who stutters, or the like.

How do you distinguish between your characters, then?

You give each *things to do* and *things to say* which are in keeping with *the kind of person he or she is*.

How do you determine the kind of person a character is? We'll get to that shortly.

This probably is also the place to bring up the matter of casting "to type" and "against type."

Casting "to type" actually is casting to *stereotype*—the traditional image of a particular type of person. Thus, "type casting" is the kind that features the "dizzy blonde," the "Italian gangster," the "Irish cop," the "nutty teenager," or what have you.

Casting "against type," in contrast, may have the accountant built like a professional wrestler, the thug wearing horn-rimmed glasses, the heroine overage or overweight.

Each approach has something to be said for it. Casting to type has the virtue of offering audiences familiar people—easily recognized, easily accepted. Casting against type offers realism, freshness, interest. You pays your money and you takes your choice.

Or, you can combine the two: type-casting some of your roles, breaking free in others.

But back to our money truck film, and the key people with whom Earl Parrish will deal in the course of the picture.

Arbitrarily, let's decide that three of these characters will be male West Virginians from Parrish's home county. Two will be females, also from that background. We'll also include a Chicago woman and a Chicago man.

Bear in mind that in conceptualizing each individual, we'll strive for contrast between them, so that each can be easily recognized on a variety of levels.

Thus, Parrish is a veteran and an ex-deputy sheriff. *In contrast,* we'll make one of his associates Appalachian-born Clyde Felders. Felders is both physically small and a small-time hoodlum, an egotistical career criminal whose pride it is that he has no Social Security number—that is, he's never held a legitimate job.

Next, *for further contrast,* let's toss in a shambling hulk of a man. We'll call him Abel Wood. Another former West Virginian, Abel's a car nut. Amoral though not basically criminal in his orientation, he frequently finds himself involved with thieves because he gets his kicks from dangerous driving, as in getaways.

Now, *again contrasting,* we'll add one Quintus James. Older than the others by 20 years or more, he's greedy and conniving, but wary—

a hillbilly shylock with a superficially clean record back in West Virginia. At present he's assistant manager of a Chicago branch bank.

The Appalachian females? Let's start with Florence Tate, retired spinster schoolteacher, an obese lump still hooked on kids. Ceil Robinson, our social worker heroine, is a trim, self-reliant, quietly aggressive woman in her late 20s. Thus, *through contrast,* she offers counterpoint to Florence (pardon me; "Miss Tate," in view of her schoolmarm role), as well as to our Chicago woman, Hilda Dinnick, Clyde Felders' girl-friend, a *Vogue/Cosmopolitan* fan so unbright she even believes what Clyde tells her.

Finally, for even further *contrast,* we'll toss in a male Chicagoan, Zeppo Perrone, a coldly efficient Mafia trouble-shooter who wouldn't carry a gun if you paid him to.

And there you are: eight story people, each summarized in a neat little word-capsule, and each *contrasted* with the others—even the sound and initials of their names are different, as an extra edge against confusion.

For bit parts, in most cases this kind of thing is good enough. For major roles, no; they demand treatment in greater depth. So before you "freeze" your people, you need to consider further factors. Casting these into categories, we have elements which we'll label *external* aspects of character, *internal* aspects, the matter of character *direction,* and character *modifications.*

1. *External aspects.*

We've already covered the matter of age and sex. Now, let's give a bit more attention to

a. *Dominant impression.*

Each of us makes some sort of impact on people we meet—blusterer, bore, braggart, nonentity. A woman may register as mouse or moose or sexpot.

In brief, each of us for better or worse is tagged—that is, labeled—by the world with an *adjective of manner.*

Such a label is ever so valuable to you as a writer, because it points you to predictable behavior. Knowing that a character is crude or brash or pompous or "duh"-stupid or wimpish gives you a guideline to plan and write to.

Similarly, society tends to categorize us in terms of the occupational role we play, how we make a living. My neighbor Sam is a carpenter; Melanie, across the street, a nurse. I'm also close friends with Jim, a professional soldier. We've been known to have a drink with Cal, a doctor. And just these words—carpenter, nurse, soldier, doctor—in large measure establish our socio-economic positions, our education, our experience, our beliefs and attitudes, and relationships.

Thus, we each may also be described in terms of function, with a *noun of vocation*.

Combine these two, adjective of manner and noun of vocation, and you have a handy way of defining a person, in life or in script. And, while it's hardly definitive, it will do very nicely to establish the *dominant impression* you wish him to convey to viewers: sloppy waitress, surly cop, sexy schoolmarm, forthright farmer, fussy florist.

So, what's with the character on whom you're working? How does he come across—his overall impact? Try to nail it down in a word or phrase; no more. Keep it clear and sharp! The more you try to fancy it up, the less likely you are to hammer it home to viewers.

Further, the clearer and simpler you make it, the easier the part will be for an actor to play, and the more believable his performance is likely to be. Complexity only confuses the issue.

Applying this approach to the cast of our money truck film, let's begin by having Earl Parrish, ex-sergeant, give a dominant impression of being a *self-reliant leader*.

Clyde Felders, in turn, is an *insolent small-time crook;* Abel Wood, a *vacuous grease monkey;* Quintus James, a *friendly/folksy banker.* Hilda Dinnick, Clyde's *mistress,* gives the feeling of being both *unbright* and *plastic.* *Retired teacher* Florence Tate, though *age-drained,* remains *dedicated.* Ceil Robinson is a *cool social worker.* We see Zeppo Perrone as a *frozen-faced mafioso.*

All these impressions are different, note; all to a fair degree in contrast. Each draws an image an actor can present on film.

So much for impression. Which makes it time to turn to

b. *Tags.*

A tag is a label. It helps to distinguish one character from another. Consequently, each character should have several.

The screenwriter, fortunately, need not worry as much about this as his friends who write for the print media. Detailed description of his characters is not only unnecessary but, as we've pointed out, for the most part undesirable. Actor and director take care of adding color nicely.

However, it's still not a bad idea to stick in a few tags, *providing you give them a direct relationship to the story.* Otherwise, count on it, they'll be ignored.

Tags, for our purposes here, are of three types: tags of appearance, tags of speech, and tags of mannerism. So, as you build each character, ask yourself,

1. *What are his tags of appearance?* In general, appearance will be that of the actor himself and that's all there is to say about it.

On the other hand, it certainly did no harm that Mel Brooks tagged the unregenerate Nazi in *The Producers* as wearing a German helmet.

Nor would Long John Silver be the same without his peg-leg, Blackbeard sans hirsute adornment, or the Hathaway shirt man minus his eye patch.

Do we need tags of appearance for any of our money truck caper people, beyond what actors and director will develop? Probably not. Yet neither would it hurt to suggest that Abel Wood limps (a neat tie-in with his passion for cars, from the standpoint of Adlerian organ inferiority theory), or that Ceil wears a swirl of hair over her forehead, to conceal a scar that somehow symbolizes her relationship with Earl or Florence or whomever.

b. What are his tags of speech?

This is a subject we'll take up in more detail when we get to our chapter on dialogue. But it's worth pointing out here that each of us speaks differently—in choice of words, in accent, in pacing, in rhythm, in intonation.

Matters of accent, pacing, and the like obviously fall largely within the provinces of actor and director. The writer, however, is the one who sets down the words which will be said. Clint Eastwood's "Make my day!" will be remembered long after Eastwood has retired, and it will be hard indeed for an alleged hoodlum to rise above a tag of "dear boy" tied to his every other speech; or for Sweet Innocence to sound convincing in her part if her lines drip double entendre.

On the other hand, it would seem appropriate for Florence Tate to tend to address her former pupils as "young man," in school mistress fashion, or to salt aging Quintus James's lines with hill-country expressions. Clyde Felders obviously would tend to Chicago street slang; Earl Parrish, to military references.

c. What are his tags of mannerism?

Remember Tom Cruise dancing around the pool table in *The Color of Money*? Captain Queeg and his ball bearings in *The Caine Mutiny*? Jane Fonda's continuing byplay with her cigarette in *Agnes of God*?

All these were tags of mannerism. They helped to make a character distinctive, memorable.

Often—as in Queeg's case—such tags are symbolic, as well as bits of business. They help to define and establish character.

Similarly, Quintus James might jingle change in his pocket, or doodle interest figures, or manipulate wire-framed glasses. Hilda Dinnick could have a thing about mirrors—she can't keep away from them. Zeppo Perrone studies the *Wall Street Journal*.

Or, they might not. You need to use careful judgment. Too much of a good thing can leave your cast acting like a bunch of freaks.

So much for character externals. Time now for

2. *Internal aspects.*

Here we'll consider three elements: point of view, dominant attitude, and interests.

a. *Point of view.*

This is a subject on which we touched in the preceding chapter. Its core is that Character—*any* character of consequence in your picture—must have an attitude towards your film's topic/premise. How does he see it? Its significance? Its implications? Its potential?

Not that this necessarily comes as a first step in character conception, you understand. It's quite possible for a story person just to pop up on the scene, sans warning, angle, or function. But there he is, and he keeps on hanging around until you feel as if you have no choice but to find something for him to do.

It also may be, too, that a character not only has no specific attitude towards your film's topic, but he isn't even aware that Topic exists—as in the case, say, of the sweet little old lady in *The Ladykillers,* who scurries about amid a gang of desperate criminals but remains happily oblivious to what's going on. All this goes to prove is that oblivion itself can constitute a viewpoint.

In most instances, however, you'll need to devise a more sharply focused point of view for each major character, based pretty much on the role he is to play; the function you have him scheduled to fulfill. Thus, Hero will have a different attitude towards topic than Villain. Heroine will look at things from another angle than Female Menace.

Does this mean we're talking only about melodrama—the standard hero-heroine-heavy?

Not at all. You and your friend both may be fine fellows. But that doesn't prevent you from liking different women, different jobs, different lifestyles . . . because each of you has a different point of view.

Thus, where *Money Truck 456* is concerned, Earl Parrish views the robbery as a challenge. Why? Because his goal is merely to help Florence Tate. He doesn't care about the cash.

Clyde Felders, in contrast, sees the heist as opportunity incarnate, alive and breathing. All his life a small-timer, he's ever dreamed of making a real score. Now, at last, the chance is with him, for money and for secret glory.

To Abel Wood, the caper is a means to money, sure. But more intriguing, from his angle, is the escape, the driving. All else lies subordinate to those wild moments of excitement in which, quite possibly, he'll match his skill as a wheelsman against the cops.

In Quintus James's eyes, on the other hand, the robbery looms only as an ulcer-aggravating hazard. Give him any choice, he'd have no part in such lunacy. But how can he say no, in the face of pressure from such types as Earl and Clyde?

Florence Tate of course knows nothing of the scheme. Neither does Hilda Dinnick. But we do have some idea of the attitude of each: Florence would reject such a plan out of hand, as contradictory to everything she's ever believed in. Hilda? Well, money's money; and besides, she believes everything Clyde Felders tells her. Too, she knows something's on his mind. She doesn't like that. It takes the stud out of him in bed; makes him hit too hard and without warning.

Zeppo Perrone, our final figure, views the whole business with wary disdain; a professional's chill detachment. He doesn't know quite what's going on, but he's certain something is. Also, it's clear that Something's principals are amateurs. But a syndicate bank, syndicate money, is involved. That makes it personally important to him. A blunder, a miscalculation, could be damaging to his career.

So there we have it: eight points of view, all centering on one central topic/premise: What if somebody pulled a robbery not for gain, but simply to switch one batch of money for another?

It's a good approach from which to start the building of any film. Not to mention a good springboard from which to plunge into consideration of our second internal aspect of character,

b. Dominant attitude.

To a large degree, personality is a matter of attitude.

An attitude, roughly defined, is a habitual mode of response to a particular type of situation. A *dominant* attitude is a person's habitual mode of response to life and life situations in general. It may be optimism, pessimism, belligerence, sweet reasonableness, or what have you. It's an implicit philosophy of life boiled down to a single sentence, and every person has one: "Good looks and sexiness will carry a woman through any dilemma." "If I keep a low profile, don't make waves, maybe no one will give me a hard time." "Don't fool with me, Buster, unless you want a flat nose."

Knowing a character's dominant attitude gives a writer a tremendous edge, for it offers him advance insight into how Character will react in any given circumstance. Thus, faced with trouble, Woman above will turn on the charm; Man 1 will try to stay inconspicuous; Man 2 is likely to come out swinging.

In a word, these characters' attitudes make them *predictable*. So Writer will have little difficulty devising ways to present them believably in dialogue and action.

Earl Parrish? He's a man to count on. In fact, let's focus on that as his dominant attitude: "Loyalty rates for more than anything, when the cards are down."

Checking the other members of our cast, we have:

Clyde Felders: "Don't try to con me, Smart-ass!"
Abel Wood: "I got no time for tomorrow. Today's all I can handle."
Quintus James: "Money makes the world go round—and I know all the prices."
Florence Tate: "I can take whatever life brings, if the children have a better chance."
Ceil Robinson: "You do what's right, no matter what the rules say."
Zeppo Perrone: "It's my mouth, but the Organization's talking."
Hilda Dinnick: "You gotta give the customers what they want."

Clear enough, right? And in case you hadn't noticed, another name for *attitudes* is *values*.

Which brings us to the third of our internals,

c. Interests.

You can tell a lot from a man's—or woman's—interests. The ball fan is a different person from the opera buff. The barfly moves in one circle, the ecology freak in another.

It would add dimension to your characters, therefore, if you give them personal interests, both to individualize them and to give them topics of conversation as required.

Thus, Earl may have a thing where weapons or hunting are concerned. Abel's eyes light up at the sight of a unique car. Hilda seeks good taste in *Vogue*, sexiness in *Cosmo*. Ceil is preoccupied with the world as people. Florence lives through her former pupils; children. Quintus James hates Chicago . . . goes back in retrospect to his West Virginia boyhood. Clyde never tires of talk of criminal cleverness. Zeppo is an enthusiastic seasonal sailor.

This interest element need not be beaten to death, you understand. But it certainly does help to have it handy when you need more than weather talk to flesh out an incident.

So much for character's internal aspects. It's time we moved on to the matter of

3. Character direction.

Direction starts with

a. Goals.

When you say a character has a goal, you mean he keeps trying to move in a particular direction; to accomplish a particular purpose.

Man's goals are of two types: immediate, and long range.

Immediate goals, immediate purposes, are pretty much the product of your story situation. You assign them to your characters, as it were, then devise rationalizations to make such behavior believable.

Goals differ from character to character. Thus, some minor characters may drift with the tide, with no strong immediate goals apparent. The goals of a central character or a villain, on the other hand, ordinarily work out best if they're so strong as to be well-nigh compulsive. Why? Because, as noted in the preceding chapter, the drive of desire is the life's blood of every film.

Take the situation in the picture, *Hennessy.* It postulates an Irishman who sets about to blow up Britain's Parliament, despite all efforts of both Scotland Yard and the I.R.A. to stop him.

What would launch a man on such a desperate course? The rationalization offered in the picture has Hennessy's wife and daughter slain in a clash between pro-I.R.A. rioters and British troops. Whereupon, vengeance-driven, grieving Hennessy goes forth to battle.

Closer to home, *Money Truck 456* makes Earl Parrish's immediate goal, his purpose, the switching of bad bills for good via robbery. Rationalization: Earl's sense of loyalty is so strong he's emotionally bound to help save his old teacher.

It should also be noted here that a character's immediate goal within a story of necessity subdivides into *sequence goals* as your story develops and the situation changes. That is, it's your job to make a character want *to do* something in each scene, each encounter; to take action to change some aspect of his immediate situation in a way that he feels will move him closer to his story goal.

The emphasis here is on the *to do* element. A sequence goal should be—shall we say it again?—immediate, specific, concrete, visual: to blow up the dam, to steal the truck, to capture the villain, to soothe the hurt child. Wishing or pondering simply isn't enough.

So much for immediate goals. Long-range are something else again, and a good deal closer to what we usually think of as characterization.

There's a phrase in an Army marching song which tells the story, it seems to me:

> "I wanta be an airborne Ranger,
> Live a life of sex and danger . . ."

Those lines represent a lifestyle epitomized—a seeking of a *kind of experience,* rather than a specific accomplishment, as a goal.

The questions to ask when you seek to determine a character's long-term goals are, "What's he looking for; what kind of experience? In what proportion is he seeking adventure, security, recognition, response?" For a character's behavior as you present it in your script should of necessity be in keeping with his lifestyle; the aspects of existence which gives him pleasure, satisfaction. Then, with that orientation in mind, we devise incidents and business to demonstrate it.

You can do worse, indeed, than to consider the future as a gigantic supermarket, with your characters impulse buyers. For far from operating on a necessarily intelligent or logical basis than focuses on long-range planning, most of us "buy" things that are in keeping with the aspects of experience that we find important—which is to say, immediately satisfying. Rightly or wrongly, and whether it works out that way or not, it's what Character sees as constituting his road to happiness. Our watchword: "It seemed like a good idea at the time."

Thus, blocking out reality with drugs or gin may just as well prove to be a goal—even if formally unformulated—as getting a raise or marrying the boss's daughter. So may postponing, or pleasure-seeking, or playing with danger. And who among us hasn't known the unhappy man or woman for whom the seeking of a goal to pursue has itself become a goal, even though it stands clear and obvious to everyone but that person that he or she never will settle down to actual striving?

In the case of Earl Parrish, he can't imagine a life in which his military skills aren't put to use. Clyde Felders dreams of a really big score. Abel Wood? He doesn't think much about what's to come. But he'll be disappointed if it doesn't include cars to play with.

Quintus James's world is money-bounded. Though he'd be hard-pressed to tell you why, he just wants more and more of it.

Florence Tate, in contrast, hopes only for an easy death . . . while Ceil Robinson, disillusioned with the red tape and basically non-human orientation of social work, yearns for something—anything—that will give her a sense of real self-worth.

Low-profile power is Zeppo Perrone's fantasy . . . a sort of business career within the Mafia, in which its leaders from coast to coast will defer as respectfully to his judgment as they would have in the past to Meyer Lansky's.

Hilda? She'd tell you she wants nothing. But everything she says and does shows that if you'd give her social acceptance, she'd be happy.

So much for character direction. Where the scriptwriter is concerned, however, there's a related factor to consider. Call it, if you will,

b. Rationalization.

It goes without saying, I hope, that you need to know your characters in order to write about them successfully.

Further, you need to know about them infinitely better than does the audience which ultimately views the film in which said characters take part.

On the other hand, it's unlikely you need to know your story people as well as many people who write on writing would have you believe.

Actually, you need to know them only well enough to rationalize their behavior.

To *rationalize* is to make logical, believable.

How do you make behavior logical and believable?

You provide appropriate reasons for it in Character's past conditionings, his past experiences.

Shall we examine this process in detail, beginning with the manner in which a character comes into being?

It all starts, of course, with a script—a story—you want to write.

Sometimes, said story begins with a character. Sometimes, the story situation is genesis.

Actually, which comes first makes little difference. Both must develop—that is, grow—side by side, in either case. Neither can spring to life full blown. Neither can survive separate from the other.

So, a character is born and then develops. But . . . how much do you develop him?

Only as much as you need in order for him to fulfill his function in the story. Why? Because the typical film averages 90 minutes running time. That gives little opportunity for fun and games where either character or story is concerned. The trick is to get the show on the road; build no more and no less than is necessary.

Which doesn't mean you don't need to give your characters their full share of attention. Otherwise they'll reach the screen stillborn, as flat stick figures . . . a sorry fate for the children of any writer's brain.

To avoid this, you provide Character with such past conditionings as are necessary to enable you to rationalize—that is, make logical and believable, remember—Character's present dimensions, present behavior.

A man is a maze of involvements in love, work, society . . . a tangle of tastes, interests, skills, boredoms.

Man develops all these on foundation stones of body and experience. A product of learned behavior, his personality is based on a multitude of procedures he has worked out, consciously and unconsciously, as best suited to coping with his problems, his inadequacies, his world.

Coping means triumphing over heredity and environment alike . . . regardless of good health or poor health or sickness or crippling . . . sharp mind or dull mind or strong mind or warped mind . . . kind parents or cold parents or neurotic parents or absent parents . . . private school or public school or slum school or reform school or no school . . . smart kids or dumb kids or sadistic kids or depraved kids . . . farm town or factory town or suburb or ghetto.

That coping . . . it takes its toll of everyone. Each of us emerges with his share of black eyes and bruises and secret sore spots . . . that sense of uneasiness somewhere deep inside that the shrinks call inadequacy, inferiority, insecurity, frustration.

Still, we have no choice but to battle on, each in his own way. So we bite the bullet and plunge ahead . . . nurse our wounds with laughter, tears, strength, weakness, virtue, vice, cleverness, stupidity, ill health, lust, anger, you name it.

Thus, Earl Parrish stands coolly competent, in command of self and situation, and endowed with a wry sense of humor.

What gave him that competence? A craftsman father? Discipline in Florence Tate's classroom? A body that lacked bull strength, so skill became a substitute?

How about the habit of command? Did it spring from mining camp scuffles? Baseball prowess? Admiration for a hard-nosed old sheriff? Or what?

And the sense of humor. Did he have sisters who sliced him to ribbons with their wit when he tried to take himself too seriously? A grandfather who poked sly fun? Boredom with a dull, drab world, so dreary he could survive it only by seeing its funny side and laughing at it?

You develop all this in notes and scribbles . . . imaginary remembered incidents from Earl's past. Generalities are of little help. What you want are the kind of bits a man might be inclined to tell for a laugh, or a tear, or a brag, or in a moment of bitterness; and frequently a perceptive listener might draw more from what he didn't say than what he did, or focus on elements that seemed at first glance to be side issues— as when you discover the tough cop has three brothers in prison.

It also just might help if you think of each of your other characters—and especially your minor characters—as being the center of a story of his or her own as he crosses paths or swords with your hero. That is, Minor Character has an existence independent of your script's pages. Give him specific things he wants to keep or change, a style of life he seeks to lead; and though you bring him on stage merely as a messenger or a spear-bearer in the chorus, don't let him forget those things important to him. Have them affect the way he behaves, the role he plays. They'll help bring him to life, lift him out of the stick-figure category.

Will all this show up on the screen? Of course not; and yes, such probing can easily be overdone. But unless you do at least a modicum of homework on such . . . brood about your hero and his friends and foes and contacts . . . get to know and understand them insofar as your story requires, flesh them out to real dimension, devise past history to help you rationalize their present character and behavior . . . count on it, they'll come through on paper and, later, film as flat and empty.

Now, our final point on character conception: that of

4. Modification.

Not all characters need modification of impression or attitude or goals or what have you. But sometimes you can add immeasurably to a portrayal if you write in incidents which help relieve your character conception's basic starkness.

Take Abel Wood. A shuffling, vacuous nonentity at first glance, he gains dimension if you allow him to display dexterity of a high order. Worn out now, Florence Tate still can show flashes of the peppery disciplinarian she once was. Let Hilda Dinnick reveal uncertainty, Ceil Robinson a warm and sentimental self beneath her cool efficiency. Quintus James can go from fawning servility to cold-eyed greed in a manner that makes clear his folksiness is a cover. Clyde Felders may reveal that he knows when to back down, just when his insolence seems sure to get him into more trouble than he can handle. Still frozen-faced, Zeppo Perrone has been known to rub his sleeve and say, "These threads cost three bills. How much did yours cost?"

As for Earl—well, he's competent and in command, but that can make for a less-than-heartening person. So mightn't it be an idea to let him play with pups, or build up his sense of humor?

Similarly, we may discover he views robbery primarily as a game, albeit a dangerous one. Quite possibly he sees his accomplices in a mellow, nostalgic glow, as if they were still the boys he knew growing up in West Virginia's hills.

How about throwing in a bit of male chauvinism on his part, too? Thus, maybe he considers robbery as men's business . . . objects strenuously to Ceil's involvement. Mightn't it be a good way to throw them into conflict?

Another thing to ask yourself, where modification is concerned, is: Has anyone a secret?

You see, it would be nice if dominant impressions were always right.

It would also be dull.

Fortunately, the human animal fools us ever so often on this score by giving us assorted false impressions.

This is God's gift to the scriptwriter. It enables him to present us with a clear-cut image . . . then slip in a logical yet unanticipated twist that adds depth and dimension.

Like this:

A cold-eyed executive type . . . who keeps a bottle in the bottom drawer.
A small, prim girl . . . with a secret taste for black lace lingerie.
A warmly winning elementary school teacher . . . who hates kids.

Do you see how it works? This kind of secret isn't necessarily a secret in the usual sense of the word. It's just something that doesn't fit the expected picture. By incorporating such a twist, a weakness, an unforeseen aspect as you build a character, you add marked viewer interest. Your audience watches eagerly as each new situation unfolds to see whether Secret will compound Character's problems.

At the same time, you don't want to overdo it. Dominant impression should remain dominant save in those moments when the nature of the situation might logically lead an individual of this particular type to expose his secret.

Note, too, those words, "an individual of this particular type." Nowhere is preparation, planting, more important than when you propose to incorporate a "secret" switch. The ingredients must be there: just not revealed. Otherwise, viewers will feel your character is inconsistent, and be appropriately outraged.

Also, for heaven's sake, don't give *all* your characters "secret" aspects. That grows old in a hurry. Be content to save such Sunday punches for key characters, crucial situations.

Do we need a secret for Earl Parrish? Not necessarily. However, for the sake of example, we'll give him one anyhow: the fact that for all his cool competence and wry good humor, he also rates as deadly dangerous. If the time comes to act and nothing else will do, he won't hesitate to kill.

Is this believable? Understandable? Acceptable? Of course. Probably Earl's demonstrated it repeatedly in Lebanon; maybe in his role of deputy sheriff also.

*   *   *

So. That's enough and too much on character conception. It's time we moved on to another vital matter: How best do you *present* your man or woman?

1. You devise establishing incidents for Character.
2. You maintain Character's character throughout.
3. You stand fast by the principles of character growth.

Each of these points deserves close individual attention. Here we go!

1. You devise establishing incidents for Character.

The only way to capture a character's behavior on the screen is through action and dialogue: the things Character does, and the things he says.

Action and dialogue are most effectively presented in terms of photographable incidents: events which reveal Character's individuality and his relationships.

You the writer devise these events, these incidents, of course. They're born of your script's plot structure. But, in addition, they should be designed in a manner to serve character-revealing functions.

To this end,

a. Establish Character early.

An easy—and hazardous—trap for a writer to fall into is that of failing to establish a given character's character at the earliest possible moment. Instead of "organizing the emotions of the audience" (to borrow playwright Howard Lindsay's phrase) towards Character at the outset, Writer allows Character to meander through a series of bland, non-characterizing scenes, in which Character might as well be part of the furniture.

Need I point out that this is not the brightest possible approach? Not only does it waste valuable screen time, but it very well may—inadvertently—create a false impression.

This being the case, *do* establish early.

b. Establish Character in character.

Failure to establish Character in character—that is, failure to develop him from the start as the kind of person he's to portray in the picture—can prove a real disaster. Why? Because such failure can, as noted above, lead to viewers getting a false impression of Character's character.

Consider, for example, a film I saw the other night. The opening sequence had the hero rough up an offending storekeeper who, in accordance with the law, refused to sell Hero a drink on Sunday. Then, as a follow-up, Hero slugged two highway patrolmen who intervened.

What the writer was attempting was clear enough: He wanted to establish Hero as a tough, belligerent type not to be trifled with.

The catch lay in the way he chose to do this. Because where I was concerned, at least, Hero ceased to be a hero, a character to cheer for, the moment he moved in on Storekeeper. He became, instead, a thug and bully, and nothing that happened in the succeeding 80 minutes of the film could change his image for me.

Yet how easily the impression could have been made positive, starting from the self-same situation! This time, instead of casting Hero in hoodlum role, let him sit down with a beer at the same time a couple of biker thugs come in. Let *them* demand the liquor and start pushing on Storekeeper. Whereupon, Hero heroically intervenes. The patrolmen arrive to halt the ensuing brawl and attempt to arrest Hero. But since an arrest is the last thing Hero can afford at the moment, there's further conflict, and we end up with the self-same situation—but with a character less distasteful.

Or, to get back to our central point, we've now established Hero *in* instead of *out of* character.

As part of this approach, it's helpful to bear down on four specific yet oft-neglected areas.

1. *Establish dominant impression.* If Character is an athletic smoothy, don't have him fall on his face in a mud puddle on first appearance. If Woman is the shy, demure nurse's aide, it's unlikely she should be introduced screaming like a fishwife at some unoffending nothing.

2. *Establish likability.* If a character in a film—particularly the central character—is supposed to be likable, do establish that likability as soon as possible.

How? By having him *do* something likable, for one thing, whether it be helping an old lady across the street, solacing a lost child, or feeding a starving dog. Yes, I agree it's possible to be more subtle about it; but that's a problem for your own imagination.

Or, you can give Character a goal that demonstrates he's on the side of right and justice. Or, you can show him to be an underdog who still clings to his sense of humor. Or, you can reveal him standing up indomitably to disaster. Or voicing views viewers are certain to agree with. Or fighting or sacrificing for others.

But whatever you have him do, do make him likable!

3. *Establish interest.* For most of us, interesting people hold an edge over uninteresting. So try to establish Character as an interesting person.

To that end, have him do something interesting. Or put him in an interesting setting. Or a changing setting. Or a dangerous setting. Or contrast him with his circumstances or surroundings: Such social opposites as rich vs. poor, young vs. old, male vs. female, urban vs. rural, landsman vs. seafarer, cops vs. robbers, and the like, offer built-in raw materials.

4. *Establish potential.* Potential in this sense is of two types: physical and climax.

a. *Physical potential.* Character is a mousy little man, scared to death at his own shadow and habitually running from trouble.

Now, at the climax, he whips out a .45 and guns down the villain.

No, I don't believe it. And I doubt that you do either.

Why don't you? Because the writer didn't bother to establish his little man's *potential* for such violence.

Similarly, the frigid girl doesn't turn into a passion flower without warning. The clod doesn't become sensitive. The illiterate doesn't write an epic.

Whatever your character is to do must be prepared for. Show us Little Man staring fascinated at the weapons in Britain's War Museum, or taking instruction on the target range. Let Frigid Woman ponder another character's suggestion that her problem is less lack of sex drive than failure to juxtapose the right man and the right mood. Give Clod sensitivity and feeling where his cat is concerned. And don't even think of casting the illiterate as a writer.

b. *Climax potential.* Climax potential, you'll recall, is a goal-motivated character's capacity for harboring two strong emotions at once.

In practical terms, this demands that you show both climax emotions, desire and whatever, convincingly in action at earlier stages. Why? Because a monster can't believably change to a hero *just* at the climax. You have to prepare the audience, make them aware that Character harbors both emotions, by showing said emotions in action earlier in the picture.

This is the process otherwise known as planting and paying off. You show a gun in a drawer; later, when it's needed—maybe half-a-dozen sequences later—somebody snatches it out and shoots the villain with it. Or, Hero and Heroine find mutual bliss to the tune of a scratchy phonograph record giving out with "Some Enchanted Evening." Then assorted issues separate them. Later—apparently spurned, scorned, and rejected—Hero is about to depart forever. But now the familiar, scratch-shredded strains of "Some Enchanted Evening" echo close at hand. Hero stops short, eyes widening . . . turns, sprints up the steps to Heroine's apartment. Clinch and close.

Similarly, when you seek to build a climax on the basis of a character's decision between desire (for a woman or a job or a million dollars) and duty (to arrest woman's father, or close down the company, or return the million dollars to its rightful owners), you'd better be sure Character demonstrates his moral fiber earlier—like close to the beginning of the picture—by jailing his own mother, or rejecting promotion, or running after the little old lady who's dropped her wallet.

Yes, I grant you that I'm murdering this point via exaggeration. But the fact remains that unless you establish your man's or woman's strength of feeling before the climax comes, said climax is likely to arrive stillborn. And just because I've corned things up to make a point doesn't mean you can't develop your own script with subtlety and taste.

Now, one final detail: No matter what anyone may tell you to the contrary, you need to build plot and character together.

Particularly does this hold true of your central character, your hero.

Indeed, you can do worse than to frame up your climax scene almost before you start, in order to get clear in your mind just what emotions will be in conflict within your hero at that time. Only thus can you block in the earlier action properly.

Which is not to say you can't attack in any other way that suits your fancy, you understand. But it does seem like an awful lot of extra work to go back planting and revising later because, at the start, you never quite thought through your climax.

And that's enough about establishment. It's time now to move on to our second point regarding character presentation:

2. You maintain Character's character throughout.

You don't just establish character once and let it go at that. Dominant impression, dominant attitude, dominant goal, all the rest—they must be brought forward over and over again; hammered home in scene after scene, so that the audience has no opportunity to forget them.

The key issue to remember? Consistency. A character who stays in character from the first frame to the last. Even when his behavior is offbeat, contradictory, it must be so within the framework of personality you've created.

A major aspect of consistency, too often overlooked, is that of *reaction.*

Reaction is a person's response to external action. Its importance lies in the fact that it reveals character as knee-jerk reflex—witness John Wayne's insightful comment that acting, at core, really is reacting.

Thus, Richard Widmark moved to new prominence in his profession when he gave vent to a maniacal laugh—an unexpected reaction— as he pushed an old woman in a wheelchair down a stair to her death in *Kiss of Death.* Similarly, when the heroine in *The Fly* embraced her hideously transmuting lover, pressing her face to his despite the fact that his ear has sloughed away in a nauseating ooze, it says more about the depth of her love than his condition.

Which is not at all to say that you must be clumsy and obvious about such. On the contrary. Small things, mere hints and touches, can keep viewers reminded that Character A is cowardly, Character B lazy, Character C the kind of woman who remembers the lessons that her mother taught her.

Finally,

3. You stand fast by the principles of character growth.

Character growth is an element critics love to belabor. It means that a character starts out one way, ends up another.

You'll have no trouble with such if you remember one simple fact: *To say a character grows in the course of a film means only that he has learned by experience.*

This being the case, ask yourself how much Character can have learned, and how—that is, through what incidents—he learned it.

The situation is, in brief, much like that we discussed in considering how to establish potential. It's a matter of planning and planting, that's all.

And most of the time, you'll find, you're better off to keep the whole thing straight and simple.

*   *   *

What about the *writing* of character material? Two things.

First, bear in mind that this is an area, like many others, where writing itself is the smallest issue. *Thinking through* your characters is infinitely more important.

Further, said "thinking through" can grow wearing. As one of my old friends, a top scriptwriter, commented not long ago, " 'But would Sam Spade really *do* that?' gets tiresome, finally—especially since Sam is just floating around in your imagination anyhow."

Second, as in all writing, the trick is not to let rules freeze you. Specifically, don't write by rote. Better by far to slop down first thoughts, then check and revise later.

Why? Because, for one thing, your characters will change as you go along. The problems of structuring your script—not to mention satisfying all the people to whose alleged judgment you must genuflect in the course of working through your project—too often will force you to reshape your ideas later.

Even in writing the story treatment, for example, you'll find your concepts developing and modifying, as we'll demonstrate in the next chapter.

CHAPTER 9

The Story Treatment

A treatment is a semi-dramatized, present-tense, preliminary structuring of a screenplay; an elaboration of the presentation.

What issue is most important in the treatment? The answer, without question, is unity; the solid development of a single story with a strong central spine. Though side issues and subplots may be introduced, ever and always they remain subordinated to the basic scheme.

This is why clear thinking on premise and starting lineup is so vital. If you've done your work on them well, they provide you with a firm foundation on which to build your treatment. In consequence, unless you deviate too wildly, your treatment, too, is likely to prove sound.

The treatment has three functions: to sharpen the proposed script's focus, to flesh out the story, and to emotionalize the handling.

Fleshing out and sharpening focus go hand in hand. The idea is to block in the story in sufficient detail that its flaws and weaknesses may be uncovered and remedied.

Not that cures are always to be found, you understand. The Hollywood hills are full of stories whose ailments proved so incapacitating that they never got beyond the treatment stage.

The emotionalization angle is a somewhat different matter. Here, the issue is the need for the treatment to create and carry forward an air of excitement such as, hopefully, viewers will experience when they see the finished film. And this, it seems to me, is an aspect oft ignored yet desperately important.

How so? Because, through most of its phases, a script is in essence a blueprint, a set of instructions for cast and crew. Its language and approach are therefore factual. The surge and flow of emotion which are the very heart of the finished film are of necessity left out, save insofar as typed description of action and dialogue reveals them.

117

The treatment, in contrast, offers an opportunity to write in all such . . . to capture mood, to experiment with emotional effects, to play with feelings.

Further, it's essential that mood, emotion, feeling, be communicated—to two people, in particular.

The first of these people is the *producer*. It's urgent that he become conscious of the spirit of the property—not just the facts—if he's to pass intelligent judgment on it.

Even more vital, the *writer* must acquire that awareness also.

This is not as ridiculous as it sounds. Though the writer may start with a feeling for his material, that doesn't necessarily mean he knows what said feeling is. Only as he works through the script, both in framing and in writing the treatment, does he discover how best to incorporate and handle emotional content.

FRAMING THE TREATMENT

How do you frame up a treatment?

The answer, of course, is: Any way that works. But for learning's sake, let's take a logical, five-step approach:

1. You block in the background of the action.
2. You establish story elements.
3. You focus your opening.
4. You plan your peaks.
5. You resolve your issues.

First step coming up!

1. You block in the background of the action.

Every story, every film, is rooted in the past, if only because the people involved in any event have pasts.

Thus, a knife flashes; a man dies. But in a very real sense, that is the end of the event, not the beginning. Knowledge of *why* one particular individual wielded the blade on a particular other is vital to any real understanding of the event.

A woman abandons her husband and her children. But that is only the tip of the iceberg. Data on the states of affairs and states of mind which led up to it are essential to true insight.

A poverty-stricken black couple take in a crippled white child in the face of neighbors' resentment. Only awareness of what has gone before can bring any degree of comprehension.

It's to your advantage as a writer to recognize this fact. Then, whatever your story, sketch in the background of the action. Lay bare its roots. Track down the events that first brought your characters to-

gether. In your own mind, at least, clarify the basis for their relationships
. . . the reasons they became involved with your topic/premise.

True, most of this will never reach the screen. But without it, you
may never have a script to begin with.

Money Truck 456 offers ever so many examples. The first to come
to mind is: How did that $60,000 in hot bills get into Florence Tate's
safety deposit box in the first place?

Well, it's a cinch Florence herself didn't put it there, soul of rectitude that she is.

Suppose, however, that Florence shared the box with a trashy
nephew, now dead. Blind to his faults, she held her box jointly with him
. . . had him run financial errands for her after she became an invalid.

Nephew's just the type who might have been involved in a bank
heist. Nor would he have hesitated to switch the loot for Florence's
savings.

Just to complicate things, though, let's pretend Nephew isn't guilty.
Rather, our villain is old Quintus James, the minor bank official. Maybe
Nephew left his box key with Quintus for safekeeping. Later, when
Nephew's killed, that gives Quintus access to the box—and a chance to
switch Florence Tate's money for that from the robbery.

You can take it from there. Had not Ceil Robinson discovered the
switch, she would never have thought of trying to involve Earl Parrish
in a robbery. Had not Earl been Miss Tate's pupil back when he was a
boy in West Virginia, he wouldn't have considered going along with
Ceil's lunatic idea.

All this constitutes *background of the action*: the roots from which
the present story springs.

Needless to say, this kind of backtracking can go on endlessly. Also,
it can be run into the ground. But without at least a little of it, plot pits
will open in your script before you like crevasses in a glacier.

It's a chance you can't afford to take. Not when you almost always
can solve your problems so easily with just a little cogitation.

Oh, yes. There's a point that fits in nicely here which you should
by all means remember: Frequently, when you start developing the background of a story's action, you'll discover there's simply no substitute
for coincidence and happenstance. Life just works out that way sometimes, that's all.

Which is perfectly all right, so long as you bear in mind that audiences will forgive you for breaks that get your hero *into* trouble; never
for those that get him out. It's like the old business of always including
bad luck in a picture's budget, but never good.

2. You establish story elements.

To establish, cinematically, is to make some element or aspect of
the film in some way recognizable and identifiable in the audience's eyes.

Thus, you have an establishing or reestablishing *shot*, which relates people or objects to a background or to each other or both.

In the story treatment, the issues are somewhat different. Here, the question is, where and how do you bring in various *story elements*—characters, situations, settings, and so on.

a. Characters.

We've already belabored this subject in the last chapter. We'll say nothing more about it at this point save than to reiterate that you establish not only the characters themselves—their physical beings—but also their *characteristics*, their *relationships and reactions* to each other, and the *impressions* you want them to make on viewers.

b. Situations.

Situations are the states of affairs in which your characters find themselves in relationship to your topic premise. Sometimes these states of affairs constitute *predicaments*—situations which arouse unpleasant emotions in certain characters. On other occasions, they don't. But whatever the situation at a given time or place, it's essential that you establish it—that is, that you let readers know about it—sharply and clearly in your story treatment, so that it will both carry full impact and avoid confusion.

c. Settings.

Obviously enough, every story is acted out against one or more settings. What writers sometimes overlook, however, is that settings have personalities just as much as do characters.

That personality should be pinned down on paper, in your treatment, in appropriate description. Keep it brief, of course; but at the same time try to capture the essence of the milieu, whether it be bar or brownstone, barn or bungalow.

d. Moods.

Moods vary from film to film—not to mention from segment to segment within a given picture. A story treatment that doesn't zero in on this vital element isn't fulfilling its function.

Nor are mere labels enough. It's one thing to say "It's a sad day for Susy;" another to flesh such out with "Everywhere, it seems, she meets with scowls. Wind whips rain down in gusting sheets. Even the cars that pass seem bent on splashing her."

Does this mean all such will be used when it's time to shoot the film? It's unlikely. But in the meanwhile, right now, a picture has been drawn, a feeling created, to help bring your story alive in the minds of those who read your treatment. And that can make the difference between a go-ahead and a cutoff.

3. You focus your opening.

Getting a film off to a good start involves two things: a hook, and a commitment. Both are ever so important.

a. The hook.

A story's one thing; the way it's presented in a script or to an audience quite possibly another.

Why? Because you start any film with an attempt to capture viewer interest. You do this by fading in on some incident or action which—you hope—will arouse sufficient curiosity or other feeling in the audience to lure them into involvement with your story as it develops.

This hook—in TV, it's called a teaser—may feature anything from a bomb burst to raindrops running down a windowpane; a car crash to a baby's gurgle. Quite often, it will run before or during the picture's titles. All that really matters is that whatever happens must appear to hold potentially disastrous or otherwise intriguing consequences for someone, on some level or other, so that the audience, anticipating dramatic developments to come, will sit enthralled.

This being the case, it's worth your while to devote a fair number of hours, a good deal of floor-pacing, to devising the most captivating hook you can.

One warning: Don't overkill.

That is, don't build a hook so strong, so hard-hitting, so attention-compelling and emotion-evoking that the rest of your story can't live up to it and so comes as anticlimax. And yes, this can and does happen upon occasion, and you can't afford it. So . . . hook your viewers—but do it with at least a little sense of proportion!

Chance are your best results will come if, while hooking, you also work on

b. The commitment.

As pointed out earlier, the central character in any story should have a *story goal*, a purpose he seeks to accomplish within the framework of the topic/premise. Indeed, on a practical level, story very well may be defined as the record of a quest: a striving and its outcome.

Your story begins—*really* begins, that is—when Character commits himself to attaining his goal, for it is only then that you establish the tale's unifying "story question": Will Character succeed in his efforts to accomplish his purpose, or won't he? Will boy get girl—or won't he? Will woman get job—or won't she? Will convict get freedom—or won't he? Will mother get child—or won't she? Will cop get robber—or won't he? Will alcoholic wife beat booze—or won't she? Will mouse win self-respect—or won't he?

Now though this simplistic approach appears ridiculous at first glance, it works. Skillfully and subtly handled, it needn't prove so artless, either. And other ingredients, without it, add up to little.

In weak scripts, all sorts of preliminaries have been known to precede the moment of commitment. A central character may move through this sequence and that, assorted incidents and events, all with no goal in view, no purpose he's dedicated to achieving.

To try to make bricks without straw has nothing on trying to build a story in which the central character has no clear-cut goal. And the sooner he's committed to that goal, the better.

On the other hand, it's by no means necessary to jump in feet first when considered judgment opts in favor of a smoother entry. Here, as everywhere, horse sense does count!

Indeed, often it's wise to *build* to Character's commitment. Perhaps, for example, you'll want to begin by establishing situation . . . revealing that Character can go in two or more directions. For him to choose to strive and struggle quite possibly will seem insane—even though Audience aches for him to do so. In consequence, when Character decides to plunge ahead despite the odds, audience satisfaction is intense. Your viewers are hooked so firmly it will take truly bad work in the sequences that follow to disenchant them.

Cases in point? They range from *Tightrope* to *Yentl. Black Widow* to *Raiders of the Lost Ark.* In all you find carefully built commitment.

Nor does any of this mean Character needs to recognize or babble about his goal or his commitment. Quite possibly all that's needed is an apparently minor action—a flipping away of cigarette, a tossing down of cards, a turning on or off of lights. The issue is merely to let the audience know, somehow, that Character has direction.

It also should be noted that sometimes we fight to retain rather than to attain. A woman may battle for the right to stay single, a man to keep his job past compulsory retirement age, a couple to defend their home against an encroaching freeway. It still adds up to purpose and commitment.

A corollary: Character's goal when the film begins may not be the goal your story deals with. Quite possibly he's "just passing through," in the words of veteran scriptwriter William Bowers, when the story situation brings him up short and plunges him into adventures unrelated to anything he's previously anticipated.

In brief, then, the whole world is open to you where openings are concerned. You can play it any way you like—from the long minutes of mood that begin *A Passage to India* or *Witness* to the wild tension and terror of *Aliens* or the scream in the night that rivets *Agnes of God*'s viewers—so long as you end up with a hook and a commitment.

What about Earl Parrish? Faced with an appeal to join in the money truck robbery, he too must make a decision, a commitment. Until he does, we have no story.

It's also important that

4. You plan your peaks.

Just as a story begins when the central character commits himself to a goal, a purpose, so it ends when he either succeeds or fails in his efforts.

Between beginning and end, in a series of confrontations, Character strives against odds to reach his goal.

The writing of confrontations is an art in itself, spelled out in our next chapter. Here, suffice it to say that a confrontation is a unit of conflict—the entity sometimes known as the dramatic scene—and is the basis on which any story develops and progresses. These units and the transitional episodes that join them, when linked one to another, make up the body of your picture.

Beyond this, in framing your treatment, three things are important to bear in mind.

a. Avoid the predictable.

Your goal in blocking in your picture should be a series of logical yet unanticipated developments, sufficiently exciting to keep your viewers intrigued with your story. Even though experience tells them that the hero will surely win, *how* he wins should come as an exciting, delightful surprise to them.

The same principle applies at every stage. Take it for granted the audience will know *something* is going to happen at a given moment. But gnaw your nails if they know *what* that something is.

How do you avoid the predictable?

In theory, it's no problem. First, you put yourself in the audience's place and figure out what they anticipate will happen. Second, you list possible alternative developments and then choose the one you feel will prove most effective. Third, at the proper points in your script you plant the elements/objects/events necessary to make the twist you've chosen come off.

Thus, in one distinctly unmemorable horror script, I had my hero prowling the Mad Scientist's lair. There he discovers a group of The Fiend's zombie-like servitors standing in a trance state in coffin-shaped boxes. Moving on, he enters another room . . . sneaks up on Scientist. But just when it seems as if he's finally triumphed, the doors of two cabinets flanking the entrance swing open. A zombie lunges from each and seizes Hero, and he's right back where he started, only worse—for now he's Scientist's prisoner.

The pattern is, I trust, clear. Audience knew something must surely happen, but not what. Since the zombies already had a known potential from earlier sequences, I simply planted them in the room adjoining Scientist's laboratory, then let Hero proceed. Obviously, in their trance state, they were harmless.

Now Hero enters laboratory . . . creeps towards Scientist. Only then, behind him, the cabinets open, revealing non-cataleptic zombies, their presence logical yet hardly predictable. They lunge, and—well, you get the idea.

Unfortunately, such tricks seldom work out quite that neatly. Hair-tearing, breast-beating, and plain old dogged hanging in there often will be required before you find the right answers.

b. Accentuate the negative.

The example above illustrates this point also. Since audiences come to the theater to worry, it follows that they enjoy themselves more if Hero gets into deeper and deeper trouble as the film progresses. To that end, follow the out-of-the-frying-pan-into-the-fire principle. Each of Hero's efforts to improve his situation should end up making said situation worse: Villain, knocked down, comes up with a knife in either hand. Heroine, saved from dungeon, turns out to have lost her mind. Treasure chest, opened, sets off a blast that sinks the ship.

Too melodramatic? Then how about Hero returning to family after 18 months' service overseas. His wife waits for him at the gate . . . ever so obviously pregnant. Or he reaches down to pick up his two-year-old son . . . and the child bursts into screams of fear. Or he opens the kitchen door of what he thought of as his and Woman's dream cottage . . . and two rats race across a filthy, garbage-strewn floor.

'Nuff said?

c. Space out your crises.

It's essential that, in planning, you decide which incidents are going to be the big, important, decisive ones. Then, having decided, space them out, so that your viewers have an opportunity to recover from one before you overwhelm them with the next.

How do you arrange your crises? It will help if you have some sort of pattern to follow until you get the feel of such. One treatment I did was titled *Wedding Week*. Because a week is comprised of seven days, it gave me a built-in structure. Action rose step by step through the daylight hours to a major crisis each evening—a cliff-hanger to ensure the heroine a sleepless night, as it were.

In television, commercial breaks offer a similar guide. Same for the acts—two, three, five—in stage plays. And there are worse tricks than to plan in titled chapters the way novelists used to do.

Thus, suppose you have six, eight, ten crises: some major, some minor; some mountains, some foothills. Ordinarily, you'll arrange them in a pattern of what's termed *rising action*, ascending intensity, with tension building from beginning to end.

The tension can't *just* build, however. You need valleys between your peaks.

This being the case, you'll need to insert quiet episodes to balance the taut . . . maybe introduce a subplot (a sort of separate-but-related minor story probably centering on minor characters), or comedy relief bits, or material that concentrates on passage of time or space briefly instead of bearing down with such emphasis on story progression.

And yes, the place to work all this out is in your story treatment . . . even though you'll deal with it in more detail later, in step outline and master scene script.

5. *You resolve your issues.*

Sooner or later, you're going to have to end your story. That means, also, that you're going to have to release the climactic tensions you've built up in 80 or 90 or 100 minutes of manipulation of desire and danger.

It will help, at this point, if you acquire some small understanding of the dynamics of ending a story/script/film.

In practice, a script's "end" portion breaks down into two segments: climax and resolution.

Climax is the point in a screenplay at which the conflict between desire and danger reaches its ultimate peak. It's the final clash between hero and villain; the win-or-lose moment where the forces of good either triumph or meet what's euphemistically known as a fate worse than death.

Obviously there are as many ways to handle this moment as there are scripts and writers. As a general rule, however, most center in one way or another on a morally oriented decision by the central character: He or she must choose between doing the right thing or the wrong, the unselfish or the selfish; and Character's choice determines whether he wins or loses. Skill or strength or smarts, alone or together, isn't enough. Ethics and principles, social or personal, also have to enter.

You can see this in its clearest form in a host of pictures, ranging from *The Maltese Falcon* to *Tootsie* to *The Karate Kid*. In each instance the protagonist made a difficult decision and was rewarded. Whereupon viewers, emotionally rewarded, rewarded the producers on a financial level.

It goes without saying, as anyone who has tried it will tell you, that arranging this isn't the easiest thing in the world to do. Yet it's far from impossible, especially if you bear a basic principle in mind.

Specifically, the trick is always, at the climax, to provide your hero or heroine with an easy way out—a course of action that will get him off the hook with minimum trial and tribulation. All he has to do is tap the till or seduce the woman or reveal the name that he's promised to keep secret.

Then, don't let him take that route. Even though all logic and self-interest push him in that direction, and despite the fact that disaster in its purest and most pristine form hangs over him in a veritable sword of Damocles should he follow conscience, let honor guide him. Heedless of impeding doom, he does the "right" thing, the moral thing.

Not that Character need be sanctimonious or verbal about this. It's better, indeed, that he play it cool. Silence or surface cynicism are quite acceptable—witness Humphrey Bogart's portrayal of Rick in *Casablanca*.

What *does* matter is that, under pressure, Character shows courage. Why? Because both in life and on celluloid, courage remains the quality most prized and admired by viewers.

Especially esteemed is *moral* courage. *Rambo* notwithstanding, film-goers recognize that they're not Superman. But they *can* imagine themselves saying no, as when Dolly Parton refuses to be seduced in *Nine to Five* . . . confessing painful truths with Adela Quested in *A Passage to India* . . . going ahead in the face of odds, the way the Cambodian photographer does in *The Killing Fields*. So while they love to fantasize themselves as Conan or James Bond or Indiana Jones, the stubborn refusal to surrender of a Paul Newman in *Verdict* turns them on at a deeper level.

So much for climax. On to *resolution!*

Despite all the odds against him, all the looming cataclysms, you make your hero win—in heart and mind, if not in body. He knows he's done the right thing; that's his payoff, even though he loses the gold or the battle or Mary Astor.

How do you manage this? You do it by manipulation of some pre-planted element, some logical yet unanticipated ace in the hole you've introduced earlier: the gun in the drawer, the death-bed statement, the previously established attitude of some character who now takes center stage. Whereupon, Indiana Jones survives the Temple of Doom, and Teen Wolf not only wins the game but at last sees which girl is the right one.

Obviously, this isn't always painted in with a barn brush. The skilled scriptwriter modifies it by introducing appropriately realistic touches. Not every victory is total. Bad things do happen to good people. But the overall picture is of what we loosely term *poetic justice* . . . of the way audiences would like life to be.

Can you find this pattern in all films?

No, of course not. Partly, this is because filmmakers grow bored like anyone else. Tiring of traditional—which is to say, predictable—lines of development, they attempt something "fresh," something "different," even though they recognize that it's a gamble.

Viewers, in turn, feel helpless and out of control of their lives, upon occasion. They want to believe they're not alone in said feeling. The very idea of irresponsibility or immorality or a world without rules pulses at them like Las Vegas neon.

In consequence, many pictures, today, stop instead of ending. Or they settle for shock instead of story. Or they present a "slice of life" that proclaims the meaninglessness of existence, or focuses on greed, short-sighted selfishness, or mindless pursuit of pleasure.

The result, too often, is a picture that depresses rather than entertains, where a mass audience is concerned. Because, actually, of course, if you want to be philosophical about it, life *is* predictable and it *does* have meaning. Predictably, birth is followed by life is followed by death; and its meaning is that the species survives a little longer.

Permit me to reduce this to ground-level, personal terms. I'm fully aware that, as my father used to say, "Life is real, life is earnest, and we all die sometime." But I also remember lying on a red-mud riverbank in southern Nicaragua not too many years ago. I had a broken rib and a smashed knee and I felt like hell and the sound of gunfire was echoing disconcertingly close.

But it was an incident, an episode; a story, if you will, not life itself. I survived it. The years since have seen good moments for me as well as bad.

The thing a scriptwriter needs to remember is that a story concerns a problem and its solution; and most of us, most of the time, do solve our problems.

We do it by hanging in there, as it were. Instinctively, we know that. So if you write scripts in which you let your characters give up, cop out, abandon hope, and deny the relationship between cause and effect, not all viewers will love you for it.

Which doesn't mean you shouldn't try it, you understand. There have been major hits that did so—remember *Easy Rider?* But there also have been major failures, a lot of them. As a rule, your chances for success will be better if you search for freshness and the unanticipated via floor-pacing and new lists of ways to kill with doorknobs to keep you clever.

How do you release climactic tensions? More specifically, how do you release them in a manner satisfying to your viewers?

Two issues are involved.

a. Releasing topic-engendered tensions.

Topic tensions are those based on largely mechanical issues: How do you get Heroine out of burning building? How do you save Hero from firing squad? How do you decipher the code, find the will, control the dread disease?

This obviously can be a problem. By the time you've built your story to a climax, odds are you've created a state of affairs that's tangled and taut indeed.

Fortunately, you've already mastered the principles of the unraveling process. It's the procedure you used in inventing logical, unanticipated, non-predictable complications and crises back in your film's middle sector.

Now, you use this same approach to resolve instead of complicate: You figure out what the audience expects . . . you devise a different alternative . . . and plant (or expunge) such elements as are necessary to bring it off.

b. Releasing character-engendered tensions.

Your viewers' tensions won't be totally released till they're satisfied with the way things worked out for the characters in your film. Solutions to mechanical problems alone just aren't enough.

Again, however, the answer is relatively simple: You give each character what he's demonstrated he deserves, on a basis of both competence and conduct.

Competence? That means only that you don't have a dub golfer winning the championship over a pro, or a janitor stumping the college physics faculty, or the town hag claiming the cup in the beauty contest. It's the element of *potential* that we discussed in Chapter 8.

Conduct is something else again. For lack of a better word, let's equate it with morality. It means that if a character has behaved the way the audience thinks he should, he wins; if he hasn't, he doesn't.

The problem here—and not just for scriptwriters—is that morality is changing, especially for the young people who make up the overwhelming majority of the film audience. "Situation ethics" increasingly is taking over, with "right" and "wrong" determined on a basis of circumstance, rather than absolutes.

Thus, not too many years ago, the penalties for sexual irregularity, for the woman, included illicit pregnancy, venereal disease, community scorn, and economic disaster.

Enter the so-called sexual revolution. The Pill gave a considerable degree of control over pregnancy. Antibiotics kept disease pretty much in line. Mobility and women's lib blunted scorn's edge. Womens' movement into better-paying jobs made economic survival feasible.

But, as the saying goes, the only thing unchanging is change. Just as the "new morality" seemed to have triumphed, herpes surfaced, and then AIDS. Together, they gave birth to what amounts to a sexual *counter*revolution. The "counterculture" of the '60s and '70s faded. Government deficits, disastrous foreign balance of trade, the devaluation of the dollar, and lost jobs increasingly played havoc with attitudes and prospects. Crimes against people and property (rationalized a few years earlier in such films as *Save the Tiger, The Sting, Charley Varrick, Cops and Robbers, Death Wish, Clockwork Orange,* and *Bonnie and Clyde*) lost much of their charm. Audiences pondered Iranscam, the Nicaraguan Contras, insider trading, and the peccadillos of TV evangelists, and began rethinking their own views on morality. And the end is not yet in sight.

That all this has influenced film attitudes goes without saying. But as this is written no clear picture of a new attitudinal set has yet emerged. Films featuring sexual promiscuity *(The Morning After, Half Moon Street)* and criminality *(Prince of the City, The Pope of Greenwich Village)* are still being made, but social values *(The Verdict, A Passage to India)* and religious themes and backgrounds *(Agnes of God, Name of the Rose, Witness)* increasingly are moving into prominence.

With society itself in such a state of flux, the scriptwriter should need no crystal ball to make clear the importance of staying ever so aware of his audience and its thinking. He dare not deal out penalties or rewards to his characters blindly or by the old standards, lest he lose contact and shatter believability in the process. Indeed, he need not—should not—ever forsake his personal code. For if standards truly make sense, and Writer truly possesses a modicum of creative imagination, he still can sell them to any audience, providing he approaches them in terms of that audience's point of view.

*   *   *

So much for the *do's* of framing your treatment. Now, how about the *don'ts?*

We'll limit them to five notes of warning:

1. Beware of idiot plots.
2. Beware of static situations.
3. Beware of diffuse opposition.
4. Beware of too many characters.
5. Beware of theme and symbolism.

Here we go!

1. Beware of idiot plots.

An idiot plot is one in which one or more key characters have to behave like idiots in order for the story to come off.

These are tales that feature heroes who defy killers, heroines who make appointments to meet murderers in isolated castle towers, villains who decide the detective has suddenly switched over to their side.

To avoid such, merely make it a practice to ask yourself, "*Why* does Joe (or Sam, or Suzy, or Griselda) do this? Is there so much pressure on him (or her) that, in the same circumstances, an ordinary, intelligent man or woman would act this way?"

2. *Beware of static situations.*

A moving picture should move, should tell its story in action. Otherwise it's not taking proper advantage of the film medium's potential.

Unfortunately, all too often, writers write scripts in which people merely sit around and *talk about* past, present, or future action.

Even worse, they choose topics which offer little opportunity for things to happen: for the story to develop in terms of people doing things. Even a highly successful stage play, for example, as a film may founder on verbosity and the innate limitations that go with its medium.

Now good films can be and have been made in which settings were restricted, action limited. But special problems always are involved, so be sure you're prepared to take on such before you dive into such murky waters.

3. *Beware of diffuse opposition.*

Simultaneously or in sequence, all sorts of elements may oppose your central character as he moves through your story towards his goal. Not only is the weather against him, the ferryman won't cross the river with the water this high, the Mennonites down the road resent his use of tractors, Banker is determined to foreclose on the old family homestead, Heroine's brother wants to knock his block off, Rival has sworn to have his blood, and Neighbor is loading his shotgun with buck instead of bird.

One of these factors should emerge as dominant in Character's struggle—and the sooner, the better. Why? So that Character will have a specific someone or something to defeat—or be defeated by—at the climax, the culmination of his fight to attain his goal: witness Rick versus Strasser in *Casablanca*, Ringo versus the Plummer brothers in *Stagecoach*, John Book versus the three crooked cops in *Witness*.

This is tremendously important. *Without* such a dominant opposing element, it will prove difficult if not impossible to bring your climax into effectively sharp focus. There will be no way to demonstrate, through your hero's victory or defeat, that he has won or lost.

A climax which does not pivot on such a demonstration will prove vague and mushy. In consequence, it will fail to give your audience that sudden release of pent-up tension that constitutes ultimate and total satisfaction.

4. Beware of too many characters.

Pay no attention whatever to how many characters you use when you set down the first draft of your treatment.

The second time round, cut out half.

The third, trim to bare-bone minimum.

Thing is, most of us tend at the beginning to bring in story people not as single spies but in battalions. Which is fine, except that (a) actors cost money (how many spectaculars has MGM released lately?) and (b) too large a cast confuses your viewers.

Further, that mass of players is seldom vital. The people you need are those who build your story, advance the conflict, stand for or against your hero in his struggle to attain his goal. Drop all others. (We're not talking about crowds, spearbearers in the chorus, and the like, you understand. The issue is characters developed as individuals, people who play distinctive roles within your story.)

Then, go over the list of those who remain and ask yourself if you can't combine one with another, or perhaps cut bits or incidents to eliminate a few more.

Yes, I grant you all this is tedious and painful. But you'll be glad you did it when, later, producer or director pokes at this role or that and you're already primed and ready to justify the character's retention.

5. Beware of theme and symbolism.

It's impossible to write a script or make a film without a theme—and this includes even the most inept of blue movies.

It's equally beyond anyone's ability to create a picture that doesn't use symbols.

However, the chances are good that the writer will have no idea as to what said theme is till the picture's released and someone tells him. And the things he'll discover about the symbols he's incorporated—well!

The reason these things are so is that a film's theme is merely the message it conveys. Thus, the theme of the blue movie cited above very well may be only that sex is on the sickening side when served up in such a package.

The trouble with themes is that if you bear down too hard on them, your films tend to grow stiff and preachy. You'll fare better, in most cases, if you follow the advice someone passed on to me long years ago. "You want to build in a message? Great! Just don't let any of your characters know what that message is!"

* * *

A symbol is something that stands for something else, on a basis of relationship, association, convention, or the like. A noun is a symbol of an object. A flag is a symbol of a country. A cross is a symbol of Christianity. A sickle and hammer is a symbol of Communism. And so on and so forth.

It follows that, in order for symbols to be meaningful, you have to know the ground rules: just what each symbol is supposed to stand for. If you don't, the whole business becomes senseless.

When a writer decides to incorporate specialized symbols into his script, he runs the grave risk that the device that seems so clear and obvious to him may totally miss its mark where his viewers are concerned. Even 75 years of Freudianism haven't yet gotten it across to everyone that they should equate church steeples and snakes with penises, windows and doors with vaginas.

This being the case, it might be wise for the scriptwriter to ignore the whole matter. No matter what he decides, symbols will be present, and he can leave it to the critics to decide what they mean.

Even better, he might make any key symbols he chooses to include clear to all—like bedbugs and cockroaches equal squalor. The audience, as well as critics, will have a fighting chance to understand!

WRITING THE TREATMENT

How do you write a treatment?

You've already heard enough and too much about my favorite tricks for getting words and ideas down on paper: focused free association, continuing elaboration, and so on. I won't repeat them here.

More important at this point, I think, is a warning not to let facts engulf or overwhelm you. A good film is feeling first of all, remember. Your task in the treatment, in large measure, is to capture same on paper.

How do you manage this? The secret is surprisingly simple. It begins with clear realization that an urge to write anything indicates, in a high proportion of cases, that the topic holds some element you find exciting.

Apply this excitement yardstick to each successive sequence of your treatment. Ignoring plot lines and bridging bits (they're the kind of thing you can stick in later as needed), ask yourself what there is about each person, setting, incident, speech fragment, or what have you that creates— or in the past created—a sense of eagerness or enthusiasm in you.

Get these exciting touches down on paper and, from them, write your treatment. Try to capture the feeling they evoke as you go along, setting your interlinked ideas down as if they were a story told in present tense: not "Joe turned," but "Joe turns." Not "Sue's eyes widened," but "Sue's eyes widen." Strive for words and phrases that will help your readers—and you too—to feel not only the flat facts of what happens, but also mood, color, tension, spirit, tone. Give heed to connotation, denotation. Make maximum use of action verbs, pictorial nouns.

Here, for example, is a passage designed to nail down the feelings that go with an opening—a time, a place, a bit of action:

```
FADE IN:

          It's a gray, misty morning on a Mississippi River inlet.

An outboard-powered johnboat putt-putts towards us in a wide arc.

It carries three men; its destination, a weathered raft/dock

secured against a steep bank at the foot of a flight of rickety

wooden steps.

          A small, neat houseboat, the Cupcake, is moored to the

dock fore and aft.  The incoming boat ties up beside it and the

men get out.  They are DEACON DOUGHBALL, a weak-faced, country-

preacher-gone-to-seed type...ANSE BLESSARD, a mean-looking river

rat who carries an old lever-action .22 rifle across his left

forearm...and Anse's raffish brother, REB, a whittler who shaves

a stick with the longest, wickedest-looking jackknife imaginable

as he walks.

          Climbing the stair, the trio get into an ancient,

battered car.  Deacon Doughball at the wheel, the car lurches

down a rutted lane and onto a gravel road that parallels the

river.  Signs tell us that we're entering GLEN FORK...POP. 1549,

and welcome us to RIVER COUNTY, HEART OF EAST ARKANSAS...SEE OUR

HISTORIC STEAMBOAT LANDING!
```

This is atmosphere stuff, of course. It's designed to establish location, set a mood, and raise questions.

The pages that follow introduce us to our hero, young Ross Copeland . . . his employer, Possum Wilberforce, publisher of the Glen Fork *Eagle* and East Arkansas's answer to Colonel Blimp . . . and Lorena Wilberforce, Possum's daughter and Ross's betrothed.

Now, the treatment gives action with a light touch, as Possum takes Ross to collect a printing/advertising bill from an appliance dealer new in town. They're accompanied by the Blessards, a pair popularly known (but not to their faces) as the Buzzard Brothers.

The dealer refuses to pay. Possum sighs gustily in
apparent defeat and heads for the door. But Anse says something
should be done about the flies buzzing about the store. When one
lands on a shiny new refrigerator, he eliminates it--and
punctures the refrigerator--with a shot from his .22.

Reb, in turn, chides Anse for wasting ammunition. To
demonstrate that such isn't necessary, he slices a second fly in
mid-air with his jackknife.

Quaking, the dealer pays up.

Currently, Ross has two major goals in life: to get Lorena alone,
away from Possum's ever-watchful eyes, and to escape Glen Fork with
her.

Regards Goal No. 1, he's secretly acquired a boat so that he can
take her, unobserved under the cover of night, to the *Cupcake,* where
he lives.

They board the Cupcake...lock the door.

Ross reaches for Lorena. She flings herself into his
arms in a wild embrace, and reveals that she's persuaded her
father to give Ross an interest in the Eagle, chaining him to
Glen Fork for all time to come in a fate which he considers
worse than death by far.

The pages that follow see Ross, in his desperation, involving himself
with such divergent types as Stacey Suggs, henpecked country-western
star who dreams of singing lieder . . . Suggs' bitchy, blue-haired wife,
Gladys, a termagant's termagant . . . tough, sexy Beverly English, an
A&R rep who's trying to talk Stacey into switching to her record company
. . . and our ultimate heroine, Carole Foster, would-be songwriter currently working as a waitress.

The wrap-up:

Carole saves innocent Ross from a shotgun marriage to
Lorena by pretending he's spent the crucial night with her.

```
         Raging, Possum departs with a worshipful Lorena, Deacon

Doughball, and the Buzzard Brothers.  Ross and Carole are left

stranded on the river bank:  broke, jobless, blacklisted.

         They do have one asset, however:  the boat Ross bought

in his early effort to seduce Lorena.  Which means that at least

they can get across the river and, from there, hitchhike to

Nashville and check out Carole's songs.

         It's a good moment.  Laughing, they scramble aboard.

Ross starts the outboard.  The boat swings out into the

Mississippi in a long arc past the Cupcake...farther and farther

into the distance in an approximation of our opening shot as we

                                          FADE OUT
```

And there you are. Your goal in your treatment is persuasion—persuasion of a very special kind: You want to convince the key personnel who read your effort that your story's strong, tight-knit, gripping: the kind of property that will pull viewers, fill theaters.

Nor do you want to leave any doubts as to your epic's cinematic practicality. That means: no holes, no flaws, no problems; no doubts but that the story will take form effectively on film.

Treatment length? Don't worry about it too much. Good treatments have been written in ten pages, and in a hundred. What counts, as more than one old hand has pointed out, is not how many words you write, but how convincingly you sell your idea.

I should also remind you here, in all fairness, that there are all sorts of ways of handling treatments. Writers range from those who like to write extremely "full" to those who prefer to keep their copy "tight" or "lean." Most fall somewhere in between. Again, you pays your money and you takes your choice.

Whichever route you choose, though, one thing is absolutely essential. It's mastery of the art of creating and building and bridging confrontations, and we'll take it up in the next chapter.

CHAPTER 10

The Art of Confrontation

A story is compounded of desire plus danger. It begins when the central character commits himself to attaining a story goal in the face of opposition. It ends when he either succeeds or fails in his efforts.

This means Character starts a story with one state of affairs and state of mind. He ends with another.

The Great Gatsby begins with Gatsby seeking new contact with his first love. It ends with him betrayed and dead in his own swimming pool.

Lady Sings the Blues begins with Billie Holiday working as cleaning girl in a whorehouse. It ends with her singing at Carnegie Hall, with newsclip flash-forwards to her continued drug addiction and death at 44. *Chinatown* begins with Jake Gittes agreeing to check on an allegedly unfaithful husband. It ends with both husband and wife dead and Gittes in a state of shock.

How do you move Character from State of Affairs/State of Mind 1 to State of Affairs/State of Mind x?

You impel him forward on twin wheels of *confrontation* and *transition*.

A confrontation is a unit of conflict; a time-unified meeting of opposing forces.

A transition is a change from one condition, one state of development, to another. In the sense I use it here, it's a topic-unified passage from one confrontation to another.

Story-wise, each confrontation and each transition changes the state of affairs and state of mind of each character involved, to some degree. In so doing, it moves the story forward towards its climax and resolution.

Thus, your story opens with your hero faced with a predicament, an emotionally disturbing situation.

In the typical film, you have approximately 90 minutes in which to resolve this predicament . . . replace Hero's disturbing situation and unpleasant emotions with something more satisfactory.

To this end, you link together a chain of confrontations alternating with transitions until, timed out, they add up to 90 minutes of screen time.

Indeed, there are worse questions to ask yourself before you start on any script than "Does my idea offer good opportunities for building confrontations? That is, will my protagonist have to fight to get what he wants, and can I devise incidents to dramatize that fight?"

Next question: How do you build confrontations and transitions?

Confrontation, first. It breaks down into three elements: *goal, conflict,* and *disaster.*

CONFRONTATION DYNAMICS: *GOALS*

Confrontations are the backbone of your script; the big moments in which your story advances.

A confrontation is a meeting of opposing forces; a time-unified clash between them. It's based on a conflict of goal-oriented actions: Someone wants to do something. Someone else doesn't want him to succeed. They struggle.

"To do something" = the attaining of a new, different, changed state of affairs.

Or, the retention of an old, same, *un*changed state.

So. A confrontation starts with goals. *Mutually incompatible* goals. Which is to say, if Character A gets his way, Character B can't have his.

A successful confrontation must first of all bring the two—or more—participants together in such a manner that they can join combat. Ordinarily, this means a face-to-face encounter. But variations are possible—witness the wars between lovers waged by telephone. The issue is merely one of imagination; the degree of creativity the scriptwriter brings to bear.

Beyond this, the confrontation should offer conflicting goals which are

a. Specific and concrete.
b. Immediate.
c. Strongly motivated.
d. Established early.

A few examples will clarify the issues.

a. Specific and concrete.

Suppose Character's goal is to win the acceptance—indeed, friendship—of the woman in the riverfront house next door, despite her tight-lipped antagonism. How can the audience know whether or not he's really succeeded? How can the cameraman film appropriate footage of anything as abstract as acceptance, or friendship?

On the other hand, let's assume the same situation—but this time, Character's goal is to borrow Woman's car. Not only is this a photographable act, instantly comprehensible to viewers, but it also demonstrates the working fact of Woman's acceptance of Character far better than could any abstraction or generality.

In addition, Character's goal should be

b. Immediate.

A good goal, for confrontation purposes, is one you can take action to attain *right now.*

In fact, it's even better if you *must* take immediate steps to achieve it. Time pressure adds urgency to any scene.

Take the case above of Character, Woman, and the car. If Character merely thinks it would be nice to be able to borrow Woman's car some day, we haven't got much to work with.

If, on the other hand, Character's infant child has just gulped down some lethal fluid, and getting Child to the hospital fast is a matter of life or death, and Woman's car is the only available transport—well, the confrontation over borrowing the vehicle is going to come on hard and fast.

Which brings up yet another important point: The goals in a confrontation should be

c. Strongly motivated.

Frivolous, unmotivated, or weakly motivated goals seldom throw a confrontation into appropriately high gear. Those strongly motivated, in contrast, may speed your story to new peaks of tension.

Back to Character and Woman. Character, with Child's life at stake, obviously is highly motivated. He'll fight to get use of Woman's car.

What about Woman, however? Where does she stand?

Suppose, for example, that refusing to loan her car isn't just a matter of whim with her. Rather, her earlier antagonism is an intentional ploy designed to hold contacts at arm's length. She's rented this waterfront house because the state prison is just across the river and her convict husband's planning an escape. He's slated to make the break this very afternoon. Unless she and the car are here and ready when he scrambles from the water, he's a cinch to be captured and dragged back.

Now: What will be her reaction to Character's demand for loan of the car?

As noted previously, it takes specific, concrete, immediate, strongly motivated goals to build a proper confrontation!

Finally, said goals should be

d. Established early.

The earlier someone involved in a confrontation demonstrates that he has a goal, the earlier said confrontation can get under way.

Next question: How does a character demonstrate he has a goal? By getting up on a soapbox and sounding off about it?

Sometimes, maybe. But not very often.

Far better, let Character create the *impression* that he has a goal by what he does. Let his actions *show* it.

Exhibit A, from our sample episode: The door of Character's house bursts open. He lunges out onto the porch . . . looks frantically this way and that . . . pivots abruptly and, leaping the railing, sprints towards Woman's house.

Not one word has been spoken, note. We don't know that Character has a child, let alone that Child's been poisoned.

But because of the way Character's behaving, we *do* know something's going on, and we have reason to believe it's on the important side.

Naturally, there are other ways this can be handled. Opening on Child's scream, for example, or Child's face, or even the can of drain cleaner. Or earlier, perhaps, with Character watching TV, or setting down a bag of groceries and unloading items which include the can.

Why make such a fuss about establishing goals early and in action? Because once said action's under way and conflict develops, a confrontation may go in any number of directions.

CONFRONTATION DYNAMICS: *CONFLICT*

Mutually incompatible goals bring characters into conflict. Which seems simple enough, save that too often too many writers fail to remember that conflict comes in a variety of shapes and sizes.

Thus, a clash may be brief, or it may be protracted. It may be major, or minor. It may be taut, or almost lackadaisical. You build it to fit the requirements of your developing story.

How do you expand or contract a confrontation, a unit of conflict?

You add intensity, time pressure, twists, complications, or whatever else comes handy, as needed.

In the case of Character, for instance, he might come charging into Woman's house without knocking. "Quick!" he gasps. "Your car keys! Buddy—I gotta get him to the hospital!"

What now? Does Woman refuse, cry out, flee, faint, or what?
And how does Character react?

Let's suppose Woman flatly refuses to loan the car. Character grapples with her. Breaking free, Woman tries to flee. Character pursues. Woman—a desperate type, obviously—hauls out a gun. Character knocks it aside, wrestles Woman for keys.

And that's the way it goes, in confrontation.

Though it should also be noted that this horrendous battle might, under other circumstances, have been brought to an end before it started had Woman said coolly, "Oh, I'm sorry. The battery's down. That's why I haven't been driving this week."

Or, were we dealing with comedy rather than melodrama, an involved scheme on Character's part to get car away from Woman for whatever reason might have ended with the vehicle—Character at the wheel—rolling into the river.

CONFRONTATION DYNAMICS: *DISASTER*

Confrontation starts with goal. Then conflict's added.

It ends, finally, in *disaster*.

Disaster: a new and unanticipated development which worsens Character's situation.

Or, if you prefer, one which offers unforeseen consequences for Character.

Or, one which raises intriguing questions in regard to Character's future.

Consider the potentialities in our car loan episode: Character knocks Woman's gun aside; wrestles her for the keys.

Only then—new and unanticipated development—Woman jerks free for the fraction of a second—and hurls the keys out the window, into the river.

Disaster, right? Character's situation is worsened. Confrontation has ended with him the loser in the conflict, just at the moment he thought he'd won.

Also, happy day, it's given us a strong curtain.

A "strong curtain"—obviously, the term is of the theater—is a striking, unanticipated development that, coming suddenly, in effect acts as a cliff-hanger, a shock device to freeze the audience's attention with an implicit "Ai! What on earth will Character do now?"

Well, what *will* he do? It's a vital question.

Further, it brings us to our second dynamic element, transition.

Transition is a bridge between battles: non-conflict action that carries your characters from one confrontation to another. For all practical purposes, it takes in everything in your film which *isn't* confrontation, conflict. The trivia of living—the chance meetings, the casual chats, the buying of groceries and eating of meals and brushing of teeth—goes into transition.

Yet it isn't all quite as loose as it seems, for transition has its own unifying element.

That element is *preoccupation:* preoccupation with the "What-will-I-do-now?" factor that's the aftermath of the preceding confrontation's disaster.

In other words, Character may drift from here to there; talk of this and that; involve himself in which or wherever. But always, one way or another, whether by implication or oblique reference or side-issue development, you the writer see to it that he's still pondering his future, his next step.

This being the case, transition constitutes a dynamic element in your story just as much as does confrontation. By no means is it mere waste space or empty lines. For through its tacit focus on the future, transition provides the motivation/justification/springboard from which Character plunges into his next confrontation.

Just as confrontation breaks down into goal, conflict, and disaster, so transition subdivides into three elements: *reaction, dilemma,* and *decision.*

TRANSITION DYNAMICS: *REACTION*

Reaction works this way: Overwhelmed by the disaster of Confrontation 1, Character *reacts* to it in characteristic fashion.

Let's take the case of a specific character and situation—a female character, this time, an executive in her mid-30s whose doctor has just told her that what she though was a touch of stomach trouble actually is liver damage brought on by years of excessive drinking. She can lay off the booze and go on a strict diet plus medication, or she can watch her condition deteriorate to cirrhosis.

Exit Executive. Back out on the street, what is her *reaction?* Shock? Rage? Incredulity? Helplessness? Hopelessness? Panic?

That will depend, of course, on her character, the kind of person she is—a matter which you, the writer, should already have pretty clearly in mind. Whatever the answer, you'll need to devise ways to reduce her response to photographable form: some sort of doings a cameraman can capture on film.

Let's make it simple. What would *you* do, if you were a long-time heavy drinker, reeling under the impact of a sudden, paralyzing shock?

Habit says: Grab a quick drink. Right? So you scuttle into the nearest cocktail lounge, there to gulp down a double vodka (vodka's an old rule with you, to keep you "breathless" on the job, as the ads say), in the same moment calling for another.

By the time Number Three's down the hatch, a greasy-looking type has moved to the stool beside yours, smiling in appropriately unctuous fashion. How's about letting him buy the next one?

You cut him off with a tart, "No, thanks." But his try shakes you. Do you look *that* bad? And whether the answer's yes or no, one thing's certain: You've got to bring yourself under control. You've got to face the salient question: *What do I do now?*

It's a state of affairs we label *dilemma*.

TRANSITION DYNAMICS: *DILEMMA*

On film, dilemma may take the form of anything from deliberation to discussion; from driving down endless roads or walking across endless landscape to praying for divine guidance.

Female Executive has her own pattern. Abandoning the cocktail lounge, she hurries home to her apartment. There, ignoring a convenient vodka bottle, she sets about stirring up a batch of thick, gooey, chocolate pecan fudge. That at least will get her away from the vodka . . . keep her hands busy while she thinks things out.

Only then a wave of guilt overwhelms her. Holding down her weight is an eternal battle for her. She even suspects there's a link between that and her drinking.

Yet here she stands, mixing bowl in hand, stirring in more brown sugar and more chocolate.

Anguish, erupting. With a choked cry, she hurls the fudge-to-be into the trash-pail, bowl and all, bursts into tears, and rushes to the bathroom.

Now, however, she finds, she can't even be satisfactorily sick. All that's left for her is to stand leaning on the washbowl, staring into the mirror at her tortured, tear-streaked face.

The real problem, she knows, is that drinking's not just a pastime for her; it's a defense. Fighting her way up through the ranks to a top executive post in a male-centered world has taken far more nerve than her background gave her. So, she's drawn courage from a bottle. And when tension stretched her too tight, she's relaxed the strain with more of the same.

Now, if the doctor's to be believed, that period's over.

If she wants to live, that is.

Yet how can she quit? Popularity has never been her strong suit; the fights she's fought to get where she is have bred far too much bitterness for that. Particularly, the male chauvinist pig-type rival who covets her job is ever hovering close, alert for any opening, any hint of weakness.

TRANSITION DYNAMICS: *DECISION*

Decision comes, finally. That is, Executive makes up her mind what to do next, what course of action to pursue: She'll quit drinking, cold turkey. Right now, effective tonight, without benefit of Antabuse, A.A., or any other crutches.

Executive's decision, please note, provides her with a new *goal*, something to strive for.

Further, to prove to herself that she really means it, she'll attend a beach-house party tonight as scheduled, despite the fact that it will put her right in the sights of her hated rival.

It's a frightening thought. A drink would do so much to bolster her resolution. . . .

Her knuckles go white as she grips the washbowl. Then, with a convulsive twist, she pivots . . . strides to the kitchen, seizes the vodka bottle . . . and pours its contents down the sink.

And there you have the pattern on which is based the art of confrontation: goal-conflict-disaster; reaction-dilemma-decision. It's a sequence which you repeat, time after time, till you reach the end of your film.

Now, one word of warning: In developing this example, note that I've left Executive alone most of the time. This can be dangerous. The screen offers few opportunities for neat asides of explanation. That means the actor must convey his inner world through action . . . must *show* us his thoughts and feelings, drives and conflicts.

A fine actor, well directed, can do this. A poor or mediocre one, ill guided, may fail, or turn us off, or win wild gales of mirth with what he hoped would be a scene of tenderness or anguish.

Be careful of asking too much in this regard, then. Better to write the bit for two, not one, most of the time, or to plan on cutting away to parallel action. The neck you save may be your own!

WHAT ABOUT RIGIDITY?

New writers sometimes make the plaint that the confrontation/transition pattern is unduly mechanical. Actually, however, the events of your own life fit within it. The only difference is that, because of time/length limitations, film forces a certain compression and neatness of ordering which life foregoes.

Thus, in life, I may spend weeks or months debating whether to quit my job, or move, or marry. On film, quite possibly I'll have only a couple of minutes' running time to do so. But the decision, if presented convincingly, is no less valid.

Take the case of our female executive. Her reaction, dilemma, and decision are perfectly logical. The only issue is how to present them most effectively on the screen. For though, in print, it's easy enough to describe Executive's thoughts and feelings, film demands that we devise ways to dramatize them; to externalize her inner turmoil.

Can such be done? Of course it can—and that as crudely or subtly as your talent will permit. We've already seen how *reaction* translates itself into a cocktail lounge and double vodkas. *Dilemma* becomes fudge and tears and mirror; *decision,* potables poured down the drain.

Now obviously this isn't the only way the situation could be handled. Some writers might have developed it in a bedroom with the greasy type from the bar. Others would have brought in concerned friends, or telephone dialogue, or psychedelic d.t.'s, or ambulances screaming through the night.

Indeed, elimination of any or all parts of a transition is sometimes not only possible, but advantageous. Thus, Doctor might have curtain-lined his session with Executive with a blunt "There it is, Miss Jones: Quit drinking, or quit breathing." She stares at him, face stiff with shock. Whereupon we dissolve to the beach-house party. Someone offers Executive a drink. She shakes her head. "No, thanks. I'm on the wagon." A crisis has been met; a decision has been made. All we see are the results.

The same principle holds true for confrontation. Instead of Character wrestling Woman for the car keys two falls out of three, Woman might simply have let his door-pounding go unanswered, leaving him no choice but to take off in a new direction.

What about the business of cliff-hangers, strong curtains? I acknowledge freely that there are those who object to such. On occasion, they're left out, by some writers and in some pictures. Yet by and large, audiences do favor them—simply because said audiences go to the theater far less for intellectual enlightenment than emotional experience. They buy tickets because they enjoy the ebb and flow of tension; and nothing brings tension into sharper focus than does the build to an unanticipated twist that threatens pure disaster.

Another conclusion easily jumped to is that the use of confrontation and transition to build rising action applies only to certain types of picture—the thriller, the chiller, the action epic.

Nothing could be farther from the truth. The moment purpose becomes apparent, whether that purpose be explicit or implicit, there stands confrontation. Wherever a character struggles to reach a decision, transition is aborning. And this is as true when a child climbs a forbidden tree, then tries to decide whether to tell the truth as to how he tore his shirt, as when a woman seduces her best friend's husband, then strives to make up her mind if she wants to marry him as well.

In a word, the patterns of confrontation and transition are eminently fluid. To assail them as false or mechanical or rigid is pure self-delusion. It indicates only that we ourselves feel so engulfed and overwhelmed by life as to convince ourselves that life itself is formless—an obvious enough misreading of the facts, if you stop to consider that all of us are born, do live, and finally die.

In much the same way, and because death and tragedy do come to each of us, we pretend that life has no strivings, no triumphs, no happy endings. Yet who among us hasn't known happiness, even if only briefly? To demand that film show only aimlessness or defeat is to distort life grossly.

THE MATTER OF SECONDARY FUNCTION

Failure to understand and use the secondary functions of confrontation and transition in your film script is to throw out some of your most helpful tools.

Thus, in addition to moving your story forward, confrontation and transition perform three valuable services:

1. Regulation of excitement and acceptance.
2. Establishment and exposition.
3. Spacing and pacing.

What can we say about each of these categories?

1. Regulation of excitement and acceptance.

Conflict, confrontation, is what creates tension in your viewers. So, to add excitement to a dragging screenplay, you increase the proportion of confrontations to transitions, in terms of number, or running time, or both. For cases in point, consider the well-nigh obligatory car chases, karate combats, and mattress maulings in a host of recent pictures.

If your script lacks logic and believability, on the other hand, the solution often is to build up the transitions. Particularly, emphasize the logic of your hero's actions and the clear good sense—nay, inevitability—of his choice of goals.

The usual word of warning, though: You can always run a good thing into the ground. Let the confrontations crowd too fast and furious on each others' heels, and the film becomes a joke. Stretch out your transitions to too great length, in striving for greater believability, and the audience goes to sleep.

2. Establishment and exposition.

I group these elements together because, by and large, they're two sides of the same coin.

Establishment, as noted in previous chapters, is making some aspect or component of your film in some way recognizable and identifiable in your audience's eyes.

Exposition is providing your viewer with information about the past which he needs in order to understand and appreciate the present and future of your story.

In general, it's desirable to limit your use of confrontation for purposes of establishment and/or exposition, *except insofar as said establishment and/or exposition are an integral part of the action.* Or, to put it another way, avoid explanations of anything in confrontation: It breaks the flow of the action.

However, it's hardly desirable to overload your transitions with background either. So, herewith a few hints on how to get maximum mileage with minimum pain:

a. Limit what your audience needs to know.

Remember what we said in Chapter 9 about building yourself a private picture of the background of the action?

Now is the time at which this homework comes in handy. Why? Because now you know all the things *you* need to know about what's gone before . . . so you can, without confusion, choose from that mass those items essential to your viewers also.

Which means you can leave out all the rest, with no fears or worries or qualms of conscience.

Well, at least not too many.

b. Make your viewers want to know the past.

The picture that sticks in my mind in this regard is an old Spencer Tracy vehicle, *Bad Day at Black Rock.* Tracy, as a one-armed World War 2 colonel, drops off a train in a sun-baked desert town in the west. Virtually from the moment he arrives, he's under attack by forces within the tiny community. Yet the town has raised a wall of silence against him. Consequently, both he and the audience are writhing in paroxysms of frustration as to just why all this should be so. And you don't get the answer till you're at least two-thirds through the picture.

c. Make your characters need information and have to fight to get it.

A variation on *b,* above, this concept takes off from the old saw that nothing is duller than information someone forces on you.

Corollary: Few things are more intriguing than information someone's trying to hold out.

Apply this principle to exposition. Instead of having Aunt Susie volunteer information about her impending gall bladder operation, let her make a secret of it. Since she's a key figure in an inheritance squabble around which our story centers, various people—probably including our central character—are going to try to worm the facts from her. Result: What might have been insipid exposition is transformed into taut confrontation. How so? Because that exposition is now an integral part of the film's action and progression.

d. Tie exposition to action.

Back in our section on the fact film, I made mention of the importance of translating information into terms of people doing things.

That same principle applies in features. Instead of telling about or discussing the height of a tower, *show* us the darn' thing. Even better, make someone have to climb it.

If you want to see a master's hand at work in such, drop by your nearest Hitchcock festival and see how he handles the issue in *Vertigo* and in the Mount Rushmore sequence of *North by Northwest*.

3. Spacing and pacing.

There are going to be times in your film when crises crowd too close together.

On other occasions, interest sags because they're too far apart.

Elsewhere, things move too fast or too slow.

In each instance, manipulation of confrontation and transition are virtually sure-fire solutions to your problem.

If the crises are too close together, the answer may be to insert a minor confrontation or two—foothills we have to climb before we reach the mountain, as it were. And each confrontation, in turn, will make necessary a bridging transition, a decision to be reached which provides the goal for the next confrontation. Or, if things really are on the frantic side, you might even consider a little cutting—reducing one of your confrontation peaks to foothill size.

Crises too far apart? Same remedy.

Things moving too fast? Slow 'em down by needling in transitions.

Too slow? Build or add confrontations.

Where do you get the raw material for insertions?

Well, imagination can be a help, of course. But I assume you're already using all you've got of that. Merely to tell you to find more would be a cop-out.

But there *is* a trick that can help, upon occasion. All it calls for is a list of characters to refer to.

Check said list, character by character. Ask yourself: *What's this man—or woman—doing, right this moment of the picture?* Or, if that comes out dull: *What MIGHT he or she be doing, in view of role and background and motivation?* Will it make for an insert or, perhaps, cutting to a parallel line of action?

So much for confrontation and transition. Master them, and you'll have tools that will serve you well in many a crisis.

As a case in point, consider the problems you'll face when you break your story treatment down into a step outline, the script phase we'll examine in the next chapter.

CHAPTER 11

The Step Outline

A *step* outline is the feature film's (and especially the TV film's) equivalent of the fact film's *sequence* outline. It is, indeed, the sequence outline applied to fiction in a dramatic presentation.

This being the case, life will prove simpler for everyone if, forthwith, you will go back and re-read Chapter 4. The basics are there.

A sequence, as noted in said chapter, is a related series of shots, a filmed unit of thought and/or action.

Where the feature film is concerned, each sequence in effect constitutes a step forward in your story's development. The step outline's function is to help you check out, strengthen, and clarify said story by breaking it down into its component episodes. To this end, it reduces each unit or sub-unit of confrontation and transition to the briefest of descriptive bits—a sentence or two or three, preferably.

The important thing to remember is that these "steps," these segments, should, when strung together, incorporate the picture's entire flow of action. Every sequence—that is, every related series of shots to be photographed—must be included. To leave one out is bound to create problems later.

Here's how a chunk of a reasonably typical step outline looks:

6. The UN General Assembly...a crucial meeting. Country
   X's delegate makes fearful threats. The delegate of
   Country Y reminds him of his nation's solemn treaty
   obligations. Country X's representative responds with
   the familiar line that treaties are just "scraps of
   paper"...and demonstrates his contempt for same by

ripping up the documents in question. Whereupon,
Villain Kurt, in the gallery with a covey of followers,
leaps into the fray with a threat of his own: If
Country X persists, not just treaties will be scrapped.
He'll destroy **all** paper. Country X's delegate and his
backers laugh aloud. Guards converge on Kurt. But
before they can reach him, Kurt whips out and smashes
a petri dish, thus freeing Papelivimus, the devastating,
paper-consuming bacterium John Reynolds has developed.
This is hardly spectacular, however, and our emphasis
as the sequence ends is on Country X's group as they
rise and demonstrate their resolve via clenched-fist
salutes, pounding on desks with shoes a la Khrushchev,
or the like.

7. On an SFX bridge of marching feet, drumbeats, or such,
    we DISSOLVE to the general headquarters of Country X's
    army. It's crowded with high-ranking officers. A
    courier enters, salutes, opens his dispatch case...
    then gapes as he finds it empty save for a few crumbling
    scraps of paper. Appropriate hubbub and byplay follow,
    with maps disappearing, files disintegrating, and the
    like. While the High Command stares at each other
    in shock, we DISSOLVE to

8. China. A warehouseman starts to lift a cardboard
    carton. It crumbles into shreds.

9. The U.S. A woman confronts a supermarket manager and
    demands to know how she's to shop...drags him to the
    nearest shelf. Rows of unlabeled canned goods stretch
    as far as eye can see. Interspersed are heaps of
    bran flakes sans boxes, sackless flour, empty paperback
    racks, and the like.

10. Paris. A couturier announces his new fall line of

paper dresses--certainly the coming thing this year.
Model steps forward, then stops short as her gown
disintegrates. Squealing, she tries to cover herself
with her hands, while the spectators gape slack-jawed
or whoop with mirth.

11. A toilet booth, camera positioned to simulate position
of stool's occupant as he reaches for the paper. The
roll dissolves beneath his fingers. Occupant gives
vent to a v.o. cry of anguish.

12. A newspaper newsroom. Shirt-sleeved managing editor
confronts the staff. Two or three girls sit at a
coin-heaped table off to one side. "It hits me just
as hard as it does you, friends," m.e. tells staff.
"But it's still a fact of life you can't have a paper
without paper. We're all being paid off." A gesture
to the money-stacked table. "In hard money, needless
to say." "But this kind of thing--good Lord, we're
going back to the dark ages!" someone exclaims. "What's
going to happen to the country?" The m.e. shakes his
head. "I wish to God I knew."

13. A shabby conference room. A grinning villain Kurt
stands before his crew. All order has broken down
throughout the world, he says. The room rings with
congratulations. Then, a question: What comes next?
Retention of control at all costs, Kurt answers. He
sees himself as The Man Who Kept the Peace. The simple
life--under his dictatorship, of course--is the answer
to all problems. Another query: What about John Reynolds?
He's upset that Papelivimus has created such chaos.
Indeed, there are rumors he's seeking a bacteriophage.
Kurt goes rigid. Any attempt to control Papelivimus
constitutes high treason, in his view. And that
makes John Reynolds an enemy of the state.

What's the simplest way to put a step outline together?

A fistful of 3 × 5 cards and a few square feet of corkboard along a workroom wall can be a major aid. A "step" description goes on each card. Then, you thumbtack cards to corkboard in sequential order. If problems of spacing out climaxes or balancing peaks and valleys arise, all you have to do is insert or remove cards, or reorganize by shifting the cards involved to more satisfactory positions. Similarly, if weak sequences turn up, or changes in plan of attack force revision, it's just a matter of retyping a few cards, not a whole manuscript.

What do you look out for in building a successful step outline? Let's put the issues in checklist form—twelve questions, grouped into three major categories:

1. The overall framework.
   a. Which are my main scenes?
   b. Are they properly spaced and placed?
   c. Do my characters come on at the right times and places?
2. The internal development.
   a. Does this sequence move the story forward?
   b. Is it necessary?
   c. Is it interesting?
   d. Is it believable?
   e. Does it have impact?
   f. Am I telegraphing my punches?

3. The presentation.
   a. Does each outline unit tell what's seen?
   b. Does it tell what's heard?
   c. Is it clear?

So much for summary. Now, a look at the elements in detail:

1a. Which are my main scenes?

Certainly you should know by the time you get to your script's step outline stage!

A useful trick to make the pattern instantly recognizable is to put a big red check on each main-scene card.

Closely related to this is our second question,

1b. Are said main scenes properly spaced and placed?

The answer, of course, comes through at a glance, once you arrange your cards in order on the corkboard. In general, you probably should have something fairly strong at the start, to hook audience interest, and your strongest scene of all, the climax, close to the end. In between— well, check any TV drama to see how a subclimax/cliffhanger is introduced just before each station break. Do *not* follow quite such a mechanical pattern yourself, however, unless your film is specifically aimed at TV—a movie-of-the-week or such. Rather, try to ride with the natural peaks your material itself develops, insofar as possible.

Helpful in spacing and placing your main scenes are three oft-used but still effective elements: subplots, parallel action, and relief scenes.

A *subplot* is in effect a secondary story, ordinarily involving secondary characters, which takes place simultaneously with the main story. Shakespeare loved these: Witness the Jessica-Lorenzo love story that runs alongside the main Portia-Bassanio line in *The Merchant of Venice.* Or, from today's films, recall the Jane Fonda romance and her son's maturing from *On Golden Pond,* or the love affair of the Jewish boy and girl in *Cabaret,* or any of the Pink Panther pictures, with a crime to be solved on the one hand, bumbling Inspector Clouzot in his ongoing conflict with Herbert Lom, his superior, on the other.

Parallel action refers to two lines of action which take place more or less simultaneously. By juxtaposing—and quite possibly contrasting— sequences from each line, you can both control time and suspense and, often, achieve neatly ironic effects. Thus, in one British picture of a few years ago, the central character is desperately—and dangerously—busy with a burglary. The occupant of the house being burglarized, in turn, is attending a concert. By alternating sequences from burglary and concert, tension is heightened immeasurably, and striking contrast achieved.

Similarly, several viewpoints may be developed within a picture, as in *Ruthless People,* where part of the time we live the story with the kidnappers; part of the time with Danny DiVito, husband of the kidnappee, Bette Midler; and part of the time with DiVito's mistress and her boyfriend.

Relief scenes or sequences offer a technique for changing mood or time or place, or reducing tension which has risen uncomfortably high, or introducing humor or contrast. At the same time, they have to tie in with the picture's general tenor and story line if they're not to prove disruptive.

Often, this is most simply accomplished through use of a comic character whose appearance signals a relief scene. A good case in point is the introduction of that master of ineptitude, Inspector Clouzot, into *The Pink Panther.*

(Note, however, how easy it is to get too much of a good thing. In *The Pink Panther,* Clouzot was side-splittingly hilarious; in *The Return of the Pink Panther,* something less.)

What about question number three,

1c. Do my characters come on at the right times and places?

Do I need to tell you that all major characters should appear on screen reasonably early? Or that they should reappear often enough to keep your audience reminded of their existence?

The answer is, yes, I do. Over and over again, I've critiqued scripts in which Hero or Heroine or Villain failed to show until the last half of the picture. Or appeared once and then vanished until the climax. Or played a major role in the opening scenes and then disappeared forever.

Any of these ploys can be managed, of course, upon occasion. Consider the way Alfred Hitchcock brought on Janet Leigh as *Psycho*'s apparent heroine, only to kill her in the first third of the film. But this kind of thing takes skill and a sure hand. You're better off to hold back on such until you gain experience.

How to check character presence? List the characters, one to a line, down the left side of a sheet of graph paper. Then, put the sequence numbers across the top, one per column. Finally, enter a check-mark in the appropriate crosshatch square if the character plays in that sequence.

What do you do if characters fail to appear where you want them? The answer, of course, is to juggle, manipulating characters and relationships and action until, at last, all pieces fall into place.

A good case in point that recently came my way was the story of a man whose brother is murdered. Try as he might, the scriptwriter couldn't figure out a way to bring in assorted key characters—including the woman who'd done the killing—until relatively late in the picture.

The ultimate solution proved to be introduction of a funeral scene, at which all the missing characters were present. Further brooding developed sound reasons for them to be there, and the script was off and running.

Do note one point, however—that focused upon in the previous sentence: . . . *sound reasons for them to be there*. One of the great curses of the beginner is a plague known as *author convenience*—which is to say, things happen in a script in an obviously phony and contrived manner, because the writer needs them to happen that way.

This is a cardinal sin, and then some. Yet it can be resolved far more easily than you may imagine.

The first step in this direction is for you to recognize that *everything* in a story is contrived—and contrived for author convenience, at that! So the real issue isn't "Is it contrived?" but "Is it contrived in a believable manner?"

This can prove a murky question. Ordinarily it will come clear, however,–if we give proper attention to the five issues involved in the *internal development* of each sequence:

2a. Does this sequence move the story forward?

The issue here is, does this sequence bring the picture closer to its climax? Or, to put it another way, if the state of affairs and state of mind of your key characters are the same at the end of a given sequence as they were at the beginning, then that sequence, that step, constitutes pure waste motion.

A case in point: Ever so much in love, Hero and Heroine visit a fair . . . ride a particularly wild loop-the-loop. The action's so violent Heroine is half sick by the time they get off. Hero is appropriately solicitous. After a moment, however, Heroine recovers completely. They go on their way without further incident, still ever so much in love.

Observe, now, the flaw in this sequence:

Beginning state of mind:
 Hero and heroine are ever so much in love.
Beginning state of affairs:
 They visit fair.
Concluding state of mind:
 They still are ever so much in love.
Concluding state of affairs:
 They continue their ramble through the fair.

Do you see what's wrong? Time has passed. Action has taken place. *But we can see no evidence of any change in Hero or Heroine's state of affairs or state of mind—at least, no change that we can interpret as having consequences for the future of our characters within the framework of the story.* Result: The sequence has not moved the story forward. Nothing meaningful has happened.

For a sequence to move the story forward believably, certain events must transpire, certain developments take place. Leave out any of them and the whole structure stands in peril of collapsing.

The situation is much like that which you face when you climb a flight of stairs. Each step consists of a riser and a tread. Leave out any one of them, and you very well may fall and break your neck.

The same principle applies where a film is concerned. Leave out crucial steps in the transition of Character from predicament to resolution, beginning to end, and that invisible entity we term suspension of disbelief quite possibly will be shattered. That is, the picture's spell over the audience will be broken; the viewers' enjoyment of the ebb and flow of tension ended. Departing the theater, they'll tell their friends, "Don't go. This one's a dog."

The essence of moving a story forward most often is the introduction of new (and, most often, unanticipated) developments which change Character's state of affairs and/or state of mind . . . actually or potentially for the worse.

Could the fair bit cited above be developed in such a manner as to move its story forward? Of course. Instead of recovering promptly, Heroine might have gotten worse. Result: a trip to the hospital, with Heroine's family holding it against Hero that he's so endangered her.

Or, an attractive carny girl helps Hero with Heroine. Result: Hero finds himself comparing his fragile flower unfavorably with the helper. He wonders if he's made the right choice of fiancees.

Or, Heroine's bag is stolen in the furore. Result: Heroine blames Hero for carelessness. The unreasonableness of this sets Hero to looking at Heroine with new eyes.

Or, seeking some medication to aid Heroine, Hero rummages through her bag. Result: He discovers information about her that casts her in a new—and unfavorable—light.

Or—to switch the situation around completely—it's Hero, not Heroine, who gets sick. Far from sympathetic, Heroine mocks him for his weakness. Result: Hero finds his feelings of love replaced by hostility.

Now none of these thoughts rate as gems, by any means. But they do show how relatively small changes in a character's state of affairs and/or state of mind can transform a sequence from static to dynamic . . . keep a story moving forward rather than standing still.

How do you come up with such twists?

One highly effective technique is to bring in a new character (the carny girl, for example) or a character already introduced who's been forgotten (perhaps some hostile member of Heroine's family).

To this end, it's not the worst idea in the world to tack a list of all characters on your corkboard. Then, when you're stuck, you can check them over with minimum waste motion, asking yourself the twist-pregnant question mentioned earlier: "What's Joe doing—or what *might* he be doing—that would jar this sequence off dead center?" Same for Sam, Rose, Eddy, Glenda. By the time you're through, nine times out of ten your problem will be history.

An even better approach is to root your thinking in thorough and intimate knowledge of your characters and their relationships to each other. The "blamer" heroine who berates Hero for letting her purse be stolen, when his only sin was solicitude for her, is a definite and special kind of human being who shows possibilities for adding extra dimensions to your story as it moves onward. So is the heroine who ridicules Hero because he can't control his stomach. And so would be a heroine who, outraged at her guy's discomfort, proceeded to punch the ride boss in the nose.

One final point: To build a strong sense of forward movement in a sequence, it's best in the majority of cases to end on what might be termed the counterpunch.

This is a concept which perhaps can stand a bit of clarification. Let's begin with reconsideration of those key story elements, confrontation and transition.

The pattern of confrontation is one of goal-conflict-disaster; that of transition, of reaction-dilemma-decision.

The counterpunch focuses on your character's response to a sequence's disaster: his mounting of a new attack via choice of a new goal and/or implementation of that decision in goal-centered action.

Thus, in our fair sequence, when Heroine's wealthy uncle arrives at the hospital and, in a rage, announces withdrawal of vital financial support from Hero's cherished project, Hero might very well conclude the episode with a chill announcement that the hospitalization concerns him and Heroine only; and that as far as the project goes, Uncle can keep his money: Hero will carry on without it.

Instantly, a question is raised in viewers' minds: What will be the consequences of this challenge Hero has thrown in the face of fate? It's a good note to break on.

On the other hand, it certainly is not the only one possible. We might also end on the disaster/cliffhanger (Uncle's announcement that he's cutting off the money), or on the dilemma (Hero's strained effort to figure out what to do in the face of the Uncle-precipitated cataclysm). But centering the sequence's conclusion on Hero's indecision tends to emphasize weakness and stasis rather than the strength and forward movement most audiences seek, while ending with Uncle's cliff-hanger announcement puts the spotlight on Uncle instead of Hero.

Which is not to say that either of these alternatives may not prove desirable in specific instances or for variety's sake. But *in general*, the counterpunch approach is stronger.

2b. Is this sequence necessary?

Now why would I raise such a question as this, after all the attention I've already given the matter of the importance of each sequence moving your story forward?

The answer is that quite possibly you've built two sequences, where one could have done the job as well.

Here, for example, is a sequence in which a friendly elevator operator helps Hero locate Villain's office. Following is one that sees Hero coaxing information from Villain's secretary. A third has him trying to find Villain's car in the building parking garage.

Next question: What is Hero seeking?

Answer: He wants to talk to Villain.

So, why not just let him talk to Villain? Elevator operators, after all, are fast becoming rarities, secretaries who talk too much are hardly unusual, and a tour of a parking garage stands a good chance of lulling your audience to sleep unless someone's taking potshots at Hero.

This business of less-than-vital sequences can be particularly important when you're running long. So don't hesitate to ask yourself, "Can I combine this sequence with another? Is it possible to merge this character/set/action with another?"

2c. Is this sequence interesting?

Again, author convenience rears its seductive head. For it's ever so easy to become so preoccupied with getting in plot lines or essential information that you forget that such can also prove dull, dull, dull, unless you give heed to keeping each sequence entertaining in and of itself.

Thus, Professor Zeitelbaum's lecture on the physics of the fourth dimension may be crucial to understanding your film's climax, or Aunt Agatha's youthful involvement with music the key to the way she reacts to Jean's joining the Hare Krishnas. But that won't help if the audience goes to sleep.

In a static situation, you see, boredom soon takes over. Viewers yawn and squirm; perhaps even leave the theater. A disastrous turn of affairs indeed!

What it all comes down to is that, all statements to the contrary notwithstanding, you don't just hold an audience's attention; you *capture* and *recapture* it.

How do you do this?

First and foremost, you do it by *manipulating tension.*

Because this is so, you'll be well advised to so plan your script that it develops that generally rising state of excitement among viewers upon which we've commented previously. Such a state will be based on the ebb and flow of fear that some immediately dreaded or desired thing will or won't happen; an *anticipation of potentially impending disaster,* as it were.

Secondly, you do it by *translating abstraction into people being human.*

This demands that you be ever conscious of the human animal and his foibles—the way people really react as contrasted with the way they're supposed to; the contradictory things they do, cutting out mashed potatoes to lose weight, even while they eat a box of chocolates; the irrationality that makes them laugh and cry and love and hate and behave the way they did on *Candid Camera.*

Thirdly, you do it by *focusing on the logical yet unanticipated.*

These are the twists of fate, the things that shouldn't happen but do, the wrong people in the wrong places at the wrong times. They're the efforts that fail, the schemes that go awry, the roofs that cave in.

And the diamond-studded cloudbursts, too.

One way or another, trickles from one or more of these three streams should seep into *every sequence* of your script. Let sinister forces be gathering outside Professor Zeitelbaum's lecture hall, with cross-cutting to give his words importance as well as build suspense. Bring the abstraction of Aunt Agatha's "involvement with music" to life via an affair with a tramp trap drummer. Or, by way of relief when tension grows too great, break the dreariness of a long afternoon by the river by including a comic character trying to retrieve a jug of moonshine from a sunken scow.

But *do* keep interest pulsing!

2d. Is this sequence believable?

Believability is largely a matter of character behavior. It comes in two parts: things your story people do and things they don't do: the same coin, but different sides.

The things your characters do raise certain crucial questions: Why does Character do this? Would the average person—or, at the very least, a character of Character's character—do it? What other, more logical paths might he take to reach the goal he's seeking?

Thus, why does Character date the ugly sister, not the beauty? Why does he support his drunken brother? Why does he back down before his boss or mother? Why does he agree to take a job that he detests?

The issue where things your characters *don't* do are concerned is even simpler. It boils down to one question: Why doesn't Character quit?

As, why doesn't he ride out before the gunmen come? Why doesn't he refuse to doctor the books? Why doesn't he refuse to marry the hellion? Why doesn't he put his father in the rest home?

If Character does things viewers see as illogical and unbelievable, their suspension of disbelief in the film is shattered. Consequently, they *must* be made to believe—and the answers the audience wants are visual: living demonstrations of the points you're trying to make. Verbiage is not enough.

2e. Does this sequence have impact?

"People never remember what they hear in a movie," Henry Hathaway once commented. "They only recall what they see."

Since Mr. Hathaway directed nearly a hundred films—including such items as *Lives of a Bengal Lancer, Kiss of Death, True Grit, The House on 92nd Street, Call Northside 777,* and *Johnny Apollo*—in the course of a long and illustrious career, his observations rate careful consideration.

The scenes audiences recall, Mr. Hathaway elaborated, the memorable moments, ordinarily center on action: bits that strike home with strong visual impact, as when Paul Newman with a single punch knocks out the woman who's betrayed him in *The Verdict* . . . Indiana Jones shoots the sword-wielding Arab menace in *Raiders of the Lost Ark* . . . James Cagney mashes the grapefruit into Mae Clarke's face in *The Public Enemy* . . . Paul Hogan is passed over the heads of the crowd in the final sequence of *Crocodile Dundee* . . . the youthful Mozart pursues the squealing girl beneath the banquet table in *Amadeus.* And while in large measure such are the product of director times actor times cameraman, the writer, too, plays a role in that he often provides the original concept.

This being the case, it will be to your advantage to try to incorporate a few such visual jolts, such not-soon-to-be-forgotten moments, into every

script you write. Take it for granted in advance that most will fall flat
or be ignored by the director. But a few will get through and touch an
audience nerve on a level that will help to build your reputation.

2f. Am I telegraphing my punches?

That is, am I being predictable?

What you're after is the unanticipated but logical development. To
get it, you need to set up an *anticipated* development . . . then pull a
different rabbit out of the hat. But don't cheat, or audiences will hate
you.

Let's suppose, for example, that your hero has faced untold perils
to get to the room where his girlfriend allegedly is waiting. At last,
panting with a combination of fatigue and passion, he knocks at the
door.

The door opens—and there stands his girlfriend's mother.

Assuming that you can make the switch logical, it's the kind of twist
that will help to keep viewers awake.

Now, what about your presentation?

3a. Does each sequence, each step outline unit, tell what's seen?
3b. Does it tell what's heard?
3c. Is it clear?

For once, in this volume, little need be said. In essence, it's enough
that you make it clear that you have something which can be
photographed.

*　　　*　　　*

So much for the step outline. It's almost time to move on to our
final feature film topic, the master scene script.

Almost, but not quite. First, we need to consider a tool essential to
writing any effective feature script, that of dialogue.

We'll take it up in the next chapter.

CHAPTER 12

Dialogue Devices

...Dr. Orbis twists back the dial, turns on the red spots,
switches off the green. The humming SOUND fades away.
The girls stop short in their exhibition of rapture...look
blankly at each other, the audience, and Dr. Orbis.

> DR. ORBIS
> So! Ladies, you weren't hurt,
> were you?

Giggling and whispering, the girls shake their heads.

> DR. ORBIS
> Nothing bad happened to you, did
> it? ...And you <u>did</u> have fun?

Complete affirmation from the girls, perhaps with AD LIBBED
COMMENTS.

> DR. ORBIS
> Then back to the fair with you!
> Have the best of times! And
> remember, all of you...
> > (arms flung wide,
> > to take in crowd
> > and girls alike)
> ...Dr. Orbis is the man who
> rules your mind!

It's been a good show. The crowd's in a good mood as it
starts to leave the tent. But now the roughneck noted
earlier breaks the spell.

> ROUGHNECK
> > (bellowing)
> Bull shit!

> DR. ORBIS
> What was that--?

> ROUGHNECK
> Bull shit, that's what I said!
> You're a fake!

161

The departing crowd stops...turns. Dr. Orbis peers down
at the man through his thick-lensed glasses.

>   DR   ORBIS
>   (dangerously
>   gentle)
>   Sir, do I understand you doubt
>   my powers?

>   ROUGHNECK
>   You bet you do. I know your kind
>   --crooks, liars, frauds--

>   DR. ORBIS
>   Of course you know. What's the
>   saying--'It takes one to know
>   one'?

>   ROUGHNECK
>   Why, you--!

>   DR. ORBIS
>   Since you feel so strongly, why
>   don't you join me up here on
>   the stage? Prove to everyone
>   just how much of a fake I am?

>   ROUGHNECK
>   You think I wouldn't!

>   DR. ORBIS
>   Oh, no, sir. I'm sure you would.
>   So, if you'll just step up here
>   now...

Dr. Orbis's reaction is totally unanticipated by the roughneck.
It dawns on him he's started something he's not sure he wants
to try to finish. He starts to turn away.

>   ROUGHNECK
>   (in fake disgust)
>   Ah--!

>   DR. ORBIS
>   You're not going, sir--? Not
>   before you've exposed me? ...Or
>   could it be you're just a bit
>   afraid I'll do the exposing?

>   ROUGHNECK
>   Bull shit!

He's eager to leave, but now the crowd won't let him.

>   MAN 1
>   Go ahead! Get on the stage!

>   MAN 2
>   What's the matter? Where you
>   going?

>   WOMAN
>   He's scared the brujo's going
>   to cast a spell on him!

                    DR. ORBIS
          Is that it, sir? Are you
          <u>afraid</u> to come up?

                    ROUGHNECK
          I'll show you who's scared!

He charges up the nearest stairs onto the stage.

                    DR. ORBIS
                 (gesturing to area
                 beneath the green
                 spots)
          Right here, sir.

Simultaneously, he backs to the light board...throws the
mind machine control switch...twists the submission dial.
The raging roughneck stops short, caught in the cone of
green light. (SOUND: humming.)

                    DR. ORBIS
          Now, my friend. Surely we can
          talk this out like reasonable
          men. ...Actually, I'm glad you
          came. I can see you have a
          problem. ...You've always
          wondered: Are you really macho?

The crowd guffaws. The roughneck cowers, wordless.

                    DR. ORBIS
          Oh! That **was** unkind of me,
          wasn't it? Your kind of man...
          who could doubt you are a
          lover? ...Here!

Stepping to the table, he whips off the rebozo...tosses it
in the direction of the roughneck. It falls at the man's
feet. The roughneck stares stupidly at it.

                    DR. ORBIS
          Yes, indeed, you are a lover.
          And every lover needs someone
          to love. For you...
                 (Turning to
                 coffins, clapping
                 hands)
          Jorge! Join him!

The worst-looking of the "undead" men steps from his box...
crosses to and enters the cone of green light. Dr. Orbis
goes back to the light board.

                    DR. ORBIS
                 (adjusting dials
                 carefully)
          A little lust, now...
                 (to roughneck)
          Isn't Jorge beautiful? Your
          heart pounds, your blood heats
          at his very nearness, doesn't
          it? ...Oh, we all understand
          how it is with a real macho
          like you!

```
                    ROUGHNECK
                 (hoarse, guttural)
           Aahhh...

                    DR. ORBIS
           Kiss him, lover!
```

The roughneck clutches Jorge...buries his face in the "undead"'s
neck in an impassioned kiss. The crowd roars.

```
                    DR. ORBIS
           Muy macho!
                 (stopping short,
                 faking shock)
           Or--could I be wrong?  Was there
           somehow something womanly about
           that kiss?  ...Sir, the rebozo!
```

Letting go of Jorge, the roughneck picks up the rebozo.

```
                    DR. ORBIS
           Wrap it around you, my dear.
           You must be modest, maidenly.
           This is your lover, Jorge, that
           you meet here in secret in the
           campo.  How your lips burn for
           his kisses!
```

The roughneck drapes himself in the rebozo...stands
simpering: head down, eyes averted.

```
                    DR. ORBIS
           Jorge!  It's your sweetheart!
           Kiss her!
```

Jorge smothers the roughneck with kisses. Again, the crowd
roars.

```
                    DR. ORBIS
                 (arms spread,
                 mocking)
           Oh, such rapture!  Oh, such
           passion!
```

In a frame-filling REACTION SHOT, the crowd roars with
laughter.

What we see above is a sample of dialogue: that portion of a script
in which people talk . . . the things they say, word for word.

The writing of good dialogue is an art in and of itself. For the film
scriptwriter, it's a vital skill.

What issues do we need to consider, where dialogue writing is
concerned? They fall into three categories: dialogue functions, dialogue
continuity, and dialogue realism.

1. Dialogue functions.

Dialogue has four primary functions; four main jobs to do:

   a. To give information.

  b. To reveal emotion.
  c. To advance the plot.
  d. To characterize the speaker and the person to whom spoken.

To a very considerable degree, these functions overlap. A given line may simultaneously perform all four jobs. Yet this is often enough not true to warrant our checking out each category separately. We'll start with

a. To give information.

At first glance this would seem so simple and so obvious as not to call for comment.

The problem is, good dialogue must not only convey information; it must do so without being obtrusive or impeding the story's flow.

Thus, in the script from which our sample above is taken, it was important to demonstrate that Dr. Orbis really does have mysterious powers. To that end, and also to lighten an otherwise heavy horror piece, this incident in which these powers are tested was written in. The situation is such that the key fact to be set forth is contained in Dr. Orbis's own grandiloquent proclamation—"Dr. Orbis is the man who rules your mind!"—yet it is so introduced that it is totally in keeping with the situation and so doesn't at all get in the way of the developing action. Indeed, it precipitates said action, by giving the roughneck an excuse to voice his challenge, thus clearing the track for the demonstration of Dr. Orbis's strange abilities. Each line that follows the initial statement builds upon it, adding new data and insights.

Is the point to be made worth this much screen time? That obviously is a matter subject to debate. My own reaction is that it is.

b. To reveal emotion.

Insofar as practical, each line a speaker delivers should reveal his mood, his feeling. Lines which fail to do so are "dead" and tend not to contribute to the sense of rising action viewers seek.

The place beginners' dialogue falls down often centers on the fact that they, writing, are not aware of the continual flux and change of a speaker's mood. In consequence, the words they put into his mouth fail to reflect his feelings.

Thus, Dr. Orbis's first three speeches in our sample reflect a genial mood, an interval of good feelings. In total command and playing to the crowd, Dr. Orbis coaxes and cajoles and radiates confidence.

The feeling flips with the roughneck's interruption. Dr. Orbis's cordiality falls away, but he stays in control. His words mirror smooth menace, as in the very formality of his line, "Sir, do I understand you doubt my powers?"

The roughneck blusters, riding the impact of his initial break-

through. But Dr. Orbis takes the sting from the roughneck's words—
and the initiative from the roughneck—by the agreement-plus-switch
he voices in his "Of course you know" line. Each line that follows puts
him more strongly in command, just as each of the roughneck's lines
reflects increasing loss of control.

For the writer, the most important issue is less the words themselves
than the changes in attitude, mood, feeling, that each line reflects. The
state of affairs and state of mind of each speaker are continually shifting.

In good dialogue, the speaker's words and manner mirror this. In
poor, the speeches are wooden, mechanical, and for the author's convenience. In consequence, they embarrass the actors called upon to speak
them, as well as leaving the listening audience bored, irritated, and
unconvinced.

c. To advance the plot.

Good dialogue should not only advance the plot: It should leave
the audience unaware that it is doing so.

Our sample offers a good case in point. On the face of it, it merely
acts out the humiliation of a hoodlum, making it more vivid through
introduction of appropriate lines. Yet simultaneously it reveals Dr. Orbis's ability to distort reality for his victims: The *macho* roughneck is first
deluded into caressing a zombie-like male . . . then warped even further, to the point where he himself takes the female role.

Now all this is entertaining enough in and of itself. But it also
constitutes preparation for later sequences in which Dr. Orbis exercises
such control in infinitely more sinister fashion. The audience accepts it,
however, because this earlier, less crucial demonstration with the roughneck has "proved" to them—"Seeing is believing!"—that Dr. Orbis can
indeed rule his victims' minds.

What has dialogue contributed to this "proof"? It has made the
demonstration infinitely more vivid, by enabling viewers to follow the
subtle ebb and flow of emotional change more closely than they could
have through sight alone. In consequence, the scene's impact is much
more convincing.

The lesson for the writer is clear: In film, dialogue does not—
cannot—exist as an element separate and apart from the picture as a
whole. To fulfill its function, it must be integrated into the overall pattern
that the writer designs in order to create that ebb and flow of tension
which we call entertainment.

d. To characterize the speaker and the person to whom spoken.

Inevitably, dialogue reflects the speaker: his background, his education, his social status; above all, his attitudes and feelings.

On the obvious side, garbage collector and college president hardly
are likely to speak the same. Dr. Orbis and Roughneck demonstrate this

clearly. "Sir, do I understand you doubt my powers?" is one person—and one *kind* of person—speaking; "You bet you do. I know your kind—crooks, liars, frauds—" another.

But it is on a deeper level, on that of personality itself, that the picture really comes into focus. Thus, Roughneck's speech labels him as a loudmouthed bully—ignorant, inwardly insecure. That of Dr. Orbis, in contrast, reflects quiet menace, coupled with the kind of sadism-laced insight that enables him instantly to pinpoint the chink in his opponent's armor.

It goes without saying, I trust, that insight precedes dialogue where this is concerned. If you don't know the kind of man with whom you're dealing and the traits which reveal his inner self, you can't write proper lines for him.

Part and parcel of this insight picture is the matter of reaction. Where Roughneck responded to Dr. Orbis's exhibition with a yell of "Bull shit!" another man might, without commotion, have asked the authorities to close down the show. A lesser figure than Dr. Orbis, in turn, might have cringed or fled or blustered at Roughneck's bellow.

Once you have your understanding of your people, dialogue becomes one of your most useful tools for bringing insight out into the open . . . putting it in such form that viewers can understand and draw full emotional value from it.

2. Dialogue continuity.

How do you make dialogue hang together?

You make use of a device called the *dialogue hook,* which insures that each speech acknowledges the one preceding it.

We see this technique at work in the very first interchange between Dr. Orbis and the girls at the show:

```
                    DR. ORBIS

          So! Ladies, you weren't hurt,
          were you?

Giggling and whispering, the girls shake their heads.
```

The hook, in this case, is *question/answer.* The girls' giggling, whispering, and head-shaking acknowledges Dr. Orbis's question. Without said question, the "answer" would make little sense.

Note also, incidentally, that though this is a dialogue sequence, the "answer" takes the form of action rather than words. An important point for anyone to remember; too often, learners insist on words, words, words and formal speech, when mime would play better. But more of that later, when we deal with dialogue realism.

The question/answer pattern is only one of a host of hooks, of course. Thus, Roughneck's "Bull shit!" stands as *disagreement* with Dr. Orbis's ". . . Dr. Orbis is the man who rules your mind!" Dr. Orbis's "What was that—?" in turn, represents *reaction*. Roughneck's later "You bet you do" and Dr. Orbis's "Of course you know" are both hooks of *agreement*—by agreeing with the previous speaker's statement, each acknowledges the speech and so establishes the element of continuity which makes good dialogue hang together.

Dr. Orbis's "Of course you know" is also a hook of *interruption*—he has broken in on Roughneck's "cheap crooks, liars, frauds—" diatribe, and the fact of breaking in is in itself an acknowledgment of Roughneck's rantings. Some lines later, when he begins, "Now, my friend," he's using a *transitional word* as a hook. The "now" is an "empty" word, like "Oh?" or "Well!" or "You don't say?" It acknowledges prior speech or behavior without taking a stand. In so doing, it constitutes an excellent pivot for changing the subject. Thus, in our example, the whole opening portion of the Orbis speech is really little more than social noise ("Now, my friend. Surely we can talk this out like reasonable men.") But what follows is a total switch which might have jarred had it not been built up to: ". . . Actually, I'm glad you came. I can see you have a problem. . . . You've always wondered: Are you really *macho*?"

Elsewhere in this script, the same transitional word device is coupled with another favorite, *repetition*, and question/answer to keep an expository passage moving:

                         LUIS
          Good God!

                         DR. ORBIS
          Why shudder? Daring is always the
          handmaiden of progress. What does
          it matter what happens to the weak
          and stupid, so long as man's
          knowledge marches forward?

                         LUIS
          So?

                         DR. ORBIS
          So, I developed my master work,
          the retinal serum...

Here, Luis uses a transitional word to answer a question with a question . . . Dr. Orbis repeats the word . . . and off we go again!

Again, we have this hook, this acknowledgment via *action*, followed by a reaction speech:

```
                    MARINDA
                  (moving head
                   dazedly)
          I--I can't see...

Luis removes her dark glasses.  Her face is still averted
and/or in shadow.  Taking her by the chin, he gently turns
her face to the window.  For the first time, light strikes
her eyes.  In CLOSEUP, we see they show only blank white
sclera...no iris, no pupil.

                    LUIS
          My God--!
```

And so it goes, with speech or action acknowledging preceding speech or action. All constitute dialogue hooks. The classifications into which I've broken them down—repetition, transitional words, reaction, action, interruption, agreement/disagreement, question/answer, and so on are totally unimportant. What counts is understanding of the basic principle involved: *Each speech should somehow "hook" to the one ahead.* Keep that in mind, and you can't go too far wrong.

3. Dialogue realism.

Where realism is concerned, the big thing to bear in mind in working up dialogue is that there's a world of difference between speech and the written word. Good dialogue strives for the tone of conversation. It attempts to avoid the stiffness and formalism that too often envelopes us when we "take pen in hand."

On the other hand, saints preserve me from the script in which the writer has tried to duplicate actual speech. Better by far that he *simulate* the way we talk. Which is to say, you should aim for the flavor and color of spoken language, but eliminate all but a salting of the banality, repetitiousness, and general meandering in which we all tend to indulge.

To that end, be sure your dialogue keeps your story moving forward in a reasonably straight line. Do *not* permit yourself the dubious luxury of bogging down in endless burblings and weather talk in the name of realism.

Beyond this, the going grows hazy. So much depends on taste and talent! An interchange handled with one man's humor comes out as light and clever. In another's hands, it would prove cloddish. The trick is to assess your own abilities, strong points and weak. Then, stay within your limitations or work with the devil's own fervor to overcome them. There is no other way.

A few observations may help you sharpen your attack, however . . . as witness these 15 far-from-all-inclusive points:

a. Dialogue should be characteristic of the speaker.

I've already given this some attention, so I'll keep my comments here brief.

The key principle is: Know your people, and let their speech help differentiate them. A Texan doesn't talk like a Down Easter, nor a cowhand like a coal miner, nor a child like a man. Each nationality, each generation, each social stratum has its own speech patterns. Only as you listen, listen, listen, pay attention to them, can you hope to capture them in your scripts.

b. Since good dialogue represents our language as spoken, rather than written, it makes full use of contractions, the second person approach, the active voice, and such.

When Roughneck in our horror film sample roars, "You're a fake!" he's using that specialized verbal shorthand that we call contraction: It reduces "You are" to "You're." In the process, it adds a touch of realism to Roughneck's speech. Same for Dr. Orbis when he asks, "What's the saying?" or says, "I'm sure you would. So, if you'll just step up here now . . ."

Second person? "When you get to the third corner, you turn right a block," instructs Character. "If you want to cut down the alley, then . . ."

This habit of using second person and active voice—the "you get," "you turn," "you want" element—is ever so common with most of us, especially when we're explaining or instructing. Indeed, the more formal third-person usage ("How does one reach the hotel?" "One proceeds three blocks in the direction you are going.") is in itself a characterizing device, useful in tagging the speaker as on the stiff and prissy side.

c. Ungrammatical constructions, clichés, and slang are a habit with many of us.

```
                    ALASTAIR
          Precisely what do you mean, young
          lady?



                    SHARON
          I mean, it do take talent, don't
          it?  Like she's a doll.  But
          rhythm counts more than rich
          relations.  You know how the song
          goes--"It don't mean a thing if
          it ain't got that swing."
```

Alastair is a man who speaks correctly. But closer to the hearts—and speech patterns—of the masses is Sharon's approach.

Note too that the contrast between these speakers helps to make for livelier, more interesting dialogue.

d. Some speakers fumble, hesitate, and/or interrupt frequently.

```
                    DR. ORBIS
        But where?  Where were they?

                    ZARA
        I--I don't know.

                    DR. ORBIS
        Was it here?  Here, in the tent,
        my show?

                    ZARA
        No...

                    DR. ORBIS
        Not the tent--?

                    ZARA
        No.  The walls...they were
        different...stone, maybe...like
        an old house...
```

As with almost everything else in the writing business, this can be overdone. But occasional gropings by the right person at the right time certainly does help.

e. Most speeches should be kept brief.

Turn back to the sample with which we began this chapter. You'll find it has 11 one-line speeches, ten two-line speeches, two three-liners, five four-liners, one five-liner, two six-liners, and one seven-liner.

Similarly, checking out a random three-page sample in the script of the much-acclaimed *Winning*, I counted 19 one-liners, six two-liners, and five three-liners; none longer. A three-page chunk from the highly successful *Ruthless People* turned up 22 one-line speeches, seven two-line, one three-line, and one four-line.

This is not to say that longer speeches are unknown. A quick thumbing of *Ruthless People* revealed one 32-line speech, two 14-line, a ten-line, and two nine-liners. *Winning* came up with one 11-liner, as well as assorted sevens, sixes, and fives.

But the overall picture, in life and in film scriptwriting, favors the short speech.

f. Action—stage business—often substitutes for speech.

```
                    DR. ORBIS
        So!  Ladies, you weren't hurt,
        were you?
```
Giggling and whispering, the girls shake their heads.

Again:

```
                    DR. ORBIS
          Now, my friend.  Surely we can
          talk this out like reasonable
          men.  ...Actually, I'm glad you
          came.  I can see you have a
          problem.  ...You've always
          wondered: Are you really macho?
```

The crowd guffaws. The roughneck cowers, wordless.

The issue in dialogue, remember, is *acknowledgment, reaction.*

Often, actions speak louder than words in this regard. What a man does clarifies his stance far better than what he says.

That being the case, your own best approach is to consider response, rather than mere words. You may end up finding silence golden.

g. Emotionalism dominates factual content in most speech.

People are not computers, nor logic machines, nor yet taped answering services. Consequently, as pointed out in the section on dialogue's emotional function, they tend to speak more in terms of feeling than of fact.

Thus, when Roughneck bellows "Bull shit!" he's giving vent to rage, rather than good sense.

Anger, even though controlled and masked, is equally evident in Dr. Orbis's "Sir, do I understand you doubt my powers?" And the sarcasm of his later "Oh! That was unkind of me, wasn't it? Your kind of man . . . who could doubt you are a lover?" clearly reveals a sadistic delight in the twisting of the knife.

Your own characters should be equally enmeshed in feelings; and those feelings should show through their dialogue just as clearly.

h. Well-nigh every speech should reflect an attempt to influence someone's attitude or behavior.

In life, much speech is empty. That's a luxury you can't afford in dialogue. Screen time is just too precious.

Avoid dull dialogue of agreement, therefore—"Oh, it's a lovely dress!" "Yes, I think so. And brown's my color." "Yes, it certainly is. Besides, when you wear your hair that way . . ."

As much as possible, your players should be goal-oriented, strivers. Then, you should focus on their confrontations, the moments when they're trying to gain their ends in the face of opposition.

i. Beware of letting any character volunteer information.

```
                    AUNT AGATHA
          This girl, George.  How much do
          you really know about her?
```

```
                GEORGE
    Please, Auntie, please!  Whatever
    I know or don't know, it's
    enough.

                AUNT AGATHA
    George, even before her teens,
    she was a problem!

                GEORGE
    Auntie, whatever it is--

                AUNT AGATHA
    An affair's one thing.  Three in
    a row's another.  And those are
    just the ones I know about.  And
    then, those poor children--
```

Beware of making life too easy for your hero—or, for that matter, for any other character. To do so takes the edge off your story.

One way of making Hero's life dangerously easy is to allow other characters to present him with needed information as a gift. Better by far that he should have to fight for it, tooth and nail, wresting it from antagonists in bitter battle. For only thus can you build a proper pattern of rising action.

How to cope with such information, if it insists on coming? One solution is to let Hero look gift horse in the mouth . . . question why he's receiving such largesse . . . and so come up with a new and unsuspected twist. Or follow the old "truth, the whole truth, and nothing but the truth" line, letting Hero receive only part of the truth, or truth mixed with falsehood, or a total lie. Or, let Hero be so eager to escape from his informant that he ignores the data he's receiving.

Whatever your solution, however, be certain of one thing: that you keep your viewers' interest aglow with some unceasing element of tension.

j. Always consider the factor of normal reticence in speech.

Few things in this world are more painful than dialogue in which the scriptwriter puts words into actors' mouths that no normal person would speak.

I'm talking about the lines in which the saintly mother describes her sex experiences in four-letter words, or the miser details the fortune he's accumulated, or the priest reveals secrets of the confessional in the course of casual gossip.

How to get such information in, then? Why not let another character hazard a guess or make an accusation?

Another aspect of all this centers on the fact that not all speech is forthright. Few of us always say exactly what we mean. Lies, evasions, euphemisms, exaggerations, irony, and the like are common.

Good dialogue reflects similar patterns of indirection, when character and occasion demand.

*   *   *

Beyond these hints, how do you learn to write good dialogue?

The first step is to learn to listen; to pay attention not just to what people say, but also to how they say it.

It will help you in this endeavor if you'll beg, borrow, or steal a tape recorder. Conceal it in locations where conversations are likely to occur—behind sofas, for example, or in the vicinity of restaurant tables or cocktail lounge booths, or concealed by a package or two in a smoking area.

Then, turn it on and exit for a while.

The dialogues you'll capture will be worth your trouble, believe me—not so much in terms of content as because you can play the tape over and over, until you catch the patterns and rhythms of speech the speakers reveal.

It will also help if, as you write dialogue of your own, you make it a point to read each passage back aloud, to see if it really sounds like people.

You'll have a lot of opportunity to do that when you buckle down to writing the master scene script in all its glory.

It's the subject of our next chapter.

CHAPTER 13

The Master Scene Script

THE EYES OF DOCTOR ORBIS

FADE IN:

1   INTERIOR - OFFICE OF DR. SUAREZ - NIGHT

The room is spookily lighted. Large colored wall diagrams
of the human eye, front and profile, are prominent, with
perhaps an optometrist's examining chair for balance. A
SLOW PAN takes us past an eye chart and any other atmospheric
touches available to a desk on which lies the corpse of
DR. SUAREZ (professional type, 30s). He's flat on his
back, face a mask of shock and horror, head and maybe an
arm hanging limp over the desk's edge. A not-new axe is
buried deep in his chest, handle thrusting up at a sharp
angle. Of course there's plenty of blood...perhaps other
hack-marks.

2   INTERIOR - CLINIC CORRIDOR - NIGHT

From OFF SCREEN we hear the SOUND of a woman's brisk
footsteps. The trim lower legs and feet (nurse-type shoes)
of PILAR CASTENON (pretty, early 20s) enter frame. We
DOLLY with them down the hall to the doorway of Dr. Suarez's
office...HOLD while Pilar (SOUND) unlocks and opens door.

3   INTERIOR - OFFICE OF DR. SUAREZ - NIGHT

Pilar (FULL SHOT now) enters...crosses towards desk. She
wears nurse-type uniform, carries raincoat over arm.

(Probably this is shot from a low angle, close beside the
desk, so we can't see Dr. Suarez's corpse.) Then, as Pilar
nears desk, glimpses corpse, and stops short, we CUT to a
shot that includes both her, as she freezes, and corpse.
CLOSEUP of Dr. Suarez. CLOSEUP of Pilar's shocked,
horrified face. She rallies...crosses to phone...throws
down coat...snatches up receiver. But even as she starts
to dial, we--and she--hear the SOUND of a man's sinister,
echoing, strangely erratic footsteps from the corridor.

4   INTERIOR - CLINIC CORRIDOR - NIGHT

In a shot similar to 2, above, the feet and lower legs of
KARL (Frankenstein monster type, 40s) enter frame. Karl's
gait is tentative and erratic because he has only peripheral
vision: That is, he sees only around the edge of the eye
rather than through its center and so is, by and large,
blind. Details are beyond him, though he can still perceive
large objects and--especially--motion. We DOLLY with him
as he moves towards Dr. Suarez's office.

5   INTERIOR - OFFICE OF DR. SUAREZ - NIGHT

Face mirroring panic, Pilar listens as Karl approaches.

6   INTERIOR - CLINIC CORRIDOR - NIGHT

Karl's feet reach Dr. Suarez's doorway. We still don't see
much above his knees.

7   INTERIOR - OFFICE OF DR. SUAREZ - NIGHT

Pilar still stands phone in hand. Karl pauses momentarily
in doorway, then lurches forward again. A tall, gaunt,
sinister figure, he wears raincoat, hat, and dark or mirror
glasses. A slow step at a time, Pilar backs away from him
in obvious fear. Closing in, Karl seizes the handle of
the axe...wrenches the blade from Dr. Suarez's chest...lifts
it for a blow at Pilar. She tries to dart past him. He
lurches into her path, letting go of the axe with one hand
to clutch at her. In silence, they struggle briefly--Pilar
desperate to break free, Karl maniacally determined to hold
her. The result is a balancing of strength that plays almost
in slow motion, with no jumping or flailing. Then, as if
realizing she can't match Karl's strength for long, Pilar
sags...claws fast at Karl's face. The blow knocks off his
dark glasses. In a CLOSEUP from Pilar's point of view, we
stare into Karl's eyes--shockingly strange eyes, in that
they're blank white; all sclera, no iris. (This effect is
obtained by having Karl and those other characters whose
eyes show blank white wear appropriate contact lenses.) A
reverse angle CLOSEUP of Pilar, in turn, sees her face
contort as, for the first time, she loses self-control.
Her mouth opens.

                         PILAR
                      (screaming)
          Aieee!!!

8   INTERIOR - CLINIC CORRIDOR - NIGHT

In a shot similar to 2, above, and while Pilar's scream
continues OFF SCREEN, the feet and lower legs of LUIS GARZA
(non-pretty hero type, early 20s) enter frame at a dead run.
Camera PANS to follow action, HOLDING on Luis in TAILAWAY
as he lunges towards the open doorway to Dr. Suarez's office.

9   INTERIOR - OFFICE OF DR. SUAREZ - NIGHT

Luis rushes in. Karl lurches to face him, flinging Pilar
aside. He and Luis struggle for possession of the axe.

Then, strength superior, Karl shoves Luis away from him so
violently Luis smashes against the wall head first. Stunned,
eyes wide and staring, he crumples to the floor. Karl
starts to close in with the axe. But Pilar snatches up her
raincoat and hurls it over Karl's head like a hood, then
hammers at him with a bookend or such. More than ever

blinded by the coat, staggering under the rain of blows, Karl makes it to the office door in a series of groping lunges.

10   INTERIOR - CLINIC CORRIDOR - NIGHT

Fighting free of the coat, Karl flees, lurching off down the corridor.

11   EXTERIOR - CLINIC ENTRANCE - NIGHT

Karl lurches out the door and to the curb...hangs there, twisting this way and that as he tries to force his semi-blind eyes to see. Simultaneously, an old-style black hearse moves into view at a measured pace, out of the shadows down the street...pulls up beside Karl. Groping, he yanks open the door...scrambles into the right front seat. Still at its stately, funereal pace, the hearse moves on again.

12   INTERIOR - HEARSE - NIGHT

Camera shoots HEAD-ON, through windshield to include both Karl and the hearse's driver, DR. ORBIS (Peter Lorre type, 40s)...then CUTS to individual or strongly favoring CLOSEUP of Dr. Orbis. He wears glasses with lenses so thick as to distort his eyes and lend him an appropriately weird appearance. He drives calmly, coolly, smiling slightly as if at a small private joke. This smile serves as a characterizing tag for him throughout the film, designed to sharpen his image as a menace. It constitutes clear visual evidence of his self-confidence and poise...says without words that everything is going according to plan and that he's in control--ever the hunter, never the hunted. In consequence, by implication, his opponents are doomed before they start. Here, now, as he drives, the smile broadens. He chuckles noiselessly. The hearse picks up speed.

OPENING TITLES OVER

In individual HEAD-ON CLOSEUP, Karl slumps panting, bloody axe clutched to his chest. Perhaps his fingers caress the lethal axe-head lovingly, as if it were a woman. His face is a sinister mask. His blank white eyes stare straight ahead.

INTERCUT with the above footage are appropriate TRAVEL SHOTS from the moving hearse.

Individual CLOSEUP, Dr. Orbis. His attention is on the road ahead now, but a noticeable trace of the smile is still with him. Camera MOVES IN to frame-filling HEAD-ON EXTREME CLOSEUP of the thick-glassed eyes.

MAIN TITLE OVER:

THE EYES OF DOCTOR ORBIS

13   EXTERIOR - HEARSE - NIGHT

On a long curve, the hearse races into frame towards and past camera. Camera PANS to follow action as hearse continues on around the curve and disappears into the night.

                                 FADE OUT

What we have here is a sample of what is known as a *master scene script:* a format which, from the writer's standpoint, frequently is the feature film's equivalent of the fact film's shooting script. A final description of what happens in your film, it spells out what's seen and what's heard, the action and dialogue within the framework of the setting. It's your story cast into such form that the director can direct it as a film, the actors can act it, and the crew members can perform their respective duties.

By and large, however, it does *not* go into technical detail, the breaking down of the action into shots or the like, save insofar as these are necessary in order to make clear a specific effect the writer hopes the director will include.

Thus, our sample probably is written with far more loving attention to such detail than normally would be desirable. Why? Because the writer is striving to create a particular mood of shock and horror while simultaneously establishing situation and key characters.

But more of that later. For now, let's consider nine key issues involved in writing a master scene script: format, visualization, point of attack, sequence development, continuity, characterization, dramatization, believability, and clarity.

1. Format.

Yes, mechanics *are* important, no matter what anyone tells you to the contrary. Why? Because your script is, in its way, your calling card. If it shows a lack of awareness of accepted practice on your part, it labels you as an amateur; and we all have handicaps enough to overcome without *that* albatross tied around our necks!

So. Mechanics.

Ordinarily, the master scene script is set up in a single column format, as per our sample pages. With the left edge of the paper at zero and a machine using pica type, give your copy horizontal spacing thus:

> 10—sequence (step) numbers
> 15—directions—75
> 30—speeches—60
> 40—parenthetical business—55
> 45—names of speakers
> 60—transitions
> 75—page numbers

Now, let's define and discuss our terms.

A *sequence number* is precisely what you'd think it would be: an identifying number in your script's left margin. The number changes every time conditions of work (INTERIOR/EXTERIOR—SETTING—DAY/NIGHT) change.

If, in the course of revisions, new sequences are added (to sequence 7, for example), they become Sequences 7a, 7b, 7c, and so on, so that no changes need be made in the numbers (8, 9, 10, etc.) that follow. Similarly, if sequences (steps, that is) are deleted, the numbers remain in the script, but are marked as omitted, thus:

> 67
> thru   OMITTED
> 69

> or,

> 67
> 68   OMITTED
> 69

Directions are those lines describing the action to be filmed.

Speeches are the words the actors voice.

Parenthetical business is any brief instruction as to some action an actor should perform in the course of a speech, or the manner in which the speech should be delivered. Thus, in the following bit, the parenthetical business is underscored. (It would *not* be, in an actual script.)

```
                    DR. ORBIS
                 (thoughtfully,
                 straightening)
         Coffins.  Faces without eyes
         coming out of coffins.  The
         girl and Garza, trapped and
         frightened.
                 (continuing, to
                 Karl, with
                 repressed glee)
         So!  That's the final set.
                 (significantly)
         At the house, you note.  Coffin
         Hall!  And for bait...
                 (a sudden leer
                 of triumph)
         ...well, what better bait then
         our friend Marinda!  'Tonight's
         Girl--Songs for Tomorrow!'
         ...Right, Karl?
```

In the same way, in the following passage, the *"(to crowd)"* line is parenthetical business. But the *"He turns the submission dial," "He twists the fifth dial,"* etc., are set up as directions because of their greater length and complexity.

```
                    DR. ORBIS
                 (to crowd)
         You see?  Dr. Orbis is the man
         who rules the mind!  Before my
         power, the strongest surrender
         ...submit totally.
```

```
He turns the submission dial as he speaks...makes a pass
in the girls' direction.  Their heads go down.  They hug
themselves, cringing and groveling.

                          DR. ORBIS
                Fear, hate, submission...ah,
                but these are bitter passions.
                Young ladies as nice as these
                deserve better.  ...Rapture,
                even!

He twists the fifth dial.  The girls' mood changes
before our very eyes.  They LAUGH (not giggle), cry out
delightedly, fling wide their arms, move in small
private dances.
```

A word of caution: Restrain yourself as much as possible when it comes to telling actors how to act or read their lines. For one thing, they "tend to act the adverb, not the line," as a friend of mine phrased it. For another, often they resent it, unless—and here's the key—the situation is such that it's important to story and character that a particular interpretation be given.

Thus, the "significantly" in our first example is probably belaboring the obvious, in view of the speech that follows. The "to crowd" in Example 2, on the other hand, is entirely legitimate, because the actor playing Dr. Orbis *could* decide he should address his line to Karl or the girls—a bad misinterpretation, in view of the image we're trying to build up for Orbis at this point.

Names of speakers are just that. Note that a speaker's name is repeated if *directions* break a speech (second example above), but not if the break is for *parenthetical business* only.

Transitions are the shifts from sequence to sequence. Ordinarily these will be optical effects—"DISSOLVE TO:," "FADE TO:," "BLUR PAN TO:," or the like. Sometimes you'll find "CUT TO:" also, especially if a cut wouldn't be the anticipated technique, but is desired for shock effect or such. Most of the time, however, a cut is taken for granted rather than spelled out.

Don't worry too much about transitions, though. Odds are no one will pay any great attention to your thoughts on the subject anyhow.

A somewhat different aspect of transition is the fairly common practice of writing "(CONTINUED)" at the end of any page that ends in the middle of a sequence. The next page starts with the sequence number and another "CONTINUED." Then, you drop down a double space and proceed.

Page numbers would appear too obvious to require comment save for one thing: From time to time in the course of producing a script, script conferences, changes of mind, or whatever, are going to put you in the position of having to add or delete pages. When that happens, treat each page as if it were a sequence. The extra pages can become 89a, 89b, 89c, and so on. And those deleted are accounted for by making the last page number before the break include those deleted. For example, page 61-2-3-4. Then, page 65.

Vertical Spacing?
Page number—two spaces below top of page
First line—three spaces below page number
Conditions of work, directions, speaker names, transitions—two spaces below preceding copy
Parenthetical business—next space below speaker name
Speeches—next space below speaker name or parenthetical business
All capital letters:
Character names (often on first appearance only), conditions of work, image size, camera movement, transitions

As per Sample Page 1, your first page will begin with an all-caps title . . . proceed to a "FADE IN:" . . . and then get down to business.

The rules on conditions of work are precisely the same as those we noted in our section on the fact film. *Always,* you establish whether a sequence is INTERIOR or EXTERIOR, its SETTING, and whether it's NIGHT or DAY; and you present them in that order.

From there on, you set forth what's seen and what's heard, with as little extraneous matter as possible. Particularly, go light on trying to tell the director how to direct your epic, save insofar as technical details are necessary to make clear an effect you're trying to achieve.

Thus, Director may not see fit to use the "SLOW PAN" in Sequence 1. But it does show him the way you visualize the scene, and that can be helpful even if he chooses to go another route.

Sequence 2 makes reference to something "OFF SCREEN"—that is, not shown—and, via the word "SOUND," lets Director know you think the sound effect (often abbreviated to "FX" or "SFX") of Pilar's footsteps would be a nice touch here. Calling for a "DOLLY" shot of her legs as she moves down the hall really is out of your domain, but we can rationalize it on grounds that we're trying for a particular effect: building audience interest via curiosity by showing only Pilar's feet and legs. Same for the "HOLD" while she unlocks the door.

Note, too, that we give each character's name ALL CAPS the first time he/she appears—a flag to warn Director that this is a new member of the cast taking the stage. The thumbnail description of the person is designed to help refresh his memory so he won't momentarily confuse Pilar with the villainess or her aging aunt.

Sequence 3 satisfies our curiosity as to whether or not Pilar has two heads . . . gives her a degree of identity through her "nurse-type uniform." We watch her discovery of Dr. Suarez's corpse . . . experience the impact of it in terms of the CLOSEUP of the corpse and the CLOSE-UP of Pilar's reaction.

Some directors might object to the writer's usurping their prerogatives by calling for closeups here. But not many. Why not? Because, you'll recall, the closeup is an emphasis shot—which is to say, its use is based on the assumption that you have something to emphasize . . . with *reason*, because you have a point you want to make.

Here, said point is (Closeup 1) the horror and ugliness that is dead Suarez, and (Closeup 2) Pilar's horrified reaction to the shock of Closeup 1.

The logic of this isn't likely to be lost on Director. Consequently, odds are he won't protest too loudly.

Will he necessarily shoot the scene according to your specifications? No. There are a dozen ways to film any sequence. It's quite possible his ideas on the subject are as good as or better than yours. But at least you've given him a notion of the way *you* see it, and the effect *you'd* like to get, and that in itself is worth the effort.

End of closeup. Pilar rallies and crosses to phone—and that in itself tells us something about her; she could equally well have fled or fainted. But either of those reactions would have made a different person of her; moved her out of the role she's destined to play.

Observe, also, that we've written this to give our girl a few bits of business—things to keep her busy and the audience's attention focused.

Take the business of keeping her busy: The Pilars of low-budget filmdom aren't likely to be played by the industry's Bette Davises or Katharine Hepburns. It does no harm to offer them a crutch or two in the way of simple action. They can always ignore it if they don't need it; and if they do, it's there and ready.

Similarly, in sequence 4, we've provided Karl with the physical tag of peripheral vision and explained how it affects him. With that motivation at hand, the actor playing the role can work to the limits of his competence—devising all sorts of business if that's within his ingenuity; plodding with just the fact that his "gait is tentative and erratic," if he can come up with nothing more.

So much for technicalities and format. On to

2. Visualization.

The first step in writing any master scene script is to visualize the action, no matter how clumsily. You can always correct flaws later.

So. The preliminaries are over. You've completed outline, treatment, and sequence outline of your new picture. Now it's time to begin the master scene script. To that end, sit down at your typewriter. Check out the first sentence of your thumbnail synopsis of Sequence 1: "Sam Jones rides into town."

Close your eyes, now. Envision that opening scene, the way your imagination would like to see it on the screen.

Next, write down what your imagination reveals as if there were a screen inside your forehead and you were describing a picture projected onto it from the nether reaches of your brain.

Maybe what you see comes out like this: "The dusty main street of a windswept western town. SAM JONES—tall, tight-lipped, saturnine, unshaven—rides in, horse moving at a tired walk. The rider looks neither to right or left, giving no heed to the loafers' curious glances . . ."

Or, maybe you see it differently: "Mud stands fetlock-deep in Pila Seca's main street. A monster draft horse, saddleless and of the type sometimes termed an Oregon puddin'-foot, plods wearily through it. Its rider, SAM JONES, stands out in marked contrast: small, dudishly dressed even unto a derby hat and pince-nez glasses, a man totally out of context in terms of both horse and setting . . ."

Or: "It's business as usual on Packrat's rutted, 1880-model main street. But then someone spots an incoming rider . . . stares slack-jawed. For the rider, SAM JONES, is mounted backwards on a particularly mean-looking mule. Tied aboard his steed, he wears only the nether half of a pair of long johns and a layer of tar and feathers so thick it's well-nigh impossible to identify the man himself . . ."

No shots have been designated, please note; no camera angles specified. Yet in each instance, a word picture of sorts has been painted, specific enough to spell out clearly just what's wanted, even while leaving plenty of leeway for the director.

How do you develop the knack of writing this kind of thing?

A first step is practice. Look out the nearest window—or from your car, or at a picture, or whatever. Then, closing your eyes, try to recreate the scene mentally and translate it into words on paper.

Or, read a chapter from a book and then, following the same process of visualization, cast it into master scene form.

Count on it, the first few times the result will be less than dazzling. But eventually the pictures you seek to paint with words will take form more and more clearly.

It will help, too, if you bear in mind the tremendous value of *contrast,* unanticipated juxtaposition of elements, as a tool, in creating any picture.

Thus, our first Sam Jones, above—"Tall, tight-lipped, saturnine, unshaven"—is the traditional spaghetti western figure: totally predictable within the story pattern. As such, he tends to be routine and so to offer little stimulus to the imagination.

Sam No. 2, the pince-nezed tenderfoot, is less of a stick figure. Consequently, he spurs us to greater flights of fancy. His contacts and confrontations come through more vividly just because they're fresher; less predictable.

Sam No. 3 is even more colorful, more stimulating. His very dilemma is suggestive of all sorts of incidents and bits of business.

This is not to say that contrast is the answer to all problems. But the injection of one unanticipated, out-of-place element ever so often will set inspirational juices to churning in you—and maybe even give you a sharper, brighter, more intriguing presentation.

3. Point of attack.

Just where do you start your story? Or your sequence?

Just where, that is, in terms of the specific image you seek to have placed on the screen.

These are the questions we deal with when we consider the problem of point of attack.

Where your picture's concerned, the opening shots are something you worked out long, long ago, in treatment and in step outline. But it's one thing to plan, another to write, as Bobby Burns observed in his line about the best-laid schemes of mice and men. Quite possibly, when the cards are down, you'll find it desirable to pick a different note on which to start than you anticipated.

The same principle applies to the beginning of each sequence, each group of related shots.

Whether the issue is story or sequence, the issue is the same. Two principles are involved:

a. Know the note you wish to strike—and strike it.

Are you shooting for impact? Mood? Characterization? Whatever your choice, know what you're after and strive for footage that will convey it.

Thus, in our *Orbis* opening, the object is to inspire horror. The point of attack is designed to achieve that end. Viewers first are given a few moments to absorb a proper mood via a "spookily lighted" room. The fact that nothing happens is intentional, in order to build anticipation of fearful things to come.

Then, the first shock note: the corpse of Dr. Suarez, complete with bloody axe and the implication of jeopardy which that implies.

(Would it have been better to handle the corpse less graphically? Using a shadow image, perhaps, rather than actual gore? Who knows? A good case can be made for either view.)

Pilar's approach and entry follows, built by the fact that our view of her at first is limited to her legs. Simultaneously, the shadow of jeopardy grows also: Where before there was only a corpse, now we have a girl who, we sense, is potentially a living victim.

Closeups build the scene. Pilar reacts courageously—that is, in character—to the shock.

Enter Karl, personification of menace. The sound of his footsteps—a non-normal sound, please note—comes first, in order to build viewer anticipation of something horrible about to happen. When we see him, his sinister appearance intensifies this feeling. But when he closes in, Pilar, though obviously terrified, still reacts with courage, So . . .

Well, you get the idea.

b. Beware the dragging windup.

Most of us tend to go for the long windup, when beginning either film or sequence.

Quite possibly, jumping into the middle of action or tension would prove more satisfactory.

Thus, is it really necessary to show Character ringing the doorbell and explaining the reason for his visit? Might it not prove more effective to cut from him hanging up the phone, say, to the moment he tells Villain he's under arrest?

More and more, in recent years, both audiences and filmmakers have shown less patience with plodding progression and long-winded explanations. From the stroke of the gavel to the clang of the cell door slamming shut is increasingly the rule.

4. Sequence development.

Developing an effective sequence is a complex business, and one learned largely through experience. But we can at least consider some of the elements involved.

a. Action.

Writers, being word people, tend to rely far too much on dialogue when they start scripting.

This is, to say the least, an error. More crucial by far is the matter of who does what, and what happens, for on the screen, especially, actions speak louder than words.

Our *Orbis* teaser offers a case in point. Not one word is spoken, unless you want to class Pilar's scream as speech. Yet the message and impact are strong and clear.

Which brings to mind an instance in which I was hired to write a science fiction script involving a future society where life centered around games. Although I struggled valiantly with it, I was cut off at the treatment. Why? Because, in large measure, my approach was too verbal, too cerebral.

The next writer fared better. He left out all the dialogue, all the discussions and explanations, in favor of simply having people moved about on a sort of giant chessboard.

Please don't make my mistake in your own writing. Analyze what happens in any given sequence, and then try to let the action tell the story insofar as possible.

b. Dialogue.

In spite of what I've said in a, above, dialogue is essential in most pictures. How to handle it? The preceding chapter gives some hints.

In addition, before you write, get the sequence's mood firmly in mind. Impose that mood on any information to be conveyed. Then, write your dialogue to fit.

c. Proportion.

Not every sequence in a film is equally important.

That being the case, you need to decide which loom large and which can be held small.

The important sequences—those in which your central characters are in greatest jeopardy, standing to lose all—should be built big. The "foothill" or transitional units can be passed over relatively lightly.

How do you build a sequence big?

You prepare for it by planting and building up its importance and potentialities of peril in preliminary episodes. Then, when the sequence itself arrives, you write it in terms of subjective time, as it were, stretching it out with detail and hazard and complications to match the dimensions of excitement you wish to create in your viewers.

(Objective time is the kind you measure with a watch. Subjective is based on emotion: your feelings, your degree of tension. It's what makes the two minutes while you climb the steps to your girlfriend's apartment seem like ten, or the half-hour spent waiting to see if your agonized, convulsing, strychnine-poisoned cat will live or die drag on forever.)

Consider, for example, the heroine's final effort to rescue a child in *Aliens*. To that end, she plunges into the monster-infested bowels of the planet's atmosphere-producing station. A dozen times she barely escapes death and disaster, blasting the hideous extraterrestrial creatures that assail her. Finally, she gets the child into a lift that carries them to the point where an android is waiting to transport them to safety. Over and over, doom seems certain, but in the end woman and child survive despite impossible odds and the "death" of the android.

Now this episode (or the chase or fight in any one of a hundred recent pictures, for that matter) could very well have been presented in flatly realistic terms—at least, as flatly realistic as this kind of action/adventure epic allows. Instead, writer and/or director chose to build it to a major crisis. To this end, (1) the emotional importance to the heroine of saving the child was clearly established, (2) the hazards involved were brought into sharp focus, and (3) the sequence itself was shot and cut with tremendous attention to detail (especially details exciting and empathy-provoking to the audience), ignoring clock time in favor of subjective time in order to wring every drop of adrenalin from its viewers.

How do you hold a sequence small?

You deal with its content as transitional or of minor importance, rather than building it up as vital or climactic. Perhaps this means bridging endless miles of travel with a few shots of landscape sliding by. Or emphasizing trivia or tedium, as when Hero questions three or four people as to Heroine's whereabouts without avail. Or restraining the emotion in a confrontation, so that Audience remains relatively calm and unexcited, as in the wryly ironic sequence in which Karen proposes to Blixen at the beginning of *Out of Africa*.

Beyond this, and as an overall guiding principle, write each sequence the way you feel it. Then, later, expand or trim as needed.

d. Pacing and placement.

In writing any sequence, consider carefully how it will fit into the picture as a whole. Specifically, bear in mind the sequences it follows, and those which will follow it.

The idea is to build to a pre-planned pattern, with crisis peaks spaced for maximum effectiveness—an individual matter with each picture—and intensification of tension from low points to high.

It helps, too, to try to avoid jerkiness, in favor of a reasonably smooth, rhythmic pace.

5. Continuity.

At last your screenplay is roughed in.

Next question: Do the sequences hang together?

Making sequences hang together is a function of continuity and, by and large, is a problem of the director and the editor. But the writer sets the stage for it, as it were, by his selection and arrangement of his material.

Thus, every event and incident should lead logically to the next. Or, as we phrased it in our discussion of dialogue, each unit should, in effect, acknowledge the existence of the one ahead.

In large measure, this comes down to anticipating your audience's anticipations. Setting up your situation, you arouse viewer interest in certain issues, thus developing the old "What's going to happen now?" angle. Then, tantalizing fragment by tantalizing fragment, you incorporate answers to the question. Simultaneously, you introduce new elements, new questions, to build tension—that is, interest—higher. But never do you lose sight of your line of development or the necessity of linking each new bit to that which preceded it.

6. Characterization.

In developing each sequence,

a. Is each character consistent?

Does your heroine act like a sexpot one moment, an icebox the next? Is your hero swaggering now, cringing then, scholarly the other time?

Consistency and believability are virtually synonymous where character is concerned. Do check for it!

b. Does Character break out of his role?

Pilar, in our *Orbis* sample, is the heroine. In keeping with her role, in the course of the script, she demonstrates courage, warmth, and concern for others.

Karl, the maniacal killer who assails her, also demonstrates characteristics geared to his role: coldness, violence, disregard for human life.

A Pilar who combined courage with coldness, on the other hand, would prove less the heroine; and, more important, would tend to confuse the audience. So would a Karl who murdered ruthlessly even while concerned for others.

This is not to say that characters must—or even should—be all black or all white. After all, Boris Karloff's *Frankenstein* was agonized victim more than fiend. But it is a fact that the subtle grays are more difficult to conceive and write. At first, especially, it's wise not to stretch your luck and skill too far.

c. Does Character have something to do?

Nothing is more deadly than a character who sits around waiting for the feathers to grow. If he has nothing story-vital to do, why include him?

d. Does Character have tags to wave?

Dr. Orbis is tagged by his thick glasses and sinister smile; Karl, by his blank eyes, axe, and erratic gait. Pilar has her nurse's uniform; Luis his reckless courage.

Granted, such billboard labels aren't always essential. But neither do they constitute a cardinal sin, especially where easy identification is desired.

7. Dramatization.

To dramatize is to present or represent in a dramatic manner—that is, in a manner striking in appearance or effect.

The essence of dramatization is the arousal of feeling.

Next question: In each sequence, are you making the most of your story's dramatic potential?

The biggest part of this work has already been done, of course, as you built outline, story treatment, and step outline.

Now, however, as you write your master scene script, the issue is to hunt down details that evoke the feeling you seek to arouse. For if you show only the facts of your saga, you'll end up with emptiness and mediocrity.

To this end, be sure that your key characters have strong attitudes in regard to each developing situation—attitudes so intense as to drive them to action and to conflict.

Reveal these attitudes in appropriate description of the details of your characters' behavior. For to capture feelings on film, the production crew must have something to shoot which will create the feeling sought.

8. Believability.

How do you make a film believable?

a. You provide justification for everything that happens.

That is, you motivate your characters to go in the direction you wish. You provide stimuli which lead them to react.

Equally important, you show your audience these stimuli, these motivations so that, seeing, they will unconsciously say to themselves, "Yes, yes. If I were this character, faced with these circumstances, these pressures, then it's conceivable that I, too, might do as Character is doing."

In other words, understanding *why* your character takes the course he does, your audience believes.

b. You proportion response to stimulus in every detail.

When a girl refuses a man a casual request for a date and he bursts into tears, most of us will feel he's *overreacting*.

When a child, screaming and bloody, comes rushing into a room and his mother fails to interrupt her bridge game, we'll tend to think she's *underreacting*.

Overreaction and underreaction are two major sources of disbelief in film. Viewers simply will not accept the character who behaves in a way they believe to be grossly exaggerated, either up or down, except in comedy.

Controlling such exaggerated actor behavior is, of course, the director's job. But again, as in so many other aspects of film making, the writer can help.

Cases in point are beyond number. But one that I particularly remember is Billy Wilder's answer to a question as to why he began *Some Like It Hot* with the St. Valentine's Day Massacre. The issue, he said, was that a truly powerful motivation was necessary to make it believable that Jack Lemmon and Tony Curtis, the two musicians, would don girls' clothes and take it on the run. Anything less than the threat of death would have made their behavior seem gross overreaction. But with the killings firmly established, their flight in drag appears plain good sense—whereupon, the picture was off to a credible start.

9. *Clarity.*

Your script, presentation of your visualizations, will be helped markedly by clarity of language. A few points to bear in mind are:

> The nouns most useful to you are those classed as *pictorial:* those that flash snapshots in your reader's mind.
>
> The specific noun ordinarily is stronger than the general, the concrete than the abstract, the definite than the vague, the singular than the plural.
>
> Active verbs, verbs that show something happening, are stronger than passive. And for film script purposes, you of course use them in the present tense.
>
> Judiciously used, adjectives help to sharpen a word picture: "tall, tight-lipped, saturnine" says something about both man and mood.
>
> Same for adverbs: "turns angrily" is different from "turns tearfully" or yet "turns slack-jawed."
>
> Short words are a virtue. So are short sentences—especially short simple declarative sentences. "Mud stands fetlock-deep in Pila Seca's main street" sets a stage with minimum waste motion.

Clarity comes first, always, in a script. But vividness is no sin if you can manage it without conflict. When we say that a man "wears only the nether half of a pair of long johns and a layer of tar and feathers," hopefully we've established an image that will inspire Director to something better than routine handling.

*   *   *

So there you have it: nine points to help you build a master scene script.

Remember, though, some things writing a script may be, but mechanical it isn't. In getting any kind of words on paper, the trick is first to learn the ropes. This, I trust, is something this book will help you do.

When you write, however, fly by the seat of your pants, following your impulses and instincts. Afterward is the time to think of rules, when you go back over your epic, checking and correcting.

*   *   *

What about writing a shooting script for your feature film?

Please don't.

Why not?

Because it will waste your time and energy for nothing.

Thing is, as I've so often said before, but now reiterate, directors feel that breaking down a script into shots is something that's strictly their business. So, even worse than resenting your efforts, they'll ignore them.

That means that, for you, the only time to write a shooting script is when Director, of his own volition, suggests that you and he sit down to work out same together.

What about your second draft screenplay, final draft screenplay, rewrites of screenplays, and the like?

Sorry. First draft is as far as we go in this book.

How so?

Because these later stages are something you have no need—or opportunity—to deal with until you've had a first draft screenplay approved by someone.

When that time comes, revision will be a subject of endless discussion and conferences. Your guidelines then will be the decisions reached by you and your colleagues. Nothing I might say here, beyond the principles already set forth, will help much.

Besides, it's more important now that you get on to an appraisal of various and sundry tricks of the trade of scriptwriting, as set forth in Part 3 of the present volume.

PART THREE

TRICKS OF THE TRADE

CHAPTER 14

Adaptation and Its Problems

How do you adapt a novel, play, fact book, or what have you for film use?

Or, to put it another way, how do you translate a printed work into script form?

The big issue is of course relative complexity. A novel may run 500 pages or more. Most films must be squeezed into 90 minutes running time. Cutting—often, drastic cutting—therefore becomes essential.

Thus, consider a novel we'll call *Monster*. Told in first person, it runs 13 chapters, 255 pages. Each chapter is comprised of one segment of present action, another of flashback background material. More than 20 characters are developed.

How might you approach the adaptation of *Monster* to film form, so far as the script is concerned? There are three major possibilities to consider:

1. You can follow the book.
2. You can work from key scenes.
3. You can construct an original screenplay based on the book.

To a considerable degree, each of these procedures overlaps the others. Yet each in its way is also separate and distinct, with individual strengths and weaknesses, advantages and flaws, to the point that each rates individual attention.

1. You can follow the book.

Wild are the anguished cries of critics outraged by the fact that a given film—which is to say, a given script—doesn't follow the book.

These ladies and gentlemen might not scream quite so loudly, however, were they themselves confronted by the problems of adaptation.

Take *Monster,* for example. Much of its impact is gained from its meshing of present and past. Chapter 1's flashback carries us to a point 263 days before the present action. But the gap narrows, chapter by chapter, until, in Chapter 12, the flashback ends just prior to the present action of Chapter 1. Chapter 13 melds both past and present in a final wrap-up.

Do I need to tell you that any attempt to approximate this pattern on the screen can lead only to total audience confusion?

Further, *Monster* is a taut, suspenseful story—perhaps too much so, for each unit of past and of present builds to a stomach-knotting climax.

How can this be handled in a film? True, it works well enough on paper, where transitions and the first-person central character's introspections provide sufficient change of pace and release of tension to balance the climaxes' mounting suspense and rising action. But development of 25 separate major crises is impossible in 90 minutes running time. To attempt it is to assure a crowded, jerky, melodramatic botch of a picture—and this without even considering the problem of how to introduce and build 20-odd characters.

The only solution, obviously, is to cut, cut, cut. The question is— cut what?

This is a Gordian knot without a sword. Whatever choice you make will unquestionably be wrong in the eyes of some; and odds are you can't conceivably blue-pencil enough to bring the picture within acceptable length, unless you resort to some version or other of procedures 2 or 3, as described below.

2. *You can work from key scenes.*

At the opposite extreme from slavishly following the book lies this approach. It has Writer shuffling the book's pages in search of scenes which appeal to him as colorful, dramatic, and at least indicative of the author's concept and story line. These he arranges in some sort of climactic order (not necessarily that followed in the book), then builds bridging passages between them, using either materials which the book provides or which he himself develops.

In the case of *Monster,* Writer might very well decide to build his script in a straight time line, ignoring such of the book's alternating flashbacks as he cannot juggle to fit the straight-line concept. For an opening, he picks a luridly esoteric scene in which a sex-oriented satanist cult is meeting. Male and female leads are both in attendance, with Male lusting after Female. But she refuses him—she won't betray her aging husband.

A scene in which Male Lead swims across a lake at night to murder Husband follows. Then, one in which he discovers that Female Lead, now his wife, has tricked him into committing the murder, simultaneously incriminating him in such a manner that he's doomed to be her slave for all time to come.

Further developments see Female Lead slay a fellow-cultist. Realizing he's next in line, Male Lead sets about to commit a series of fake lust killings, in the course of which he can also murder Female Lead; and so on.

His key scenes chosen, Writer now sets about bridging the gaps between them in such a manner as to give the final product some sense of continuity and logic. Thus, he decides that the incriminating evidence against Male Lead will unknowingly be held by Female Lead's younger sister, a girl as innocent as Female Lead is evil.

This touch particularly pleases Writer, since he recognizes that the characters in the original novel are too distasteful and perverted to serve as hero and heroine in any film of consequence. By playing Sister as heroine, he can in effect make the picture one long chase, with both Male and Female Leads secretly trying to kill her, complete even unto a quick save at the climax.

It's not hard to see why many viewers will find this filmed version of *Monster* unsatisfactory. In effect, they've been given a whole new picture—one with little resemblance to the novel save for the characters and buckets of blood.

Shall we draw a kindly veil and move on to our final approach?

3. You can construct an original screenplay based on the book.

This technique follows the line laid out in Chapter 7. To make a film script of *Monster*, attack the adaptation as if you were putting together an original screenplay. That is, start by nailing down what you consider to be the story's premise. (*"What if a man sets out to fake a series of lust murders to mask his killing of his wife—and then discovers he's actually a real lust murderer at heart?"*)

Next, decide on a point of view. (The novel stays with the murderer himself. But is that best? Would it be better to use the angle of the wife, for instance? Or a psychiatrist? Or a detective?)

Now, lay out a starting lineup. (*"Unable longer to endure the harassment inflicted on him by his evil, sadistically domineering wife, Celeste, Blair Hilliard determines to kill her, masking the slaying with a series of fake lust murders. But can he succeed when his arch-foe, mysterious cult chief Master Satan, refuses to stay dead?"*)

And so it goes, as you move on through your story, step by step . . . determining beginning, middle, end . . . writing a story treatment . . . breaking the treatment down into a step outline . . . building up a first draft master scene script . . .

Will this prove easy? Hardly. For where *Monster* the novel may capture thoughts, develop interior monologues, range through years of flashbacked time and the whole United States, and explore an infinity of bypaths and subplots, you the scriptwriter can't afford such.

Instead, you must reduce the mass to filmable dimensions. Which is to say, you must decide which of the maze of potential story lines you wish to follow . . . which characters should be built up, which jettisoned . . . which relationships offer most potential . . . which scenes hold greatest dramatic strength . . . which incidents must be devised and incorporated to draw the various bits together.

Flashbacks? In essence, they constitute someone remembering in the present something which happened in the past. Unless that remembrance is vital to the story, you very well may skip them entirely.

If, on the other hand, a flashback's content must of necessity be included, you may (a) reduce it to dialogue references—that is, let someone reveal the essential data verbally, or (b) play it out as a dramatized incident, dissolving from present to past and letting the characters involved live through the experience, then dissolving back to the present.

As a general rule, however, it's wise to avoid flashbacks wherever possible, simply because they bring your story's forward movement to a halt. This may either bore or confuse your viewers. In consequence, most of the time, it's better to stick with present action: what's happening now.

Yet the task with which *Monster* confronts you is relatively simple, compared with that which faced the writers of the scripts for such books as *Gone With the Wind, War and Peace, Out of Africa, Dune, Clockwork Orange*, and a hundred others.

Clearly enough, too, the three plans of attack I've outlined are far from exclusive. At one time or another, on any adaptation, you'll jump from tight adherence to the original here to working from key scenes there, to drawing out a premise and starting lineup from your material elsewhere in order to tie otherwise disparate elements together. And that's fine too. As I've said so many times, the big thing is to get the job done.

Over and beyond broad reformulations such as those discussed so far, the question of what details to cut always arises.

The answer is, cut facts—whole incidents, if need be. Why? Because the heart of any film is *feeling*.

This is diametrically opposite to the tendency of most beginners. Faced with a series of seven incidents centering on a boy's or girl's departure, the new writer invariably will try to crowd all in.

What he should be doing instead is asking himself one vital question: What dominant feeling is the novel's author trying to convey through the incidents? Passion? Poignancy? Relief? Or what?

Thus, suppose it soon becomes apparent that Girl feels poignancy, Boy relief, at their impending separation.

Obviously, seven scenes aren't necessary to convey this. All Writer needs to do is write—or rewrite—one to make clear the characters' divergent feelings, and he can move on again with pages saved.

Of course, this is not to say that cutting is necessarily the writer's only problem. Indeed, the opposite may be the case, as when he finds himself forced to expand a short story to fill 90 minutes. Yet that too can be managed—witness the brilliant work of Dudley Nichols in expanding Ernest Haycox's *Collier's* story into the classic *Stagecoach,* the Mark Hellinger adaptation of Ernest Hemingway's *The Killers,* or any of the many expansions of Stephen King's tales of terror. The issue is merely one of taking the original story as a springboard, then building a broader work upon it.

Play adaptation? It offers its own headaches. Trapped within the limits of the proscenium arch or arena staging, relying heavily on dialogue for its effects, the play's thrust is far different from that of film. To adapt it for screen use demands a willingness to cut it loose from the stage's confines and conventions . . . open it up to a wider sweep of action and of setting. Too slavish adherence to the playwright's conception can only destroy it.

Adaptation of factual material—a biography, say, or an account of some sort of adventure, discovery, or expedition? Your main problem quite possibly will be avoidance of that overdramatization which embarrasses and infuriates participants, heirs, and assigns. Wives of departed heroes rarely enjoy seeing their husbands portrayed as leering rakes; scientists cringe when colleagues kid them about the simplism or inaccuracy of filmed laboratory techniques; and no tough cop likes it when his buddies in the squad room play their own version of his deeds of derring-do.

I wish I had remedies for all such headaches. Too often, unfortunately, the writer is trapped between producer demands and subject sensitivities. Your biggest assets in such situations are a real determination to give your subject a straight count; honest sympathy for survivors; a willingness to develop your people as warts-and-all human beings, and enough of a sense of humor to incorporate such immortal lines as the one I picked up from a detective describing a blood-curdling shoot-out: "Warning shots, hell! I was just plain missin'!"

*   *   *

One final thought: Whatever your adaptation assignment, often the result will be a script—and film—which on the surface shows little relationship to the material from which it's taken; and viewers and media alike—and, quite possibly, the original author—will rave at the way you've "corrupted" the work.

Yet if you've done an honest job and played in luck, without too much interference from actors or director or front office or elsewhere, quite possibly you will have created a work which not only holds firm to the spirit of the original, but actually offers better entertainment.

If, on the other hand, you try to cling too tightly to chapter and verse of your source material, you very well may end up with a script which never quite jells: a straggly thing replete with loose ends, abortive scenes, jerky development, and characters who never quicken.

On that thought, we'll move on to another subject: the story conference, the writer and his people.

Read it. It's vital!

CHAPTER 15

Surviving Story Conferences

It may come as a shock to you, but your success as a film scriptwriter probably depends less on your skill with words than it does on your ability to deal with people.

How so? Because scriptwriting is no ivory tower occupation. Too much money is involved in filmmaking for that—so much it makes people in power nervous. Result: They're forever looking over your shoulder: picking holes in your work, shooting angles.

This is true in both fact and feature fields. The scene of the battle ordinarily is a small meeting known as a story conference, in which your script project is dissected and discussed in an effort to produce the best (or at least the most profitable) product possible. To that end, you sit down with a group of script-wise experts—executive producer, producer, story editor, director, other writers, their aides and assigns, or the like—and analyze what you've done, are doing, and propose to do, with special emphasis on what the Powers That Be consider weaknesses or problems.

Since the people involved are certainly experienced, and quite possibly brilliant, where scripts and films are concerned, the result can be fantastically helpful on occasion. But it can also be frustrating, not to mention destructive of your enthusiasm—and more so, since you'll be expected to work within the framework of the conference's decisions. Nevertheless, it's an accepted way of doing business in all phases of filmmaking, so you might as well get used to it.

Ideally, the man in charge of a story conference should be an individual who (a) thoroughly understands the process and problems of filmmaking; (b) knows what he wants, even though he's not inflexible about it; (c) expresses his views freely, clearly, specifically, and persuasively; and (d) makes all necessary decisions without delay and then stands firmly behind them.

Such men do exist. It's been my pleasure to work with a number of them.

Unfortunately, however, they tend to be rather rare birds. More common are those unhappy specimens who don't know film, who demand the impossible or undesirable, who can't make up their minds, who won't commit themselves, and who refuse to take responsibility. The results, for the scriptwriter, can prove very sad.

Sooner or later, you too will encounter one or more such types.

Next question: How can you best cope with each?

The man in the first category, the one who doesn't know film, isn't a variety you encounter often among feature picture executives these days. Among fact film clients, on the other hand, he's as prevalent as ants at a picnic.

For you as a not-yet-seasoned film writer, this type constitutes a special problem, in that it may take you a while to recognize him for what he is.

Thus, when Mr. Jones suggests that your feature's hero turn out to be a transvestite, or that dancing girls costumed as the components of your client's gear train perform a ballet at your fact film's climax, you may be taken somewhat aback. Yet the solution is reasonably simple.

First, unless you're being questioned directly, keep quiet—someone else among those present may burst out laughing, thus both getting you off the spot and letting you know how Herr Jones' thinking rates.

Second, make it a point to stay properly respectful, no matter how stupid or senseless an idea/suggestion/question seems to be.

Third, explain your own position and reasoning as clearly and convincingly as you can. Because before you're through, count on it, enough will have been said to clue you in as to just where your man stands.

Quite possibly, you'll even find he's also Man No. Two, the one who makes impossible demands.

If this should prove the case, honesty is your best refuge. Tell him the truth about Busby Berkeley chorus lines in $30,000 industrials, or the chances of Charlton Heston in drag hitting the box office jackpot. (And yes, I do remember Jack Lemmon and Tony Curtis in *Some Like It Hot*.) Then, if he still insists, go ahead. As to whether you also ask him whether he brushes off the advice of his doctor and lawyer too—well, how much of a gambler are you?

What about the man who can't make up his mind, or won't commit himself? One way out is to misstate his position purposely—not sarcastically, but soberly; straight-faced: "You mean, you want to play this

so Sitting Bull is really Custer's lost half-brother?" "Are you crazy?"
"Well, if you don't mean that, what *do* you mean?"

Quite possibly, all this will infuriate your man, but it does force
him to take a stand. Indeed, if your twist is sufficiently far out, Man's
sense of humor may get the better of him, whereupon the conference
tension eases and things start falling into place.

The man who refuses to take responsibility can give you special
nightmares. Ordinarily, the game he plays is "pass the buck," with you
as the receiver. To that end, scared rabbit that he is, he delegates duties
to committees which you are supposed to coordinate, sends you "F.Y.I."
critiques from people who have nothing to do with the project, and
otherwise lays the ground for hanging any failure around your neck
and well wide of his.

A case in point: Walking into an alleged story conference at a major
governmental agency, I discovered 20-odd "advisors" assembled. All I
was supposed to do was incorporate their off-the-cuff notions into my
script, and take the rap in case anyone later disagreed with same.

Instead, I walked out. Which may, in its way, be as good a method
of resolving such dilemmas as any.

Not that it will often prove necessary. Most often, impasses break
as soon as you explain how eager you are to do the job; it's just that you
don't want to infringe or take advantage by making decisions outside
your jurisdiction.

But this recital is beginning to sound choleric. Let's move on to
something more positive—specifically, an experience-gleaned list of ten
ways of approaching problems that may help you through your own
first story conferences:

1. Go in loaded.

I still recall a meeting I once had with an agent I wanted to impress.
Eagerly, I plunged into a description of the opening of my script. It was
a good opening, too, believe me.

Finally I paused for breath.

Agent gestured impatiently. "All right. What happens next?"

I gaped. Because while I certainly did know what happened next,
I—well, I didn't know it on quite the same level as I did the opening.
Matter of fact, when I thought back on it, I'd somehow assumed that
everyone would be so stunned with my magnificent beginning the rest
would just sort of develop naturally.

I really did know the rest of the story, though, after a fashion, so
I managed to grope my way through it.

To say the agent was unimpressed with my presentation is to put it mildly. Our association began and ended in that one meeting. Which was sad, but it taught me a lesson, cheap at the price.

That lesson was: *Go in loaded!* Know everything there is to know about your story, be it fact or fiction. Be prepared for every objection, every question. Even if you do, indeed, your colleagues still will find enough loopholes in your logic!

2. Play to your audience.

In story conferences, a scriptwriter needs to a degree to be an actor, adapting himself to the tone of the group.

Thus, you may be the lone, youthful outsider in a group of aging corporate executives. Or the college graduate confronting self-made men up from the foundry. Or the civilian among military, the layman among doctors, the high school dropout among professors, the kid with three one-acts to his credit up against a hundred years of major studio experience.

Your best beginning stance, in each case, is one of pleasant, relaxed friendliness.

Beyond that, play to your audience, the other men and women present. If they're all deadly serious, don't crack jokes. If they talk football, come in on the chorus with a few reminiscences of your own favorite games. Are hangovers the issue? Be sympathetic. Does someone try to bully, or play big dog, or put you down? Stay courteous anyhow.

Which is not to say that you should fawn or grovel, you understand. Self-respect is never out of style. But this is the other man's turf, not yours, so within limits you'll do best to fit yourself to his pattern.

3. Be prepared to take the lead.

Some years ago I signed on to script a series of six films for a national organization. The pay was good, the subject interesting, and the steering committee with which I was to work congenial. Yet the first couple of sessions made it apparent nothing constructive was ever going to happen.

Why? Because, most often, unless a strong man is in charge, a committee tends to go in circles. Or, to put it another way, somebody has to take the lead in any creative effort.

In this particular instance, I was the one who took it, laying out a complete—if unauthorized—plan of attack on the project even unto brief synopses for each of the six pictures.

The committee, delighted, promptly approved the whole package, and we got down to work. But the fact remains that if I hadn't taken the first step, Lord knows when or if we'd have gotten started.

Bear this thought in mind with regard to your own projects. Ever so often, walking in cold, you'll discover that no one knows quite where to begin. When that happens, be sure you have some thoughts of your own in mind—some sort of concept or approach to serve as springboard. For even if your associates reject it, it at least will serve to jar them off dead center.

On the other hand, don't be *too* quick to jump. The human ego is easily bruised, and your "presumption" can give you headaches that go on well-nigh forever.

4. Be prepared to TELL your story.

So there you are, in the story conference. A neatly duplicated copy of your epic lies on the table in front of each participant. Eagerly, you wait for their reactions.

Only then the man at the head of the table pushes the sheets aside. "Let's dispense with this stuff, Joe," he says. "What we want's the story. Just tell us about it."

Yes, it does happen, and more often than you might imagine. Why? Well, for one thing, it gets pretty dull in a few minutes if everyone sits around the table reading. But more important—and believe me, I'm not kidding when I say this—reading is a problem for a lot of people, and that includes even intelligent, educated, allegedly highly literate types. They simply can't cut it comfortably where a script page is concerned.

Result: "Just tell us about it."

So, just tell them, as clearly and effectively as you know how.

It goes without saying you'll tell them *more* clearly and *more* effectively if you've thought through the possibility of verbal presentation beforehand. A bit of rehearsal might not even hurt.

5. Talk scenes, not story.

"Telling" a script can be a tricky business. Often, before you're through, you find yourself tangled in such a maze of plot details that your audience hangs on the ropes.

Two small stratagems will help you:

First of all, *simplify* your presentation. The closer you can come to stripping it to bare bones, the better. (It's alleged that the line which sold Joe Levine on *Panic in Needle Park* was "Romeo and Juliet on junk.") Work for the "Who wants to do what and why can't he?" approach, the Objective-Obstacle-Outcome synopsis. Not too difficult a task, either, if you've built your script solidly, up step by step from a foundation of premise or core assertion. The mushy, unstructured jobs are the ones that kill you.

Second, insofar as practical, *talk scenes*.

That is to say, talk confrontations, color incidents, conflict units: the big, exciting moments that you can build the way you'd build your account of a bank robbery or marital battle that you witnessed. Tell them vividly, dramatically, so that they come alive in your listeners' minds and capture their imaginations, joining each episode to the next with a minimum of transition.

Is this a legitimate technique? It is indeed. As director Henry Hathaway has pointed out, "People never remember what they hear in a movie. They only recall what they see. The big hits have unforgettable scenes in them, usually action. Pictures that are filled with dialogue do not do as well." You're just capitalizing on that angle. Others will bring up any discrepancies of logic later.

6. Be animated.

If you tell a story as if it were dull, that's the way it's going to seem to your listeners. If, on the other hand, you come on strong, with maximum enthusiasm, your audience will respond in kind.

Obviously, you have to adjust this approach to your own style, your personality. And it doesn't mean pouring on the superlatives or adjectives. But if you can, in your own way, show that this is a story that excites you, you'll have won the biggest part of your battle.

7. Listen.

The reason other people are attending your story conference is to help improve your script. Most of them will be clever, creative, experienced. Often, they can and will give you new twists, improved ideas, sharper concepts.

They can do this, however, only if you do your part—that is, listen.

8. Hang loose.

Close corollary to point 7 is that your mood as well as your ears must be receptive. Obviously, you're not going to agree with every idea that's tossed at you, but you should give each and every one honest consideration. A chip on your shoulder will only turn people off, and that you can't afford. Remember, damn it: They're here to *help* you!

9. Don't be afraid to keep it light.

Years ago I knew a used car salesman who always was good for a laugh. It got to where I looked forward to seeing him each morning as I walked past his lot to my office, just for the way he brightened my day with his latest gag.

Later, I learned his secret: His company provided its crew with a fresh, new one-liner daily.

You can do worse than to acquire a store of such yourself. Even the serious business of scriptwriting can stand a smile or two when there's a conference in the offing. No need to be a clown, you understand; but no need to wear a long face either. A cheerful group works better.

10. *Stop.*

Few things in a meeting are more painful than the man who won't let go. Whether he's ridden by insecurity, lacks judgment, or has nothing to go home to, the fact remains that he makes everyone dread sessions with him.

It's worth your while, therefore, to cultivate a sense of timing; a feel for the moment when all that's pertinent has been said.

When that moment arrives, don't hesitate to beam, straighten up your papers, and say, "Well, that shapes things up, right? At least, so far as I'm concerned. . . ." Then, if anyone else sees fit to halt the exodus, that's up to him. At least, you won't have been the one to play albatross.

Which makes this a good stopping-place for this chapter, too. For it's high time we were getting on to that most vital chapter of all in this epic work: How to sell your scripts.

CHAPTER 16

The Scriptwriter as Businessperson

This chapter will devote itself almost entirely to economics, pure even if not so simple. We'll tackle the subject on four levels:

1. How to get assignments.
2. How to handle assignments.
3. How to survive as a scriptwriter.
4. The agents and the Guild.

Ready? Let's go!

1. How to get assignments.

How do you find work as a scriptwriter?

Let's take it for granted you've already explored—or will explore—all the usual routes: help wanted ads, college employment services, personal contacts, you name it.

If you're on the Coasts, East or West, in New York or Los Angeles, you can shoot assorted other angles. I've known people who took jobs as studio typists, for example, just in hopes that pounding through the pro work would teach them pro skills, or give them contacts, or what have you. Others have signed on as page-boys or gofers (go for coffee, go for cigarettes, go for my lucky piece that I left on the dressing table), cheap labor on non-union productions, and the like.

Sometimes, if you have enough of what our Jewish friends call *chutzpah,* you can scrape acquaintance with some old hand who's tired or has a liquor problem . . . get him to let you do the dog's work on a TV episode in exchange for a shared credit.

Again, reading *Variety* or the *Hollywood Reporter,* occasionally you'll see ads from producers wanting scripts or writing help. And though the boys in the know will tell you that all such are frauds and wastes of time, I've still cashed checks from a few of them.

Writer's Digest, The Writer, and other such publications periodically offer lists of film and television companies in the market for scripts. And magazines dealing with the industry sometimes carry classified ads soliciting writers.

The American Film Institute's training programs are also worth investigating, as are the internships announced on rare occasions by various of the studios. And opportunities sometimes appear on the bulletin boards or by word of mouth at such film schools as the University of Southern California and the University of California at Los Angeles.

Regional producers of both fact and feature films also are becoming more numerous. You'll find many of them listed in the classified telephone directory under "Motion Picture Producers" in your area's larger cities.

Also, it's worth your while to check out your state's film office.

Whatever path you choose, however, getting assignments and/or selling scripts is seldom easy. But on the other hand, it's seldom quite as impossible as it sometimes seems to the beginner; and the first step is always the hardest.

The problem is, as you know if you've ever hunted for any kind of job, that the boss always says he won't hire you because you have no experience. Yet how are you to get experience if no one will hire you?

Well, in film scriptwriting, fortunately, there *is* an answer. Not a simple answer, you understand, nor a quick one, nor even a sure one. But then, who ever promised you a rose garden in this business?

So: Your first step is to get yourself a film to script to prove your worth.

To this end, you take the same road as does the freelance writer in any other field. That is, you find yourself a subject and then you write a script.

No, this isn't easy. But it *is* easier than it sounds. The trick is merely to think and act *as if* you already were a scriptwriter, and so script a film.

Thus, let's assume you're a beginner, without contacts and stuck in a town or city far from any major production center. Money is something you're short on, but you do have a certain amount of free time. So, what do you do?

Take it in four steps:

a. Pick a worthy cause.

The world is full of "public service" causes that can't afford commercially-produced films. So, pick one—anything from the United Fund to the Listless League for Lost Leprechauns.

Research this group and its goals a bit. Develop some sort of core assertion you think might help them on their way.

Then, make contact with the people in charge—informally and casually, if you can. In the course of things, let it drop that you think a film might do Group some good, and that you'd like to script such—for free, of course. Would they, in their role of experts, help you get their position straight?

Count on it, they'll help. Or, if they won't, the officials of some other similar body will prove more farsighted.

At this point, you

b. Write the script.

Do this as your contribution to your career. Do it step by step, just as painstakingly as if you were being paid top dollar.

Approach? The big thing is, keep it simple. Avoid sync sound in favor of voice-over narration, or even live commentary by a speaker. Any angle is acceptable, so long as what you produce serves your group's cause and fills its need.

Once you've got a script, and your associates' agreement that it does the job,

c. Shoot some film.

Here you may go in a variety of directions. Maybe, since you can get by with a sample sequence or two or three, you'll find it easiest simply to buy a few hundred feet of film out of your own pocket, borrow an 8mm camera, and shoot and edit the stuff yourself. Or, get hold of a video recorder and some tape and work with that. Or, there may be a movie bug in the group you're promoting. Or, a college film production class might prove willing to take over. Or, a local TV station conceivably will agree to do the picture as a public service project.

However you work it, hopefully you'll end up with a completed film or, at least, part of one.

Whereupon, take said film to every advertising and public relations agency, film production company, and TV station you can find. Show them film and script, tell them you're the guy who wrote it, and would they kindly consider giving you a whack at any script chores that come up in the days ahead?

You'll be surprised how many brownie points this approach will get you. For one thing, the fact that you come to an agency or producer or station with a can of film in your hand automatically will set you head and shoulders above the competition, if for no other reason than that most people involved with film are constitutionally unable to resist looking at the other fellow's product.

In addition, the fact of having that film says you really *are* a scriptwriter: You've conceptualized an idea in film form and set it down in words that someone, somehow, has translated into moving pictures.

Finally, the fact that you're free-lance and not asking to go on the payroll will give you an extra edge, because it offers the man you're talking to extra talent sans outlay. Given half a chance, he'll try to use you just so you'll stay available.

Beyond all this, there's no law that says you can't show your film and present your ideas to companies or organizations which you think might be in the market for a picture of their own. Talking around and reading trade journals might even see you taking off as a shoestring producer.

Also, it's entirely possible you'll find yourself in a film-related job in spite of yourself. TV stations, especially, often make room for a man or woman handy with ideas and typewriter.

But let's not pipe dream too far ahead. The big thing is, you've done a script—an at least partially produced script—and made some contacts.

Next step: Work at keeping said contacts alive. How? Well, one way is to send some sort of reminder—a note or postcard will do, providing you make it lively and clever—reminding each person on your list that you're still looking for scripts to write. Be sure to feature your name, address, and phone number prominently; and it won't do any harm to brag up any assignments you've won since you last saw Contact.

Another visit? Sure, providing you don't make yourself a nuisance by coming too often or staying too long.

Finally, any spare time you have can very well be devoted to working up yet another script/film, for two *are* better than one, if only to prove your first effort wasn't a flash in the pan.

What if you could care less about industrial/educational/documentary/promotional films? What if nothing save cinematic storytelling will satisfy you?

Well, you can shoot some angles there, too. I've never known a college drama department that didn't like original one-acts, for example. For a good reason: no royalties to pay.

So, write yourself a one-act. Then persuade said drama department—or a little theatre group, or a church school unit, or a union, or a lodge, or a high school—to stage it. Take it from one who's been there, you'll learn by it.

But your target's film, not theater, right? So, the very night your play makes its debut, ride the euphoria of the applause with a suggestion: "Hey! Let's film it!"

You're taking on a job, I warn you. But given a little luck, it will prove worthwhile.

First, of course, comes a script: an adaptation. Then, the recruiting of a crew to shoot it, probably in Super 8.

Again, you'll have a script and a can of film to show. Again, you'll be ready to make contacts.

*   *   *

Now one word of warning: Count on it in advance, the overwhelming majority of those of you who try this are going to fail. But that's the way it is in the film business. It's rough, and you need every one of those nine attributes I listed in the opening chapter if you're to survive.

On the other hand, if you have backbone, persistence, talent, and whatever, this is at least a chance for you to put them on display. And that's all anyone can ask.

2. How to handle assignments.

You've already learned a high proportion of what you need to know on this subject from Chapter 2, "The Proposal Outline," and Chapter 15, "Surviving Story Conferences." But certain key points still can stand attention, as follows:

a. Do ask to see a sample script.

This book has, I trust, given you some idea of how to put a script together. But well-nigh every outfit has its own idiosyncrasies where style and format are concerned.

It follows, therefore, that it's worth your while to learn about these before you start. And the simple way is to ask the producer to loan you a script whose style he likes.

b. Do nail down deadlines.

Day before yesterday can be a pain—especially when it develops that's when you were to have turned your script in.

You see, in the early stages of a job, clients and producers can be ever so casual about when they expect a finished product. But that attitude may change overnight when it dawns on someone that they just might be able to show their gem at the June convention.

For your part, you can't afford that kind of unanticipated nonsense, nor yet the client's sudden assumption that you can produce rabbits out of hats if you just work 48-hour days like he doesn't. So, nail it down at the start just when you're expected to deliver what.

And then come through.

c. Do be certain who has final authority.

I learned about this the hard way, when I devoted a week's hard work to hammering out a proposal—and then discovered that the people who'd hired me didn't have the power to do so.

Point 1: The kind of authority you need to be interested in is, who has final authority over acceptance of your script?

Point 2: Does everyone else in the operation agree that this man has the authority?

Both of these are questions I'd surely raise in the very first conference, in the course of explaining how a script is written, and setting up an operating procedure to follow.

d. Do be sure you have a technical advisor.

I've already yakked at length on this point. This time, I bring it up just so you'll remember it.

Equally important, be sure Technical Advisor knows what's required of him. Neither you nor he will be happy otherwise.

e. Do insist on signed approvals.

Unhappy is the writer who, starting on his shooting or master scene script, finds that Client has suddenly changed his mind, so now they're going to start over again with a new concept.

He'll be ever unhappier if his agreement hasn't provided for Client approval signatures of proposal, treatment, sequence outline, and so on, so that Client must pay extra for any approved work which, later, must be changed/done over.

f. Do spell out payment terms.

How much are you paid for scripting a film?

Obviously, that depends in large degree on Client, your skill, your reputation, your availability, and the situation.

There's a marked difference, too, between the rates for fact and feature films. Indeed, the circumstances vary so much we'll take up features in a separate section of this chapter.

Fact film hangs much looser. All kinds of rates and deals are possible. Thus, some producers pay by the reel—ordinarily, that's a 360-foot, 10-minute, 16mm reel. Others pay by the film, regardless of length. Most pay on a one-shot basis, without royalties or residuals. On the other hand, I have a contract now in my file that provides that I get $1,000 for the job, with another thousand if the returns on the film go above $20,000. (I'm not spending it until the check not only arrives, but clears the bank.)

A common target writers shoot for is 10 percent of the cost of production. In other words, if the film is to cost $10,000, the writer wants $1,000 for the script; if it costs $30,000, he wants $3,000.

Another approach is to try for $1,000 per reel, settling for less if that seems too rich for the client's blood. (If you're tops, on the other hand, you may get more.)

Still a third way of tackling the problem—especially if the film shows signs of being a long, drawn-out project in which everything is certain to go wrong and eat up extra time—is to ask to be put on retainer or on the producer's or client's payroll at so much a month for the duration of the project, with the understanding that you're free to work on other scripts when nothing's doing on Client's picture.

It's also vital that you schedule the payments for your work properly. Personally, I like a four-payment system, set up like this:

25% on signing of letter of agreement.
25% on submission of treatment.
25% on submission of shooting script.
25% on completion of film.

Why the business about "submission" of treatment and shooting script, rather than "acceptance"? Mainly, because you never know what may happen between the time you start writing these items and the time you turn them in. For example, appointment of a new advertising manager may result in the junking of your script's basic concept. Death of an organization's president may put a different philosophy in command. Absence of key personnel may result in months of delay.

None of these things is your fault. Yet if your agreement says you must wait for approval, you very well may spend months cutting financial corners even though you delivered a script that fitted all specifications perfectly.

Above all, you must not under *any* circumstances agree to wait for payment until a film is completed or approved. A personal experience may show you why.

The instance in point saw me writing an introduction-of-the-new-model film for a subsidiary of a major manufacturing company. No producer was involved, because the company wanted to put the job out for bids on the basis of the finished script.

As usual, I stipulated that I was to receive my money in four equal payments, as outlined above.

The parent company's representative bridled at this a little—after all, why shouldn't I be willing to guarantee my product by deferring payment until the film was finished and the client satisfied? I in my turn explained that I had no control over the finished film, or whether it would be approved, any more than a lawyer can guarantee to win a case or a doctor can guarantee that a patient will recover. All I could do was my best, just as Company Rep was doing. Indeed (ha-ha), I'd be willing to defer payment, if he'd be willing to defer his salary for the same period. . . .

Anyhow, I finally got my way. Things went along reasonably smoothly thereafter, with no more than the usual number of hassles. (I was interested, though, to discover that this firm's accounting department classed a film script as in the same category as bituminous coal, limestone, and cinder blocks.) Eventually, the script was completed, ready for production. I pocketed my third payment, then went on to other projects while I waited for whoever won the production bidding to finish shooting and editing the picture so that I could do the final polish and draw 25 percent No. 4.

A year passed without further word. Wondering what had happened, I called the subsidiary firm in whose behalf the film was being made.

To my bewilderment, not one of the men with whom I'd had dealings was still employed there. Those who'd replaced them denied all knowledge of the film project.

Now I wrote to the man who'd been my contact in the parent company. In due course, back came a letter from another name I didn't recognize. Mr. Jones, the first man, was no longer with the firm, this epistle explained. Further, a decision had been made to phase out the product my script was designed to promote, and to retool Subsidiary for work in an entirely different field. Consequently, no film would be needed, and my services were no longer required. Very truly yours.

Well, that was that. I'd been cut out of a quarter of my fee—the quarter I'd counted on as profit—and no one had even thought it important enough to write or call me about it.

But—and here lies the important point—if I'd agreed to accept the original, payment-on-film's-completion offer, in all likelihood I wouldn't have received a cent for my efforts.

Bear that in mind when you check out your own letter of agreement.

g. Do hang loose.

Do I sound as if I thought everyone was out to rob the writer? I don't mean it that way. Many times, I've gone to work on the basis of a telephone call or a handshake, with any letter of agreement an after-the-fact proposition.

Ordinarily, though, this was with small operations, where I knew and trusted the individuals involved. With larger concerns, the letter of agreement is a good idea—not because the people are less trustworthy, but because more of them are involved and things have more opportunity to become confused in the course of moving up or down the chain of command.

About letters of agreement in and of themselves: I'm not a lawyer; whereas my clients in most cases have attorneys on retainer. It therefore makes sense for me to let said attorneys draw up any and all agreements, with me merely checking to make sure Client and I understand each other. What I get is nothing resembling a complete contract, nor do I care about such. You never can hope to plug all the loopholes, if someone's really out to clip you.

More important by far, in my own estimation, is maintenance of a relaxed and friendly atmosphere where all phases of your work are concerned, for it's disconcertingly easy to get a reputation as a paranoid or a prima donna. Take my word for it, you're better off with neither label. To that end, hang loose!

h. Do try for credits.

A writer is judged by the credits he accumulates—credits being those film titles which name you as the man or woman who scripted the picture. Indeed, titles are a matter of sufficient moment that the Writers Guild goes so far as to spell out such details as "The Company must include the writing credit in all publicity, handouts, screening invitations, etc., if the names of the individual producer and director are included, even if such credit is in the form of a presentation or production credit."

In the fact film business, unfortunately, some companies make it a policy to give no production credits whatsoever. That means that your only recourse, if you feel strongly enough on the subject, is to refuse to script for said companies.

More often, the question is negotiable. If you fuss enough about it, you get a credit.

So, do fuss! Some potential customer may see the line on a picture you've done that he likes. The result might be yet another contract.

3. How to survive as a scriptwriter.

Would-be writers, script and otherwise, tend to be (a) gamblers, and (b) optimists. Which is fine, but do calculate the odds before you take cards in the game!

Herewith, four ways to improve your hand:

a. Line up clients.

You need scripts to write before you tackle full-time free-lance work: clients and producers who like your copy and who can be depended on to throw a fair number of assignments your way each year.

This of course implies that you've sold enough scripts already, catch-as-catch-can, to build yourself a reputation.

If you haven't done so, do it now!

b. Put yourself on salary.

In addition to clients, you need a strong financial backlog: money enough to carry you till you get established. How much will that be? Enough, I'd say, so that you can survive at least a year—or, better, two—without too much pain if assignments fail to materialize as quickly as you'd like.

It's important in this regard not to overestimate your potential. Or, to put it another way, a good week doesn't necessarily mean a good year.

Thus—and I have been as guilty of this as anyone else and sometimes more so—it's easy to look at a check that says you've made $3,000 for two weeks' work, and kid yourself that this means you're now a $75,000-a-year man.

Fortunately, there's a simple solution to this problem: Instead of dreaming, put yourself on salary. To this end, divide your total resources ($23,000, let's say) by the number of weeks you want to give yourself to succeed or fail (52, for example).

Breaking this down into roughly even numbers, this gives you a salary of $400 a week, plus a small buffer for emergencies. You're free to spend it as you will, with a clean conscience—though it would make good sense to calculate your probable business expenses and put that amount aside each week so you won't run short.

Now, here comes check number one. It's for $2,250, and it arrives less than a month after you make the break.

Congratulations! But do be careful what you do with your bonanza. I'd recommend that you put it in a separate bank account and forget about it. Indeed, until the year ends, you should remain a $400-a-week person. Then, if the record shows you can afford it, and you think you deserve it, maybe you can give yourself a raise.

There's also another, oft-overlooked factor to consider: the matter of you and Uncle Sam and New York (or whatever) State and any other tax-levying bodies that may be lurking in the bushes. So long as your current income is in the bank, you'll have no trouble paying off when Judgment Day arrives. If you spend it, you may find yourself in the unhappy situation of having to go hat in hand to beg a boon of your friendly neighborhood loan shark—he of the cheerful smile, sympathetic mien, and brass knuckles. (Why the loan shark? Because your banker may not consider you, as a writer, the best risk. It's just one more occupational hazard. Only later, when you make it into the Writers Guild, will you have a credit union to give you a hand.)

c. Keep proper records.

I once knew an accountant about to retire from a major film company. Eager for words of wisdom, I asked what kind of a system he planned to use in handling his finances in the days ahead.

Dead-pan, he answered, "Whatever money I get, I'm going to put it in my right pants pocket. Anything I have to spend, I'm going to pay it out of there. At the end of the month, if there's anything left, I'll know I made a profit."

Well, ask a stupid question, you get a gag-line answer.

Where you're concerned, however, I'd strongly recommend that you keep some kind of financial record. The best will itemize every penny you receive, and every cent you spend. With good reason, too. No one can fault you if you have a record of *every* transaction, not just tax deductible expenses. One scriptwriter friend of mine in Hollywood, with $100,000-plus annual earnings, has gone blithely through audit after audit from the IRS on just that basis.

In addition to these income/outgo figures, it's a good idea to keep some sort of time sheet to show how many hours you devoted to each project.

Such a record is valuable for three reasons.

First, it lets you know how much you worked, and this can be a more important point than you realize. Thus, you may have assumed that you've been putting in eight hours or more a day minimum. But when you get the facts down on paper, taking out the coffee breaks and bull sessions, you discover that you actually spent little more than three at actual writing.

Second, it lets you know how much your work paid off per hour. Again, the results may shock you, as when you come to realize that the little narration polish job you took on for a flat $250 paid you $25 an hour . . . or $10 an hour . . . or 73¢ an hour.

Third, it lets you know how much to charge the next time.

This last can be a truly vital point, for too many of us tend to set our fees with a ouija board. This was clearly illustrated to me when an advertising agency asked a number of writers and producers to submit their prices for a small job. Incredulously, I discovered that one producer's bid for the complete film was dollar for dollar the same as my price for the script. Needless to say, it came as no shock to me some months later when said producer went bankrupt.

On the other side of the fence, a public relations outfit once asked me how much I wanted to write narration for a tape cassette. The job sounded fairly simple, so I named a low price—and knew instantly I'd made a mistake when the man to whom I was talking laughed and said, "Well, I guess we can afford *that*."

I learned later that they'd charged the firm for which the job was done precisely ten times my price.

d. Develop good work habits.

How do you develop good work habits?
By working.
Specifically, by not just sitting, staring out the window.
No. What you need to do is turn out copy.
To this end,

1. *Make preparation a part of your schedule.* One of the most difficult problems in writing is "starting cold"—going at a project without having thought it through beforehand.

A good way to beat this is by setting up a regular schedule for preparation. A program I've found effective is to arrange for a daily quiet time of relaxed thinking—a period when you *don't* have to be grinding out anything or being in a hurry.

Set an hour to do this. Late evening's a good time.

Thus, let's say that your appointment with yourself is for 10 p.m. each night, Sunday through Friday. (Why include Friday, unless you're going to work Saturday? Because you need a bridge from which to start on Sunday night; a springboard from which to leap, as it were.)

When 10 p.m. arrives, take scratchpad in hand and sketch in the work you're going to do tomorrow—detailed notes, a rough draft of shots, or what have you. Let your fancy roam free, so long as it stays on the subject in a sort of focused free association. Don't try to organize too tightly. Bear down more on feelings, emotionally colored thoughts—a state of mind that's alert for what's exciting about the project.

When your hour's up, put away your pad. Go on to bed or your chosen leisure.

Now it's next morning. Get to your desk on schedule. Put a sheet of paper in your typewriter, take up your "preparation" notes, and start typing. Not thinking, you understand; not judging or organizing or weighing phrases, but *typing:* words onto paper from your notes, copying or changing as the spirit moves you. Adding, too? Sure thing; but just the bits that come to you. No straining. No forcing.

By the time you're finished with your notes, I guarantee you'll have your day's work on the road. And I mean *really* on the road. Your interest will have been caught. You'll be rolling, turning out a flow of copy. Not window-staring.

Does 10 p.m. possess some magical property that makes me recommend it? On the contrary. Any consistent routine is acceptable. Thus, suppose you find that the last hour of the normal working day, 4 to 5 p.m., ordinarily is dead time for you, waste motion so far as your regular schedule is concerned. Why not put it aside for preparation?

With that in mind, knock off your customary writing at 3:30 and go for a walk or a Coke or whatever. But promptly at 4 p.m.—and I do mean promptly—report back to your desk and scratchpad and start doodling on tomorrow's work.

Do this from the start of your career. Why? Because when you're young your initial flush of enthusiasm for creating will carry you. But as you grow older at the game, you'll tend to drag your feet more and more . . . spend long hours dawdling. Whole days quite possibly may

pass in which you'll get little or nothing done. Soon you'll grow depressed
. . . wonder if you've shot your wad or lost your marbles. It's a damaging,
nerve-wracking state.

The purpose of preparation time is to keep such from happening
. . . to drill the right work habits into you before you're desperate for
them.

O.K., end of lecture.

2. *Line up assignments ahead.* Writers sometimes have a weird way
of viewing assignments. They think of them as work orders someone
brings to them. Consequently, they sit back and wait for them, the way
too many actors in Hollywood sit gnawing their nails by the telephone,
yearning for the call that never comes.

Believe me, friends, that's not the way to go about it. For while
such miracles sometimes happen—be grateful for them!—they tend to
be rare birds indeed. You can starve to death while you wait for them.

What you need to do, rather, is *develop* potential assignments. In
other words, keep digging up and expanding upon a steady stream of
ideas of your own.

Once you've found a concept that you like, one that strikes you as
having possibilities, start pushing it in what seems the most likely direction: to agent, client, producer, director, actor, friend—just about anyone whom you can see as helping you get it into production.

Will it sell? Who knows? But whether you place it or whether you
don't, it still will get you into contact with film-oriented people and
remind them of your existence.

This is important. To finish a film, then wait for a new assignment
to pop up, is a sure road to disaster. You need to be constantly promoting,
so that jobs overlap. Otherwise you'll have endless wasted days in those
periods between the time you finish a shooting script and come in weeks
or months later to do the narration polish job.

Incidentally, this business of working up your own assignments is
not to be confused with what the Guild terms "speculative writing," in
which a producer says, "Hey, that's a great idea, boy! Why don't you
work it up into a treatment and then if I like it I'll buy it." No, indeed.
Your ideas should remain just that—ideas, presented in a page or two
or three at most. If anyone wants you to work them up further, it's up
to him to pay you for it.

e. Beware friends.

No one except free-lance writers really believes a free-lance writer
works. Consequently, all feel the writer is fair game for idle moments.
The amount of your time they can waste is absolutely incredible. Not to
mention disastrous, in view of the fact that all you have to sell is time

and talent; a different situation by far than that which exists for the man happily ensconced on someone's payroll.

I know of no solution to this problem save rules—and the rules should be yours, not the other fellow's. Thus, some writers refuse to give out their office addresses, or they have unlisted phone numbers, or they see visitors by appointment only. My own system in recent years has been to hold what amounts to open house—from 5 p.m. on. Before that time, I simply see no one.

What about the friend who takes offense at your thus protecting yourself?

Who says he's your friend, when he won't understand your need for work time? Let him lie where he falls. You can do better.

f. Beware bottles.

Once upon a time there was a fact film producer in Santa Fe, New Mexico, for whom I occasionally did work. I remember him fondly for one particular gimmick he developed for use at client lunches.

Thus, Producer would take us to his favorite place, and the first order of business would be a drink around, with Producer ever beaming and convivial. "The usual for me, Vi." he'd tell the waitress.

So then we'd have a drink or two or three and talk some business, with Producer ever hale and hearty with his "usual"—a screwdriver, we all assumed, since that was certainly what it looked like.

Only after a considerable acquaintance with Producer did I learn the truth: His "usual" was straight orange juice, nothing else.

"Booze is great stuff," he told me, when I finally stumbled on the truth. "I like it fine. But I'm not about to try to talk business with two or three belts of vodka or gin or bourbon in me. Good deals are hard enough to make without that. So, the girls here all know that when I say 'the usual,' I want orange juice."

It's not the worst thought for a writer to bear in mind; for writing, too, is hard enough to handle sans liquor. To work with a bottle on the desk beside you—or even with a couple of beers under your belt—can develop a pattern of conditioning that soon proves a prelude to disaster; and Alcoholics Anonymous has the writer-members to prove it. Drinking is something to do *after* work, not during or before it.

4. The agents, and the Guild.

Writing feature films is a somewhat different kettle of fish than anything we've discussed before. There are two main reasons for this. One is the involvement of agents; the other, the activity of the Writers Guild of America, East and West.

Agents, first.

In that never-never land which Hollywood terms "the industry," writing and selling tend to be two different businesses. The man or woman who does the selling is known as an agent. He markets your scripts and/or services, negotiating prices and contract terms.

For this, he receives 10 percent of your earnings.

It is, for all practical purposes, essential that you have an agent if you wish to sell feature film scripts. Without one, your chances of breaking in are limited indeed.

The reason this is so is that virtually no producer will consider— or even look at—a script submitted by an "unrepresented" writer—that is, a writer without an agent. Scripts mailed in unsolicited are returned unopened.

There are several explanations for this. One, of course, is that most producers are busy people indeed, and the copy of the typical beginner is so unutterably bad as to constitute a total waste of time. Whereas, when a script comes through an agent, that very fact indicates that the product has passed a preliminary screening and so is at least half-way in line with standard practice, format, level of literacy, and the like, as well as having entertainment value.

Secondly, in the view of producers, reading a script submitted by a person unknown to him is an open invitation to a plagiarism suit. Nor is this an idle fear. There actually are cases on record of would-be screenwriters who have had scripts read and rejected later copying down lengthy passages of dialogue from a picture released by the rejecting producer, incorporating it in a new version of the rejected script—and then suing on grounds that the producer had stolen their lines!

This is perhaps as good a spot as any to observe that plagiarism charges in regard to film are almost always groundless. How so? First, because it's easier—and cheaper in the long run—to buy material than to steal it. Second, because similarities between scripts well-nigh invariably are due to what might be termed the coincidence factor, with two writers coming up with the same idea more or less simultaneously.

Thus, I recall one case when I sent a TV producer a treatment for an episode of his show.

Producer returned it in the next mail, together with a copy of a brand-new script which duplicated the story line I'd developed in almost every detail. "I had to send you this," he wrote, "because if I hadn't, you'd have sworn I'd stolen your idea."

Well, he had a point there, of course, because the similarity between the two jobs was absolutely uncanny. Yet the time element was such that plagiarism became a physical impossibility.

After you've had such happen to you three or four times—in both directions—you get so you hesitate to be too quick on the trigger with accusations.

But back to agents. An agent, in California, where the largest part of theatrical film and TV production is centered, is licensed annually by the state, and bonded. He has to maintain an appropriate office, give character references, and have no criminal record.

Beyond this, naturally, there are both good agents and bad agents—and the one who's superlative for your friend may be awful for you, or vice versa.

Since his income comes from his commissions on works or services sold, no agent can afford to be a total altruist. He therefore is unlikely to help you just for love. Promise, to him, is more important—particularly, that type of promise that indicates you may become a big money-maker.

If he thinks you have such potential, an agent can push and promote you in a host of ways, from upping your price to getting you into shops that otherwise might never look at you.

Of course there's a negative side to this, also. Thus, any agent tends to favor his "hot" properties—perhaps to your detriment. Some are more astute than others, too, as quite possibly may be brought home to you when you discover the deals they've signed you to. And each has his own personality, which may or may not jibe with yours.

How do you acquire an agent? The first step is to get a list of such from the Guild: the Writers Guild of America, east, Inc., 22 West 48th St., New York, N.Y. 10036, or the Writers Guild of America, west, Inc., 8955 Beverly Blvd., Los Angeles, Calif. 90048. (Jurisdiction divides at the Mississippi River.)

The Guild is the scriptwriters' union, with approximately 6,500 members in the WGAW and 3,500 in the WGAE. It holds minimum basic agreements with most producers (including broadcasting networks and stations), covering theatrical and television films, live television, documentary film, and news programs.

One of the best things about the Guild, from the newcomer's point of view, is that though it maintains a closed shop, it's an open union. This means that no hurdles are put in your way when it comes to selling your first script. If you can write anything a producer will buy, says the Guild, go to it!

Script No. Two is a different matter. To place it, you have to join the Guild. Requirements are set forth in Appendix E.

In joining, you must agree to abide by the Guild Constitution, By-Laws, and all rules and regulations issued or promulgated by the Guild.

Among these rules—and now we get back to the matter of agents—is one (Working Rule No. 23) that says, "No writer shall enter into a representation agreement, whether oral or written, with any agent who has not entered into an agreement with the Guild covering minimum terms and conditions between agents and their writer clients."

This is why you get the Guild's list as a first step towards finding an agent. No agent not on said list is acceptable to the Guild. And since the Guild exercises a marked degree of control over whether you work or not, choosing a non-signatory agent shoots you down in flames before you start.

Once you have the list, your next step is to persuade one of these agents to agree to handle your work. The simplest way to do this is to get some friend who's a client of a given agent, and who also thinks you might have the markings of a scriptwriter, to recommend you.

Lacking the right friend, you can make your play the hard way: phoning an agent about whom you've heard good things, telling him you're a writer who wants to work in film/TV, and asking if he'll consider representing you. If Agent agrees to talk with you, take yourself and a sample script to see him. (It will help if the script is one about which you're particularly enthusiastic.) With luck, he'll accept you. If he doesn't, try another agent.

Is your fight won, once you make this connection? To the contrary. An agent is a salesman. That means he needs something to sell.

Especially when you're just getting started, you yourself simply haven't enough to offer to ring up any jackpots. You have no name, no established market value, no arm-long list of credits.

That means there's promoting to be done. And you're the one who's going to have to do it.

As a writer, your best stratagem to this end is to write something someone might conceivably want to buy. Indeed, agents have been known to tell beginners that their most direct road to success is to author a best-selling book so that Agent then can peddle screen rights to it.

If your major interest is in the film script form, this offers little encouragement. However, a highly acceptable alternative exists: You can write an original screenplay, in outline, treatment, or master scene form. (A complete master scene screenplay is probably your best bet. So much depends on a script's development in actual dialogue and action that many agents won't even bother to read beginners' outlines or treatments.)

This gives your agent the "something to sell" I mentioned . . . brings your name before producers and demonstrates your skill and talent, if any. Even if no one buys your gem (and odds are strongly that no one will), you quite possibly will arouse interest and perhaps even get offers in relation to other projects.

Further, this is an entirely legitimate approach. For while the Guild's contract specifically forbids speculative writing, it also states that "this does not limit the submission of original stories . . ." Indeed, I know a few writers who, though Guild members and old hands, have no desire to develop properties on payroll. Admittedly mavericks, they prefer to write what they want to write, then turn it over to their agents for placement.

How does this differ from "speculative writing"? In the Guild's sense of the phrase, as mentioned earlier, speculative writing means writing in which a producer in effect says, "You go ahead and work up this idea you've told me about. Then, if I like it, I'll buy it." This the Guild will not allow. If a producer *asks* you to do work for him, or otherwise gives you a go-ahead, he's considered to have hired you and, in consequence, is expected to pay you the going union rate for your services. That is, you are in effect put on salary for the period it takes you to develop your script—though you can be cut off at various points if the producer decides he doesn't like the way your assignment is going.

The table in Appendix E will give you some idea of how much such work brings, and perhaps make it clearer to you why most scriptwriters love their union. Other benefits include a pension fund, a health and a welfare plan, a credit union, assorted awards, a newsletter, a directory, a TV market list, and the like.

There is, of course, a negative side to the Guild's approach. It centers, for my money, on the concept known as corporate authorship. Under it, when you sign on to develop a script for a producer, you lose all control over what you write. He can change it in any way he sees fit, abandon the project at will, or whatever. Once you take his money, your work becomes his, to do with as he wishes.

Most Guildspeople don't like this idea any more than I do. But for the time being, at least, they're stuck with it since producers by and large view the granting of "creative control" to writers in about the same light the Vatican would see turning over direction of church affairs to the Communist Party.

One final point: Theatrical film production is concentrated in the Los Angeles area and, to a markedly lesser degree, in New York City. Since the development of any theatrical film script almost always involves extensive discussion and rewriting, it follows that it is well-nigh impossible to break into the field if you do not live (or are not willing to move to) these areas.

(On the other hand, the times they are a-changin', and regional producers are playing a larger role every year, so don't take the paragraph above as total gospel. By the time you read this you may be able to hit a few jackpots right in your own state.)

*   *   *

So much for the business end of your work as a scriptwriter. But there still are a lot of miscellaneous items and technical details about the film field which you should know.

We'll strike a few of them a glancing blow in the next chapter.

CHAPTER 17

What You Should Know About . . .

Writers have an unfortunate tendency to consider themselves writers only. In the film business—especially in the fact end of it—that's a luxury they can't afford. The more they know about all phases of production, the more likely they are to survive. Indeed, a host of the brethren have carried this to the point of abandoning the exclusively "writer" classification altogether, in favor of the increasingly common tag of "hyphenate"—writer-director, writer-producer, or even writer-producer-director.

There's a sound reason for this switch. In the first place, the hyphenates make more money. But beyond that, screen writers get almighty tired of seeing their scripts butchered. By adding directing and/or producing to their repertoire, they insure themselves greater control over the films they write.

Even if you have no desire to produce or direct, however, it's still worthwhile to learn all you can about production. Why? Because the more you know, the better you can tailor your script to a producer's needs. Particularly, you can to a marked degree help to hold down the budget, simply by limiting the requirements you set up and simplifying the way you handle your material.

A writer with such skills is ever and always in demand. So here we go, with a first lesson in regard to at least a few of the things you should know about . . .

Actors: As every fact film producer soon learns, amateurs generally can carry out actions satisfactorily—especially if said actions are those the actor performs in life, as when a plumber plays the role of a plumber. Often, however, these sterling citizens find it almost impossible to deliver lines well. They're also prone to tire of the whole tedious business of filmmaking as soon as the glamor wears off—whereupon, disastrously, they may quit in the middle of a picture.

How to avoid such? Hold Amateurs' lip-sync dialogue to a minimum; substitute voice-over narration wherever possible.

Regards action, stick as close as possible to the kind of thing found in Amateur's life experience, so that the necessity of retakes—and consequent irritation—is reduced to a minimum.

Professional actors? They tend to be hams, too often—lazy about learning lines; more interested in building their own parts than in fitting into the needs of the production; difficult to work with.

Especially are these things true if Professional is working with an inexperienced or unsure director, or on a job he considers beneath his dignity. Should you perchance be called in to help remedy the situation, try these ploys: (a) flexibility—stand ready to change lines if need be; (b) flattery—do your best to convince the ham that *your* lines show him off to best advantage; (c) lines that play—you find out about this the hard way, by having your harelipped friends read them into a tape recorder . . . then playing them back to see if they really sound like people talking.

Cutting (also known as editing): Film editors are unsung geniuses of the business. The miracles they can perform with inept writing, directing, and acting are absolutely incredible, upon occasion.

You can help your film's editor by providing him (in the script) with plenty of inserts, cutaways, reaction shots, and the like, so he has footage available to cover the errors and ineptitudes that crop up in any picture.

It's to your advantage, in the course of all this, to learn as much as you can about Editor's problems. How do you learn? You study such volumes as Livingston's *Film and The Director,* Mascelli's *The Five C's of Cinematography,* Gaskill and Englander's *How To Shoot a Movie Story,* Bare's *The Film Director,* Reisz and Millar's *The Technique of Film Editing,* Dmytryk's *On Film Editing,* Arijon's *Grammar of the Film Language,* and the like. After which, it doesn't hurt a bit to spend any spare time you can manage hanging around the cutting room, watching the viewer/Moviola as Editor runs his work print back and forth and makes his choices, and listening to any gems of wisdom he may let drop.

Directors: Start with the assumption that the director knows a lot more about the film business than you do. So, learn from him, and don't get your feelings hurt when he hacks up your pet sequence.

On the other hand, if you've worked in a clever handling, Director just may use it. As a matter of fact, your only real headache is to figure out a way to make sure Director actually has *read* the script before he starts changing or shooting it.

As with actors, flattery can be a good gimmick here. Tell the Great

Man you want to learn from him (true enough!) and therefore will beat your brow on the floor before him if only he'll go over the script with you, line by line.

Many of the best directors will want you close by their warm side while they prepare for shooting. It will be a time to test how well you've done your homework, believe me. Action that previously existed only in your script now quite possibly will be diagrammed in relation to actual sets or locations. Weak sequences will fall by the way. Strong will be rearranged. Characters will appear and disappear and take on new depth or coloration; and you'll be asked, "But would Seth *do* that?" until you'll swear your skull will split.

Will the final script that results be better than your original? Maybe; maybe not.

But one thing's for sure: *You* will definitely have learned by it.

Lighting: The bigger the area you ask a crew to light, the more men and equipment and power it's going to take. While there are tricks old pros can use to achieve the impossible, you're really sticking your neck out if you ask them to make a factory interior look like an MGM imperial ballroom. Try, instead, to use your head to come up with something just as striking that makes its points via closeups, or a couple of exteriors followed by a quick dissolve to a modest office.

Locations: For greater realism and in order to avoid the problems inherent in set construction, a high proportion of pictures today are shot "on location"—that is, in a "real" environment, away from the sound stage.

But before you specify location shooting, remember that (a) transportation can prove both costly and a headache, (b) bad weather can bomb you out, cataclysmically, (c) extraneous sound can make anything but silent shooting impossible, and (d) an eight-foot ceiling has proved a disaster for many a lighting crew.

Movement: Two key elements move in any picture: the actors, and the camera. Though control of each is fundamentally the problem of the director, you can add greatly to your popularity if you'll (a) learn the nature of the so-called "imaginary (180°) line" which limits camera movement in the interests of maintaining screen direction; (b) master the simple principles of overlapping movement that help to create an effect of continuity from cut to cut; and (c) make it a habit to *act out yourself* anything you intend to ask the actors to do, so you're sure it's physically possible. Believe me, getting people on and off screen, following action, reversing, dealing with obstacles—all are more complex than you might imagine. But you can take them in stride if you'll study the books mentioned in the section on cutting, above. Even better, augment the books by sneaking onto a set whenever you can, in order to observe the principles in action.

Sets: Building a set is a difficult, expensive, time-consuming business. The more you can work with what's readily available, avoiding elaborate construction, the happier everyone will be. Really, it's amazing what you can accomplish with a couple of flats, a curtain, some molding, and a few pieces of second-hand furniture! And the resources of any studio scene dock can enable you to perform virtual miracles, budgetary and esthetic.

Set-ups: In lighting any interior, four basic types of light are involved: the *key light,* the *back light,* the *fill light,* and the *background lights.* Eventually you'll learn the whys and wherefores of each of these.

The important thing right now, however, is that you understand that every change in lighting takes time and thus costs money. It is no accident that so many old-timers state flatly that the secret of staying within the budget lies in cutting the number of set-ups.

Consequently, if you can plan ways to limit set-ups by means of simplified sets, narrowed range of action, reduced number of locations, "cheater cuts," or the like, producers will love you and you'll get more work.

Sound: It's always quicker, easier, and cheaper to shoot silent. The moment sound comes in, you not only have extra personnel and equipment, but the problems that arise from power lines, inept actors, traffic noise, planes passing overhead, air conditioning machinery, and (if you're outdoors) the whisper of the spring breeze in the microphone.

Does this mean abandoning sound forever, then? No. Even filming under the worst possible circumstances, voices can be dubbed in later, or voice-over narration substituted.

But it does stand to reason that the writer who's conscious of the problems involved may do a more satisfactory job than one who isn't.

Video: Videotaping is a cost-cutter that encourages cost-cutting—and that can be expensive.

This is another way of acknowledging that video offers the filmmaker—and the scriptwriter—fantastic new opportunities. Shot at minimal expense, with limited crew and low-budget staging, it makes it possible for the small operator to mount productions which previously would have involved major money.

Because this is so, producers sometimes are tempted to try to slash expenses even further. Whereupon, the finished product may not only reflect same but, on occasion, turn into pure disaster, as witness a TV museum mini-series I scripted a couple of years ago. To cut costs, the producer eliminated background lighting. In consequence, the foreground subjects lost definition and separation, and the overall effect became one of blurred confusion, client outrage, and cancelled contracts.

*   *   *

If you think this covers all the ground of what a writer should know about filmmaking, or even a fraction of the headaches he'll encounter—don't kid yourself! From beginning to end, this business is a torturous if fascinating nightmare—with the scriptwriter getting the blame whenever anything goes wrong.

The solution? Time, study, experience.

Meanwhile, however, you might like to take advantage of veteran scriptwriters' techniques; learn by studying the way they tackle writing problems.

You'll find it all in the next chapter: Lessons from the Pros.

CHAPTER 18

Lessons from the Pros

There are a lot of ways to do things right.

That's why this chapter includes excerpts from the work of seven different scriptwriters. The idea is to show you not The One True Path, but a variety of styles and techniques and approaches.

Since today's film industry is in a constant state of flux, with emphasis strongly on the "different" slant, the "different" touch, all these case studies are new with this edition, with two exceptions. In those two instances (Charles A. Palmer's *The Gullies* and Jack Turley's *Terror on the Fortieth Floor*), I felt that handling was so uniquely instructive that it would be doing you a disservice to leave them out.

Circled numbers in the margins of the script excerpts/materials that follow refer to the numbered comments that follow each excerpt.

Where each of the five new scripts is concerned, I'll comment on points illustrated as we go along, starting with:

NIGHTMARE ON ELM STREET (original screenplay)
by Wes Craven.

Originally from Cleveland and hooked on film from his teens, Wes Craven gave up college teaching (Freshman Writing, Modern Drama, Survey of Western Civilization) to try for a career in the field of motion pictures in New York. There, within a year and a half, he won the chance to write, direct, and edit a low-budget picture, *Last House on the Left*.

All of which makes it sound easier than it was, of course. Jobs that intervened ranged from grocery stock clerk to apprentice meat cutter, professional guitarist to illustrator to translator for a Lithuanian poet, apprentice cable splicer to nightwatchman to Manhattan cab driver. As a writer, he began with poetry, at 14; did a humorous column (*Craven's*

232

Raven's) for his high school paper; edited (and later was fired from) his college's literary magazine; and wrote (and failed to sell) a mass of fiction before hitting the cinematic jackpot.

The far-out has become his trademark. His credits include such titles as *The Hills Have Eyes, Deadly Blessing,* and *Swamp Thing,* plus a number of two-hour TV movies and some "Twilight Zones." As this is written, he's in Haiti, directing *The Serpent and the Rainbow,* a film based on a book by Harvard ethnobiologist Wade Davis. Craven says it represents a radical departure from his past work; it has an adult theme, looks at voodoo as a real religion, and has "a cast, literally, of thousands."

Nightmare on Elm Street remains special, however. Its success is attested to by the fact that it has generated two sequels and a bulky paperback book.

The film focuses on supernatural horror, a recurring nightmare that comes to life. To make it all the more terrifying, it's played against a totally down-to-earth setting.

Throughout, Craven demonstrates his awareness that the issue in any superior film is feeling, emotion. His ability to devise incidents and pick significant details to communicate the feelings he seeks to rouse in his chosen audience is outstanding, as is the way he manipulates the ebb and flow of tension to the film's nerve-shattering climax.

A NIGHTMARE ON ELM STREET

an
original
filmscript
by

Wes Craven

Registered
WGA 1984

1   Rev. 4/30/84

1A. INT. (MONTAGE).   1A

(1) NIGHTMARE MUSIC THEME begins as we FADE UP on a SERIES OF SHOTS, all CLOSE and teasing.

(2)
  -- A man's FEET, in shabby work shoes, stalking through a junk bin in a dark, fire-lit, ash-dusted place. A huge BOILER ROOM is what it is, although we only glimpse it piecemeal. Then we SEE a MAN'S HAND, dirty and nail-bitten, reach INTO FRAME and pick up a piece of METAL.

(3)
  -- ANOTHER ANGLE as the HAND grabs a grimey WORKGLOVE and slashes at it with a straight razor, until its fingertips are off.

  -- CLOSE ON SAME HANDS dumping four fishing knives out of a filthy bag. Their blades are thin, curved, gleaming sharp.

(4)
  -- MORE ANGLES, EVEN CLOSER. We can HEAR the MAN's wheezing BREATHING, but we still haven't seen his face. We never will. We just SEE more metal being assembled with crude tools, into some sort of linkage -- a splayed, spidery sort of apparatus, against a background light of FIRE, and a deep rushing of STEAM and HEAVY, DARK ENERGY.

  -- And then we see this linkage attached to the glove.

  -- Then the BLADES attached to all of it.

(5)
  -- Then the MAN'S HAND slips into this glove-like apparatus, filling it out and transforming it into an awesome, deadly claw-hand with four razor/talons gleaming at its blackened fingertips. Suddenly the HAND arches and STRIKES FORWARD, SLASHING THROUGH a DARK CANVAS, tearing it to shreds and REVEALING BACKGROUND (OPTICAL) --

1   EXT. LOS ANGELES. NIGHT. (2nd Unit)   1

(6) A PULSATION OF LIGHT AND SHADOW. MUSIC DROPS AWAY to a hushed RUSHING OF WIND and DISTANT SIRENS. CAMERA RACKS INTO FOCUS on a HIGH PANORAMA of the San Fernando Valley, its night sky lit from within by a strange GREENISH LIGHT. TITLES BEGIN.

CAMERA TILTS DOWN and ZOOMS SWIFTLY into the valley's web of light.

         CUT TO:

1A   Rev. 4/30/84

2.   INT. CONCRETE PASSAGEWAY.   2.

(7)   TITLES CONTINUE as TINA GRAY, a strong girl of fifteen in a thin
      night shift, moves towards us down a dark concrete corridor. Her
      steps quicken as TITLES appear in the portion of frame she leaves
      free.

      A subliminal COLLAGE of SOUND threads in and out of the MUSIC.
      Distant insane LAUGHTER. Slamming iron DOORS. A bleating animal
      CRY. A LAMB, white and blank-faced, skitters across her path and
      on into the dark. No reason why it's there.

      Then another SOUND, much nearer -- the slithering SCRAPE of
      something like <u>fingernails</u> across slate. It sets our teeth on
      edge, twists the MUSIC, and sends TINA running.

3.   INT. BOILER ROOM.   3.

      Suddenly TINA's a tiny figure running among huge boilers steam
      pipes and catwalks -- a shadowed forest of iron and stone. She
      stops, listening intently as the SOUND of tiny hooves suddenly
      turns into the rattle of DISTANT RAIN. Long tendrils of saliva
      are catching in TINA'S hair. She stumbles back, clawing the
      stuff off her face. Then she hears RIPPING FABRIC.

      Someone is shouldering behind a ragged screen of dirty canvas,
      approaching TINA.

      CLOSER ON THE CANVAS. The long curved fingerblades suddenly
      punch through, flashing in the firelight, and begin ripping
      through the thick fabric, as easily as scalpels through flesh.
      They make a hideous, extended RIPPING SOUND.

      TINA rushes away, hands over her ears.

      ANOTHER ANGLE -- as the blinded girl stumbles backwards. Then
      the canvas flaps free. The blades are gone. The TITLES END ,and
      everything goes silent.

      CAMERA CIRCLES until TINA'S looking right into our eyes. The
      light from a nearby boiler pours through her thin night dress,
      leaving her naked and vulnerable. Then a deep, ragged VOICE
      whispers at her as CAMERA CLOSES IN ON HER FACE.

                          VOICE (O.S.)
(8)   One two, Freddie's coming for
                   you...

(9)   TINA opens her mouth to scream but only a dry, yellow dust pours
      out. And at that precise moment a huge shadowy MAN with a grimey
      red and yellow sweater and a weird hat pulled over his scarred

2   Revised   5/8/84

3 CONT.   3 CONT.

face lunges at her. And it's <u>his</u> fingers that are tipped with
the long blades of steel, glinting in the boney light and giving
the hulk the look of an otherworldly predator.

TINA dodges away, her legs suddenly elephantine and slow. The
MAN seizes the trailing hem of her nightgown and hauls her back.

The MUSIC shrieks as TINA manages to tear free -- the MAN lurches
after her with a hoarse SHOUT as we --

                                      SMASH CUT TO:

4.   INT. TINA'S BEDROOM. NIGHT.   4.

⑩   TINA convulses in bed with a SCREAM, looking around wildly.
     Someone is KNOCKING on her door.

                         WOMAN'S VOICE (O.S.)
                 You okay, Tina?

TINA'S MOTHER sticks her head in with a worried look. TINA sits
up and blows out a breath, groggy.

                              TINA
                 Just a dream, Ma...
                         (more to herself)
                 Damn dream, is all...

The woman, once attractive, ventures a step into the room. A MAN
hovers BACKGROUND. TINA's mother waves him away without looking,
shoving a strand of bleached hair from her eyes. She appraises
her daughter.

                         TINA'S MOTHER
                 Some dream, judging from that.

She nods at TINA's nightshift.

⑪   TINA looks down at her nightgown, only now aware of the chill

                                                         CONT.

3   Rev. 4/30/84

penetrating it from the room. There are four long slashes up its
middle, cleanly cut as if by scalpels.

                              MAN (OS)
                         (distant, annoyed)
                    You coming back to the sack or
                    what?

                              TINA'S MOTHER
                    Hold your horses.
                              (lower, to Tina as she
                              stands to leave)
                    You gotta cut your nails or stop
                    that kind of dreaming, Tina. One
                    or the other.

The woman shuts the door behind her. TINA looks back to her
nightgown.

                              TINA
                         (low)
                    Oh, shit.

⑫ She suddenly snatches up the cross that hangs over her bed, her
    face white as her sheet.

                                        FADE TO BLACK

                                        BURN ON   5.
5.

                         THE FIRST DAY

                              CHILDREN (OS)
                         (singing)
⑬   One two, Freddie's coming for you...
                    Three four better lock your door
                    Five six grab your crucifix...

6. EXT. HIGH SCHOOL. DAY.   6.

⑭   FADE UP ON SHOT OF this large highschool and its crowds of
    STUDENTS. FOREGROUND, TINA climbs out of a cherry-red 1959
⑮   Cadillac convertible with two other students, best friend NANCY
    WILSON, and Nancy's boyfriend and owner of the car, GLEN LANTZ.

    FOREGROUND several GRADESCHOOLERS are playing jump-rope, and the
    old ditty they sing continues unbroken from TINA's bedroom.

                              ROPE JUMPERS
⑯   Seven eight, gonna stay up late!
                    Nine ten -- never sleep again!

7. MOVING ANGLE FAVORING NANCY. She's a pretty girl in a letter 7.
    sweater, with an easy, athletic stride and the look of a natural
    leader. GLEN, holding her hand, wears one of the school's

                                                            CONT.

86

Next moment the young man's body is dragged straight down into the bed, as if some huge beast had grabbed him and heaved him down! His feet and his arms shoot up -- there's another hauling jank -- and the boy disappears except for his hands and fingers -- down into the pit in the middle of the bed! His hands are last to go, clawing for a hold. But soon they vanish as well, dragging blankets and bedsheets, wires and stereo across the caved-in bed and into the abyss.

There's HIDEOUS SCREECHING of MUSIC jamming in with GLEN's ECHOING SCREAMS -- then an unholy, sudden silence.

Next moment what's left of GLEN is vomited up from the pit of the nightmare bed...a horrible mess of blood and bone and hair and wires...streaming out and over the bed. Then the pit in the bed is gone as if it were never there.

Drawn by the terrible screams and struggle, GLEN's mother bursts into the room. The woman stares for one moment of horrified disbelief, then reels back and lets out the most god-awful SCREAM imaginable. The cry splits the night.

W

165 EXT. ELM STREET. NIGHT.

The SOUND of the SCREAM CROSS-FADES WITH the WAIL of the AMBULANCE as it screeches to a halt at the curb, followed by two BLACK AND WHITES and an UNMARKED CAR. Uniformed POLICEMEN spill out FOREGROUND.

LT THOMPSON and PARKER exit the unmarked car. By habit or by premonition THOMPSON glances at the house that was his home. His eye is caught by a movement; his daughter is at her upstairs window, white-haired, hollow-eyed, looking down on him through her bars. She gives a little wave.

Unnerved, THOMPSON waves back, then walks rapidly for GLEN's home. MR LANTZ, pale as a ghost himself, waits on the porch; we can hear the mother's WAILING inside.

INT. NANCY'S ROOM. NIGHT.

CLOSE ON NANCY'S BIG OLD WINDUP ALARM CLOCK. Its big and little hands sweep together at midnight.

                                        BURN ON:

                            THE NINTH DAY

There's a BABBLE of POLICE RADIOS, SIRENS WINDING DOWN, RUNNING FOOT-STEPS, SHOUTS, NEIGHBORHOOD KIDS and DOGS BARKING as CAMERA LIFTS TO NANCY'S FACE. Set. Unafraid. Ruthless.

The girl pulls the window shade on it all, then looks at her *watch*.

87

Rev. 4/30/84

166 CONT   166 CONT

> NANCY
> Okay, Krueger, you bastard.
> We play in your court.

167.   INT.   GLEN'S LIVING ROOM/NANCY'S KITCHEN -- INTERCUT. NIGHT.   167.

168.   LT THOMPSON is halfway across the living room when he stops.   168.
        Something dark and red is welling from a crack in the ceiling.
        One of his men is rigging a bucket beneath to catch the leaking.
        The telephone rings and PARKER picks it up.

> PARKER
> Lieutenant. It's your daughter.
> Says it's urgent.

THOMPSON turns away from the dripping.

> LT THOMPSON
>   (low)
> Tell her I'm not here, tell
> her ...

> PARKER
> Uh, she just saw you, sir...

THOMPSON nods, crosses and picks up the telephone. SCREEN
SPLITS; we see both.

> LT THOMPSON (CONTD)
> Hello NANCY.

> NANCY
> Hi daddy. I know what happened.

> LT THOMPSON
> Then you know more than I do --
> I haven't even been upstairs.

> NANCY
>   (guessing)
> You know he's dead though, right?

THOMPSON debates, then admits it.

> LT THOMPSON
> Yeah, apparently he's dead.
> How the hell'd you know?

A tear coarses down NANCY's cheek, but her voice remains firm.

> NANCY
> I've got a proposition for
> you. Listen very carefully,
> please.

CONT.

88   Rev. 4/30/84

168 CONT   LT THOMPSON   168 CONT
                  Nan, I --

                            NANCY
                  Please. I'm gonna go get
                  the guy who did it and bring
                  him to you. I just need you
                  be right there to arrest him.
                  Okay?

                            LT THOMPSON
                  Just tell me who did it and
                  I'll go get him, baby.

                            NANCY
                  Fred Krueger did it, Daddy,
                  and only I can get him. It's
                  my nightmare he comes to.

          The detective flinches at the name.

                            LT THOMPSON
                  Where'd you hear about Krueger --

          NANCY presses, very firm, very rational.

                            NANCY
    (18)   -- I want you to come over here
                  and break the door down exactly
                  twenty minutes from now -- can
                  you do that?

                            LT THOMPSON
                  Sure, but...

                            NANCY
                  That'll be exactly half past
                  midnight. Time for me to fall
                  asleep and find him.

                            LT THOMPSON
                  Sure, sure, honey. You just
                  do that -- get yourself some
                  sleep -- that's what I saying
                  all along.

                            NANCY
                  And you'll be here to catch
                  him, right?

                            PARKER
                  Lieutenant -- they're waiting
                  upstairs.

          THOMPSON waves curtly, still speaking to NANCY.

                                                    CONT.

89

Rev. 4/30/84

168 CONT.   168 CONT

                               LT THOMPSON
                   Sure, okay, I'll be there.
                   Now you just turn in and get
                   some rest, sweetheart. Please.
                   Deal?

                                NANCY
           Deal.

NANCY hangs up. LT MARKS starts upstairs. But then he stops,
and as an afterthought he could never really explain, turns to
PARKER.

                                LT THOMPSON (CONTD)
                   Get outside and watch her house.
                   If you see anything funny call
                   me.

                                PARKER
                   'Anything funny' like what?

THOMPSON shakes his head, embarassed.

                                LT THOMPSON
                   I don't know -- but one thing
                   for sure, I don't want her
                   coming over here. She's way
                   too far gone to be able to
                   to handle this.

(19) As PARKER exits, ANGLE CUTS TO NANCY'S KITCHEN as the girl hangs
up and sinks back against the wall, trapped by her own
resolution. She looks at her watch.

169.   INSERT -- five past midnight. NANCY switches modes to stopwatch 169.
and sets the COUNTDOWN going at twenty-five minutes.

170.   INT. GLEN'S BEDROOM. NIGHT.   170.

LT THOMPSON steps into GLEN's room, anxious to be done with it.
He hits a wall of stench and horror even before he takes it in
with his eyes, and as soon as he sees the bed he claps his hand
over his mouth, pivots and walks right back into the hallway.

171.   INT. HALLWAY. NIGHT.   171.

He sags against the wall, unable to look at the COPS who hover
there.

                                COP
                         (faint)
                   What the hell did that,
                   Lieutenant? There ain't even
                   a head left.

                                      CONT

171. CONT.

                            LT THOMPSON   171 CONT.
                    Goddamed if I know.
                            (tries to straighten)
                    What's the Coronor say?

                            COP
                    He's in the john puking since
                    he saw it.

172.   INT. CELLAR. NIGHT.   172.

(20)   NANCY pulls tools and hardware out with grim resolution. Hammer,
        nails, spools of wire, an old square of heavy fishneting, some
        old shot gun shells, a file -- referring only once to the booklet
        in her hand.

173.   INT. NANCY'S LIVING ROOM. NIGHT.   173.

(21)   Barely able to control her shaking hands, NANCY starts stringing
        off the spool of wire across the living room, crying and swearing
        at the same time.

        DISSOLVE TO HER HANDS wrapping bare lamp wire around two
        thumbtacks stuck into the insides of the pinchers of a common
        wooden clothespin. The wire goes OFF SCREEN.

        ANOTHER ANGLE as she inserts a Lifesaver between the two prongs.
        One end of the fishline is tied to the lifesaver. The whole now
        is stretched taut about three inches off the living room carpet.

        ON NANCY carefully filing a hole in a LIGHTBULB.

        ON HER pouring powder and shot from shotgun shells into the
        opening in the bulb until it's full, then sealing it with tape.

        DISSOLVE TO HER screwing the bulb back into the floor lamp, and
        placing the thing near the foot of the stairs.

        SC 174 (DELETE)

175.   INT. NANCY'S UPSTAIRS HALLWAY. NIGHT.   175.

        -- NANCY completes installing a sturdy sliding bolt to the
        outside of her own bedroom door.

        -- NANCY screws a hinge into the wall directly above her door.
        Attached to the hinge is the shank of something -- some kind of
        tool. We can't see what it is because CAMERA never quite frames
        the whole thing.

        -- NANCY tiptoes to her mother's door and peeks in.

91   Rev. 5/6/04

176.   INT. MARGE'S BEDROOM/N   176.

MARGE lies propped in her bed looking back at NANCY. Her
drunkeness has been altered by the SIRENS and BABBLE outside into
a sort of comatose clarity.

                              MARGE
                    Guess I should'n'a done it.

                              NANCY
                    Just sleep now, Mom.

                              MARGE
                    Just wanted to protect you,
                    Nan. Just wanted to protect
                    you...

MARGE slides over on her side. NANCY smooths her hair, covers
her as she would a child, then exits the room

DELETE SC 177

INT. NANCY'S ROOM. NIGHT.

The girl enters, turns out her bedside light, slips out of her
dress and puts on her nightgown. Then she kneels by her bed.

                                             CONT.

92   Rev. 4/30/84

178. CONT.   NANCY (quietly)   178CONT
                   Now I lay me down to sleep,
                   I pray the Lord my soul to keep.
                   If I should die before I wake,
                   I pray the Lord my soul to take.

     She gets into bed and pulls the blankets to her chin.

(24) CLOSE ON NANCY's face. She stares straight up at the ceiling for
      a long moment, then closes her eyes.

                                        CUT TO:

179.   INT. GLEN'S LIVING ROOM. NIGHT.   179.

     LT THOMPSON trudges down the stairs and confronts GLEN'S FATHER.

                              LT THOMPSON
                   I know it's hard to think at
                   a time like this, Walter, but
                   can you think of anyone who
                   could've done such a thing?

     The father stares away, his voice low and dull.

                              MR LANTZ
                   He done it.

     THOMPSON looks at the man, baffled.

                              LT THOMPSON
                   Who? Who did that?

                              MR LANTZ
                   Krueger.

                              LT THOMPSON
                   Krueger?

     The father gives him the strangest look.

                              MR LANTZ
                   Had to've done it. No one
                   else was in there.

                              LT THOMPSON
                   How you know that?

                              MR LANTZ
                   Cause I thought Glen was
                   gonna sneak out to see your
                   lunatic daughter, that's why.
                   So I locked him in his room!
                        (getting control)
                   Sorry. Anyways, the door was

                                        CONT.

104   Rev. 5/8/84

                You're nothing. You're
                shit.

And then she turns her back on him.. KRUEGER bunches his
fingers, producing a single ragged bundle of razor talons and
raises his hand over the back of her head and neck.

NANCY closes her eyes and steps to the door.

CLOSE ON HER HAND, touching the door knob.

CLOSE ON KRUEGER'S KNIFE-FINGERS poised.

MUSIC BUILDS then SHRIEKS as KRUEGER stabs down, right through
NANCY -- as if she were an optical illusion -- loosing his
balance and falling down, down, down... And he's gone.

                              CUT TO:

EXT. ELM STREET. DAY.

(25) CLOSE ON NANCY'S FRONT DOOR AS NANCY jerks it open and blinks in
the bright, diffused light. The MUSIC FADES on a transitional
note, into light.

We hear BIRDS.

CHILDREN playing.

Early morning SOUNDS.

                        NANCY
                     (to herself)
                God, it's bright.

MARGE sticks her head out, squinting, and nods. Sober.

                        MARGE
                Gonna burn off soon or it
                wouldn't be so bright.

NANCY turns and looks her mother over.

                        NANCY
                Feeling better?

                        MARGE
                They say you've bottomed out
                when you can't remember the
                night before.
                     (shakes her head)
                No more drinking, Baby, suddenly
                I just don't feel like it
                any more.

105   Rev. 5/8/84

She touches NANCY.

                    MARGE (CONTD)
          Didn't keep you up last night,
          did I? You look a little
          peeked.

NANCY smiles.

                    NANCY
          Nah. Just slept heavy.

The girl gives a wave and goes off. MARGE calls after.

                    MARGE
          See ya.

NANCY turns and waves.

                    NANCY
          See ya.

(26) WIDER ON NANCY as she walks to the curb. The whole scene is
     wrapped in an unseasonal tule fog, bright yet diffuse. We notice
     that NANCY's house no longer has bars on its windows. Then we
     see a familiar convertible pull up at the curb, top down. TINA
     and ROD are in the back seat. They all wave to MARGE as NANCY
     climbs in.

                    GLEN
                  (calling)
          You believe this fog?

                    MARGE
                  (laughs)
          I believe anything's possible.

TINA slaps five with NANCY.

                    TINA
          Lookin' good, girl!

(27) ANGLE INSIDE THE CONVERTIBLE. GLEN slips into the seat next to
     NANCY. Someone else is driving, it seems. NANCY looks up to the
     DRIVER. The big MAN turns and grins at NANCY, a terrible,
     scarred, hideous leer of a grin -- FRED KRUEGER'S grin!

(28) ANGLE BACK OUTSIDE THE CONVERTIBLE as its top clamps over the
     kids within -- a bright red and yellow top that closes as fast
     and hard as a beartrap! NANCY'S frightened face flies to the
     window, pressing against the thick glass as the car roars away
     from the curb and into the thick fog.

(29) CAMERA PANS TO a group of LITTLE GIRLS, half-hidden by the fog,
     jumping rope and singing gayly.

106   Rev. 5/8/84

                         GIRLS
              One two --
              Freddie's coming for you!
              Three four --
              Better lock your door!
              Five six --
              Get your Crucifix
              Seven eight --
              Gonna stay up late!
              Nine ten --
              Never sleep again!

MUSIC CROSSFADES WITH THIS SONG, expanding the simple tune to
symphonic, boundless dimensions as the little girls fade into
thin air, and we

                    FADE TO BLACK

              ROLL END TITLES.

The numbered paragraphs that follow refer to the marginal numbers in the script excerpts.

1. Actions speak louder than words, a point well demonstrated in this montage. The pictures tell the story. Further, they're pictures chosen to capture emotion . . . establish a menace-pulsing mood, with music to help create and build the feeling.

2. Note how Craven heightens tension through his selection, arrangement, and description of shots. We don't see the man . . . merely his feet, stalking through a fragmented and hence sinister place. Then, we see his hand—a "dirty and nail-bitten" hand as it performs a simple act . . . unexplained but, we assume, foreshadowing something fearsome.

3. Still no explanation, but the razor and the slashing project further menace.

4. More mysterious action, with tension heightened by the faceless man's breathing, the steam sounds, the background firelight.

5. Climax of the buildup: We see the pattern, the purpose, behind the earlier shots. A horrifying weapon has been created; its potential for destruction revealed.

6. Title background. Setting's established . . . then menace.

7. We meet a victim-to-be, Tina . . . move into footage designed to establish that this is a nightmare . . . *her* nightmare, the nightmare from which the film takes its title.

   Why start with Tina, rather than our heroine, Nancy? Because her doom foreshadows Nancy's potential fate; gives viewers something to fear will happen.

   "The device of killing Tina was quite premeditated," Craven observes. "Investing the audience's confidence in the apparently stronger of the two girls, I then destroyed that confidence along with Tina. It left the audience to identify with what it could only assume upon initial evidence was the weaker woman. I like that psychic situation— the discovery of greater strength out of what first appears to be greater weakness."

8. At last, a voice . . . introducing us to the doggerel chant that's to constitute our theme.

9. Our villain—a "shadowy" figure, in keeping with the dream atmosphere, but tagged with "red and yellow sweater," "weird hat," and "scarred face" for easy identification later.

*   *   *

Note how this opening has clearly set up genre, mood, and color, yet has done so with minimum footage and without dialogue.

*   *   *

10. Reality at last. The opening's all just a dream.

11. Well, maybe.

12. The cross brings the intensity of Tina's fear into focus.

13. Our running theme: the jump-rope song, foreshadowing the horror to come.

14. Which reality shall Tina—and we—believe? Craven has set up a contradiction that's a cinch to lock in any horror film audience for the duration of the picture.

15. Enter our heroine, Nancy . . . introduced visually, sans a lot of verbal exposition.

16. Our theme and threat spelled out: . . . *never sleep again . . .*

*   *   *

17. The long jump from *Nightmare*'s page 3 to page 86 sees Craven develop his characters as warmly human young people—individuals we can understand and believe in. Also, there's a lowering of immediate tension from time to time, plus the introduction of more information on the menace.

    These are important issues in the building of any picture. Stick-figure story people just aren't good enough. Viewers need to see characters in such circumstances that they can come to care about them, worry as to what's going to happen to them.

    They need periodic relief from high-voltage tension, too. If they don't get it, sheer nervous strain may take over and lead them to burst out laughing at the most suspenseful moments.

    So it goes with *Nightmare:* an alternation of peaks and valleys that builds tension higher and higher by the very fact that periodic relief *is* provided.

    Then, at last, page 86, the pinnacle of a particularly harrowing scene, and heroine's reaction to the horror. And that, too, is important, for it's not enough for a heroine, jeopardized, to palpitate in panic. Your audience wants to see her rise to meet the challenge.

    Here, Craven lets Nancy realize that she's on her own; that she's going to have to fight her own battle if she's to survive. And since that's the case, he gives her intelligence, nerve, a plan of action . . . then has her *do*, not just talk; counterpunch as well as quiver.

18. Focus on audience psychology . . . the teenage conviction that adults don't really pay attention to them or take them seriously. In line with this attitude, viewers take it for granted that Lt. Thompson will give no serious heed to Nancy's pleas. Thus the scene extends time and the anticipation/fear of what's to come, and tension builds even higher.

19. Setting the stopwatch is Step 1 in Nancy's plan of attack. It's specific action, and everyone can understand it. But we don't know *what* she plans to do, what Step 2 is to be, so we're glued to the screen, panting to find out.

20. We still don't know what's ahead. But clearly, something is, so we'll keep watching.

21. More unexplained action to intrigue us. It all adds up to some kind of booby-trap designed to trap Fred Krueger. But how?

22. Craven inserts a brief scene designed to isolate Nancy further. Clearly, her mother has no potential for helping her.

23. A young girl, challenging the powers of darkness with her own courage and a child's prayer. It builds on every level.

    Craven says: "This scene completes one of the more subtle but powerful transformations in Nancy's character—the total reversal of roles between her and her parents in a time of utter crisis. I believe this is one of the most profound passages in life— one we all must some day do. Nancy, as Everyman, does it at the beginning of her third act, much as we all do personally within the 'movie' of our own life. In the next scene, with her child's prayer, she includes her most precious, creative self—the child. Then she takes action as the full adult—child, parent and Present Self unified in one powerful whole—utterly awake, terrified by this unvarnished awareness, but in possession of will—and acting in free autonomy to survive and prevail."

24. The truth dawns on us. Despite all peril, Nancy is going to play bait for Krueger by letting herself go to sleep.

*　　　　　*　　　　　*

25. From page 92 to page 104 Craven builds through scene after scene of violent, blood-chilling action, pulsing with horror as Nancy meets and defeats her unearthly foe—a brilliant example of how a skilled craftsman manipulates time and circumstance to create a climax.

    Then, at last, on page 104, resolution—we think. The end of nightmare and tension, dissolving into day's release and light, birds singing, children at play.

26. Full circle back to reality. The menace faded to memory, the dead risen. Only the strange fog strikes a discordant note . . . hints that not everything is quite as it seems.

27. And then—Fred Krueger. Total switch, total reversal, total shock.

28. The slam of the car-top, the snap of the trap. The final twist, to bring adrenalin surging.

29. We FADE OUT on a reiterated note, our jump-song/horror theme.

*   *   *

There's more to *Nightmare on Elm Street,* of course. A lot more. But by now the pattern should be clear. From beginning to end, Craven works with threat, menace . . . the fear that something will or won't happen. At no point does he allow his audience to truly relax or get off the hook.

Further, ending as he does, we conclude with a blaze of new peril; and, in so doing, leave viewers something to shiver over and talk about after the show. It's an open ending, the kind designed to bring audiences back to the theater for yet another round.

Was Craven's approach successful? *Nightmare's* box-office jackpot and the fact that more than two sequels already have followed tell the story.

SECRETS OF THE TITANIC (original film-on-tape script),
by Nicolas Noxon.

On the night of April 14-15, 1912, the "unsinkable" British liner
Titanic, largest ship afloat, struck an iceberg on her maiden voyage and
went down with a loss of more than 1,500 lives. It was the greatest
maritime disaster of all time.

Seventy-three years later, in the North Atlantic 350 miles southeast
of Newfoundland, a deep-sea expedition sponsored jointly by the Woods
Hole Oceanographic Institution and the U.S. Navy reached and explored
the sunken *Titanic,* 2½ miles down.

The National Geographic Society felt that a film should be made
to bring the full impact of his well-nigh incredible feat to the public.
Preparation of the film's script was assigned to Nicolas Noxon. He was
also named the producer.

London born, Canadian reared, U.S. educated and a citizen here
since the 1950s, Noxon was a natural selection. Enamored of film from
childhood, at Antioch College he majored in "what in those days was
called Mass Communications. That meant drama and theater arts and
sociology." His first student film was a pantomime of about 15 minutes
called *Masquerade.*

Preferring "true" stories to fictional ones from the beginning, his
first major post-college film was *Time of Migration,* a documentary about
a herring "run" in New England. Since then, films produced and/or
written by him have won virtually every award in American television,
as well as prizes at many film festivals. His work for The National Geographic Society includes writing and producing *The Sharks,* the highest
rated program of any type ever broadcast on PBS. Other Noxon productions have been in association with David L. Wolper, Columbia Pictures, MGM, and *Sports Illustrated.*

Today, after 25 years in film, Noxon sees himself as equally writer
and producer; to a lesser degree, as a director. His work in *Secrets* is
particularly notable as an example of his outstanding ability to find the
tension and drama in factual and technical material. Here, history comes
alive in his script as he captures, builds, and communicates the interest
and excitement that went with the location and exploration of the *Titanic.*

The pages shown here are from his final script.

THE TITANIC PRODUCTION
For National Geographic Television ①

DATE: December 8, 1986

PRODUCTION: "SECRETS OF THE TITANIC"

WRITTEN BY: Nicolas Noxon

AS AIRED SCRIPT - FINAL

PAGE: 1

VIDEO	AUDIO
②	NARRATOR ③
Establishing shot - Belfast	It began here in Ireland - at the Harland & Wolff shipyard in Belfast.
Construction seq.	Three thousand men would labor here for more than two years. They were building a monster - the largest ship the world had ever seen.
	In the spring of 1909, a mountain of steel began to rise against the sky.
Construction seq./ "scale" shots	The ship would weigh sixty-six thousand tons; Her hull would span four city blocks. Each of her colossal steam engines was the size of a three story house.

THE TITANIC PRODUCTION
For National Geographic Television

DATE: December 8, 1986

PRODUCTION: "SECRETS OF THE TITANIC"

WRITTEN BY: Nicolas Noxon

AS AIRED SCRIPT - FINAL

PAGE: 2

VIDEO	AUDIO
	NARRATOR
Anchor on wagon	The huge scale of these things was a source of delight. It was a scene out of Gulliver's Travels when twenty draft horses were needed to haul the ship's anchor through the streets of Belfast.
Men and anchor	Some few observers found this giant threatening and wrote of her "nightmare scale." But their forebodings fell short of the event. For the fate of this ship still
Pan to name – "TITANIC"	fascinates the world, and her name is a synonym for tragedy.

—— MAIN TITLES ——

SECRETS OF
THE TITANIC

PRODUCED BY
THE
NATIONAL GEOGRAPHIC SOCIETY

WRITTEN & PRODUCED
BY
NICOLAS NOXON

NARRATED BY
MARTIN SHEEN

THE TITANIC PRODUCTION
For National Geographic Television

DATE: December 8, 1986

PRODUCTION: "SECRETS OF THE TITANIC"

WRITTEN BY: Nicolas Noxon

AS AIRED SCRIPT - FINAL

PAGE: 11

VIDEO	AUDIO
	NARRATOR
Autograph seekers	There are only about 24 known survivors alive today, but the number of people interested in Titanic is growing.
Titanic fans check in and check out memorabilia.	And this fascination reached a fever pitch when the wreck of Titanic was found.
Establish "A - II"	July 13th, 1986, the first attempt to reach Titanic by submarine is planned for this morning.
Ballard & crew get into Alvin	Bob Ballard and two companions will ride to the bottom in the research submarine, Alvin.
	④ In his enthusiasm, Bob Ballard has perhaps made things seem too easy. This morning, he has many promises to keep.

THE TITANIC PRODUCTION
For National Geographic Television

DATE: <u>December 8, 1986</u>

PRODUCTION: <u>"SECRETS OF THE TITANIC"</u>

WRITTEN BY: <u>Nicolas Noxon</u>

<u>AS AIRED SCRIPT - FINAL</u>   PAGE: <u>23</u>

VIDEO	AUDIO
⑤ Inside submarine	<u>NARRATOR</u> ⑥ The crew compartment of Alvin is a sealed seven foot titanium sphere, jammed with equipment and three uncomfortable humans.
Alvin in water	Alvin is a tried and trusted design. It has mapped undersea mountains, located a lost H-bomb and now is poised over the most celebrated shipwreck of modern times.
Alvin launch	Once launched, Alvin is independent of its mother ship. The crew can communicate with the surface, but in the deep they are so far from help they might as well be on the moon.

THE TITANIC PRODUCTION
For National Geographic Television

DATE: December 8, 1986

PRODUCTION: "SECRETS OF THE TITANIC"

WRITTEN BY: Nicolas Noxon

AS AIRED SCRIPT - FINAL

PAGE: 24

VIDEO	AUDIO
	NARRATOR
CU as Alvin sinks into water	To conserve electrical power, Alvin will fall to the ocean bottom only as fast as gravity allows. The slow plunge will take two and a half hours...a time of tedium and growing suspense.
	(Top lab - Alvin checks in and gets directions)
	A-II: Alvin, this is A-II, over.
	⑦ Alvin: Roger, Ralph. We have the tracking running well. The bow section should be in range at about 800 meters; bearing 230 degrees, over.
More waiting	⑧ Ballard reports that Alvin's batteries are leaking and its sonar system has failed. He must rely on imprecise directions from above. And he cannot stay down much longer.

THE TITANIC PRODUCTION
For National Geographic Television

DATE: December 8, 1986

PRODUCTION: "SECRETS OF THE TITANIC"

WRITTEN BY: Nicolas Noxon

AS AIRED SCRIPT - FINAL

PAGE: 25

VIDEO	AUDIO
	⑨ <u>SYNC/V.O.</u> Topside Control Room: Alvin, this is A-II. Acording to tracking, you just drove over the forward section. Suggest you come to course: 2 - 8 - 0 and travel for 2 - 3 hundred meters, over. I can't believe they can only see 20 - 30 feet. Ballard Alvin Sub: Atlantis II, Atlantis II...this is the Alvin. We are at the Titanic, over. Topside Control Room: Roger, Alvin, we understand you have found the Titanic, over. Alvin: Roger, we're sitting at the base, appears to be near the tear in the stern, but a misconception. We're deciding what to do next, and we're running low on power.
Alvin recovered	⑩ No sooner is Titanic found then the dive must be abandoned. It takes another two and half hours for Ballard to regain the surface.

THE TITANIC PRODUCTION
For National Geographic Television

DATE: December 8, 1986

PRODUCTION: "SECRETS OF THE TITANIC"

WRITTEN BY: Nicolas Noxon

AS AIRED SCRIPT - FINAL

PAGE: 26

VIDEO	AUDIO
	SYNC
	Ballard: We've got bad problems with the submarine. So, we had to abort the dive and immediately head up. So I saw it for 10 seconds and that was it. So, we'll have to go back and do it tomorrow. Interviewer: What hapens next? Ballard: Well, they're going to be up all night, they've got a sick puppy - and they've got to fix it. And it's going to take them all night.
Another launch	Alvin is quickly repaired, but the mood next morning is uncertain. Everyone has been reminded that technical problems, bad weather or a combination of both could terminate the expedition.
Sea botom/POV	This time, everything goes according to plan.

THE TITANIC PRODUCTION
For National Geographic Television

DATE: December 8, 1986

PRODUCTION: "SECRETS OF THE TITANIC"

WRITTEN BY: Nicolas Noxon

AS AIRED SCRIPT - FINAL

PAGE: 39

VIDEO	AUDIO
	NARRATOR
(12) Pan of wreck model	Most strikingly -- the wreck lies in two major sections, eighteen hundred feet apart. This supports some eye-witnesses who said the ship broke in two as it went down.
Move through debris ∧field	Between the two sections of the wreck lies a vast field of debris. And scattered throughout the wreckage are many commonplace objects.
Various objects	A bottle of champagne still corked...and a cup sitting on a 57 ton boiler, where it gently came to rest seventy-four years ago.
	Ballard brought nothing up from Titanic and had vowed not to interfere with the wreck. But that was before Alvin came upon the assistant purser's safe.

THE TITANIC PRODUCTION
For National Geographic Television

DATE: December 8, 1986

PRODUCTION: "SECRETS OF THE TITANIC"

WRITTEN BY: Nicolas Noxon

AS AIRED SCRIPT - FINAL   PAGE: 40

VIDEO	AUDIO
	NARRATOR
Mechanical arm turns the safe handle	The handle turns, but the door won't open. At any rate, experts say it was emptied by the crew before Titanic went down.
⑬ at ∧ Painting of Titanic night	As the wreck is explored, the Titanic story is re-lived and, in some cases, revised to suit new evidence.
Dissolve to crows nest on wreck	It's 11:40 p.m. April 14, 1912.
Fleet CU	From the crows nest an iceberg is spotted dead ahead by lookout Fredrick Fleet. Fleet immediately rings an alarm bell and calls the bridge -- where the First Officer,
Murdock CU	William Murdock, orders the wheel hard-a-starboard and the engines full astern.

THE TITANIC PRODUCTION
For National Geographic Television

DATE: December 8, 1986

PRODUCTION: "SECRETS OF THE TITANIC"

WRITTEN BY: Nicolas Noxon

AS AIRED SCRIPT - FINAL

PAGE: 41

VIDEO	AUDIO
	NARRATOR
Pan wheel	Titanic grazes the ice – posibly causing only a few crumpled hull plates – but enough to tell Captain
⑭ Smith CU	Edward Smith that his ship is doomed.
Radio room on wreck	Captain Smith personally walks back from the bridge to the radio room where, soon after midnight, the first distress call is sent.
Radio room signal	Radio is in its infancy and the newly adopted signal "SOS" is a novelty to operator Jack Phillips.
Gymnasium entrance on the wreck	Orders are given that women and children must board lifeboats. Near the boats, some first class passengers gather here in the gymnasium.

For National Geographic Television

DATE: December 8, 1986

PRODUCTION: "SECRETS OF THE TITANIC"

WRITTEN BY: Nicolas Noxon

AS AIRED SCRIPT - FINAL   ⑮   PAGE: 45

VIDEO	AUDIO
	NARRATOR
Window on wreck	In a single first class cabin, there was a wealthy woman travelling alone. She was a tough and earthy character requiring no assistance.
CU Molly Brown	She boarded a lifeboat, boldly took over command and was known from then on as "the unsinkable Molly Brown."
Painting – ship going	And now, at last, fifteen hundred people began to realize that soon they were going to die.
.Move in on band	But, on the boat deck, near the entrance to the grand staircase, the band played on.

THE TITANIC PRODUCTION
For National Geographic Television

DATE: <u>December 8, 1986</u>

PRODUCTION: <u>"SECRETS OF THE TITANIC"</u>

WRITTEN BY: <u>Nicolas Noxon</u>

AS AIRED SCRIPT - FINAL

PAGE: <u>46</u>

VIDEO	AUDIO
	<u>NARRATOR</u>
Still of the band	No one could agree later what tunes were played. And all the musicians drowned. But Titanic's band and its
Still of Hartley	leader, Wallace Hartley, became immortal heroes of this disaster on the sea.
Hartley Statue	
Still of E.J. Smith	Few honored Captain Smith who had ignored many warnings as he sailed boldly into history. He went down with his ship, his last words disputed.
Pull back from Smith	Some said he told the crew, "Be British," others "...it's every man for himself."

THE TITANIC PRODUCTION
For National Geographic Television

DATE: December 8, 1986

PRODUCTION: "SECRETS OF THE TITANIC"

WRITTEN BY: Nicolas Noxon

AS AIRED SCRIPT - FINAL

PAGE: 47

VIDEO	AUDIO
⑰ CU of plaque	NARRATOR ⑯ When the Titanic expedition ended, Bob Ballard left behind a plaque honoring those who died here. Titanic is their monument -- more than 2 miles beneath the sea.
Photo of Titanic ⑱ Underwater footage	BALLARD V.O. ⑲ It's a memorial to this period of time. To that mistake of arrogance. It's a whole bunch of things, all bundled up and now, down at the bottom of the ocean. It's a very peaceful place, very quiet place. And it's sitting upright on the bottom, very nobly and at rest. --- END CREDITS --- DIRECTED BY GRAHAM HURLEY DR. ROBERT D. BALLARD ASSOCIATE PRODUCER TERESA KOENIG PHOTOGRAPHED BY PAUL HOULSTON LEE MANDER EDITED BY GEORGE STAMER MUSIC BY CRAIG SAFAN

1. The National Geographic Society follows the traditional two-column informational film format in its productions: video on the left, audio on the right.
2. The video side here, what the audience is to see, clearly is "pickup footage," documentary coverage chosen from various film archives.
3. The narration track is packed—infinitely more wordy than would be the case in the average picture. Yet as Noxon points out later, the information given is essential to understanding of the film's subject.

   Note, too, how Noxon translates generalities/abstractions into concrete terms that viewers can understand: "3,000 men", working "more than two years", "a mountain of steel", a hull that would span "four city blocks", engines "the size of a three story house".

*   *   *

Jumping ahead to the present day, and page 22 of Noxon's script, we're introduced to the first attempt to reach the *Titanic* by the Woods Hole/U.S. Navy expedition:

4. An interest-focused device: the hint that something may go wrong almost automatically grips viewer attention.
5. Curiosity satisfied: a look at the submarine's interior.
6. On the one hand, information about Alvin. On the other, a testimonial as the submarine's merit in terms of past accomplishments.
7. Intensely aware of how much narration he's packed into this script, Noxon takes advantage of an opportunity to add life by introducing a fragment of lip-sync speech.
8. Lip-sync has its limitations too, however. Often, as in this bit, narration conveys information more concisely than can speech.
9. Virtually an entire page of lip-sync builds a sense of "experiencing" (and tension) in the audience. Lines like "I can't believe they can only see 20–30 feet" and "we're running low on power" build viewer excitement higher and higher.
10. Back to narration, covering a decision and 2½ hours of tedium in 24 words.
11. Confidence, competence, indomitability, served up in a single speech by an authority figure.

*   *   *

On to page 39:

12. The *Titanic* located and the *Alvin* repaired, exploration of the sunken ship continues. First the exterior is surveyed; then, the interior probed. Thousands of pictures are taken, a detailed map of the *Titanic*'s remains developed. A model of the wreck site makes the situation underwater more easily understandable. Ingenuity in devising such approaches is tremendously important for a writer.
13. Here Noxon uses animation and footage from old feature films to take us into the past . . . the night the *Titanic* sank.
14. Still photos help to build a sense of reality. Others follow, plus underwater footage and more animation.

*   *   *

The script's final pages—45, 46, 47:

15. Narration, visuals, and human interest build to the conclusion.
16. Noxon wraps up the Titanic's story. But he leaves it to Dr. Ballard, as the expedition's leader, to voice the great ship's epitaph.
17. A shot of the plaque provides a lead-in to Ballard's voice-over closing words. It's a touch that helps to avoid audience confusion.
18. A film like *The Secrets of the Titanic* develops a spirit all its own, born of the insights the writer develops into his subject and his feeling for it. Noxon captures that feeling/insight when, concluding, he links this final photo of the *Titanic* with underwater footage.
19. It's in total keeping, too, with Ballard's words . . . a memorial that acknowledges arrogance as a form of fate, laid to rest now in the quiet of the ocean's depths.

*   *   *

NOXON ANSWERS SOME QUESTIONS

Do you work entirely free-lance?
Noxon: I'm free-lance, but I do projects that tend to be long-range. This thing I'm working on now will be at least a year.
What's the project?
Noxon: It's another for the National Geographic Society—a film for its centennial. I'm in charge as far as the script is concerned.
How did you get the Titanic *assignment?*
Noxon: I guess I got chosen because I'd done a lot of underwater subjects before. Also, I was acceptable both to Ballard (Dr. Robert Ballard, the geologist and undersea explorer who headed the expeditions to locate and explore the *Titanic*) and to the Geographic Society.
How long did the Titanic *script take you?*
Noxon: Beginning to end, the whole *Titanic* production took about four months. The actual narration writing took two-and-a-half weeks.
What made it go so fast?
Noxon: The immense advantage I had was actually going along on the expedition. It gave me unpressured time to think and plan. I did most of my *Titanic* reading on the ship, right over the wreck. It was a crash course. If the script's good, in part it's because it had very good preparation.
Clearly, your script isn't a complete shot list.
Noxon: It couldn't be. On a job like this, you can't predict precisely what will happen. Sometimes things you plan just don't work out. Others, you run into details you didn't anticipate that add interest. You'd be a fool not to take advantage of them. So your best bet is to hang loose, play by ear, move with the flow of developing action.

But the script was *written before the fact? Where the live action of the expedition was concerned, you pre-planned the line of development insofar as possible? You didn't just write to the footage after the fact?*

Noxon: On *Titanic* and most of my films, no narration is written until the editing is complete. Until then the written evolution of the film is as follows:

> Sales presentation or treatment (if necessary)
> Shooting outline (often revised during shooting)
> Editing outline (also often revised)
> "Scratch" rough narration for approval screenings
>   (if required)
> Final narration—written to fit final picture

To explain the process as briefly as possible, you plan everything you can and change the plan to accommodate reality. But in the end pictures dominate words and the final narration is written to support the visual story.

Do you consider this film a compilation job: a gathering together of bits and pieces from all sorts of sources?

Noxon: Yes and no. Some of the background stuff was pickup, of course. But the bulk of it—the preparations for the expedition, the expedition itself—we shot ourselves.

In other words, you were actually able to prescribe the footage that you wanted.

Noxon: To a degree. I was working in cooperation with an English crew, so both their requirements and ours had to be satisfied. A certain amount of negotiation was involved. But I did get a good bit that I wouldn't have had otherwise.

Would you class Secrets of the Titanic *as primarily film, or primarily videotape, or what? Or, if you see it as a mix, what do you consider to be the advantages of each method in this particular situation?*

Noxon: *Titanic* is a "film on tape." We shot tape exactly as we would have film and the editing process was very similar. In this context the big advantage of tape is the ease with which you can shoot great amounts of footage. That's the disadvantage too. You get careless and lazy.

Were you in on the editing?

Noxon: Yes, I directed the editing. I do that in almost every case.

For what reason?

Noxon: You know what you're thinking, how you've conceived the film. Someone else is bound to see it differently. More often than not, they'll miss the points you want to make. When that happens—well, it can be pretty hard to come in at the end.

It struck me that as scripts go, this one is short in terms of the number of pages.

Noxon: Yes, but I think anyone in the business is going to notice that it's also very heavily narrated. It's by far the longest script I've ever written for an hour; it has far more words. I belong to the school that less is more. I try to write as little as possible. I get very suspicious of my own motives if anything is even slightly long. I wonder if I'm falling in love with my own words.

You found that here?

Noxon: This script is so enormous I doubted my own sanity. I went back over it and back over it and back over it. I gave every line the acid test of necessity. And I found that I needed it all. I mean, it worked very well, even though it's very, very wordy. I don't think the story could be told as well in many fewer words, but it still worried me.

Why do you think it ran so long? Can you pin down any general reason?

Noxon: Well, I think that sometimes people need to know more than they need to sit and look at things that otherwise are meaningless. To understand this film, people needed background, and words, narration, were the only way to give it to them.

Putting aside the script for a moment . . . the meld of video and music in Secrets *struck me as tremendously effective. Did you—as writer; as producer—play a major role in its selection?*

Noxon: I worked with the composer and decided when and where music was needed. This close involvement with every phase of production is my "method." Every writer (at least in documentary) should strive for this if only to gain experience and respect for the different arts and crafts involved. This is how and why many writers become producers. They discover that merely writing a film doesn't guarantee its quality. Seeking better control, they end up as producers. There are few "pure" writers in documentary. The authorship is too much a part of the process of production.

The film was an enormous success, wasn't it?

Noxon: It certainly was. To me, though, what's even more interesting is that it's been an equally big success in home video. In fact, it's the best selling non-fiction video to date. At one point it was number five in video cassette sales. Which makes it a breakthrough for all of us who do this kind of work. I knew that it would get on television, but at the time I was working on it, I didn't know when, and I wasn't sure how the commercial breaks would be arranged. But I was face to face with my television editing console every day, so I found myself thinking about it in terms of how I'd react and what I'd want to know if I was watching it in my living room. So that became my guideline; I edited it in terms of that.

Titanic continues to amaze me with its success. When aired by Turner Broadcasting it posted the highest rating ever for a basic (non-pay) cable program. It's very pleasing to have a film run away from the competition as this one has. Now the question is, "Can we do it again?"

THE GULLIES (fact film proposal), *by Charles A. Palmer.*

THE GULLIES (shooting script, Episode B), *by Charles A. Palmer and Audrey Kaczenski.*

Once upon a time there was a highly successful New England businessman named Charles A. ("Cap") Palmer. Later he became a highly successful film writer. Then, tiring of the major studio routine, he abandoned it in order to set up his own corporation to produce business films for such firms as Kaiser Aluminum, Western Electric, International Harvester, and Hilton Hotels, among others.

Two-hundred-fifty pictures and innumerable awards later, Palmer continues today as executive producer of Parthenon Pictures, the firm he founded.

He also continues to develop and script films, with *The Gullies* an intriguing example of how to promote and package a fact piece.

The proposal

How do you sell a concept? It's a fine art, certainly, and each picture demands its own approach. But this excerpt from Palmer's handling of his *Gullies* proposal is a good example of a highly skilled pro in action.

PARTHENON PICTURES

HOLLYWOOD

2625 TEMPLE STREET, HOLLYWOOD, CALIFORNIA 90026
DUnkirk 5-3911

PROPOSAL

"THE GULLIES"

LAYOUT TREATMENT FOR
A PUBLIC SERVICE FILM SERIES
ON CONSUMER EDUCATION

by
Charles "Cap" Palmer
5/20/74

DOCUMENTARY FILMS FOR BUSINESS

PARTHENON PICTURES

"THE GULLIES"

①
A package of 5 5-minute "short stories" featuring the Gully family, each concerned with a consumer "gull."

②
The proposed treatment is unique, and the best way to explain it is via stating the initial assignment and retracing the analysis which led to "THE GULLIES" solution.

③
The initial problem is that we are entering into a field where there is already a great deal of competition. Many pictures have been made on consumer fraud. Some are really pretty good. So what we had to do was find some way of handling Consumer Education -- consumer gulls and cons -- in some new way that would earn us a general audience by somehow overleaping the things that are already on the market.

④
Well, the conventional way of approaching it would be the usual 20-25 minute documentary type movie. That had disadvantages to it in the beginning, regardless of marketability. Because for one thing, we'd have to lump too many different things into the one package and by the time the audience would walk away from that screening they'd have say 8 or 10 or 15 diffent kinds of gulls in their minds, and the only residual impression they'd go away with would be, "There sure are a lot of crooks in the world -- I'd better not ever buy <u>anything</u>." They couldn't sign a "resolved that" at the end of it. For another thing, the 20 or 25 minute picture wouldn't reach its adult audience effectively.

THE GULLIES

PARTHENON PICTURES

You can get almost anything to a school audience -- these kids
have to sit there and take it. That is, they have to <u>sit</u> there --
but they don't have to absorb the message. We've got to earn
their honest interest. And the adult audience -- which is spending money all the time, and a lot of it wrongly -- is even harder
to impress.

More -- even supposing we were to make a perfectly wonderful
28-minute picture and take it to the TV stations to run on their
"free time," the TV stations may run it because they've got that
public-service log to fill for the FCC -- but unless it's entertaining and interesting, they'll run it at a poor time with
little or no audience. Worse, even if we get a good time slot,
<u>our message will have only this one shot at the audience</u>, and
they won't be looking at it with concentration. So we're not
going to get much impact -- at best a melange with little or no
lasting <u>effect</u>.

Our job here is to make the consumer-con message really sink
into people's heads. And to do that we've got to have <u>repetition</u>.
All good advertising is based on repetition: one ad doesn't get
you much of anything -- the second ad helps, the third helps
some more. You've got to hit it, hit it, hit it, hit it, hit it.

So we've got to have some way of doing the same thing. But we
cannot give a series of 20-25 minute pictures for TV -- the
stations wouldn't run them and there isn't that much money
around to produce them.

THE GULLIES   -3-

PARTHENON PICTURES

So, to get to our proposed solution, we propose a sort of mini-
series of several pictures; but "little pictures" of around
5 minutes; each devoted to <u>one</u> con -- one consumer gull -- and
very interesting and entertaining -- because it's a crime show
in effect, and it's happening to people like <u>us</u>, to our neighbors
down the street -- so we'll identify with it. And since we see
just one fraud, when we've seen that 5-minute picture we go
away realizing the next time we see an ad for a brand-new sewing
machine at $20, we'd better be prepared to resist the switch to
the "better" one at $200. That's all we go away with -- Bait
and Switch. Next week, we get educated on Mail Order. The week
after that, perhaps Home Improvement, then Land Investment; Door
to Door. And each one sinks into us. As a parallel; in school
we teach one lesson at a time, we don't dump the whole semester
course over their heads in one three-hour lecture. It's only
logical that we educate the consumer in the same way. And if
we find a format for this which is interesting enough to people,
we can get them to come back next week and the week after that,
and the week after that.

Our next step is to figure out how to make our shows interesting
enough so that the television stations will accept the series,
and on a scheduled basis, hopefully in "good time."

Well, what's "interesting"? What catches people and holds them?
One proven answer is family shows, situation comedies -- The
Waltons, All In The Family, The Brady Bunch, and so on. So it

1. Fact films come in all shapes and sizes. Witness that this proposal is concerned with a series of five five-minute pictures.
2. Palmer says he's simply a good explainer, not a salesman. Here he explains why he's giving his explanation.
3. The prevailing situation, briefly outlined.
4. Why Palmer feels the traditional approach isn't the best, in view of said prevailing situation. Observe that this is presented in terms of purpose and audience.
5. Having shot down the traditional approach in flames, Palmer now introduces his first sales—pardon me; explanation—point: the virtue of repetition.
6. Point 2: an attack on the normal-length picture as a solution to the client's problem.
7. Now, the Palmer solution: a series of mini-pictures, each devoted to one technique by which consumers are conned.
8. Next: What approach to take in order to catch and hold an audience.

. . . and so it goes, point after point. The final product adds up to a pleasant, informal, low-key presentation.

Is it effective? This time it was, certainly: Palmer got the contract!

The shooting script

   A proposal, outline, or treatment can, to a degree, stay general. A shooting script, in contrast, must spell out what happens in such detail that a production crew can capture the desired action effectively on film, as witness these excerpts.

PARTHENON PICTURES

HOLLYWOOD

2625 TEMPLE STREET, HOLLYWOOD, CALIFORNIA 90026
· DUnkirk 5-3911

"THE GULLIES"

by
Charles Palmer
and
Audrey Kaczenski

EPISODE "B"

"BAIT AND SWITCH"
(10-minute Version)

3/31/75
Prod. 211

DOCUMENTARY FILMS FOR BUSINESS

10 MINUTE VERSION

PARTHENON PICTURES

"THE GULLIES"

EPISODE "B"

"BAIT AND SWITCH"

①

② 10-B-1	FAST ZOOM-IN TO HOLD ON CU NAME ON MAILBOX - "THE GULLIES" (SHOOT 15 times @ 5')	⑤ STET MUSIC THEME

NARRATOR

How do you do, I'm Frank Nelson,

bringing you another visit with

(SERIES OF FLASHES OF GULLY CHARACTERS IN ACTION (LIKE MTM INTR'O) TIMED WITH THE NARRATION: (SHOOT 50')

that intriguing family, the Gullies.

③ 10-B-2 GUS
10-B-3 GUS AND GRACIE

Gus, and his wife Gracie ...

④ 10-B-4 GIL
10-B-5 GIL AND GLORIA

younger brother Gilbert, and his
wife Gloria ...

10-B-6 GRANDMA

feisty Grandma ...

10-B-7 GALSWORTHY

and, the teenager's teenager,

Galsworthy.

10-B-8 SLOW ZOOM IN TO EXT. GULLY
HOME (NIGHT) -- ACROSS MAIL-
BOX ... CAR IN FRONT, MOTOR-
·CYCLE IN DRIVE (CARTOON)

What makes them intriguing is

their devotion to the great

American tendency to fall for

10-B-9 MAIN STORY TITLES SUPER'D
OVER ABOVE SCENE

consumer cons, frauds, pitfalls,

and gulls. In short, utterly

unlike you and I, the Gullies

are -- gullible.

MUSIC THEME CONCLUDES

BAIT & SWITCH (10)   -2-

PARTHENON PICTURES

10-B-10   GULLY LIVING ROOM.   As this episode opens, Galsworthy,
          GUS, GRACIE, AND
          GRANDMA LOOKING AT   as is his nightly habit, is easing
          TV ... GALSWORTHY
          STUDYING AT TABLE   the pains of homework with the
          IN BG WITH STEREO
          NEARBY ... ZOOM TO   musical accompaniment of Malice
          CU GALSWORTHY
                               ⑦   Glooper and his All Electric

                                     Aggravators. (WE HEAR IT)

                                     Er -- musical?

10-B-10A 3-SHOT AT TV   Not to his father who, after some

                                     months of this nightly decibel

                                     debauchery is finally going out of

                                     his skull.

10-B-10B CU GUS   ⑤ₐ   Galsworthy, my son, knock off that

                                     expletive-deleted uproar or I will

                                     set your hair on fire.

10-B-10C GALSWORTHY GETS UP,   Galsworthy, somewhat surprisingly,
          MOVES TO TV AREA
          AFTER TURNING OFF   obeys. Showing his father a news-
          STEREO
                                     paper advertisement, which he has
⑥ 10-B-10D CU ADV - "CRAZY AL'S   cherished since clipping it from
          DISCOUNTS"
                                     the Sunday paper,

10-B-10E 3-SHOT FAVORING   he says, stay cool, Father, all
          GALSWORTHY
                             ⑤♭   will soon be well because I have

                                     grown tired of this tasteless

                                     music

BAIT & SWITCH (10)   -3-

PARTHENON PICTURES

10-B-10F   GRACIE REACTION   and I will soon purchase an 8-track
           (WHAT'S HE UP GO?)   tape deck on which I can play

                                     selections of

10-B-10G   GALSWORTHY   my own choosing in the sound-proofed

                                     privacy of my room.

10-B-10H   GUS   What is holding you back, my son,

                                     asks Gus.

10-B-10J   GALSWORTHY   Ten bucks, says Galsworthy --

10-B-10K   GRACIE - "NOW I GET IT" here is the ad, does it not look

                                     wonderful?

10-B-10L   GUS   All ads look wonderful, his father

                               replies. But - a complete tape

                                     deck for $29.95! Kid, this Crazy

                                     Al is driving without his head-

                                     lights! Why do you not go to

                                     Michaelson's Music, which we know

                                     to be reliable, and get a set

                                     you can depend on?

10-B-10M   GALSWORTHY   Because, Father, Michaelson's

                                     cheapest deck is many dollars more

                                     and you will have to listen to this

                                     tasteless music for months before

                                     I can save up the required amount.

BAIT & SWITCH (10)   -10-

PARTHENON PICTURES

10-B-19   EXT. MICHAELSON'S   MUSIC BRIDGE
           MUSIC STORE --
           "RESPONSIBLE" LOOK

10-B-20   INT. STORE STEREO DEPT.   Oh, yes, says Mr. Michaelson; Crazy
           (ART). CONSERVATIVE
           LOOKING MAN LOOKING AT   Al's $29.95 come-on, I know it well..
           THE CRAZY AL AD WHICH
           GALSWORTHY HAS HANDED   it is not much good for music, but
           HIM. (MR. MICHAELSON)
                                        it works just great at bringing

                                        victims into his store.

10-B-20A   GALSWORTHY   But sir, says Galsworthy, $29.95 is

                                        all the money I have, and I do so

                                        want a tape deck.

10-B-20B   MR. MICHAELSON WALKS   Well, let's see -- over here is a
           O.S. - GALSWORTHY FOLLOWS.
                                        demonstrator of a really nice set
10-B-21   INT. TAPE DECK DEPT. OF
           MICHAELSON STORE - GALS-   which soon is to be replaced by a
           WORTHY FOLLOWS MR. MICHAEL-
           SON INTO SCENE   newer model, and if you can wait

                                        until the new shipment comes in, I

                                        will let you have this one at the

                                        reduced price of --

10-B-21A   MR. MICHAELSON READS $58.50.
           FROM BACK OF TAG

10-B-21B   FAVOR GALSWORTHY   Galsworthy's eyes light with

                                        happiness for a moment, but then his

                                        face falls as he has to say, but,

                                        sir, I do not have that much money.

                                        Could I purchase it on installments?

BAIT & SWITCH (10)   -11-

PARTHENON PICTURES

10-B-21C FAVOR MR. MICHAELSON	To which Mr. Michaelson replies, do you have a job? Good, then I will take your $29.95 as a down payment, and finance the balance.
10-B-21D CU GALSWORTHY	Galsworthy, now wary, says, one question, sir -- will I get a new-set warranty? And where is your service department? Three thousand miles away?
10-B-21E FAVOR MR. MICHAELSON	My goodness, young man, says Mr. Michaelson, what a strange thing to ask! It's right here in the store.
10-B-21F MR. MICHAELSON STARTS WRITING UP ORDER (SALES CONTRACT)	So now if you wish, we will write up the contract, taking plenty of time to fill in all the blank spaces so we're sure everything is understood.. then you can take it home for your folks to look at, sleep on it, and if you still feel the same way tomorrow, come in and we've got a deal.

                                         DISSOLVE

10-B-22 GALSWORTHY'S ROOM -- GUS, GRACIE, GRANDMA (SAME SET-UP AS BEFORE)	And here we are, a few weeks later, ready for the grand op -- er, listening. And <u>this</u> time ...

BAIT & SWITCH (10)   -12-
PARTHENON PICTURES

10-B-22A   GALSWORTHY HITS THE
            SWITCH
                                              MUSIC STARTS - THE SOUND
                                              IS GREAT, BUT THE SONG IS
10-B-22B   GUS STARTS TO REACT   THE SAME GROUP GUS HATED
            TOUGH, BUT GRACIE PUTS   IN THE LIVING ROOM SCENE
⑪   A HAND ON HIS AND COOLS
            HIM DOWN AND HE MANAGES   And so, as they say, all's well
            TO FOLLOW GRACIE'S LEAD
            TO ENSEMBLE APPLAUSE   that ends well ... for the Gullies.

                                       But you and I can't run our lives

                                       backward when we goof, we've got to

                                       be right the first time around.

                                       So remember --

10-B-23   RECAP MONTAGE OF   since in this world one seldom gets
            PREVIOUS SCENES
                                       something for nothing, if a
⑫   ⑬   proposition seems too good to be

                                       true, it probably is ... and when

                                       people put pressure on you and say

                                       that tomorrow will be too late --

                                       what they mean is, too late for

                                       them.

10-B-24   OVERLAY END CREDITS   So in conclusion, remember --

                                       before you buy -- be wary.

                                              MUSIC UP FOR FINISH

1. Like most fact film producers, Parthenon favors the two-column format—visuals to the left, sound to the right.
2. Shooting instructions are abbreviated to a sort of shorthand. In some instances orders are extremely specific ("SHOOT 15 times @ 5' "), but often they're looser and less rigid than in many shops. Which same is a good example of why it makes sense to ask to see a sample script when you tackle a job for a company with whose format style you're not familiar.
3. This picture and the others in the series are basically brief fact films. But because they're also designed for TV use wherever possible, as per the proposal, they're set up in TV series style, with fast establishment of characters, setting, and general circumstance.
4. Ordinarily the proliferation of "G" names here (the Gus, Gracie, Gil, Gloria, etc., thing) would be a no-no. But *The Gullies'* slant is comedic, so the matching initials add rather than detract from the effect.
5. Voice-over narration cuts costs and simplifies shooting. Note that only one narrator is used, although many passages (5a and 5b, for example) simulate speech by individual actors as they mime their roles. It's one of the many devices by which life and interest can be added to a narrated film.
6. This is the kind of thing that in many scripts would be labeled "INSERT."
7. Frequent use of exaggeration and incongruity help give the narration/dialogue a comedic tone to help build the overall style set for the film.
8. The basic "bait and switch" angle—a low-price come-on, to bring in customers who then will be coaxed and cajoled into buying something more expensive—of the episode is established.

Now we move ahead to page 10: the episode's climax and payoff.

9. By using an art background—that is, one painted on a flat or the like—instead of dressing and lighting an elaborate set or shooting on location, costs are reduced.
10. A time lapse, and a DISSOLVE to cover it.
11. A final twist, a final laugh: After all the furore, Gus still ends up with the music he loathes.
12. Well-chosen fast cuts (that is, a montage) from what has gone before is a useful device for visually summarizing the points previously made.
13. Meanwhile, our narrator hammers home the message.

PLATOON (original story and screenplay), *by Oliver Stone*

Himself 15 months in Vietnam with the 25th Infantry Division, complete with Bronze Star for bravery and multiple Purple Hearts, Oliver Stone created *Platoon* as a labor of personal passion, a blood-drenched morality tale that arouses fierce emotion and clings in memory like a jungle leech. Surely one of the most controversial films of recent years, it focuses on the experiences in the field of a young soldier, a "cherry," from his arrival at a base camp airstrip through his survival of four patrols to his shot-up, pain-racked evacuation by helicopter at the end.

Born in 1946, Stone grew up in Connecticut and New York City. He was tuned in to writing from childhood, but otherwise tended to a loose-ends style of life—traveling, dropping in and out of college, writing a novel that failed to sell.

Then, Vietnam. Discharged and returning to the United States in 1968, he wrote *Platoon* in 1976. The years between saw him attend New York University on the G.I. Bill, studying film under famed director Martin Scorsese. Graduated in 1971, he wrote and/or directed a spate of minor films, largely horror, later connecting more solidly with such scripts as *Midnight Express* (which won him an Academy Award in 1979), *Scarface,* and *Salvador.*

Platoon remained words on paper only, however. Although it was shopped around to virtually everyone in Hollywood, no one was willing to gamble on its commercial potential for nearly 10 years, until 1986.

Once the picture was released, reaction flipped over. Audiences and reviewers alike came to appreciate the devastating realism Stone brought to his work, and the way he interwove explosive action with aching lulls and anticipatory tension. Even viewers who argued that much of the picture he painted was distorted acknowledged his skill at capturing character and the manner in which he suffused the whole panorama of war in Vietnam with a strange, bitter lyricism.

The end result was a film that packed theaters, won the cover and featured treatment in *Time,* and claimed Academy Awards for both script and Best Picture.

①   <u>THE PLATOON</u>

②   Original Story and Screenplay by
       Oliver Stone

Copyright 1976. Oliver Stone

Ixtlan, Inc.
9100 Sunset Boulevard
Suite 355   February 10, 1986
Los Angeles, California 90069

1.

FADE IN:
1. A QUOTATION AGAINST A BLACK SCREEN: 1.

④   "REJOICE, O YOUNG MAN, IN THY YOUTH..."

                            ECCLESIASTES

The sound now of a C-130 air cargo plane roaring over
us and we cut sharply to:

2. EXT: AIRSTRIP -BASE CAMP - VIETNAM - DAY   2.

As the C-130 coasts to a stop, the hatch rotating
down on a hot, dusty lifeless airstrip somewhere in
Vietnam. Nothing seems to live or move in the midday sun.

TITLES RUN.

⑤ A DOZEN NEW RECRUITS step off the plane, unloading their
duffel bags, looking around like only the new can
look around, their hair regulation-clipped, crisp,
new green fatigues fitting them like cardboard.

⑥ CHRIS TAYLOR is just another one of them - as he
turns into a tight closeup, to look at a motorized
cart pulling up alongside...He's about 21. Newmeat.
His face, unburned yet by the sun, is tense, bewildered,
innocent, eyes searching for the truth.

⑦ They fall now on a heap of BODY BAGS in the back of
the cart. Two Soldiers begin loading them onto the
plane. Flies - hundreds of flies - buzz around them,
the only cue to their contents.

                    GARDNER (next to Chris, Southern accent)
              That what I think it is?

                    SOLDIER 1 (a look)
              I guess so...

An uncomfortable look between them.

                    SERGEANT
              Okay, let's go...

⑧ As they move out, Chris' eyes moving with the body
bags being loaded onto the plane. Moving over now
to a motley HALF DOZEN VETERANS bypassing them on
their way to the plane. They look happy. Very happy,
chatting it up.

15.

20.   CONTD   20.

> CHRIS VOICE OVER (continuing his letter)
> ...'Course Mom and Dad didn't want
> me to come, they wanted me to be just
> like them - respectable, hard-working,
> making $200 a week, a little house, a
> family. They drove me crazy with their
> goddamn world, grandma, you know Mom, I
> don't want to be a white boy on Wall
> Street, I don't want my whole life to
> be predetermined by them.

A large RIPPING SOUND as the wind blows down a big
tree branch onto the jungle floor. He starts,
peering out. Nothing. He looks at his watch again.

> CHRIS VOICE OVER
> ...I guess have always been sheltered
> and special, I just want to be anonymous.
> Like everybody else. Do my share for my
> country. Live up to what Grandpa did in
> the First War and Dad the Second. I know
> this is going to be the war of my
> generation. Well here I am - anonymous
> all right, with guys nobody really cares
> about - they come from the end of the
> line, most of 'em, small towns you
> never heard of - Pulaski, Tennessee,
> Brandon, Mississippi, Pork Bend, Utah,
> Wampum, Pennsylvania. Two years high
> school's about it, maybe if they're lucky
> a job waiting for 'em back in a factory,
> but most of 'em got nothing, they're poor,
> they're the unwanted of our society,
> yet they're fighting for our society and
> our freedom and what we call America,
> they're the bottom of the barrel - and
> they know it, maybe that's why they call
> themselves "grunts" cause a "grunt" can
> take it, can take anything. They're the
> backbone of this country, grandma, the
> best I've ever seen, the heart and soul -
> I've found it finally, way down here in
> the mud - maybe from down here I can start
> up again and be something I can be proud
> of, without having to fake it, maybe...
> I can see something I don't yet see,
> learn something I don't yet know...I
> miss you, I miss you very much, tell Mom
> I miss her too - Chris.

74.

98.   CONTD.   98.

Chris makes a conscious decision, moves up - bit by bit,
shielding himself with tree stumps, ant hills, laying
out fire, trying to get closer to Lerner.

Francis following his progress, bug-eyed.

Fu Sheng now comes up with his M-60 -- Harold his
loader, belts of ammo flapping against their bodies.
He fires from the hip, providing cover fire for Chris,
then pops down.

99.   <u>EXT: FORWARD POINT - JUNGLE - DAY (DRIZZLING RAIN)</u>   99.

Chris, firing out another magazine, crawls closer to
Lerner, trying to ascertain if he's still alive.

                        CHRIS
            Lerner! Lerner, can you hear me man?

Lerner groans. A fresh burst of AK fire rakes the area.
Lerner jerks smasmodically with the impact of the rounds.

Chris spots the sniper. In a hole in the ground. Twenty-
five metres off. Snapping the magazine out of his AK
to reload. A live gook.

Chris tears off a volley at him but the gook disappears
in the hole. This is the moment, Chris realizes it,
it's now or never if Chris intends to get the gook.
He's got to make a move before the man has reloaded
his weapon.

He pulls his grenade, pops the pin. He lets the spoon
fly off, activiating the grenade-timer, as he jumps
to his feet and runs for the gook hole, concentrating,
concentrating. That head is going to pop up any second
with a freshly-loaded weapon and tear his head off.

Chris won't make it to the hole. The throw has to be
perfect. He won't get another chance. He heaves the
frag, drops and rolls away. The throw <u>is</u> perfect, the
golden arc of flight from the outfield nailing the
baserunner. It twists cleanly in the hole. The
explosion muffled but deadly.

Chris scrambles to his feet, a look of almost total surprise
on his face. He can't seem to believe he did it.
Pointing his M-16 before him, he advance on the hole,
looking over the muzzle to see the badly-mangled NVA
man twisted at the bottom.

ENDING "A"   122

161.   EXT: PERIMETER #3 - DAY   161.

Rhah, at the edge of the treeline, vigorously shakes
his walking stick at him, his other hand a fist,
waving them, emitting his cry.

                         RHAH
(16)   Baaaaaaaaaaaa!!!!!!!!!!!!!!!

Defiance. Pride. Dig me, I'm Rhah - and there isn't
nobody like me in the world.

162.   EXT/INT: PERIMETER #3 - LZ CHOPPER - DAY   162.

The chopper -- with its huge red cross painted on --
now rising to meet God. Smashed on morphine, Chris
looking out at the waving ants below.

Now the trees, the skyline and the chopper is moving
fast over the devastation. The jungle forever locked
in his memory, Chris looks back, copious, quiet tears
flowing from his eyes.

                    CHRIS VOICE OVER
              I think now, looking back, we did not
              fight the enemy, we fought ourselves -
              and the enemy was in us...The war is
              over for me now, but it will always
              be there - the rest of my days. As I
              am sure Elias will be - fighting with
              Barnes for what Rhah called possession
(17)   of my soul...There are times since I
              have felt like the child born of those
              two fathers...but be that as it may,
              those of us who did make it have an
              obligation to build again, to teach
              to others what we know and to try
              with what's left of our lives to find
              a goodness and meaning to this life...

The music surges now to its full strength as we replay
bits of film with each actor's name listed - some with
silly, clowning looks, others sober, haunted. Gardner,
(18)   Tex, King, Rhah, Lerner, Sanderson, Manny, Big Harold -
all the boys...and then Barnes staring quietly into
the camera, and lastly Elias - shirt off, bowl of
grass in hand, his big, beautiful smile.

                    THE END

1. Note that the film's title was *The Platoon* in Stone's script, but the picture was released as *Platoon*. Clearly, someone somewhere along the line felt that the title carried more impact without the article.
2. The script was totally Stone's work. He claimed credit for both story and screenplay.
3. The 10-year lapse between script and Ixtlan's production is brought into focus by the two dates.

Page 1 of the script:

4. Irony and bitterness in a Biblical quotation keynote the opening shot.
5. New recruits come on center stage. Their condition and status is established visually, without words, by their haircuts and new fatigues.
6. Our central character, Chris Taylor, is introduced, his importance made clear via the "tight closeup," an emphasis shot. Stone also makes it obvious that he's out to "sell" a mood, a feeling, by his line, "eyes searching for the truth"—"eyes searching" can be photographed; "for the truth" can't. It's the kind of device Stone uses frequently in this script.
7. The tension-building shock of contrast: life, personified in the recruits, played against the shadow of death carried by the body bags and flies.
8. Veterans: more contrast, more tension. These are survivors. Their happiness sharpens the implication of the danger ahead for the recruits.

Page 15:

Too often, critics of *Platoon* have viewed the picture in terms of blood and violence, focusing on dope, rape, blood lust, degradation, and the murder of soldier by soldier. Its philosophical elements and ethical concerns have been lost in its rush of action.

Actually, there's more than a little thoughtful dialogue sifted through the rage and turmoil. Character development is strong and solid, as witness Stone's work on this page of script.

9. Chris's letter to his grandma . . . another of Stone's devices for introducing ideas not easily set forth or interpreted in pictures. Here, we gain insight into Chris's goals and feelings, his reactions to his previous life.
   Also worthy of note is the fact that Chris's letter is to his grandmother. In having his central character write to her, rather than to his parents, Stone has made it possible for him to express his deepest feelings more honestly and candidly, with less restraint and inhibition, than he might otherwise.
10. Pride and duty, we see here, are prime components of Chris's character. He has a heritage he wants to live up to.
11. Stone's Vietnam–shaped attitudes and insights where his fellow-grunts are concerned are seen here through Chris's eyes.
12. Clearly, the soldiers who serve with him have helped to shape him. He sees through the ego-armor war has forced them to wear to hide their doubts and fears and inadequacies. And out of the understanding he's gained he's found new values for himself . . . a humility that acknowledges that what you want often is what you're afraid you haven't got.

Page 74:

13. Moving through the jungle, Chris's squad comes under fire—an ambush. One of those hit is Lerner, the point man. He's isolated, cut off from the others. Chris, coming forward, sees him.

The page of battle action that follows is developed in master scenes. Stone describes what's happening, what the audience is to see and hear, leaving it to the director (Stone himself in this case, as it worked out) to break it down into shots. It's a veteran's battlefield experience made visual, translated into photographable action-images, the kind of thing Stone does ever so well.

14. Stone establishes danger—and with it, heightened audience tension . . .
15. . . . then releases that tension (at least temporarily) with Chris's successful throw of the grenade.

Page 122; the script's final page:

16. Rhah, a strongly tagged secondary character, here emerges as a climactic symbol both of defiance and of the eternal conflict of love versus hate which Stone has built.
17. This voice-over monologue by Chris is a good example of why *Platoon* is as much philosophy and morality play as action film. When he says that Vietnam's survivors have an obligation "to try with what's left of our lives to find a goodness and meaning to this life . . ." duty and rectitude and principle are put into words.
18. The wrap-up. Clips of the film's various characters sum up *Platoon*'s message of the oneness and differences of all men as brought into sharp silhouette by war.

Especially to the point is the fact that we conclude on Barnes and Elias, for in essence the picture hinges on them. Both sergeants, both superior soldiers, each in his own way personifies the clash between evil and good that lies at the heart of *Platoon:* Barnes, who earlier has been described by Rhah as "That man is *mean,* man, red in his soul . . . Barnes comes from hell . . . He's roaming these jungles looking for little yellow devils to kill"; and Elias, the handsome, graceful Indian three years in Nam who thinks killing's cheap, "the cheapest thing I know," and who describes death as "like a giant garbage can," and hopes that if he's reincarnated he'll come back "as wind or fire— or a deer."

Stone's message could hardly be clearer.

TERROR ON THE FORTIETH FLOOR (outline), *by Jack Turley*.

TERROR ON THE FORTIETH FLOOR (sequence cards), *by Jack Turley*.

TERROR ON THE FORTIETH FLOOR (treatment/step outline), *by Jack Turley*.

TERROR ON THE FORTIETH FLOOR (elaborating notes), *by Jack Turley*.

TERROR ON THE FORTIETH FLOOR (teleplay), *by Jack Turley*.

Jack Turley prepared for a scriptwriting career with TV production experience in such places as Oklahoma City and Albuquerque, then moved to Los Angeles and enrolled in TV writing courses at UCLA. His first sale was to *Route 66*—a collaboration with his instructor, Milton Gelmer. Now, with 20 years' experience behind him, he is turning more and more to the movie-of-the-week type of thing. *Pray for the Wildcats*, *Hurricane*, and *The Day the Earth Moved* are among his recent credits.

Terror on the Fortieth Floor, airing as a two-hour, seven-act show, kicked off NBC's 1974 season. It also has been released in Europe as a theatrical film, as well as rerun in the U.S.

Turley's handling of *Terror* offers excellent insights into the entire process of script development. Here we see how it was built step by step from a story by Turley and Ed Montagne.

The outline

Jack Turley

①

"THE ONLY WAY IS DOWN"

This is not meant to be a storyline. It is a preliminary
sorting of possibilities...a springboard.

②
③

THE PHYSICAL ELEMENTS

④

Christmas Eve. An office party on the top floor of a
modern skyscraper. The building is empty except for those
at the party--and even these people are finishing their
drinks so they can hurry home to families for the long
holiday week-end.

An exodus to the elevator. No one is aware that a small,
die-hard group of revelers has slipped away to continue
the party in the plush inner sanctum of the boss' private
office. There is, however, one witness to the secret--
the OFFICE MESSENGER BOY. But one of the party participants,
an Executive, swears the Office Boy to secrecy, half by
implied threat, half by allusion to promotion.

⑤

The mass of departing office workers get off the elevator
at the main floor, unaware that they have left a few
revelers behind. The people say goodnight to the WATCHMAN,
tell him that they are the final remnants of the office
party. No one else left upstairs. The Office Boy,
protecting his Executive conspirator, says nothing as
he leaves with the others.

2

The remaining seven or so people still on the top floor
in the boss' private office have effectively isolated
themselves from discovery, stealing a little more time
to enjoy themselves. No one knows they are there, except
the Office Boy--and the Executive assures his friends
that their secret is safe

THE DISASTER

Because it is a holiday week-end and the building will
be totally unoccupied during that time, the Maintenance
Supervisor has left orders for some minor repair work to
be done on the building's heating system. The Maintenance
ENGINEER comes on duty this Christmas Eve begrudging his
lot for having to work at all. He is assuaging his
discontent with a bottle of cheer he has brought with
him.

The Engineer begins his repairs, getting drunker as he
works. There is a gas leak, then a spark caused by a
careless mistake. A massive EXPLOSION knocks out all
the support systems in the building--lights, phones,
heating, elevators, etc.--enveloping the basement in a
blazing fire.

The Engineer is killed and the watchman, making his rounds
and pausing to pass the time with the Engineer, is critically
injured.

Firemen answer the electronic alarm and a frantic effort

3

begins to get the fire under control before it guts the
skyscraper. The Watchman is conscious enough to inform
the firemen, erroneously, that the building is deserted.
The Fire Commander utters a fervent "thank God." If the
explosion had occurred two hours earlier, hundreds of
people could've been killed.

THE PEOPLE

and their separate stories will begin to unfold now against
the ominous threat of the raging fire far below, which
appears to be climbing toward the top, floor by floor.
The people are trapped, aware of the danger below them
but unable to make their presence known to the firefighters
below. Communication systems are gone...no lights...stair-
wells are choked with heavy, deadly smoke...windows designed
for gale force cannot be broken.

Let us consider these trapped victims, identifying them,
for the moment, by the simplest of names:

> MISTER PLAYBOY
> MISTER SENIOR EXECUTIVE
> MISTER DESPERATE
> MISS NAIVE
> MISS LONELY
> MISS OPPORTUNIST
> MISS PREGNANT

Contrary to the names, these people should not be
interpreted as caricatures. They are, and must be,

4

real, very real, people...flawed in instantly recognizable
ways. These people could be found at any office party
anywhere. They must contain the essence of familiarity
for anyone who has ever worked in an office.

Let's look at each character a little closer:

⑧ MISTER PLAYBOY is a young, good-looking stud, four button,
wing-tipped, attache-cased make-out artist. He lives the
virile Hefner image--ski trips, sports cars, flashy
acrylic bachelor pad. Mister Playboy has one primary goal
in life--to make one more conquest, to get one more woman
in bed. It might be interesting to find out that, even
with all his macho and super charm, Mister Playboy doesn't
have anyplace to go on Christmas Eve...or anyone to go to
that he really wants to go to.

MISTER SENIOR EXECUTIVE is a tired memorial to all the
tough years he's spent beating his way to a comfortable
existence. All the right appurtenances are finally his.
The fashionable suburban home...private school for the kids...
the country club membership...an attractive wife perfectly
trained to the executive role. But something is missing.
A spark...a reason for Mister Senior Executive to want to
go home. He's staying at the private party because it
gives him a little longer reprieve, a chance to flex a
rapidly-diminishing male ego before those he mistakenly
thinks actually care.

11

She knows she's starving herself, that her neighbor has
been, innocently enough, what a man should be for her.

THE OVER-ALL STORY APPROACH

(9) The crisis in the skyscraper, the fire and the threat
that it will climb upward through every floor to the people
trapped on top, will encompass most of Christmas Eve
and into the early morning hours of Christmas Day. During
this time, we will interstice--against the ongoing drama
(10) of the trapped victims--individual cameos of the "connecting
people" and how their own lives are being affected by
the crisis.

(11) For a period of time within the dramatic story, the firefighters below would be unaware that the trapped people
are even in the building. It seems deserted by all outward
appearances and, also, there was the reassuring statement
from the unknowing watchman that all the people were gone.
But the Office Boy, the only one who knows about the
secret party in the boss' office, is the ultimate key to
alerting firefighters to the new complication.

Now it becomes not a matter of saving the building, but
(12) of saving people who are trapped on the top floor.
Helicopters seem to be a logical and dramatic answer.
Portable lights are dropped onto the building's roof.
Rescuers acetylene their way through the locked steel door
leading to a stairwell from the roof. They work their

12

⑬ way down through the smoke-filled passage to find the trapped people. In these few minutes, personal drama is suspended in favor of pure action. The victims are led back to the roof and carried away by the helicopter in a rope-slung litter.

⑭ At a nearby city park, in a hastily-organized rescue area, the victims are reunited with their individual "connecting people"--to resolve, however we choose, their lives from that point forward.

⑮ This final scene, or rather scenes, should not, I think, be handled with quick one-liners and then fade out. The resolution of each prime character should, by this point, be more essential than all the drama and action preceding it. We should then savor it, play it out full; not simply treat it as a wrap-up finish to an action adventure story...

1. Titles do tend to change. *The Only Way Is Down,* Turley's choice, stayed with his script most of the way.
2. Turley's presentation of his materials is an interesting variation on the traditional outline. His use of subheaded groupings of data ("THE PHYSICAL ELEMENTS," "THE DISASTER," "THE PEOPLE," "THE OVERALL STORY APPROACH") breaks a complex mass down into easily grasped components.
3. "THE PHYSICAL ELEMENTS" is really a statement of the background of the action, the circumstances under which the story takes place.
4. In choosing Christmas as the time for the action, Turley establishes a strong joy/tragedy contrast. Similarly, the disaster stands out starkly against the background of office party revelry.
5. Here Turley establishes the plausibility and logic of his situation, anticipating and answering possible viewer questions even before they arise.
6. More holes are plugged, the sense of jeopardy intensified.
7. It's easy to lose readers—even experienced script-readers—in a mass of details. By simplifying his people to the label level, Turley makes them instantly understandable stick figures.
8. The image of each person established via label, Turley now elaborates them into believable human beings, giving them attributes and backgrounds as required.

Skipping ahead to page 11 . . .

9. "THE OVER-ALL STORY APPROACH" reveals the broad outlines of Turley's plan of attack in thumbnail form.
10. No one exists in a vacuum. Here characters are revealed in greater depth by showing their interrelationships with others beyond the scene of the fire.
11. Plot angles, tension factors, are developed.
12. The mechanics of resolution. No producer wants to take chances on a writer writing himself into a corner.
13. Character's great, but viewers like excitement too.
14. Tension released; physical problems and peril resolved. But a good character has a future as well as a past, and an effective denouement must at least foreshadow it.
15. Tone and residual impression are important. Turley sets forth his own views on the subject.

The sequence cards

A few of Turley's sequence cards: a writer's notes to himself on how to develop his play. These all are from Act 1.

TOP FLOOR   ① a

OFFICE PARTY WRAPPING
UP — XMAS EVE.
A SPLINTER GROUP
SNEAKS OFF TO BOSS'
OFFICE — UNSEEN BY OTHERS
AT PARTY.

BASEMENT   ① e

STOSH MAKING REPAIRS,
NIPPING bottle,
getting DRUNKER.

LOBBY   ① f

LAST OF MAIN PARTY
LEAVES, TELLS WATCHMAN
NOBODY ELSE UPSTAIRS.
OFFICE BOY SILENT.
(mention that cleaning
personnel won't be in
UNTIL MON.)

TOP FLOOR   ① g

PARTY get's cozy.
Playboy hitting on Ginger
Overland hitting on Darlene
Jerry Foster making drinks
to Lee and Rich,
discuss what's happening.
Lee turns inward, to
her own thoughts.

FLASHBACK   ① h

Lee and Jim Pearson
and his two young
daughters on outing.
Lee tells him she's
pregnant. Pearson
stunned, withdraws

BASEMENT   ① i

Mister Sawes drops in to
visit Stosh, making
Rounds. Stosh makes
drunken mistake.
Explosion—FIRE
END ACT 1

The treatment/step outline

Turley prepares neither a treatment nor a step outline as such, preferring instead this combination form that includes elements of each.

"THE ONLY WAY IS DOWN"

Jack Turley
May 23, 1974

ACT ONE

TOP FLOOR - MODERN SKYSCRAPER - AT DUSK

①

② Christmas Eve. An Office Party in progress...drinking...
laughter...presents exchanged. The building has already
emptied out except for this last celebration. Now, even
these celebrants are finishing their last round so they
can hurry home to families for the long holiday week-end.

TOP FLOOR - BOSS' OFFICE

A plush private office. We watch a separate contingent
of die-hard celebrants slip away <u>unnoticed</u> from the main
party to continue their own party privately in the boss'
office.

TOP FLOOR - CORRIDOR

STOSH, the night watchman, gets off the elevator, locks
it open. He pauses to watch the office celebration a
moment, then turns downthe corridor to lock the steel
security door at the stairwell. As he turns around, some
of the celebrants exit from the party to jokingly inquire
if Stosh is locking them in for the night. Stosh grins.

③ No such luck. He's locking the floor because of a recent
office theft. Orders from Mister Overland.

Stosh waits as the mass exodus begins, the celebrants grabbing
their coats and their presents in a noisy, festive crush
to get to the elevator.

TOP FLOOR - BOSS' OFFICE

The three men and four women who have slipped away unnoticed
from the main party are now silently waiting until the others
leave. They listen behind the closed door, smuggling amused
glances at each other, offering a silent toast to themselves
on their success. We take this moment to meet each one:

DANIEL OVERLAND - a tired memorial to all the tough years
it's taken him to beat his way to near the top. Overland
is greying, mature, and long-suffering from a marriage on
the rocks. Like countless other executives who go to office
Christmas parties, Overland is stealing some extra time
to bolster a fading ego, to gain reprieve from the chore of
just going home.

KELLY FREEMAN - the office stud, a young, good-looking
macho chaser who worships at the Hugh Hefner shrine.. Kelly
has a single goal in life--to get one more woman into bed.
There are some suitable prospects here at the party. As
Kelly sees it, it's only a matter for his choosing.

HOWARD FOSTER - a hustler, a fast-talking loser who is
caught somewhere in the no-man's middle of the corporate
ladder. Howard Foster has already peaked in his career
and knows it. He has trapped himself in a wasted lifetime
of playing the angles, of working deals that never work.

1. Presentation is, in effect, by sequences. Each is labeled as to location and, if necessary, by DAY/NIGHT or the like.
2. Handling in this sequence ranges from impressionism to "telling" summary.
3. Key plot factors are included, even though not yet fully developed.
4. Characters also are introduced, within the same general framework in which they'll come on in the final script. Now, too, the characters have names as well as traits and backgrounds.

The elaborating notes

    An actual screenplay or teleplay requires infinitely more detail than the summarized versions that go before. Turley works these out on yellow legal pads.

Parker answers: Negative. ~~~~ We've ~~~~ brought out five fatality and one injured. Building ~~~~ watchman has reported no one else in building.

Voice from ~~radio~~: "Ten Four, ~~Battalion~~ one. ~~~~ We're dispatching engines three, eight, two oh eight, fourteen, 72, and trucks 8, 82 and 43. And Utilities nine, 13 and five.

I'm setting up command
Post on first floor
lobby by elevators.
The incoming Captains
report to command
Post for assignments
We have we can able
use elevators, not
involved. I've
committed 1st alarm
assignment to one
on the 11th floor. We're
going to try to hold
it on 12.
Batt. one,
Voice from source: "Do
you have a rescue
problem?

The teleplay

"THE ONLY WAY IS DOWN"

Teleplay

by

Jack Turley

Story

by

Ed Montagne

and

Jack Turley

FIRST DRAFT
June 21, 1974

<u>ACT ONE</u>

FADE IN:

EXT. DOWNTOWN STREET - LOS ANGELES - DUSK

Traffic...pedestrians...the thinning residuum of rush hour.
It is <u>Christmas Eve</u>, on the edge of early evening. We're at
an intersection, CLOSE on a volunteer SANTA CLAUS who stands
a lonely vigil beside his coin kettle. Santa is shaking his
tiny bell at passersby, but there are few interested
contributors. People are hurrying homeward to their holiday
weekend, presents and packages tucked under their arms.

CREDITS BEGIN as Santa wearily gives up the bell-ringing, paws
under his uniform to fish out a pocket watch. He consults it,
decides it's quitting time. Santa folds up his portable
kettle rig, slings it over his shoulder, trudges off across
the street. As he passes by in front of an office building,
CAMERA HOLDS, watching him disappear into the distance.

Now, CREDITS CONCLUDE as CAMERA SWEEPS UPWARD on the tall
office building, taking us for a dizzy ride toward the top
floor. OVER THIS, the SOUNDS of an office party in progress...
voices...laughter...

INT. OFFICE BUILDING - TOP FLOOR - THE PARTY

A suite of offices, obviously part of a large corporate
operation. Desks have been pushed aside, a temporary bar set
up on a filing cabinet, a decorated Christmas tree, a few
decorations hung from the ceiling. The voices and laughter
continue to fill the scene as we gently nudge our way through
the crowd of celebrants -- Executives, secretaries, various
office personnel. This is the wind-up of what has obviously
been a wet and festive afternoon.

Perhaps as we circulate our way through the crush, we hear
bits of conversation, familiar bits that might be heard at any
office party:

                    AD LIBS
        "We should have a party like this
        at least once a month--"

        "If I don't get a raise by the first,
        I'm quitting. I mean it--"

        "Look, this is the first time we've
        had a chance to talk...really talk.
        Why don't we get out of here and
        go someplace for a drink?"

②

③

2.

One of the celebrants, a slightly tipsy office-manager type,
SAM LEWIS, is making a speech...or trying to. We move in
CLOSER.

                         SAM
               Now I know this is not what you
               would call a 'serious occasion'
               but--

Snickers, some good-natured jeers.

                         SAM (CONT'D)
               But I still think something should
               be said...I mean...the real spirit
               of Christmas...all of us, you know...
               good friends sharing a little fun
               with the hard work...

The celebrants don't want to hear this crap. People turn to
search for coats, to gather up packages.

                         VOICE
               We know, Sam. That's what you said
               last year!

Laughter. Sam can't help but give his audience a bleary grin,
shaking off his attempt at sentimentality.

                         SAM
               Yeah and I'll probably say it next
               year!

More laughter as somebody shoves a drink at Sam.

ADJACENT OFFICE

an open doorway connects it to the main party area. BETTY
CARSON, a plain, slightly-overweight secretary in her middle
20's, is talking on the phone, cupping her hand over her ear
to block out the din:

                         BETTY
               When I get there, that's all!

Betty is angry. She glances over at her friend waiting for
her in the doorway, GINGER MACKLIN, another secretary. Betty
gives Ginger a long suffering grimace as:

                         BETTY (CONT'D)
               Mom, quit talking to me like a
               child!!

Ginger is younger than Betty, prettier, and a new initiate to
the office force. Eager to get back to the party, Ginger
gives Betty an impatient gesture. Betty nods, still suffering
her martyrdom.

41.

④
>   KELLY
>   Yeah...and we've both come a long
>   way. You're Regional Sales
>   Manager, I'm Executive Assistant
>   to the Senior Vice President. He
>   listens to me, he respects what I
>   have to say. Would you say that's
>   'paying the freight' now, Howie...?

HOLD a beat, Kelly's smile turning more brittle as he gazes at
the older man, watching him crumble.

INT. FIRE FLOOR (SPECIAL SET) - ACTION CUTS

⑤
The battle continues against the raging flames. Firemen are
moving down a passageway, spraying tons of water into the
crackling holocaust. SMOKE...INTENSE WILTING HEAT...A ROARING,
bellowing monster out of control, lashing in all directions.

EXT. ANGLE IN STREET

⑥
A REMOTE TV TRUCK wheels to a stop. DAVE HARPER jumps out,
gestures his crew to hold a minute. Harper is a local TV news
personality, a professional. He quickly scans the situation,
moves in to intercept a familiar face.

>   HARPER
>   Captain Thomas!

ANGLE - INCLUDING CAPTAIN THOMAS

caught in mid-stride. He stops, frowns impatiently. The
Captain's face is smoke-blackened, his coat stained and water-
streaked. Harper beelines to him. No wasted talk. They know
each other.

>   HARPER
>   What've we got?

>   CAPTAIN THOMAS
>   A bad one. Fire started on
>   twelve, it's up to fifteen. If
>   you're setting up cameras, give
>   us room, Harper. We've got more
>   equipment coming in.

>   HARPER
>   Right. Radio report said you've
>   taken out two victims, one dead.
>   Anymore trapped in there?

42.

                         CAPTAIN THOMAS
⑦   Far as we can determine, there's
          no life hazard on the upper
          floors. Building was deserted
          for the holidays.

                         HARPER
          That's a break.

                         CAPTAIN THOMAS
          It's the only one.

Captain Thomas pivots away. HOLD on Harper a beat, his gaze
scanning upward, toward the top of the building.

INT. OFFICE SUITE - THE PARTY ROOM - TOP FLOOR

⑧   Lights off. Ginger, weaving slightly, crosses to pick up her
coat, hastily puts it on, gathers up some Christmas packages.
She moves to a doorway and out into the corridor.

CORRIDOR

Ginger pauses, looks off toward Overland's office. The door
is ajar, the SOUNDS of conversation -- Lee and Overland and
Darlene talking. Ginger ruefully considers saying goodnight,
but discards the idea. A quick departure might be more
prudent. She silently hurries on.

ANGLE - THROUGH GLASS DOOR

leading from the elevator lobby into the reception area of
the offices. We see Ginger come around a corner, struggling
to get her packages securely tucked under her arm. As she
⑨   reaches the glass door, she looks up to push it open...but
stops, frozen where she stands, her hand still suspended on
the door's handle.

POV - REVERSE ANGLE - THROUGH THE GLASS

⑩   and Ginger's horrified expression mirrored on it. Beyond the
door, in the elevator lobby itself, deadly ominous wisps of
smoke are spewing through the slits of the closed elevator
doors, roiling lazily upward to gather on the ceiling. HOLD
as MUSIC STINGS and we--

                                           FADE OUT:

                  END ACT TWO

43.

ACT THREE

FADE IN:

EXT. OFFICE BUILDING - NIGHT

⑪ The floodlights...Firemen hurrying into the building...
emergency vehicles...the Crowd...all ESTABLISHING the
continuing fire fight. SMOKE seeps from the narrow band of
windows at the 12th floor, getting heavier. We can also see
a flickering <u>red glow</u> through the windows two floors <u>above</u>
the 12th. The fire is climbing toward the top.

INT. OFFICE SUITE - RECEPTION AREA - TOP FLOOR

⑫ Ginger has sounded alarm to the others. Overland, Darlene,
Lee, Howard, Betty and Kelly converge into the reception
area from every direction. They gather at the glass door
with Ginger, grimly looking out into the elevator lobby. The
smoke, although thin and wispy, is still visibly seeping from
the closed elevator doors, accumulating against the ceiling.
It doesn't take Overland but a second to make a command
decision:

                    OVERLAND
                (coolly, quietly)
        I think we better get out of
        here--

                    GINGER
        What is it, Mister Overland?
        What's wrong--??

                    OVERLAND
        Probably an equipment fire or
        something in the basement.
        Nothing to worry about, Ginger.

                    DARLENE
        My new coat!! I've got to get
        my new coat!!

She darts off before anybody can stop her.

INT. STAIRWELL - BELOW FIRE FLOOR

⑬ A tangle of water hoses snake up the criss-cross stairs,
making the already-narrow passage that much tougher for the
Firemen hand-carrying equipment upward. Other Firemen are
also coming down the stairs, the two streams of traffic
bucking each other in a constantly-congested flow.

102.

POV SHOT - THELMA AND OVERLAND

from across the parking lot. They're locked in each other's
arms, oblivious to everything around them.

REVERSE - DARLENE

⑭   watching them with a brittle detachment. Her gaze shifts.

HER POV - BETTY

Arm in arm with her <u>Mother</u>, crying on her shoulder as they
walk away.

BACK TO DARLENE

She considers it, a bit wistfully, then glances up.

HER POV - A CHRISTMAS DECORATION

⑮   hanging from a nearby street lamp. The light dims OFF,
shutting down as morning approaches.

BACK TO DARLENE

She sighs, brushes at her tattered fake fur coat, turns, looks
off. Somebody else is sharing her loneliness -- <u>Kelly</u>. He's
⑯   hunched down on the bumper of a Paramedic unit, head drooped
in despaired brooding. Darlene crosses to him, reaches out to
touch his shoulder, keeping it light. She doesn't want any
heavy dialogue right now.

                         DARLENE
               Hey, we're alive. That's worth
               something, isn't it?

Kelly looks up, tears in his eyes.

                         KELLY
⑰   I was scared. I didn't want him
               to get killed.

                         DARLENE
               Look, I've got an idea. Why don't
               a couple of losers get together
               for Christmas day? We can talk
               about everything if it'll help.

                         KELLY
               Nothing helps...

103.

Kelly's head droops down again, resigned to his misery.
Darlene reaches to offer her hand, a gesture of sympathy.

                              DARLENE
                    Come on, Kelly baby. We might
                    even find something to like about
                    each other...

Kelly looks up at her, hesitates, then takes her hand and rises,
walks off with her.

                              KELLY
                    You understand, don't you...about
                    Howie?

                              DARLENE
                    Sure...I understand.

WIDE ANGLE - FROM HELICOPTER

Taking in the full street scene, this aftermath of disaster.
We're lifting into an <u>early</u> <u>morning</u> <u>sky</u>. OVER THIS:

                              HARPER'S VOICE
     ⑱   Although the fire is still burning
                    through parts of the lower floors,
                    Chief Packer says they now have it
                    under control and he expects to
                    have it completely stopped within
                    several hours...

The Helicopter is rising <u>close</u> alongside the building, floor
after floor after floor. We get brief glimpses through some
of the windows, the fire damage, the smoking debris. Over
this, continuing:

                              HARPER'S VOICE (CONT'D)
                    It's been a long and grim night for
                    a lot of dedicated Firemen...and
                    for the six people who somehow
                    managed to survive this disaster.
     ⑲   If there's one thing we can be sure
                    of, we'd be willing to bet those
                    four women and two men just got the
                    best present they'll ever open...on
                    this or any other Christmas morning.

CAMERA RISES UP over the edge of the building, past the
lingering smoke, STILL RISING to take in the vast sweep of
     ⑳   Los Angeles spreading far to the horizon. A clear bright day
has come.

                                             FADE OUT:

                              <u>END</u>

1. Credits are important to every scriptwriter. Here, Turley gets a joint story credit, plus solo teleplay credit. (And though the script terms this a teleplay, remember that the finished picture was released as a feature film in Europe—a clear indication of how much the two media tend to overlap today.)
2. Check the first sequence of Turley's treatment/step outline, above, against these three paragraphs. Time and place now are established in terms of specific images. Thus, the Santa Claus in effect says Christmas; the bit with the watch and kettle sets the time. The camera's upward sweep tells us where the party's taking place.
3. Mood and general situation are established swiftly. Turley begins to zero in on his story people.

A jump ahead to page 41 now:

4. Action here is at the party.
5. Now, a cut to parallel action: strong contrast, extreme jeopardy.
6. A different scene; more parallel action. Turley brings in necessary exposition via the dialogue between the TV newsman and Captain Thomas.
7. An important plot line here. Captain Thomas's assumption that the top floors are deserted can't help but heighten viewer suspense as jeopardy to the trapped party leaps higher.
8. Back to the party again, but centering on Ginger, one individual, with a consequent concentration of attention.
9. Suspense is heightened and attention focused even more sharply by shooting Ginger's panic reaction before revealing its cause . . . an excellent technique, but dangerous unless motivation not only follows immediately, but is instantly understandable to viewers.
10. Now, the payoff to Ginger's reaction—not to mention the jeopardy pinpointed in 5, above, and Captain Thomas's assumption (in 7) that the building's upper floors are deserted. A tremendous visual cliffhanger for an Act 2 curtain, it's intensified even more by the music "sting"—a sudden, jarring musical note struck for emphasis, like an exclamation point at the end of a sentence.
11. The pickup after the act break: swift, wordless reestablishment of peril.
12. Back to the fortieth floor. Our characters react characteristically to the crisis—Overland coolly, Ginger naively, Darlene in terms that, in effect, make possessions worth more than life itself. All of which is, of course, highly important storywise—for our story concerns not just a fire, but the reactions of people with whom viewers are emotionally involved to the character-testing jeopardy the fire represents.
13. A suspense-heightening return to parallel action.

Again we jump forward . . . this time to the final scenes of the picture's resolution.

14. The fate of one character after another is resolved. And since we see this through Darlene's eyes, she becomes increasingly the focal point of viewer interest.
15. Christmas morning has arrived. The night of terror is over.
16. There's still no happiness for Darlene, or for Kelly. But Darlene has strength. She's still in there fighting. It's the kind of thing that makes a character admirable to viewers.
17. Kelly, too, gains sympathy, as we discover he has a conscience. And since Darlene understands, at least there's hope for them, even if not instant happiness. Which is fine, for a quick save would have come through as both corny and unbelievable.
18. There's a larger world beyond the problems of Turley's story people, however. Now, it takes over, with Harper clarifying the situation where the fire is concerned.
19. Harper voices a feeling which most viewers will share.
20. A new day . . . peace, and a return to reality for viewers, in contrast to the night's fear and tension.

INTERNAL CRIME PREVENTION (informational video script), *by Benjamin S. Walker.*

Scriptwriters come from all kinds of backgrounds and operate on all sorts of levels.

Benjamin S. Walker offers a good case in point. Born in Omaha, Nebraska, and brought to Washington, D.C., at the age of 11, he won a scholarship to Auburn and earned a degree in chemistry as a Navy ROTC student.

He wound up not caring much for chemistry, however—"I always was a reader and a writer," he says. After paying for his education with an obligatory three years of Navy service, he took a job as a technical writer with RCA, later worked for other firms, and ended up in 1960 with a newly formed film group at Johns Hopkins University.

Today, he's supervisor for production with Johns Hopkins' audio-visual team, successor to the film unit, turning out slide shows, films, and (mostly) television. As such, he estimates he's written more than 300 scripts for Johns Hopkins.

That's only part of the story, however. For 20 years Walker also has free-lanced scripts (at least 200 of them) for other organizations: a total of more than 500 writing jobs completed, on topics ranging from medicine to computers to satellites to human interest to recruitment to training—"and just about anything else you want to name."

Most of Walker's outside chores are on assignment. The rest he wins on bid. His free-lance client list includes the U.S. Postal Service, for whom he did *Internal Crime Prevention.*

It's a script particularly worth noting for the manner in which it combines interest with information, interweaving factual content—that is, the client message—with a presentation designed to catch and hold its target audience. Yet it does this in a straightforward, down-to-earth fashion in keeping with its topic, with none of the hype or hoke that too often is injected into informational films.

```
                    D R A F T

          for a television production




          INTERNAL CRIME PREVENTION




                    Produced for

                    POSTAL MANAGEMENT ACADEMY

                    by

                    Benjamin S. Walker
                    11317 Marcliff Road
                    Rockville, Md. 20852
                    301-493-5556



                    August 29, 1985
```

INTERNAL CRIME PREVENTION

<u>Video</u>   <u>Audio</u>

① 1. High-angle down   MUSIC: ROCK MUSIC, AS IF FROM
on Post Office workfloor.   AN EMPLOYEE'S RADIO. MUSIC
VERY SLOW PAN of area: DUCKS UNDER NARRATION.
we see many workers at
their jobs. SUPER titles:

THE U.S. POSTAL SERVICE
   presents ...

  INTERNAL CRIME
  PREVENTION

② Titles FADE OUT, and PAN
stops to HOLD on scene
with several employees
working: sorting mail,
working with packages,
etc. Narration begins.

③ NOTE: The Narrator also ④ NARRATOR (Voice-Over): Just your
appears as an on-camera
Postal Inspector.   typical Post Office workfloor --

            everyone doing their usual good job.

          ⑤ But, are they?

2. MCU On inspection walkway. Postal Inspector (PI), who is the Narrator, pulls back from looking down through observation window, and talks to camera. PI is wearing his badge.

MAKE A SHORT, SLOW ZOOM INTO A HEAD-AND-SHOULDERS SHOT.

NARRATOR (Lip-Sync): Some of your employees may not be doing a good job. They may be stealing -- from the Postal Service, from the American public. Postal workers -- you, me, the people down there -- are pledged preserve the sanctity of the seal ... to protect the integrity of the mail. If we fail, the public won't trust us with their personal mail, or companies with their products, or the government with its valuable documents. So, let's take a closer look at the problem of crime in the Post Office.

TURNS AND AGAIN LOOKS THROUGH OBSERVATION WINDOW.

3. High-angle shows same scene as before. Now we see one of the workers occasionally, nervously looking up at the observation window. He's in the rewrap section. On cue, "this clerk" HIGHLIGHT the clerk.

NARRATOR (VO): Who commits these crimes? Well, it's usually someone with a problem -- like this clerk in the rewrap section.

⑨ 4. MCU On the floor. Clerk looks furtively around, then takes an item out of a damaged, parcel, hides it, then begins rewrapping the parcel.
NOTE: Don't overdo the looking around action.

NARR (VO): Fred takes drugs. He needs money. When he sees something valuable in a damaged parcel, he takes it before rewrapping the parcel. He's a thief and he works for you.

5. MCU Female window clerk getting money from customer, writing numbers on parcel, putting it aside. She faces next customer with a big smile and hello.

Joyce is in heavy debt, hooked on gambling. She's setting up a small theft that she'll commit later. Everyone likes her.

6. MCU Carrier yells at someone, then returns to task of casing mail. He holds one of the letters up to the light before throwing it into a slot by itself.

Not many people get along with Al. Someone said he's been having family problems and last week he had a minor accident on his route. Why is he examining the mail like that?

7. MCU PI on workfloor. In background we see Postal activity.

NARR (LS): People with problems -- they're the ones most likely to commit internal crimes.

⑩ Local Postmaster walks by, says hello to PI.

(TO P.M.): Hi, Larry.
When you have solid information that an an employee is a heavy drinker, on drugs, or has financial or domestic problems, we want to know about it.

3

30. MS From customer's
view, establish Joyce
working at counter.

NARR (VO): And remember pleasant

Joyce, at the window? Let's listen.

31. MCU and CU's:
Lip-sync exchange
between Joyce and
a customer with a
parcel.

CUST: How much is it?

JOYCE: Altogether, with the insurance,

              it's $9.00 even.

JOYCE is writing
on corner of
parcel

CUST: It's for my grandson, I hope

              it gets there in time.

JOYCE: We'll certainly do our best --

She gets the money
from the customer

              have a nice day (BIG SMILE).

Customer leaves.

CUST: Thank you.

32. CU Joyce puts
stamps on parcel.

NARR (VO): At least we know Joyce is

having a good day. She took $9 from

the customer, ...

33. ECU Joyce's
hands putting $6 in
stamps on the parcel.

... put $6 on the package, and ...

34. MLS Finish at
racetrack. We see the
toteboard in the
background.

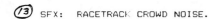 SFX: RACETRACK CROWD NOISE.

... $3 on the tri-xacta at Pimlico.

So -- what are the odds on stopping

such thefts in your Post Office?

39. MCU PAN with   NARR (VO): We personally review and
Inspector over to
files (maybe a computer)   analyze every 1510 we receive. Send
where she looks up
additional information.   them to us.

40. MCU Narrator, with
Post Office activity in
background.   NARR (LS): Of course, the first line

                                of defense against internal crime is

ZOOM IN SLOWLY to a   here, in the Post Office. We
tighter shot. At
end of narration, he   depend on you to observe and report
(16) looks away from
camera.   any suspicious activity --

                                employees who ...

41. CU Carrier casing
mail holds it up to
light.   ... over-examine the mail;

42. MCU Clerk looking
around for supervisors.   ... constantly look around to see

                                where supervisors are standing; ...

43. MCU Clerk in the
wrong place, perhaps   ... who are always in the wrong place.
by the window counters
or near the cage.

44. MS ZOOMING INTO
a window clerk writing
on parcel and putting
it aside.   Notice clerks who don't put on the

                                             postage in front of the customer; ...

45. MCU ZOOMING INTO
a clerk's hands
overlabeling a parcel.   ... who put labels over other

                                             labels; or ...

46. MS Clerk working
by himself in nearly
empty surrounding.   ... who always seem to be working by

                                             themselves during lunchtime or before

                                             others report for work.

47. MS Several employees   And take a second look at people
leaving Post Office. One
carries a small athletic   wearing bulky jackets in work areas,
bag. ZOOM INTO him/her.
                                             who frequently carry a bag to and

                                             from work.

48. TRUCKING SHOT: NARR (LS): Don't investigate any of
TRUCK BACK slowly as
Narrator walks forward,   these people or activities yourself.
talking to the camera.
This is along the Postal   Don't talk to others about your
workfloor and we see
activity going on.   suspicions; don't confront the

                                             employee. Tell us and we'll follow up.

TRUCK STOPS. Narrator
stops at head-and-
shoulder distance.   Now if you remember, this presentation

                                             is called "Internal Crime Prevention."

                                             The key word is "Prevention." We would

                                             rather prevent a crime than catch a

                                             thief. Here's what you can do.

                              12

57. MONTAGE: Several
scenes of Larry, the
P.M. around the Post
Office -- talking to

people, looking (not
snooping) at what's
going on everywhere.

LARRY (VO): As far as I know, no one's
ever stolen anything from here. I'm
sure I'd know -- I've worked up from a
carrier and seen just about everything.
I'm on the floor a lot. I talk to
people, and see for myself what's going
on. I can actually feel the *rhythm*
of this place -- can sense when
something's about to go wrong. Then
I communicate.

58. MCU Larry the P.M.
talking. Slow continuing
ZOOM BACK reveals
employees listening
to him. (Narrator will
be standing at the back
of the crowd.)

LARRY (LS): I notice that some of
you have been taking those toothpaste
samples from the trash. I want it
to stop. I don't care if it is
trash -- it doesn't belong to us.
Any questions? Okay, next item ...
some customers have been complaining
about ... (FADES, BUT CONTINUES,
UNDER NARRATOR'S WORDS).

15

58 (cont'd). Narrator, standing at back of crowd of employees but closest to camera, turns and talks to camera. After delivering lines, he turns back to look at Larry, who still is speaking.

NARR (LS): "Talk to the people ... see what's going on ... feel the rhythm ... communicate." What it all adds up to is internal crime prevention. My job and your job.

59. MCU As soon as Narrator turns back to Larry, CUT to an MCU of Larry speaking. We can see 6-8 people in front of him, listening to him.

LARRY (LS): .... so he offered to swap me a vehicle for a clerk. I said "does it work?" He said, "Does yours?" (EVERYONE LAUGHS). Okay -- some of you have audits coming up. Please make sure that ... (HE FADES UNDER MUSIC)

60. MS Wider shot from new angle on Larry and employees as he continues to speak.

SUPER tail credits.

TAIL MUSIC SWELLS UP AND ENDS WITH A CLIMAX.

THE END

1. Setting/situation and a degree of interest are established from the start by the background against which the titles are superimposed. And the rock music indicates that handling isn't likely to be overly pontifical.
2. A wordless focusing of attention on the kind of people who are going to make up our cast.
3. The producer's warned of a potential casting problem: the narrator's going to do double duty—acting, as well as reading commentary.
4. Narration here is voice-over. Which both simplifies the job and cuts costs—by and large, no location sound man will be needed in this show, save where there's lip-sync dialogue.
5. The narration itself uses contrast—"But, are they?"—to raise the tape's lead-in question fast.
6. Walker flips our narrator from disembodied voice to living person—an authority figure, identifiable by badge and doing his job as an observer.
7. The motivational message, delivered lip-sync for impact . . . narrowing down at the end to the immediate issue.
8. We begin a sequence in which both major types of thieves and techniques of theft are established, via zeroing in on individuals.
9. This "capturing the moment" continues as Walker picks specific action, significant behavior, to make his points.
10. Interweaving of lip-sync and voice-over narration continues, and we meet a second authority figure, the local postmaster, a key target of this film.

*   *   *

11. Skipping forward in our *Internal Crime Prevention* script, we again encounter Joyce, the window clerk whom we first met on page 3. But where there we caught her in the briefest of capsules, here we observe her theft technique in more detail. Equally vital, Walker shows us that a thief doesn't necessarily look like a thief.
12. A fragmentary scene in lip-sync—but limited lip-sync. Why? Because not everyone can read lines effectively. Also, shooting lip-sync means controlling set/location noise, not to mention adding a sound man to the crew.
13. Racetrack noise creates atmosphere with no strain on the budget.
14. Again, keeping it simple, holding down costs. Joyce doesn't even have to be present.
15. No law says fact films have to be dull or devoid of humor. Here, Walker has combined a play on words and action into unanticipated contrast that's a cinch to get a laugh even while it drives home a point.

*   *   *

16. Page 10 has our narrator explain steps to take to help prevent thefts. Here, on page 11, Walker gives further practical help to his audience, as well as information. Action and narration pinpoint behavioral red flags, things to watch for that may indicate thievery in the offing.
17. Walker and his technical advisors are aware that paranoia can be just as dangerous as playing patsy. Hence this warning against any temptation on viewers' part to develop a Sherlock Holmes syndrome. The message is clear: Leave action to the Postal Inspectors. They know the law, the rules; what can and can't be done.

18. Page 15, now; next to the last page of the script. With the film's conclusion approaching, Walker introduces the time-tested psychological device of a testimonial: Larry, the postmaster, is an authority figure, but a friendly one. Up from the ranks, broadly experienced, he points up a specific fault that illustrates the kind of thing that can lead to problems.
19. Finally, another laugh line, to close the film on a positive note and leave viewers feeling good, not browbeaten or hostile.

*   *   *

How did Walker research and develop *Internal Crime Prevention?*

"I talked to an inspection service agent," he reports. "She told me what sort of guidelines they had in mind—what they wanted the show to do. Their goal was to alert postmasters and other supervisors on how to spot and therefore prevent theft by postal employees.

"Then I went to a post office and spent half a day interviewing the postmaster there. He showed me the ways that theft ordinarily is accomplished. And of course I grabbed all available printed information.

"After that, it was just a matter of thinking through and writing the script and having it checked."

On a technical/format level, note that Walker has limited his use of optical effects to FADE IN and FADE OUT. This isn't unusual today, both because there's a tendency to eliminate dissolves and wipes in favor of straight cuts wherever possible, and because directors are inclined to ignore them even if the writer does insert them.

CHARIOTS OF FIRE (original screenplay), *by Colin Welland.*

In his native land they call Colin Welland a "professional North-erner"—north of England, that is. Well known as a TV actor and writer, characterized by a frizzy mop of curls and upon occasion described as "Harpo Marx with a double chin," he's achieved even greater respect in cinematic circles as the man who scripted *Chariots of Fire,* winner of the 1981 Academy Award for "screenplay written directly for the screen." The film also claimed that year's "Best Picture" honors and went on to become the highest-grossing imported film in the United States up to that time.

Chariots of Fire was by no means Welland's first success. His previous major screenplays included *Bangelstein's Boys* (1969), *Roll On Four O'Clock* (1970), *Kisses at Fifty* (1973), and *Leeds United* (1974). And in the years since, he's gone on to *Chaplin* (1983), and *The Yellow Jersey* and *Twice in a Lifetime,* both still in the scripting stage.

Produced by famed David Puttnam for Britain's Enigma Productions, *Chariots* is a totally unique picture. It centers on the true story of two sprinters as they clash in the 1924 Olympic Games. One, Harold Abrahams, is English and Jewish. The other, Eric Liddell, is the son of Scottish missionaries. The contrast between their divergent personalities, attitudes, and motivations, coupled with Welland's refusal to resort to cheap shots and traditional hype in his script, is such as to create one of the period's most memorable films.

People clearly are Welland's passion. In every film he's written, they are the focus.

Yet beyond this lie the factors of judgment and choice. A dozen times, a hundred, he must decide on the dynamics of each personality, and then pick and develop the incidents and color and details of setting that will best reveal the true nature of the man—or woman—under consideration.

It's here that *Chariots* best provides us with insight into Welland's talent. With deep practical knowledge of both psychology and film technique, he translates anti-semitism into Abraham's experiences at King's College, Calvinism into Edinburgh and the Scottish Highlands and Liddell's preaching. Races become far more than running. Tags, traits, and relationships are made meaningful in terms of speech and action.

Rather than attempt to dissect the script itself, we'll concentrate here on the creativity which Welland brought to bear on his project.

1924 RUNNNERS ◯◯◯◯

BY COLIN WELLAND

A TREATMENT FOR A FILM – JULY 1978.

②

Three young men, runners, gentlemen in a gentlemen's world. But each with his own peculiar driving force, ~~his own particular need~~, his own battle he has to win .... and each with the one common aim .... AN OLYMPIC GOLD!

1-

Introduction

'The Olympic Games'.! They never fail to
fire the imagination — They are the ultimate in
contests, and of all contests nothing beats a race,
and races between the best in the world, so they're
irresistable. Furthermore, but foot races have
a fundamental appeal far beyond any other —
no elaborate equipment, no trappings, no vast
organisation — just one against one against
a distance — and all for that title 'The fastest
man alive on earth'.

Its 1924, and a generation — whose heels have
been nipped by the first world war, march around
the Stade Colombes in Paris, perky, defiant,
decked in barmy blazers and boaters determined
to cock a brave snoop at its still lingering
stench. Many men
and women from 40 Nations in Germany
excluded, follow their flags and with them
go stride the hopes of millions for a return to
international sanity and mutual respect.
The 1920 games in Antwerp have been
a brave but austere and often bitter occasions —
Europe just hadn't had time to
recover — but now, six years after the Armistice,
the stage is set for a triumphant return to
all that is "best and honourable".

But wars aren't just physically traumatic,
they shatter the whole order of things. Pre war Britain
had been an Edwardian domain. The playing
fields of Eton reigned supreme and consequently
as did those of Oxford and Cambridge, and now
as the war dust settles a return to 'normality'
is simply of mistakenly taken for granted.
Oxbridge undergraduates still appear to live in their
quaint totally male orientated society of boater
back slapping and tea and buns, Behaviour
is still based on Dr Arnolds pro concepts of living,
learning and playing. Sport is still a training for
life and leadership, Individual glorification

2

④

'RUNNERS'

Breakdown of Story Line

RUNNERS

⑤   HAROLD ABRAHAMS   ERIC LIDDELL

Both loners. Both exceptionally gifted.
Both feeling intensely about their 'roll'
and responsibility.

⑥ UP ON   MEMORIAL SERVICES AND INTERLUDE 1924. SEASIDE

1919   1922

Abraham's
introduction   Liddell at Highland
to Cambridge.   gathering. Sprints' for
Meets MONTAGUE   fun ... Talks to crowd.
LINDSEY and   IMPRESSES both ROB his
STALLARD.   brother with his oratory -
Through initial   and Sandy his host with
anti-semitism to   his running.
KING'S COLLEGE   FAREWELL SUPPER TO FAMILY.
DASH.   Pressures on him to preach
                                          and to run.
                                          FATHERS ADVICE - Rejoice
                                          in all gifts.
                                          SISTER'S opposition sensed
                                          as he trains for first time
                                          at Powderhall.
                                          His reaction to Pro's and
                                          Whippets.

M O N T A G E   O F   B O T H

⑦ ABRAHAMS   LIDDELL

Harold's develop-   Eric's development over the
ment over next year.   year 1923 in: ATHLETICS
1923 in:- ATHLETICS   Student triumphs in Edinburgh
Student triumphs in   colours.
Cambridge colours, with   STUDIES
Stallard, Lindsey, and   Deep into science. Working
Montague.   in lab etc.

1.

ABRAHAMS (Cont.)

STUDIES
Harold at Old Bailey
observing -- debating
society showing erudite
wit.
Gilbert and Sullivan
singing in production
with pertinent lyrics.
ALL covered with
cuttings from TIMES
on his athletic
exploits read by him-
self.
"GOING TO GET MYSELF
A COACH" up North.

LIDDELL (Cont)

SPIRITUAL
Preaching outside football
ground with ROB and SISTER.
Gathering in confidence.
Preaches in towns in which
he runs .. 'Posters' proclaim
both events.
Audiences increasing dramatically.
ALL covered with cuttings
from GLASGOW HERALD read by
two Svengalis - ROB and SANDY.

C O N V E R G E

Meeting at Newcastle

ERIC COMPETING - HAROLD OBSERVING. They meet. "Professional Foul" Incident
in 230 yards start - resulting, despite odds, in incredible win by Liddell ....
Abrahams watching. Contrives pub meeting with SAM MUSSABINI - asks him to
coach him - refused. Meanwhile in taxi Eric rejects Sandy's bet.

 TWO ATTITUDES hardening now. ABRAHAMS ultimate victory all important.
LIDDELL - Everything in perspective - MIND, BODY and SPIRIT.

Amateur Athletic Association Championships 1923

Liddell and Abrahams both up in London to compete. Harold at Savoy to
see 'Gondeliers' with his 3 friends. Entranced by Sybil in leading roll.
Meets her in dressing room, invites her to supper - she accepts - to surprise
of Andy, Harry and Aubrey.

She's in the crowd to see Harold run ... He's beaten by Liddell. Sybil sees
his moody aggressive side - He's approached Mussabini in Chelsea pub. "I
can't give you another yard". They agreed to work together. He immediately
brightens. Sybil now wary of him.

2.

3 Beverley Rd
SW13

Dear David.

Here's the provisional first thirty pages
of 'Runners'.

It's an atmospheric film this depending
so much on mood and the creation of
a visual time and place – If this is
done successfully then my characters will
suddenly take on a reality.

I'm now deep into Liddell up in Edinburgh
– even greyer, stonier, mistier and more
austere than Cambridge. There's a
calvinistic simplicity about the man and
his world that make Abrahams set-
up book positively baroque.

But I have the complete story line laid
out now. I'll have it typed and Andre
can send it on to you.

Hope you enjoy meeting Harold, Aubrey
Andy and the gang.

Have a nice flight.

Colin

"CHARIOTS OF FIRE"

A Film

by

COLIN WELLAND

First Draft
April, 1979

01-876-0168
3 Beverley Road
Barnes, London, SW13

UP ON 1. INT. ST. BRIDES CHURCH, FLEET STREET, DAY

Flying angels vaulting across the screen, gilded and triumphant amidst the pipes of a great church organ reaching for the sky.

The light is the pale pastel of a Georgian church interior.

THE SOUND OF SINGING OVER:-

CONGREGATION (o.o.v.)

He who would valiant be

'Gainst all disaster.

Let him with constancy

Follow the Master.

There's no discouragement

Shall make him once relent

His first avowed intent

To be a pilgrim.

The singing soars, the angels leap, the pipes tremble with vibrato. The voices are strident - mainly masculine - forceful yet strangely toneless .... school assembly like.

PAN DOWN   Searching for the source.

Down past the organist enthusiastically pounding his keys with hands and feet alike - down past the candles and clean cut alter silver.

LEVEL OFF at the rosy glow of Anglican priests in the medals and white regalia of the English established church.

THEN PAN RIGHT past the Rabbi with black flowing beard .... THE RABBI? HERE?

YES. THE RABBI. There's no mistaking his calling or the cut of his cloth. He's singing lustily with the best of them.

ROUND past the choir of cherubic boys aged it seems from nine to ninety.

ROUND to the congregation itself.

1.

5/-

"CHARIOTS OF FIRE"

A Film

by

COLIN WELLAND

⑫   ~~First Draft~~ 2nd Draft.
~~March 1979~~ June 1979

01-876-0168
3 Beverley Road
Barnes, London, SW1.

UP ON 1. EXT. FLEET STREET. DAY

(13)

Filling screen - big close up - a medal, a gold medal - hanging
on a 'sky blue' East German chest.

The D.D.R. dirge ploughs on above the image. Then pull back to
see the recipient - erect - bland - smiling a practised smile,
programmed. Back further to encompass his team mates, second
and third - cast from the same mould. They stand - a triumphant,
manufactured trio.

Back again to reveal they are images on a screen - a T.V. screen.
Back further - more screens - the image multiplied a score or
more.

Reflections flash before us - passing pedestrians - London buses,
cabs.

The anthem is lost in the sound of traffic as a shop window
emerges, filled with TV screens. London passes them by - and
their all too-familiar, boring story.

THEN out of the noise of Fleet Street, rises the sound of
singing ... a congregation.

5/2

(14)

> "He who would valiant be
> 'Gainst all disaster.
> Let him with constancy
> Follow the master ...."

The camera pans left - seeking the singing's source. To the left
of the shop is an alley - down it we can see an open church door.
Inside the rear of the congregation.

Close on them ... erect, sombre suited - solemn.

1.

CHARIOTS OF FIRE

A Film

by

COLIN WELLAND

Second Draft
(13 February 1980)

Enigma Productions Ltd.
2-10 Tavistock Street
London W.C.2.

Tel: (01) 240-5684

PREFACE

"This first experience with "official" sports was
conclusive.   Wherever public authorities
undertook to meddle with any sports organization
they introduced the fatal germs of impotence and
mediocrity.   The body formed by the good will
of all the members of an autonomous sport group
becomes swollen to gigantic and uncertain
proportions upon contact with this dangerous
thing called the State."

> Baron Pierre de Coubertin
> Founder of the Modern Olympics
> Paris, July, 1900.

These are sour days in Olympic history. The bureaucracies of
big business and nation states have finally demanded more of
the original slender ideal than it can possibly bear and it's
fatally begun to crack. This year's Olympiad could possibly
be the last.

But it wasn't always so.   Back beyond Moscow and Montreal,
Bundage and the big brass bands, Hitler and the Zieg Heils,
was a time when the young people who gathered under the five
rings and flame did so of their own volition.   They were
fired by their own purpose, inspired by their own dreams, and
seeking only to test themselves, on their <u>own</u> behalf, against
the fastest, the strongest, the highest on earth.

Such men were Eric Liddell and Harold Abrahams. The one the
son of a Scots missionary destined to follow in his father's
footsteps and to die in Japanese hands in 1945.   The other the
son of a German Jew who battled against prejudice and the might
of the English Protestant Establishment to become the last
Englishman and the only Jew ever to win the Blue Riband of the
Games - the 100 metres. Liddell and Abrahams, in 1924 are to
become the two fastest men in the world, yet both have their
own individual driving force.   They run because they have to,
Liddell for God whose cause he upholds almost to the point of
athletic suicide, and Abrahams as a means of dealing a final
blow to the humiliation and bigotry which have haunted his life.

They both reach Gold, but on their own terms.   Riding their
"Chariots of Fire" they fight against and finally sweep aside
those newly emerging Goliaths, nationalism and political
expedience, those same monsters which today have resulted in
the probable demise of the whole magnificent ideal.

Their stories deserve to be told again, if only to inspire
today's young men and women the world over to pick up a new
torch, to rekindle it and to find for themselves that old
Olympic spirit once more.

UP ON

1   EXT.   FLEET STREET   DAY   1

Filling screen - BIG CLOSE UP - a medal, a gold medal -
hanging on a 'sky blue' East German chest.

The D.D.R. dirge ploughs on above the image.   Then PULL BACK
to see the recipient - erect - bland - smiling a practised
smile, programmed. . Back further to encompass his team mates,
second and third - cast from the same mould.   They stand - a
triumphant, manufactured trio.

Back again to reveal they are images on a screen - a T.V.
screen.   Back further - more screens - the image multiplied a
score or more.

Reflections flash before us - passing pedestrians - London
buses, cabs.

The anthem is lost in the sound of traffic as a shop window
emerges, filled with TV screens.   London passes them by -
and their all too-familiar, boring story.

THEN out of the noise of Fleet Street, rises the sound of
singing ... a congregation.

                    "He who would valiant be
                     'Gainst all disaster.
                     Let him with constancy
                     Follow the master ..."

The CAMERA PANS LEFT - seeking the singing's source.   To the
left of the shop is an alley - down it we can see an open
church door. Inside the rear of the congregation.

CLOSE on them ... erect, sombre suited - solemn.

                                        MIX TO

Flying angels vaulting across the screen, gilded and triumphant
amidst the pipes of a great church organ reaching for the sky.
The light is the pale pastel of a Georgian church interior.

THE SOUND OF SINGING CONTINUES.

                        CONGREGATION (O.O.V.)
           " ... There's no discouragement
                 Shall make him once relent
                 His first avowed intent
                 To be a pilgrim."

The singing soars, the angels leap. The pipes tremble with
vibrato.   The voices are strident - mainly masculine - forceful,
yet strangely toneless ... school-assembly- like.

PAN DOWN still searching for the source.

1. The cover sheet on Welland's original treatment. Note that at this time, the project was titled *1924 Runners*, rather than the ultimate *Chariots of Fire*.

    Observe, too, that the date is 1978.
2. The concept for the film, captured in a single brief paragraph: "Three young men, runners, gentlemen in a gentlemen's world. But each with his own peculiar driving force, his own battle he has to win . . . and each with the one common aim . . . AN OLYMPIC GOLD!"
3. The first page of Welland's handwritten notes for the picture. Although he heads the presentation "Introduction," it clearly is a laying-out of his own thinking as he ponders the background against which the proposed film must develop: a Europe still reeling in the aftermath of World War I, with all the political, sociological, and psychological trauma that implies. The very fact that Welland probed the situation in such depth can't but have had an influence on the way he built the script.
4. "Breakdown of Story Line": another step forward in the concept's unfolding.

    Note, too, that the title is now simply *Runners*.
5. The two major characters: their development; the events and heritage that have shaped them.
6. Passage of time, too. These men don't spring onto the screen full-blown, nor are they one-dimensional. They're different, unique human beings, each with a depth that gives him individual fascination for us, the audience.
7. As timespan and exploration of divergent aspects of characters' lives grows, footage lengthens. Welland uses montage to hold it down, compress it.
8. Welland has thought through his characters and their contrasting values. Which means that he has a standard to write to for each. He's established guidelines not only to tell him in advance how each will react in any given situation, but to help him devise appropriate, tension-building scenes and incidents . . . essential even in a "true" account such as this one.
9. We find more insight into Welland's thinking in this undated letter to producer David Puttnam: "It's an atmospheric film this," he writes, "depending so much on mood and the creation of a visual time and place. If this is done successfully then my characters will suddenly take on a reality."

    The paragraph that follows makes clear how he's feeling his way into the atmosphere he knows is so important and, simultaneously, is integrating his characters into it.

    He also has "the complete story line laid out now"—worth noting here because it points up the step-at-a-time procedure that goes with scripting; a denial that screenplays flash into a writer's mind full blown.

    This is perhaps a good place, too, to note that Welland is working with David Puttnam, a brilliant producer. Without in any way diminishing Welland's role, undoubtedly the final script reflects the interplay of two creative minds.
10. First draft of the script. It's now April, 1979; nearly a year has elapsed since Welland submitted his treatment. Also, the title now has changed from *Runners* to *Chariots of Fire*.
11. Note the church interior setting.
12. June, 1979, and the second draft.
13. The church interior of the first draft has changed to a Fleet Street exterior, with television screens picking up East German Olympic winners.
14. Not for long, though. We return to the church interior from the first draft, with only minor changes.
15. February 13, 1980, and another version of the second draft.
16. A preface has been inserted. It helps to orient the film's audience to the time, place, and circumstance of the picture. Yet in all likelihood it also was rooted in more than

a little nail-gnawing and floor-pacing, for in film any delay in getting into the action is bound to constitute a calculated risk where the box office is concerned.
17. The script page that follows remains as before, however.

*　　　　　*　　　　　*

The point to be made here is that writing a film script—*any* film script—is a big job. To produce one as superior as *Chariots of Fire* is even more so. It took at least two years—probably more—of Colin Welland's time and talent, not to mention the tedium and frustration that go with what sometimes seems like endless revision. Which is to say, it's not a job for anyone who lacks staying power and the ability to work with others.

Observe, too, how many bits and pieces and ideas have been introduced and discarded in the course of the script's development.

And if you've seen the finished film, you'll recognize that even more changes took place while the picture was being shot and edited . . . par for the course in the very nature of things, no matter how upsetting to the person who wrote the script.

*　　　　　*　　　　　*

So, at last, we end these lessons from the pros; this glimpse at the way the old hands solve script problems.

But there's still the question of where you fit into the world of film. It's the topic of our final chapter.

CHAPTER 19

The Other Side

It's one thing to write scripts, another to talk to the people who work with the scripts you write. Their outlook is different, their approach geared to the problems involved in turning words on paper into images on a theatre or television screen. Yet precisely because this is the case, their thoughts often are of infinite value to the scripter.

That being the case, here are the insights of six experienced people in the business: a story editor, a writer/director of entertainment films, a producer/director of home video entertainment films, an agent, a manager of a major video production facility, and a story analyst of print material.

STORY EDITOR: Judy Burns.

Intrigued early on by film, and totally captivated by "Star Trek" during her college years at UCLA (Irvine), Judy Burns broke into script-writing at that show, gained additional experience with "Mission Impossible," later was an apprentice writer at Paramount Studios, and then went on to earn credits at a wide range of top shows.

Currently, she produces the hit "Stingray" action adventure television series. Before that, however, she was story editor for "The Six Million Dollar Man," "American Girls," "Vegas," "The Powers of Matthew Star," and "T.J. Hooker." She was also coproducer on "MacGyver." Her insight into what makes for a successful script is both shrewd and practical.

Just what does a story editor do, Judy?
Burns: That differs, I think, on the phase of production. At the beginning, you sit and listen to writers as they pitch their material, present

their ideas for new episodes for the series. Then you try to shape those pitches, direct them so that they fit the show's pattern, help the writer to work out a line that takes his story from Act 1 to Act 4. Also, you try to steer them away from worn-out stories, plots that have been done before.

So basically you work with ideas as much as writing.

Burns: Yes. You take it for granted that people here know how to write, so you operate more in terms of concept than putting pencil to paper. Typically, with a new writer, you'll sit in a meeting with the producer and one or two staff writers and listen to the outside free-lance writer tell you his story.

How does the free-lance get in to see you to make his or her pitch?

Burns: There are three major ways. First, there's the writer with a lot of credits. Usually his agent can get him a pitch meeting based on his credits—that is, assuming his credits are along the line of the kind of stories you need. A comedy writer generally wouldn't get an invite to an action adventure show unless he had action adventure credits too.

How about the writer who's agented, but hasn't sold before?

Burns: If the agent says he's good, and can submit unsold material that looks interesting, then you might talk to him, let him make a pitch.

What's the third possibility?

Burns: The cold submission, the spec script, the script the writer's written for your show on a pure gamble. I always have my hands open for those. I got into the industry on a spec script myself. I can't remember anyone who hasn't. Often they'll catch the flavor of the show. So even though the script itself isn't right, you may allow them to come in and pitch.

So here's the story conference . . . the producer and the story editor and a couple of staff writers, plus the free-lance. What happens then?

Burns: You give the writer, the free-lance, whatever help you can, plugging holes and what not. Basically, you just talk to him as a creative individual.

What's the most common mistake you find in scripts? What turns you off the worst?

Burns: I think if you haven't been gripped by a character or a situation in the first five or six pages, the story's in trouble already.

Why is that such a danger?

Burns: Because every good writer, every story editor, learns from the start that every scene has to have a purpose. It may be a character purpose sometimes, but usually it progresses the story, moves it along towards the climax. And if I don't see the story progressing from the first page, then I'm probably going to toss that script back to the writer.

What are the most important areas of the script?

Burns: Almost always, the first ten pages are critical. If you're receiving spec material [material submitted on speculation, written by the writer as a gamble, without assignment], or if you're reading for the first time, you'll usually know if the writer's on key by the first ten pages.

You'll also know whether or not they have some talent.

Are there any other critical areas in particular to watch for?

Burns: The last ten pages. Oftentimes a writer will get into terrible trouble with the last act.

How so?

Burns: He gets lazy, lets his hero take the easy way out. Opts for the obvious solution, that is. So the viewer gets no real satisfaction from the climax, the resolution.

What else do you look for?

Burns: Good characterization.

What do you think makes for a strong character?

Burns: I think it's a character who has something to say in this particular script. If a character who has something to say and something to do doesn't come alive, then it's the writer's fault. Usually if you come across a character who has conflict in the story or with the other characters in the piece or who has a personal dilemma to resolve in that particular script, then you have a good script, or at least you have the basis for a good script. And that's whether it be comedy or action adventure or high drama.

What's the other side of the coin?

Burns: If you have a character who *doesn't* really have anything to do, or doesn't have any conflict, or doesn't have a goal to be attained in that script, or who can't be turned around in that script, then you're in trouble. Usually if you're going to write an hour-long action adventure, you have to have at least one main character besides the characters who are intrinsic to the show. In other words, you need someone against whom you can play the story. Oftentimes you have three or four such people, such characters. Typically, in an hour show, you're running with about nine or ten characters. Out of these, maybe three or four—in "Stingray's" case, one—is your lead.

That means that some of those other people are going to have to carry major parts. If each of them doesn't have a goal or a motive in that script, then there's no reason for the script in the first place.

Where does dialogue come in?

Burns: Dialogue that plays, lines that move along and that the actors can speak, is important. My personal taste is for dialogue that moves, snappy dialogue that isn't flat.

What constitutes flat dialogue?

Burns: It's a term we use too loosely here. We've all been accused of "flat writing" at one time or another. I guess what I mean is that I like to see the dialogue move along. If somebody stands around and talks non-stop for five pages I know that we're in trouble unless it's Shakespeare writing.

How can you learn to write effective dialogue?

Burns: Tape only the audio part of a television program. Then when you listen to it, pretend it's radio. You'll know when it's a clinker and when it isn't. If it's well written, the people will talk well. You'll hear it. If you can't see the video, your eyes won't fool you into accepting bad lines.

How about things in a script that turn you on?

Burns: You need story. Typically, I'm looking for stories I haven't seen every week.

Which means?

Burns: Just something different enough to catch my mind. Sometimes what seems a little far out is what turns me on. I'm tired of the typical action adventure, shoot-'em-up, bang-bang, and so on. So if something comes across my desk that somebody thought about a little bit, something I'd like to be involved in personally, then I'm going to read the rest of it. It's hard to put your finger on what you're looking for exactly. I mean, you can't say that a car crash will turn you on. What you *can* say is that the character comes in with an interesting problem and really unique ways of solving it. That's going to turn me on, and I might have an interest in it.

What makes a bad script?

Burns: The lack of all the good things, of course.

Beyond that, when a script comes in that hasn't been thought out scene by scene, it leaves me cold. A good script has a dynamic all its own. It has its beginning and its middle and its climax. It introduces a problem, it contemplates that problem, and it resolves the problem.

Each little scene does the same thing, in a way. It introduces something, then plays around with it. Sometimes it resolves it, sometimes it doesn't; sometimes you have to wait till the next scene to resolve it.

If someone writes scenes that don't introduce and resolve, or at least attempt to resolve, a problem, or if he writes scenes that just go on forever, then he's in trouble.

It also helps if writers write grammatically. I don't mean that the dialogue has to be grammatically correct, but you at least have to approach the description and the dialogue in a fashion that says you're intelligent about your script. I've had scripts turned in that looked like a second-grader probably wrote them. People should take care about how they present their material, present it within a proper form and do the best editing they can on it before they turn it in. That gives them the best shot at being read. The Guild doesn't exist as a 300-member Guild any more. It's a 6,000-member Guild now, so the new writer's in heavy competition. He needs to look up how to write a screenplay and then do the best job he can to make sure it works dramatically and grammatically when it comes across the desk. You still work a lot by instinct, you understand. But you know the rules, too.

Do you prefer master scene scripts, or shot-by-shot?

Burns: Master scenes are very much in. If you write two-shots and three-shots and long shots and closeups, it probably means you're behind the times. Today, scenes are written either as masters, or in a very flowing style in which you might pick up running feet, say, without ever calling a shot.

How about production costs?

Burns: Nobody should inhibit himself by thinking about cost in his script. But he might think about whether something really can be done. If you ask for the world to end on page 48, it might be difficult for us to do that. But if you just ask for a plane to crash, we might be able to accomplish that. Common sense is what counts. If you ask for something outlandish in the first five pages, your credibility as a writer may go down.

What about guidelines?

Burns: Some shows have them, some don't. It's not like it used to be, when every show had a bible. If "Stingray" comes back, I'll probably write a 10-page bible—what we know about the main character, the places he's been, what he thinks, about our production problems, about anything I think is pertinent to the show. Plus a synopsis of what's been done, so that we don't come too close to shows we've run.

Where guidelines are concerned, the only way the new writer can learn is to watch the show he wants to hit. If there's a two-hour pilot that you think may make it, tape it and then write a script on spec. When I started trying to break in, I'd just call a story editor whose name I saw on the credits and ask him to tell me about his show or send me some scripts. Or maybe I'd ask him if I could tell him about an idea, and better than half the time the editors were pleasant people who picked up the telephone and talked to me. Professional writers are on the whole pretty nice people, people who care about other people who are trying to break in.

Any last bit of advice?

Burns: Don't give up after the first try. Or the second. Or the third. That's the best piece of advice I can offer. Because if I'd given up after the first or the second or the third tries, I wouldn't be here today.

WRITER/DIRECTOR (ENTERTAINMENT FILM/TV): Burt Kennedy.

Burt Kennedy is a highly successful film director who also writes and, upon occasion, produces. Born in Muskegon, Michigan (in a trunk, he says—"My folks were dancers, a next-to-closing act for 20 years"), he came to California after World War II, and started to write.

"Ten years later I got a job, and I haven't been out of work since," he reports. "If I can make it, anybody can."

More specifically, he broke into films in 1953 when he sold John Wayne's company the script for *Seven Men from Now.* His credits include such films as *The Rounders* (screenplay and director), *Return of the Seven* (director), *Support Your Local Sheriff* (director), and *Dingus Magee* (produced and directed)—a total of 20 pictures, plus more than 50 television episodes, 16 of them "Simon and Simon" segments. Among his recent shows have been *The Alamo,* a three-hour NBC special (directed) and *Down the Long Hills* for Disney (directed).

Burt, what are some of the things that turn you off when you read a script?
Kennedy: Everybody tries to tell too much story in the first 10 or 15 pages. Usually if I go to the first fade-out and don't look at those first 15 pages, dodge that opening exposition, nine times out of ten the story's much more interesting, just because I don't know anything they try to fill me in on up front.

What's the solution?
Kennedy: My own experience is that when you write you have a tendency to want to lay the whole situation out in the beginning. So maybe you should write it that way and then go back and drop any portions that you don't necessarily have to have. You'll undoubtedly say it again three times before the script is over anyhow.

And beyond the situation?
Kennedy: Many writers describe far more than they need to. I guess they just want to fill up the page. When I'm reading a script that is very terse in its description, it's good for me. I don't have to know every stick of furniture in the room in order to read a scene.

You understand, if I'm writing it myself, an original, I might have to do that so that I know what's going on in the room. But that's because I'm the director as well as the writer. Most of the time, people just overdescribe things. And believe me, there's nothing worse than to turn a page and see solid directions.

You don't have to do it that way. Take Neil Simon. He very seldom describes anything. He uses dialogue—just gets some characters into a room and away they go.

What was your own biggest mistake when you were starting out? What taught you the most?
Kennedy: Mostly, I think, I wouldn't let scenes play as long as they should. I'm going through a thing now in this Peter Viertel book, *White Hunter, Black Heart.* It's a wonderful novel, but when he did the screenplay he was afraid to write a ten-page scene because he thought it was too long. He didn't realize that you can always cut the film.

My own tendency was the other way. My scenes weren't long enough. They were long enough for me; I understood them. But the audience didn't. Now, I seek answers to every question from actors, no matter what.

Do you have any theories about optimum scene length, beyond the "whatever it takes" kind of thing?

Kennedy: I think you just have to see how it plays. And we all know that when something really happens, when a scene really works, the elevator operator or Mayflower service man can tell it. It just happens.

There's a certain rhythm that has to come from the lines, though. If someone asks a question, the actor doesn't necessarily have to answer it in the next line of dialogue. Sometimes he can pose a question himself instead.

And that works?

Kennedy: It has a tendency to work. It's almost like editing the scene as it goes. The writers who can do that are very good writers. Jimmy Grant [the late James Edward Grant, whose unpublished story, "Latigo," was adapted as the screenplay for *Support Your Local Gunfighter*] used to be able to do that. He'd have two people talking, both of them asking questions and neither one of them answering the other guy's questions. Lawyers do that all the time. They always ask questions in everything that they do, and if it's a smart witness and he answers another question it makes for better testimony.

How about the tendency to fragmentary scenes that seems to be growing more and more prevalent? Particularly in the soaps, I've noticed that they'll do bit-bit-bit-bit, jumping around so fast in their efforts to hang onto their audience that they seldom develop a scene fully. Do you think that this is a good or a bad idea?

Kennedy: I think it's a very bad idea. It's born out of the fact that they've practically done away with dissolves in pictures. That's because dissolves cost money. Now everything is a cut, and you end up with fragmentary scenes. I find them confusing. Logical development tends to get lost. They're just doing it for excitement. But as John Ford used to say, "Let them bore me, but don't let them confuse me." It's better to stay with the scene awhile and make it play.

How about wipes [a transitional optical effect in which one image appears to push another off the screen in any one of dozens of patterns]?

Kennedy: Wipes are wonderful—vertical wipes, horizontal wipes, diagonal wipes, iris wipes, you name it. They're out of style now, of course, and they certainly can be overdone. Using them, though, you can stay with the same scene and move it ahead days.

In the past I've heard you say that you always look for honest characters, believable characters. What makes a character honest and/or believable?

Kennedy: Character has a lot to do with the writer. I learned that a long time ago, when I took a night class in short-story writing. The idea has stuck with me ever since. Take a writer like Max Evans with *The Rounders*. He's as down-to-earth as the people he writes about. So he writes very down-to-earth, honest characters. They're not phonies.

They're very straightforward. Hemingway did the same thing. He wrote straight-out, good characters that you like. I don't know how you do it, but it's certainly something you should strive for.

What are your thoughts on what makes a line memorable?

Kennedy: Simplicity; and the best illustration I can think of is one of the great lines Jimmy Grant wrote years ago in *Hondo*. John Wayne was the star, of course, and he comes into an army camp and throws a guidon, a military pennant, down on the colonel's desk. When the scene's over the colonel says to Wayne as Wayne is leaving, "The Indians that you got this guidon from, were they dead Indians?" And Wayne answers, "Finally." That one word speaks reams. One-word lines like that, if they're used right, can be very good.

How about the times when action speaks louder than words?

Kennedy: Oh, those can be great too. Like in *Support Your Local Sheriff*. Walter Brennan is holding a pistol on Jim Garner. Only then Garner sticks a finger down the gun barrel and Walter doesn't dare shoot for fear the gun will blow up.

I remember. I thought I'd choke laughing. Garner underplayed it so beautifully.

Kennedy: That was a good one, all right. I've always like working with Jim. And of course the late Bill Bowers was a great writer; his script was a winner. And the scene with Walter Brennan made Garner's bit even better.

What's your favorite scene from your own pictures?

Kennedy: Actually, my favorite scene's from a picture Budd Boetticher directed, *Seven Men from Now*. It was the first script I ever wrote, and probably the best scene I've ever written. It was between Lee Marvin, Randy Scott, and Gayle Russell robbing a bank. Gayle had a weak husband. There's a storm going on, and he was in a wagon with her. Scott and Marvin are there, too. They're all practically touching each other. Randy is the hero, and there's clearly a great attraction between him and Gayle. Marvin keeps egging on the husband, telling him in effect that he once was in a situation like this with a girl, like Randy is. He plays it almost as a monologue. At the end, they all get out, and Randy finally knocks Lee Marvin on his rear.

Burt, you're both a writer and a director; but these days you think of yourself primarily as a director.

Kennedy: Right.

What moved you over from writing to directing?

Kennedy: I think it's a natural progression. Also, remember that I'm still writing. I'm working on three screenplays right now.

But on directing . . . did you just get tired of directors who butchered your scripts?

Kennedy: That's what lots of writers say, but I never felt that way. Budd Boetticher did a lot of my scripts, and they were very good, maybe even better than they were on paper. My feeling is that you write and then you finally move over into directing because that's what you're doing anyway when you write a script. You're directing it on paper. The trap you can fall into is to get to thinking, "Oh, I wrote it and I'll direct it and that's the best there is."

Then I started directing other people's scripts and found that when you direct from a weak script you have to work harder, trying to make it good. It's easier and better getting the script right in the first place.

You've done major work in both films and television. What's the difference between a film script and a TV script? What do you look for in each?

Kennedy: I don't think there's any difference. I just did *The Alamo* for a three-hour NBC TV special. I wouldn't have shot that any differently if it had been a movie. They just cut it differently, cut out the big closeups. That's what television thinks they have to do. But the writing's no different.

What do you feel is the outlook for the young writer trying to break in today? Is there still a chance for him, even now when there are 6,500 members already in the Guild?

Kennedy: Of course there is. Sure, there are 6,500 members. But how many real *writers*?

PRODUCER/DIRECTOR (ENTERTAINMENT HOME VIDEO): Christopher Lewis.

Call him an innovator.

His name is Christopher Lewis, and he's a man who had an idea: the idea of mating film and television technologies to produce movies especially for home video. For though video tape doesn't project too well on a movie screen in a theater, it plays just fine on a TV set.

The son of Loretta Young, famed Hollywood star, Lewis in effect grew up in the film business. Training at the University of Southern California's School of Cinema, he worked on a succession of low-budget TV shows, both before and after graduation.

By 1982, he was producing and co-hosting television's "PM Magazine" in Tulsa, Oklahoma.

Then he met a man named Bill Blair whose business was buying movie titles and licensing them for home video use. Distributors and video stores sold his product.

Together, Lewis and Blair decided to see if they could bring Lewis's video movie idea to practical commercial life. "The basic concept was to get into the project really inexpensively, by shooting on video tape and then never going to a theater with the product," Lewis explains. "In effect we wouldn't even make features; we'd make television shows for home video."

Naturally, there were production problems—problems that went with a budget so low that it allowed a crew of only twelve or so; problems of shooting virtually everything on location to save money on sets; problems of working with actors who lacked film experience, so that scenes had to be shot top-to-bottom instead of in Hollywood's traditional bits and pieces.

"You have to design your own system for making these pictures," Lewis comments wryly.

What made it all the more difficult was that Lewis had decided in advance that he wanted his finished product to look like film. Not TV, not soap opera, but film.

"Thirty-five millimeter [theatrical release size] film gives you one look," he explains, "16 millimeter another. And video has its own look to it."

To attain that theatrical film look, Lewis used film lenses, film filters, film techniques.

Lewis has three successful—that is, profitable—films in the can as this is written, with more to come.

How do you get your stories, your scripts?

Lewis: There's a lot of stuff around. This script *[The Ripper]* was written by a fellow who went to Tulsa University. He's a movie nut.

Is he typical of your writers?

Lewis: More or less. Mostly we're dealing with people right out of college. Or, they're people who understand what we're doing and will do it very cheaply because they have other jobs and will get a point or two of the picture.

Back to The Ripper. *How did your man come to write it?*

Lewis: He did it as a senior thesis.

You mean you shot from his thesis?

Lewis: No. It wasn't in script form, so it wasn't anything we could use. But we sparked on it because the idea was good.

What then?

Lewis: I did a rewrite. He polished that. Then I went back and did the final.

A lot of work.

Lewis: Yes, but the basic idea was there and the basic scene outlines were there. That's what counts.

And that was your first picture here?

Lewis: No. The first we did was a story that Bill Blair had written with Stewart Rosenthal, a local doctor.

Did they write it with your movies-for-home-video idea in mind?

Lewis: No. It was written in 1971. Rosenthal's now living in Portland. He's become a movie critic.

How about picture number three?

Lewis: It was a sequel to the first one. We hired a writer who was an actor in the first one and who's also an award-winning playwright here. He's a young guy, a teacher at Tulsa University.

Number four?

Lewis: It's a story written by two movie critics who work on the paper here. My wife had a TV show with one of them. Now they've sold a script to Wes Craven for "Twilight Zone".

What do you look for in a script? What makes it salable, where you're concerned?

Lewis: We want our first 12 pictures to be like a television series. Each of them should have the same elements of suspense and gore as those we've already done, basically the same production values, so that they can be sold as a package. Also, in all our pictures, we try to have a little twist at the end, like Hitchcock always had, just a little twist at the end.

Are there any key points a writer needs to remember when he's putting together a script?

Lewis: Once you get into feature films you're not dealing with a three- or four-minute attention span. You're dealing with an hour and a half, 90 minutes.

And beyond that?

Lewis: You have to tell a story.

What advice would you give to would-be writers?

Lewis: Don't get too ambitious. Don't write in the fall of the Roman Empire. Start with a project you can cut your teeth on, one where you can tell a story. Always, focus in on the story. The most important thing is the story line. All the gizmos, all the effects, don't mean a damn if you don't get the audience caring about what they're seeing on the screen, and it doesn't have to be the fall of the Roman Empire. It can be one person's fight against muscular dystrophy.

What's the best way for a new writer to present an idea to someone like you?

Lewis: First, write a story outline. Because the producer's going to want to change it to his vision of how to tell that story, and if you get too detailed a script, he has to throw it out and start from scratch. So I'd start with a story idea in as few pages as possible. Maybe even put some graphics in with it. Not a picture book, not a story board; not that detailed. But something to make it stand out from all the other things that come across a producer's desk.

And once the story is there—?

Lewis: Try to get a feeling into the script as to how you approach the screenplay, the movie. In other words, if it's a "Miami Vice"-type thing, put some of the lingo in. If it's Old West, read some Louis L'Amour books; find out Old West terminology. Do your research, so that in that really short presentation you can get a feeling not only of what the story's about, but how you would approach the characters, what little eccentricities these characters would have.

What's the next step?

Lewis: If the producer likes it, the next step would be to go in for a story conference. Discuss what you'd like to do. That's when you bring out your outline or your script or whatever and say, "Well, what do you think? Is this the right approach?" But the thing to hit him with first is just a couple of pages to lay out the idea.

What other advice can you give writers as to how to get the most out of story conferences?

Lewis: Just be sure you communicate. Too many of the writers who meet with me here don't come across on the same level as when I go into Norman Lear's office to do a story conference. I open my mouth about story points, not lighting. In story conferences here, someone will bring up special effects or changing the story line. I say the script is already here and there's no use saying "Let's change this character to Blackman," or something. The script is already here; let's take it from this data base.

Next question: What goes into the script?

Lewis: I find that in a lot of pictures today, there is no story. Kids are being raised on modern television, where there is no character development; all there are are car chases and explosions and things like that. But actually, what counts is the show where you give a damn about who's on stage. You've got to care about somebody, and in order to care you've got to have a hook, a story line. That's the bottom line.

Does any particular thing seem to be lacking in the scripts you see?

Lewis: Clarity. I constantly have battles with my editor about being so obvious. My opinion is that you can never be too obvious. If you have a dialogue scene, better it be too long and you can cut it than too short and not cover your story content.

What other major headaches do you run into?

Lewis: The writers whose scripts I see haven't all learned format. In Hollywood everyone was coming from the same data base. You got to be a scriptwriter at a studio and knew the production problems and there was a common knowledge of what a medium shot was and a closeup, and when you said "I want this on a closeup," it meant a closeup, not a two-shot. What I find in working with people who haven't been to USC Cinema School, who haven't paid their dues, things are interpreted differently.

To a lot of kids, the fundamentals aren't all that important. They think all there is to it is just to get the idea down. To me, the fundamentals are very important. It makes it easier for the production manager to break it down, makes it easier for the director of photography to know what elements he has to look for in the script.

So then it's rewrite time.

Lewis: Yes, we insist on feature film format. If it says FADE OUT, you should know where to put it. It goes in the lower right hand corner; that's just standard. You capitalize all the props and the characters' names and that stuff. We do it like a movie script. We just photograph it like a TV show.

What's your solution to the rewrite problem?

Lewis: In my case, I find it simpler just to do the rewrite myself. Then I get it the way I want it. But as we go into production faster and faster that may become impossible because of the time involved.

How long does it generally take you to handle a rewrite yourself?

Lewis: I usually go through a script in four or five days and straighten it up. Five days. Something like that.

What kind of money do you pay for a script?

Lewis: Script purchase price generally is about one percent of the proposed budget for the picture. Sometimes it's a flat deal and sometimes it's against a percentage of the picture when it's out. One hundred thousand dollars pays one thousand.

A lot depends on the experience of the writer. A writer with no experience, where I have to put in a lot of time will probably get a flat deal, no proprietary rights, but he'll be able to make a deal with anybody after the film.

Even so, in home video there's not enough money for a writer to make a decent living. You'd have to sell a script a week.

What's the best way for a writer to handle the money angle?

Lewis: Get your money up front. Don't take a percentage deal, or if you do, don't expect to see your money. What we've done, typically, is to pay half the money on signing the agreement, and the other half on delivery of the product if it's accepted.

Then, if there's a rewrite—well, you negotiate so much more for another polish of this particular version.

You're giving us an honest view, a realistic view.

Lewis: That's because I see scriptwriting in perspective. It's real important, but to me it's just a step in the total process—the most important step, because if you don't have a script, there's nothing to shoot. If it doesn't make sense on paper, it ain't gonna make sense up there on the screen. That's your bottom line.

But writers have to understand, too, that the script's not the Bible. It's just a map, like a road map, and you can take any road you want. But whatever road you take, you still need the map. If you don't have a good map, a good script, don't even roll film or roll tape.

Do you feel the movies-for-home-video field is going to be a big market?

Lewis: One day it's going to be the biggest. Together, home video and television will surpass theater. For beginning writers it's going to be a huge market.

AGENT: Barry Perelman.

Originally from Chicago, Barry Perelman got his start in the agency field in the William Morris mailroom as a trainee. Later he spent four years at CMA, then went on to such firms as IFA, Motown, and Eisenbach-Greene. He opened his own company four years ago. Active in both film and television, he handles writers, directors, and producers.

As an agent, Barry, what do you look for in a new writer?
Perelman: I judge by the material the writer produces.
Then personality isn't a big issue?
Perelman: Not really. It can make a difference if he's pitching an idea to a story editor, of course. But where an agent's concerned, it's what the writer writes that counts.
When you're evaluating material, what do you look for?
Perelman: I look for originality, imagination, professional-type writing.
What do you mean by "professional-type"?
Perelman: I mean professional in the sense that it's cast into the proper form. And that it's the kind of screenplay that's a studio-type project.
What in particular tends to turn you on where a script is concerned?
Perelman: That's tough to say, because it's so subjective. It's got to be well plotted, well structured, of course. But what you keep looking for is something that seems really exciting—a fresh approach to something, a wonderful comedy, a marvelous drama, a story that thrills you because it's presented in a whole new way. It's got to show some kind of brilliance, because a new writer needs that. He has to be better to start off than some guy who's already known to the studios.

Also, it's got to have a professional feel to it, so to speak. It's got to capture you, it's got to hit you, it's got to jump off the pages at you. If it's just, "Well, you know, I've seen that film before"; if it's an imitation of films that have already been out there, it usually won't work. It's really got to have a freshness to it. And I think it's got to have something that excites you about the piece and says, "Hey, this is a film that I know I can sell because I know the studios want to make this picture and are looking for something like this." Something that excites me. It's got to excite me.

What turns you off?
Perelman: There are a lot of things. If a script is way too talky, or if the opening is unimaginative, or if there's no hook to get you into the picture, it's hard to work up any interest. Something that just lays there isn't likely to strike a spark. You need movement, not just talk. Otherwise you haven't got a film.

Naturally, every new writer wants to get representation, an agent. But does he stand any chance of finding one if he's not in the Los Angeles area and can't make face-to-face contact?

Perelman: Yes, he can. But it's tough to get somebody to read your material if you're not known. No one who's honest is going to deny it. Most of us that are known in town here really don't take unsolicited material. I'm not likely to consider anyone who doesn't come through some kind of recommendation unless he dazzles me with some kind of fancy footwork.

On the other hand, I handle a fellow who's an airline pilot out of Texas. He came to me through a lawyer, and he's a very bright writer, and we've sent his material out, and we've gotten very good responses. We haven't sold it, but we've gotten excellent responses.

Do you often find that even if a script itself doesn't sell, if it's a good script, it ends up by getting the writer assignments?

Perelman: Well, it gets them known. And then maybe somebody will say, "I'm interested in seeing what they do next," or "I'm interested in hearing a pitch from them and finding out what they want to do next."

Of course, they're going to have to sell from an actual script, rather than pitching, until they get established, though. Right?

Perelman: Usually so, yes. A writer who tries to make it without having an actual script to show is dead before he starts. He needs something he's written, something he's really worked hard on that shows talent and an awareness of the market.

Do you have any trouble finding really acceptable clients?

Perelman: Yes, I do. It's very tough to find really good screenplays. As a whole, I believe Hollywood must get about a quarter of a million scripts minimum per year, and you see how few films are made. What it takes to hit is a quality script. Look what Oliver Stone did with *Platoon*. Anyone with the ability to write can do that, get attention. They might not get it made, but it's a first step. It gives someone a reason to put a director to it or to put a star to it and to be able to package it and to sell it to a studio.

Which doesn't mean it still isn't tough to break in.

Perelman: It's very tough to get in today, even with hard work and talent. Somebody's got to see something in you, some potential, and give you a break.

So the breaks are important.

Perelman: Oh, are they ever! I mean, I'll tell you that more than anything what it takes is luck. Luck and timing have everything to do with it, as much as what's on the pages.

And finding a mentor, what amounts to a sponsor, doesn't hurt a bit.

Perelman: You're absolutely right. Young kids coming out of film schools have a much better shot than others. USC, UCLA, the New York film schools like Columbia. It gives them access to Hollywood and New York. Then, if they've got the right words, the ideas, the talent—well, at least they've got a chance. And in this town, this business, a chance is all anyone can ask for.

PRODUCTION MANAGER (INFORMATIONAL VIDEO):
Richard Thorp.

Active in film and media production since 1961, Richard Thorp currently manages educational media development for the U.S. Postal Service at its video production facility in Potomac, Maryland, a suburb of Washington, D.C. He is a pioneer in the area of computer-based training and interactive video optical laserdiscs.

Thorp's experience ranges from film production for the National Institute of Mental Health to production credits for ABC's "Wide World of Sports" and NBC's "Animal Secrets", plus work for a variety of industrial and commercial clients. He is also president of Micro-Marketing Systems, Inc., a management consulting, marketing, and production company.

Although Thorp works primarily for the Postal Service, his observations apply equally to the procedures followed by many other large informational film units.

Just what does your organization do?

Thorp: Today it's an operation devoted mainly to in-house video production, though it also turns out film, textbooks, workbooks, and press materials. Last year, our unit produced 1,203 minutes of finished screen-time video—72 productions. I'm very proud of that, because it represents a two-million-dollar costs savings to the Postal Service over contracting out the same amount of production.

How large an organization do you have?

Thorp: We employ five senior producers and three production crews. Often, that's supplemented by use of outside contract crew members. There's a lot of travel involved. More than 70 percent of our projects are shot on locations throughout the country.

What about scripts?

Thorp: Almost all scriptwriting is contracted out. I can make more cost-effective use of my staff by keeping my producers in production rather than bogging them down with scripting.

Then the issue's primarily cost . . .

Thorp: Not necessarily. Use of outside writers keeps scripts fresh and creative, and that's important. Today's viewers watch over 30 hours of commercial television every week. They're very sophisticated. That means our productions have to earn their attention. We get that through extra staff effort and attention to detail.

Where do you find your writers?

Thorp: Generally, they find us. We're always in need of good writers. We periodically conduct workshops for interested writers.

What do you look for in a writer? What standards must he meet in order for you to consider him?

Thorp: I look, number one, for reliability. It's the most important factor.

If a person works diligently on a project, communicating with the client and meeting schedules, that's a primary virtue. What's bad is when our staff people get together for a script meeting and the writer doesn't show up, or shows up 30 minutes late, or comes on with a flippant attitude. Most people we work with are responsible professionals. Unfortunately, a lot of basically unemployable misfits with attitude problems call themselves scriptwriters. Those we can do without.

You speak about meetings . . .

Thorp: Yes, most scriptwriting for us requires personal contact. There's a good deal of story conferencing. It's not a good spot for anyone who can't stand talking over projects.

What other factors do you consider?

Thorp: We like the person who's realistic towards our needs. A competent writer takes time to become familiar with our production standards and capabilities. I don't like someone to call for a lot of visual effects that are very complex and expensive unless we discuss it first and I can build it into the budget to have it done under contract.

What experience do you demand of someone starting?

Thorp: We ask for samples of their work in script format.

How about films that they've scripted?

Thorp: Generally, writers just don't get copies of their films, so I'm willing to judge them solely on their scripts.

However, I've started a policy of giving writers a copy, either VHS or Beta, of anything done for us.

Are all your scripts done on assignment?

Thorp: Almost all, but not everything. Most of the time, we spell out our requirements: We're going to do a video, it's going to be about 20 minutes long, and it's on the operation of a mail-sorting machine. Then the writer works with the subject matter expert and the producer assigned. You go at it that way.

However, there also are times when we're doing, say, motivational things for employees and you're not locked in. Then we're looking for that very abstract element called creativity, a way of conceptualizing the entire training program. We're using the video to relay something more than just technical data. An example is our new employee orientation program. Every year the Postal Service hires approximately 47,000 people. Every one of those new employees goes through what is essentially a week-long acclimation. They meet managers, tour the postal facility, talk about what their responsibilities are, learn about leave and retirement benefits, the health plans, all that. How you don't steal mail, how the Postal Inspection Service makes sure it doesn't happen, how grandmothers sending birthday gifts to their grandkids and major businesses count on the mail service being reliable, how all employees must do their part to assure the sanctity of the mail.

What we'll do is get a number of writers together and we'll talk over the general concept of what we'd like to accomplish with this familiarization. We won't discuss specific films or videos or media, but we'll say, "These are the topics that have to be covered, and we want to have a unified approach." Different department heads probably will be present at such a meeting, available to explain what they want to have new employees know at the end of the orientation.

Then we'll ask the writers each to submit a treatment for handling the material to be covered. Everyone's paid for their treatment.

All the treatments are evaluated, and a contract awarded. The award's based on script cost, but you also get points for certain things you cover, and your approach, and your creativity, and so on.

A third approach is that anyone can turn in what's called an unsolicited proposal. A proposal for a motivational training program to solve a carrier problem, say—it must be evaluated and responded to within a certain length of time, and you can end up with a contract.

What's the average length of your films or videos?
Thorp: I try to keep them as short as possible. We're running from 12 to 20 minutes.

What percentage of your films are purely technical?
Thorp: About 60 percent are technical information.

What percentage are dramatized?
Thorp: Remember, I'm in management and craft training. I use a lot of role playing. So about 40 percent are dramatized.

When you look at a script, what are some of the things that turn you off?
Thorp: I'm turned off in a hurry when someone comes in with a real dramatic opening, something that sounds like it's going to be dynamite, but when you get to page three you find there's really nothing unique about it. I like to look at the total script. The holistic approach, you could say, though I don't like to use cultist terms. I like to consider what's happening to our trainees during the 15 minutes that the video is supposed to be demanding their attention. Is everything all bangs and whistles at the beginning and the closing, and the students snore through the rest of it? Is there a reason for using the effects that are worked in? Is the thing interesting throughout? I'm looking for that "throughout" business as opposed to concentrating everything at the beginning and the end.

We give our writers a content outline at the start—a rough listing of the information we want included in the video production. We also give them what we call performance objectives—four or five little statements that say, "Upon completion of the viewing of this video, the viewer should be able to . . . ," and then you write three or four sentences that spell it out, whether it's "Replace a framistan" or "Understand the importance of business mail to our revenue base" or "Be able to correctly classify third class mail." These are things you can quantify or use as a checklist or a report card against the script. I go through the script to see if they're adequately covered—laid out in such a manner that we can expect the student to understand what it is we're trying to put across.

Do you ordinarily ask the writer to do necessary rewrites?

Thorp: Absolutely, unless I'm so dissatisfied with the writer's work that it makes more sense to pay him off and shove in another person to do the rewrite.

Do you see any key factor in getting good scripts?

Thorp: Yes. It's good communication between producer, the writer, and the subject matter expert—an understanding of common objectives.

I mean, not every video we make is worthy of *Gone With The Wind* or *Ben Hur* treatment. Basically, we produce three categories of videos, three levels of production values. They divide on a basis of size of audience, longevity of materials, and nature of materials, among other things. The Postal Service has over 800,000 employees. If all of them are to see a video, I can justify a pretty expensive initial production. In one recently we used the stars of "Miami Vice", along with a lot of visual effects and so on.

Same way, how long will a production be in use? One year, five years, one showing to Congress or a board of directors? A lot of things we do are subject to change annually. We don't want to go for high production value in order to show how the merit performance system is going to work this year, when we know darn well there'll be another set of rules next year.

The nature of the materials makes a difference, too. This year we produced a video on internal theft. It was essentially a remake of a film we produced 12 years ago. The original was narrated by Jack Webb. Theft, being honest on the job, doesn't change from year to year, so it's good for a long time. But eventually it has to be remade, because uniforms change, vehicles change, the way people dress and move around changes. You can't afford to have people laugh at the film because it's so out of date.

Writers have to realize that categories of film differ, levels of production differ. I don't want to open everything with a free-fall jump from an airplane. There's a place for a good voice-over narration, run-of-the-mill, level-one type of production too. Something that we can shoot in a short time on location with people or equipment working, with studio inserts to fill out. It's a finished production and it's out quickly and it's doing the job—good, clean, well done, but not elaborate.

In between, there's the production where we might have some role playing, some dramatic scenes. But instead of trying to carry a story line throughout, we might have a narrator on camera and cut away to the illustrative incidents, the drama.

With all these possibilities, I like a writer to be adaptable. And lots of times, of course, I'll select a writer on the basis of the subject matter of the script. I wouldn't pick someone who uses a manual typewriter to do a script on computer security. I look for someone with that kind of technical background who's also a writer.

About how many different writers do you ordinarily use in a given year?
Thorp: We have contracts with ten free-lance writers for continuing work. They're paid according to the number and kind of scripts they do. Whenever new writers come along we try to find small jobs that we can try them out on.

Frequently, new writers aren't in tune with our requirements, so we end up nursing them along through one script and then it's "Good luck, don't call us, we'll call you." But when we come across someone who has a background, a portfolio of scripts they've done for a variety of clients who have goals similar to ours, we latch onto that person and keep him busy.

I would much rather hire a contract writer to do a script than I would to have our in-house staff do it. In-house people get bogged down by the bureaucracy, but a contract writer can push for action, get decisions from postal executives that an internal staff can't.

Anything else?
Thorp: I like a script writer who has an interest in what we're doing beyond the check. I love it when a writer calls me and says how did the production go? Did it work out o.k.? That follow-up says you're not alone with the script; the writer is there too—interested in what you're doing; proud of the script. That makes me want to call that person back next time a job comes up.

Same way, when you go out on location and you find things don't work in the real world the way they did in the script. The willingness of the writer to come in and help out means a lot. We pay for it, but it's patchwork pay, not as good as for a new script. A lot of writers don't like to do the $200 rewrite after you've shot something. The ones who are still willing to work together with you, that's the thing that builds a long-term relationship that keeps you together.

THE WEDNESDAY NIGHT KILLERS (novel manuscript appraisal), *by Beth Sullivan*.

What does a story analyst look for when he/she appraises print material as to its possibilities for film use?

Herewith, a reproduction of an actual analyst's report, submitted on May 25, 1976, on a book which later became the basis for an NBC Movie-of-the-Week, aired during "Sweeps Week" (the time when the television networks are vying for top ratings) on January 13, 1985.

The novel was Oliver Crawford's *The Execution*, the best-selling story of five women who survived degradation and torture in the concentration camp at Auschwitz only to discover 20 years later that the man who directed their torment there is alive and prospering in Los Angeles.

Originally from Chicago and a former actor, Crawford turned to Hollywood following army service in World War II. In the next 30 years he earned an enviable record as one of television's top scriptwriters, as well as story consultant on assorted shows. His awards include Emmy nominations for *Climax!* and *Lineup* scripts, and a Writers Guild nomination for *Outer Limits*. He is a winner of the National Conference of Christians and Jews Brotherhood Award for a *Death Valley Days* script. A member of the Dramatists Guild and the Authors Guild of America, he is the ranking member of the Board of Directors of the Writers Guild of America West, having served on that body for twelve terms. He also is a former Associate Professor of Film and Television at Loyola Marymount University.

The Execution was Crawford's first novel, published in 1978 by St. Martin's Press. Submitted to Twentieth Century–Fox for possible film adaptation, it was turned over to Beth Sullivan, then a story analyst in the television division of Twentieth Century–Fox.

Since 1980 Ms Sullivan has herself been a screenwriter of numerous TV movies-of-the-week and feature films. Formerly a development and production executive at Twentieth, she has also been associate producer of a number of independent feature films, and was executive producer of the dramatic short film, *One Fine Night*. She has also taught screenwriting at UCLA, a university from which she also holds a degree in film production. Like Crawford, she currently serves on the Writers Guild's Board of Directors.

Ms Sullivan's comments on Crawford's novel by and large are self-explanatory, with time, place, and drama category immediately established. A brief capsule ("Theme") summed up the story. Evaluating the work in terms of six factors (characterization, dialogue, structure, uniqueness of story line, uniqueness of setting, and other production values), she rated all as excellent, and estimated cost of production as in the medium bracket.

A four-page synopsis followed; then a final paragraph of comments.

The overall result is a concise but clear picture of *The Execution/ Wednesday Night Killers'* film potential.

Note that a scanning of the first page provides enough information to enable an executive to decide whether it's worthwhile to read further. And what follows both fleshes out the picture and allows a skilled story analyst to express judgment and call attention to any additional pro or con factors.

Where *The Wednesday Night Killers* was concerned, Crawford reports, "Twentieth and I entered negotiations. I wanted a motion picture. They insisted on a TV film. Negotiations broke down. Ultimately, after two subsequent motion picture options, I succumbed to a TV production by Newland-Raynor Productions. Twentieth bought the property, and I co-produced the picture and co-wrote the screenplay."

"The Wednesday Night Killers" story coverage provided courtesy of Beth Sullivan and Twentieth Century Fox Film Corporation.

Type of Material: <u>302 page manuscript</u> Title: <u>THE WEDNESDAY NIGHT KILLERS</u>

Pub. as THE EXECUTION

Submitted by: <u>Oliver Crawford</u>   Author: <u>Oliver Crawford</u>

Analyst: <u>Beth Sullivan</u>   Circa: <u>Present</u> Location: <u>Los Angeles</u>

Date: <u>May 25, 1976</u>   Drama Category: <u>Drama</u>

THEME: Five women who have shared a Wednesday night Mah-Jong game every week for twenty years, also share the common history of being brutalized in the female compound at Auchswitz under the command of DR. WILHELM GEHBERT. When one of the members discovers Gehbert now posing as a restauranteur, the women decide to eliminate him. The consequences of their act become complicated, but justice is done.

	Excellent	Good	Fair	Poor
Characterization	X			
Dialogue	X			
Structure	X			
Uniqueness of Story Line	X			
Uniqueness of Setting (And other production values)	X			

Check One

Budget: High____ Medium <u>X</u> Low____

(FOR <u>SY SALKOWITZ</u>)

SYNOPSIS: THE WEDNESDAY NIGHT KILLERS

Five women. They played Mah-Jong every Wednesday night. The
game is in its twentieth year. FREDA FRIEDKIN, HANNAH EPSTEIN,
SOPHIE LANGBEIN, GERTRUDE SIMON and ELSA SPAHN also share the common history of having been interred in BIRKENAU, the female compound
at Auchswitz, where they were subjected to the most inhuman, vile
offenses imaginable including 'experimentation' that left Freda and
Elsa sterile. Though none of the women knew each other at the time,
they have since learned that they also share the outrage of having
been brutally raped by the head of the compound, DR. WILHELM GEHBERT,
(among countless others) whose savage attacks left an indelible imprint on their memories.

Elsa's sudden statement that she has seen Gehbert brings this
week's game to a silent halt. The youngest and outwardly the frail-
est, Elsa is in fact as sturdy as an oak. To their barage of questions, she answers that she came across their dreaded enemy now
posing as 'PAPA GROSSMAN', proprietor of a flourishing little
German restaurant in Topanga Canyon. The others agree to pay a
visit to the establishment during the following week to verify the
identification, though no one will yet admit the motivation behind
such a move.

The following Wednesday, the five friends agree that the man
is indeed Gehbert, with Freda (the 'Foul Mouth') claiming in the
most adamant of terms her desire to destroy the man, thus giving
voice to what the others have been thinking, but hesitating to admit.
Being the gutsiest of the bunch (as well as the most vivacious and

THE WEDNESDAY NIGHT KILLERS -2-

attractive), she pushes the others to take a vote on whether or not
they wish to take revenge. The others manifest their own inner
strengths in the affirmative, but everyone agrees that they must
make an absolute identification before proceeding. The only way
to make sure is to check for the large dog-bite scar on his left
shoulder. Freda insists that she be the one to do whatever necessary, since, as a widow, she has no one to have to explain any
unusual behavior to.

Freda cleverly maneuvers 'Papa Grossman' into taking her home
when she pretends that a date has stood her up at his restaurant.
Though her stomach turns the entire time, she allows him his sexual
advances in order to steal the look that will seal his fate. She
has packed a small pistol with her and plans to kill him if he is
indeed Gehbert, but one thing gets in the way. By the time she's
able to get his shirt off to see the scar, he has ironically broken
through the frigidity that has plagued her since the time of his
first assault.

Freda reports back the possitive identification of Gehbert,
and the women agree to draw lots to see who will actually have the
hand in his murder. Freda secretly palms the slip of paper with
the swastika and puts five blanks in the bowl. They agree that
none should ever know who among them actually commits the deed
and that five weeks be allowed to carry it off. If after that time
Gehbert is still alive, they must let the matter drop.

Freda is torn between her awakened sexual appetite and her

commitment to the thousands maimed and murdered by this ice-hearted
man she has taken for a lover. Each week at the Mah-Jong game, the
unspoken acknowledgement of failure to eliminate Gehbert hangs over
the festivities. Freda lives in torment. Gertrude decides in the
fifth week to take matters into her own hands and begins to case
out the restaurant.

But, Freda's conscience comes through at the last moment. When
Gehbert stays home from the restaurant with a cold one night, she
goes to him with what she assures him is some soothing tea mixture,
but is in fact a poison. As he begins to lose consciousness, he
realizes what has happened and makes a feeble struggle. Freda is
forced to suffocate him with a pillow.

The following night's Mah-Jong ritual turns into a rowdy celebration, until the women learn that a MARTIN RENNER has been charged
with the murder of 'Papa Grossman'. They are dumbfounded as to how
such a mistake could have happened, but it seems that this man had
the misfortune of having an automobile accident nearby at the time
of the murder and now suffers from amnesia. His inability to supply
a traceable background adds to the suspicions of Head Deputy Dis-
trict Attorney of Van Nuys, DINO FERRARA, and Los Angeles City
Attorney, JONAS WHYTE.

The women can't allow an innocent man to stand trial for their
crime, so they again draw lots to see who'll publicly take the blame,
very much against the wishes of Freda, who insists that her single
status makes her the obvious candidate. Elsa draws the lot, and

based on an anonymous confession drawn up by Freda, she turns herself in.

The facts revealed are enough to get Martin Renner off the hook,
but Elsa's idyllic marriage is made a shambles by the confession.
This quickly leads to a series of confession on the part of the
others, ending with Freda having to go to Ferrara and reveal her
special knowledge of the murder in order to prove that she and she
alone committed the actual crime. Ferrara is impressed not only
with the history behind the women's action, but also with Freda
herself. A widower, this is the first time he's been drawn to a
woman since meeting his beloved late wife. He decides to put
pressure on Whyte, who has an upcoming election at stake, to drop
the case on grounds of insufficient evidence. The latter agrees.

The women meet tentatively for their first Mah-Jong game since
the upheaval over Renner. No one is sure whether or not they'll
be able to reestablish the old comraderie they felt before, but
Freda brings out a letter that changes the entire atmosphere. It's
from a man in Brazil who admits to having posed as Renner in order
to kill Gehbert himself. He had been in the house and about to do
just that when Freda showed up with the poison. He observed the
suffocation, ready to come to her aid if need be. When she left,
he checked Gehbert, who was still alive, and proceeded to finish
the job with the pillow. When Freda finishes the letter from their
fellow freedom fighter, the women digest the news for a moment, then
the stillness in the room is punctuated by the mixing of the Mah-jong
tiles.

COMMENTS: THE WEDNESDAY NIGHT KILLERS

If I may, this is a well-written, involving piece with some of the most vivid characterizations I've come across in a long time. The material, which has itself been brutalized through the years in so many books, films, etc., is here dealt with from a fresh standpoint. There are flashbacks into each woman's previous experiences interspersed through-out the story, treated as vital exposition, rather than any heavy-handed historical indictment. Also, the insights into the various marital and familial relationships are almost as interesting as the central line of action.

CHAPTER 20

You and Film

So there you have it: how to write film scripts, complete in 3½ easy lessons.

Or, who's kidding whom? Nothing in this world worth having comes that simply.

One edge is yours, however. In writing, above all fields, you stand as master of your own destiny. Your genes and chromosomes and conditionings shape your tastes and talents. Beyond that, you call the shots. Which way you go is your own decision.

The only way to learn to write is to write, it has been said.

It's also the only way to find out if writing is your thing.

Hopefully, this book has helped you acquire a degree of professional technique. But the fact that you have training and talent is not enough. You also need desire and drive—a continuing desire and drive, specifically; one that functions day in and day out, week in and week out, assignment after assignment, year upon year.

That kind of focus isn't easy to come by, for building any script is hard work. Often the day arrives when you just don't have the push to want to go on. Nor does such a faltering come only to the losers or the fringe types. Even top performers have been known to succumb to it.

Exhibit A: A friend, retired now. Things reach the point where scripting even one more film was just too painful.

Exhibit B: Friend 2. Too bored to write another line, he said; he became a gentleman farmer.

Exhibit C: Yet another friend. "There comes a time when you want to be judged for your own incompetences, not someone else's," was the way he put it.

All these were good writers, believe me. Still, they quit.

Theirs aren't unique plaints. You'll hear them over and over again, from men and women who've reached the peak of their profession. Victims of the old "I hate to write but love to have written" syndrome—it strikes each and every one of us sometimes—they come to the moment where all they want to do is back away.

And yet . . . And yet . . . can you really quit, once you've tasted the excitement that comes with architecting films? I wonder.

Take "A," above. I'd have sworn he was out of the business forever—only then, the chance to script a picture came along, and once again he was off and running.

"B" continues in his role of gentleman farmer. But I notice he seems to find other things to do upon occasion—things involving the scripting of further films, regardless of whatever he may say of boredom.

"C" still hates the way producers and directors and actors blame writers for their own weaknesses and errors. But periodically, he too still involves himself in doctoring scripts in trouble.

You see, there's a sort of fever that goes with film work, no matter whether you're doing loops or feature pictures. Some succumb to it more completely than do others—to the point, sometimes, that they not only catch fire, but continue to burn in spite of themselves.

Such burning is hardly an unmitigated blessing. Frustration comes with it, too often, and so does emotional involvement on a level that amounts to paranoia, and a well-nigh obsessive-compulsive preoccupation with work.

On the other hand, it has its good side also: the excitement that surges up as you face the challenge of each new project; the sense of commitment that grows as the work progresses; the feeling of fulfillment you get when words—*your* words—at last take form as pictures on the screen. . . .

Or, as I remarked back at the beginning of this epic work, one of the nicest things about film scriptwriting is that it offers not just a living, but a way of life which allows you to make full use of your potential.

That can prove a satisfying thing, believe me; one worth finding.

Again, good luck!

APPENDIX A

The Storyboard

A useful tool in scripting either fact or feature films is the device known in the trade as a storyboard. It consists of a series of small sketches of proposed film action, thumbtacked to a corkboard or other background in sequence so that the picture's line of development is presented in visual terms. Ordinarily descriptive comment, narration, or dialogue accompanies each sketch. The finished product is much like a comic strip, with individual panels presenting the film's highlights in such fashion that any and all concerned may understand.

Why bother with working up a storyboard? There are three good reasons.

Reason One is the difficulty fact-film clients and feature-film producers sometimes have in visualizing action from words. A storyboard lays this to rest by letting said client or producer *see* the story as it develops.

Reason Two is the way the storyboard enables a writer to nail down precisely the effect he wants, making his point with pictures instead of struggling vainly to translate complex images into verbiage.

Reason Three is that even the most talented of inexperienced writers—indeed, writers far from inexperienced, upon occasion—sometimes have difficulty knowing whether or not a given sequence will translate well from script to screen. The storyboard offers an excellent way to find out, by forcing Writer to show rather than talk about precisely what he means. Or, to put it in other terms, it's a first-class method to train yourself to think pictorially.

Storyboard art ranges from the roughest of rough stick figures to semi-polished work. The most elaborate example I ever encountered was developed as an ambitious executive's gimmick to sell his firm's top management on making a film. Far from constituting a preliminary step in or aid to writing, it came into being only after I'd turned in the shooting script for the proposed picture.

At that point, an artist was engaged to do color sketches of the action, shot by shot. Thirty-five millimeter color slides then were made of the sketches and set up in sequence in an automatic projector, the film's tentative narration timed and taped to play with it, and the whole package presented to the firm's board of directors.

Unfortunately, the board didn't buy the idea. Since the presentation was, to say the least, an expensive venture, I still wonder how Executive hid the costs in his branch's budget.

This incident also illustrates that storyboard art may take a wide variety of forms. Though most boards feature sketches, I've seen some that utilized snapshots, clips of pictures from magazines, and assorted other approaches. So don't let the fact that you're not an artist stop you. Indeed, learning to sketch well enough for storyboard purposes needn't prove too traumatic. Thumbing through a few books on cartooning self-taught and the like at your local library will give you all the information you need. Or, for a whole chapter on sketching for storyboard purposes, get hold of Leo Salkin's *Story-Telling Home Movies* (McGraw-Hill, 1958). It's excellent.

Does this mean you should always storyboard your scripts? On the contrary. While a storyboard can be an exceedingly helpful aid upon occasion, it also represents an extra—and extremely time-consuming— step in the scripting process. Employ it, therefore, only when a client demands it, or when you see definite benefits as accruing from it—as, for example, in working up or getting across some bothersome point.

APPENDIX B

Judging Screen Time

Few topics generate more debate among beginners than the question of the ratio of script time to screen time. That is, how many pages of script does it take for how many minutes of film?

Of course this is ridiculous. It's obvious that the whole issue can be resolved with a simple formula or two.

Or is it?

Let's try to figure it out, starting with the simple formulas mentioned above:

1. It's ordinarily considered that two pages of a fact film's two-column shooting script averages out a minute of screen time.
2. Similarly, a page of a feature film's master scene script allegedly is equal to a minute of screen time.

Is this true? Well, now, that all depends.

Suppose, for example, that the two pages of fact-film shooting script is made up of descriptions of 15 shots of mechanical components. Each shot is scheduled to run not more than two seconds. In consequence, it doesn't take a mathematical genius to figure out that 15 shots times two seconds comes out at 30 seconds—one-half minute.

Or, suppose a page of your feature film script includes that immortal line, "Five hundred Indians ride over the hill." How much running time does that take?

The issue, you see, is that each page of script is different.

But—and here we get the other side of the coin—they're not *all* different, and they're not often *wildly* different. Put together, one after the other, the *average* fact film script will run about 30 seconds per page; the *average* feature, about a minute.

Which is not to say that it still doesn't pay to use your head at least a little. Thus, if you have a whole series of pages that strikes you as running extremely slow or fast, make allowance for it.

Ordinarily, that allowance should take the form of including a few too many pages, rather than a few too few. Why? Because your script is going to pass through many hands, and be filmed under circumstances you can't control. In consequence, you need to take it for granted that a few lines or shots or scenes just may be blue-penciled somewhere along the line. Also, that when the crew gets out on location, they'll discover that it takes Harold Hero only 17 seconds to climb the cliff, or that the dog flatly refuses to frolic for more than seven, no matter how his trainer curses.

And then, when the boys view the dailies, they discover that two-thirds of the footage in the shot of Hilda Heartlorn swimming across the creek is light-struck, to the point it can't be used.

That kind of thing explains why the old hands would rather write a little fat than thin, as in the case of two TV scripts now beside me. Each is designed for a one-hour show—which is to say, 60 minutes minus commercials, for an actual on-screen time of 42 minutes. Both scripts were done by old pros with years of experience behind them. One runs 72 pages, the other 75.

'Nuff said?

Beyond such generalities, here are ten factors to bear in mind when judging timing:

1. Number of locales.

Every time you change to a new setting, you have to establish it in your viewers' eyes. Establishing takes footage. Footage takes time. So, the more changes of setting, the more screen time will drain away. And if these changes are of a type that take only a line in the script (INT. - SPACESHIP - DAY), the normal balance between pages and minutes can get seriously out of kilter.

2. Subject.

A shot must be held on the screen long enough to convey the essential information about it to the audience visually. Obviously, less footage will be needed if the subject is a simple monument than if it's a complex piece of machinery.

3. Action of the subject.

I've already mentioned the classic gag about the Indians riding over the hill. In general, simple action will be more easily understood—and will take less screen time—than complex.

4. Distance.

A long shot takes more time to grasp than does a closeup. Why? Because Viewer may have to search the long shot for seconds before he can decide the point being made ("What the Sam Hill gives with all that desert? Oh, I get it! There's a rider over there in the corner"), whereas a screen-filling closeup of Chief Running Sore makes its impact instantly.

5. Composition.

The shorter the shot, the simpler the composition is going to have to be. Long S-curves in the D.W. Griffith tradition, patterns within patterns, and the like, take time to comprehend.

6. Color.

Footage in color takes longer to understand than footage in black and white. I learned this the hard way via a shot of a herd of Black Angus cattle grazing on lush green pasture land. Given enough distance to show the herd *as* a herd (see point 4, above), black cattle and green grass so blended that we had to throw out the footage. In black-and-white workprint, in contrast, you had no trouble at all separating them.

7. Size of screen.

A "normal" film frame has an aspect ratio (ratio of width to height) of four to three. The various "wide screen" gambits change this ratio—Cinemascope, for example, offers a ratio of five to two.

The normal screen allows for faster cutting, simply because the audience doesn't have to scan so large a span in search of each shot's point, the thing it's emphasizing. Result: A film designed for wide screen will actually include fewer shots than one shot for normal.

(Incidentally, *do* bear in mind that many theaters project *all* films wide screen, whether they were shot for it or not. Which explains why so many actors' heads are cut off just above the eyebrows, and why audiences leave theaters frustrated and baffled when the final, crucial action happens to take place a bit too low. Television is even worse, of course, in the way it not only trims edges but, because of small screen size, virtually eliminates anything meaningful where shots at any distance are concerned.)

8. Depth.

It's easier and quicker for viewers to grasp what's going on if action takes place on a virtually two-dimensional plane. The greater the effect of depth—that is, three dimensions—in a shot, the slower the cuts must be.

9. Camera movement.

Pans, tilts, zooms, dolly shots, and the like tend to control—and to slow—cutting. Consider, for example, the shot in which Our Hero makes a crucial announcement. Camera pans to Heroine so we can see her reaction. Fine, but less time and footage would be involved if we merely *cut* to her shocked face.

Which is not to say camera movement should never be used, of course; merely that it *does* have negative aspects which should be weighed against possible advantages.

10. Context.

Closely related to point 1, above, is the fact that if your audience has already seen given settings, people, equipment, or what have you, they'll catch it faster in succeeding scenes.

Bearing this in mind, you as writer can use such familiar material to speed up the cutting and thus reduce footage and screen time.

On the other hand, you don't dare forget that, overdone, too much of the familiar creates a devastating—and deadly—sense of monotony.

APPENDIX C

For Further Reading

I know scholarly screen writers, and I know others—equally successful—who have never read Word One on the subject. Nevertheless, most writers of my acquaintance show a tendency to learn by reading; and I myself owe a monumental debt of gratitude to the printed word.

Here, then, is a selection of works I've found interesting, informative, and in some way useful to me as a scripter. Perhaps you, too, will enjoy thumbing through a few.

Obviously, this is anything but a systematic or definitive bibliography. Nor do all the volumes included deal with scriptwriting as such, for much of what you'll need to know comes from other fields. Thus, my own *Techniques of The Selling Writer* is basically an analysis of fiction dynamics. But, hopefully, a little thought will enable you to apply its principles to motion pictures as well as the short story and novel.

Similarly, Stuart Palmer's *Understanding Other People* offers psychology simplified to a level where it's actually useful in creating characters. Aesop Glim's books on advertising include much that's of value to the fact film writer. Marian Gallaway's *Constructing a Play* and *The Director in The Theatre* are stage-oriented, but full of ideas and approaches equally valuable for film. The various technical books on film production contain information that will help orient you to the practices and problems of the medium.

One final point: Don't let the age (dates) of publications necessarily turn you off. Pudovkin and Nilsen still have much to offer that's applicable today, and so do Frances Marion, Arthur Krows, and *The Film Book*.

The editions listed are those that happen to be on my own shelves. Good reading!

A.N.A. Film Steering Committee. *Criteria for Business-Sponsored Educational Films.* New York: Association of National Advertisers, Inc., 1955.

A.N.A. Film Steering Committee. *The Dollars and Sense of Business Films.* New York: Association of National Advertisers, Inc., 1954.

Arijon, Daniel. *Grammar of the Film Language.* Boston & London: Focal Press, 1976.

Baddeley, Hugh. *The Technique of Documentary Film Production, Third Edition.* Boston & London: Focal Press, 1973.

Bare, Richard L. *The Film Director.* New York: Collier Books, 1971.

Barsam, Richard M. *Nonfiction Film.* New York: E. P. Dutton & Co., Inc., 1973.

Barzun, Jacques, and Graff, Henry F. *The Modern Researcher.* New York: Harcourt, Brace & World, 1957.

Blakeston, Oswell. *How to Script.* London: Focal Press, 1949.

Bluem, A. William, and Squire, Jason E. (eds.). *The Movie Business: American Film Industry Practice.* New York: Hastings House, 1972.

Blum, Richard A. *Television Writing from Concept to Contract* (revised edition). Boston & London: Focal Press, 1984.

Brady, John. *The Craft of the Screenwriter.* New York: Simon & Schuster, 1981.

Brown, William O. *Low Budget Features.* Hollywood: William O. Brown, 1971.

Buchanan, Andrew. *Film Making from Script to Screen.* London: Faber & Faber Limited, 1937.

Burder, John. *The Work of the Industrial Film Maker.* Boston & London: Focal Press, 1973.

Butler, Ivan. *The Making of Feature Films.* Baltimore: Penguin Books Inc., 1971.

Carrick, Edward. *Designing for Films.* London: The Studio Publications, 1949.

Corliss, Richard. *Talking Pictures: Screenwriters in the American Cinema.* New York: Penguin Books 1975.

―――. *The Hollywood Screenwriters.* New York: Avon Books, 1972.

Curran, Trisha. *Financing Your Film: A Guide for Independent Filmmakers and Producers.* New York: Praeger, 1986.

DeWitt, Jack. *Producing Industrial Films.* New York: A. S. Barnes & Co., 1968.

Dmytryk, Edward, and Dmytryk, Jean Porter. *On Screen Acting.* Boston & London: Focal Press, 1984.

Dmytryk, Edward. *On Screen Directing.* Boston & London: Focal Press, 1984.

Dmytryk, Edward. *On Screen Editing.* Boston & London: Focal Press, 1984.

Dmytryk, Edward. *On Screen Writing.* Boston & London: Focal Press, 1985.

Eastman Kodak Co. *Basic Production Techniques for Motion Pictures.* Rochester, New York: Eastman Kodak Co., 1971.

―――. *Basic Titling and Animation for Motion Pictures.* Rochester, New York: Eastman Kodak Co., 1970.

Edmonds, Robert. *Script-Writing for the Audio-Visual Media.* New York & London: Teachers College Press, Columbia University, 1978.

Egri, Lajos. *The Art of Creative Writing.* New York: The Citadel Press, 1965.

Fadiman, William. *Hollywood Now.* New York: Liveright, 1972.

Feldman, Joseph, and Feldman, Harry. *Dynamics of the Film.* New York: Hermitage House, 1952.

Field, Syd. *Screenplay: The Foundations of Screenwriting.* New York: Dell, 1979.

Fielding, Raymond. *The Technique of Special Effects Cinematography, Fourth Edition.* Boston & London: Focal Press, 1985.

Froug, William. *The Screenwriter Looks at the Screenwriter.* New York: Dell Publishing Co., Inc., 1972.

Fulton, A. R. *Motion Pictures.* Norman: Univ. of Oklahoma Press, 1960.

Gallaway, Marian. *Constructing a Play.* New York: Prentice-Hall, Inc., 1950.

———. *The Director in the Theatre.* New York: The Macmillan Co., 1963.

Gaskill, Arthur L., and Englander, David A. *How to Shoot a Movie Story.* New York: Morgan & Morgan, 1959.

Geduld, Harry M. *An Illustrated Glossary of Film Terms.* New York: Holt, Rinehart & Winston, 1973.

Gerrold, David. *The Trouble with Tribbles.* New York: Ballantine Books, 1973.

Glim, Aesop. *Copy—The Core of Advertising.* New York: Dover Publications, Inc., 1963.

———. *How Advertising Is Written—And Why.* New York: Dover Publications, Inc., 1961.

Goldman, William. *Adventures in the Screen Trade: A Personal View of Hollywood and Screenwriting.* New York: Warner Books, 1983.

Halas, John (ed.). *Visual Scripting.* Boston & London: Focal Press, 1976.

Herman, Lewis. *Practical Manual of Screen Playwriting.* New York: World Publishing Co., 1952.

———. *Educational Films: Writing, Directing, and Producing.* New York: Crown Publishers, Inc., 1965.

Higham, Charles, and Greenberg, Joel. *The Celluloid Muse: Hollywood Directors Speak.* New York: New American Library, 1972.

Kirsch, Maurice. *How to Write Commentaries for Films.* London: Focal Press, 1956.

Knight, Arthur. *The Liveliest Art.* New York: New American Library, 1959.

Krows, Arthur Edwin. *Playwriting for Profit.* New York: Longmans, Green & Co., 1928.

Lasky, Jesse L., Jr. *Whatever Happened to Hollywood?* New York: Funk & Wagnalls, 1975.

Lawson, John Howard. *Theory and Technique of Playwriting and Screenwriting.* New York: G. P. Putnam's Sons, 1949.

Lee, Robert, and Misiorowski, Robert. *Script Models: A Handbook for the Media Writer.* Boston & London: Focal Press, 1978.

Lewin, Frank. *The Soundtrack in Nontheatrical Motion Pictures.* Hollywood: Society of Motion Picture and Television Engineers, 1959.

Leyda, Jay. *Films Beget Films.* London: George Allen & Unwin Ltd., 1964.

Livingston, Don. *Film and the Director.* New York: The Macmillan Co., 1953.

MacCann, Richard Dyer. *Film: A Montage of Theories.* New York: E. P. Dutton & Co., 1966.

Macgowan, Kenneth. *A Primer of Playwriting.* New York: Random House, 1951.

———. *Behind the Screen.* New York: Dell Publishing Co., Inc., 1967.

Madsen, Roy. *Animated Film.* New York: Interland Publishing Inc., 1969.

Marion, Frances. *How to Write and Sell Film Stories.* New York: Covici-Friede, 1937.

Marner, Terence St. John. *Directing Motion Pictures.* New York: A. S. Barnes & Co., 1972.

Mascelli, Joseph V. *The Five C's of Cinematography.* Hollywood: Cine/Graphic Publications, 1965.

May, Mark A., and Lumadaine, Arthur A. *Learning from Films*. New Haven: Yale University Press, 1958.

Mayer, Michael F. *The Film Industries: Practical Business/Legal Problems*. New York: Hastings House, 1973.

McGraw, Charles J. *Acting Is Believing*. New York: Holt, Rinehart & Winston, 1955.

Mercer, John. *Introduction to Cinematography*. Champaign, Illinois: Stipes Publishing Co., 1971.

Miller, Tony, and Miller, Patricia George. *"Cut! Print!" The Language and Structure of Filmmaking*. Los Angeles: Ohara Publications, 1972.

Nash, Constance, and Oakey, Virginia. *The Screenwriter's Handbook*. New York: Barnes & Noble, 1978.

Nilsen, Vladimir. *The Cinema as a Graphic Art*. New York: Hill & Wang, 1959.

Osborn, Alex. *Your Creative Power*. New York: Charles Scribner's Sons, 1948.

Palmer, Stuart. *Understanding Other People*. New York: Thomas Y. Crowell Co., 1955.

Parker, Norton S. *Audiovisual Script Writing*. New Brunswick, N.J.: Rutgers University Press, 1968.

Pudovkin, V. I. *Film Technique and Film Acting*. New York: Grove Press, Inc., 1960.

Reisz, Karel, and Millar, Gavin. *The Technique of Film Editing, Second Enlarged Edition*. Boston & London: Focal Press, 1968.

Reynertson, A. J. *The Work of the Film Director*. New York: Hastings House, 1970.

Rilla, Wolf. *The Writer and the Screen*. London: W. H. Allen, 1973.

Root, Wells. *Writing the Script*. New York: Holt, Rinehart & Winston, 1979.

Rose, Tony. *How to Direct*. London: Focal Press, 1949.

————, and Benson, Martin. *How to Act*. London: Focal Press, 1951.

Rosenblum, Ralph, and Karen, Robert. *When the Shooting Stops . . . the Cutting Begins*. New York: Penguin Books, 1979.

Rouverol, Jean. *Writing for the Soaps*. Cincinnati: Writer's Digest Books, 1984.

Salkin, Leo. *Story-Telling Home Movies*. New York: McGraw-Hill Book Co., Inc., 1958.

Shavelson, Melville. *How to Make a Jewish Movie*. Englewood Cliffs, N.J.: Prentice-Hall, Inc., 1971.

Smith, Richard W. *Technical Writing*. New York: Barnes & Noble, 1963.

Snyder, Robert L. *Pare Lorentz and the Documentary Film*. Norman: University of Oklahoma Press, 1968.

Spottiswoode, Raymond. *Film and Its Techniques*. Berkeley: University of California Press, 1951.

Stephenson, Ralph, and Debrix, J. R. *The Cinema as Art*. Baltimore: Penguin Books, 1965.

Stork, Leopold. *Industrial and Business Films*. London: Phoenix House, 1962.

Strasser, Alex. *The Work of the Science Film Maker*. Boston & London: Focal Press, 1972.

Swain, Dwight V. *Scripting for Video and Audiovisual Media*. Boston & London: Focal Press, 1981.

————. *Techniques of the Selling Writer*. Norman: University of Oklahoma Press, 1974.

Taylor, John Russell. *Hitch: The Life and Times of Alfred Hitchcock.* New York: Berkeley Books, 1980.

Toeplitz, Jerzy. *Hollywood and After.* Chicago: Henry Regnery Co., 1975.

Trapnell, Coles. *Teleplay.* San Francisco: Chandler Publishing Co., 1966.

Truffaut, Francois. *Hitchcock.* London: Panther Books, 1969.

Vale, Eugene. *The Technique of Screenplay Writing.* New York: Grosset & Dunlap, 1972.

Wilson, William H., and Haas, Dr. Kenneth B. *The Film Book for Education, Business and Industry.* New York: Prentice-Hall, Inc., 1950.

Wolff, Jurgen M. "How to Pitch Ideas," in *Journal of Film and Video,* vol. 36, no. 3, Summer 1984. University Film and Video Association, River Forest, IL.

Yoakem, Lola (ed.). *TV and Screen Writing.* Berkeley: University of California Press, 1958.

APPENDIX D

Terms You'll Use

Every field develops its own specialized in-group jargon, and the film industry is no exception.

A number of lexicons of this terminology have been compiled—Harry M. Geduld's *An Illustrated Glossary of Film Terms,* Tony and Patricia Miller's *"Cut! Print!,"* and the University Film Association *Journal*'s "Terms Used in Production of 16mm Non-Theatrical Motion Pictures," for example. Indeed, there's even a handy pocket volume (*Film Vocabulary,* published by the Netherlands Government Information Service, Film Division, 43 Noordeinde, The Hague, Netherlands) which gives the equivalents for 1,024 film terms in French, English, Dutch, Italian, German, Spanish, and Danish.

The glossary I offer here is indebted to these others, but obviously makes no pretense to being anywhere near as comprehensive as they are. However, it does place special emphasis on terms the beginning scriptwriter is likely to encounter and hence may save him at least a few moments of bafflement.

action. Movement of the subject within the camera's field of view.
adaptation. A script in which fact or fiction is translated into a presentation suitable for filming.
angle shot. A shot continuing the action of a preceding shot, but from a different camera angle.
animation. The cinematic creation of an impression of movement by inanimate objects or drawings.
answer print. The first combined picture and sound print, in release form, of a finished film.
antagonist. The person, element, or force which opposes the central character of a film in his efforts to attain a goal.
anticlimax. An inadvertent drop in tension following the climax of a film because

of the scriptwriter's attempt to top the climax with additional material dealing with some secondary issue. The cause ordinarily is the writer's failure to recognize the key element of danger which threatens his central character's desire. Once this threat is resolved, the film is over, save for the tying up of loose threads in the denouement.

art director. The person who designs and supervises construction of a film's sets.

audio. Sound, including dialogue, voice-over narration, music, and effects. The "audio side" (that is, the right side) of a two-column script is the side which tells what sound elements are to be included.

back light. A light thrown on foreground actors or objects from farther back in the set, separating them from the background and giving an impression of depth to the picture.

back lot. That portion of a studio's property equipped with streets, false-front buildings, and the like for use in simulated location shooting.

background. Action, objects, or setting farthest from the camera in a given shot or shots.

background light. A light used to illuminate a shot's background.

beat. A momentary, predesignated pause in an actor's action or delivery of a speech.

big closeup. British term for extreme closeup.

business. Action introduced in order to build up or reinforce characterization, a sequence, a plot point, or the like.

busy. A shot or sequence in which inclusion of too much unnecessary action or setting detail distracts from the impression desired.

camera angle. The point of view from which the camera surveys a subject. Thus, "high angle" means that the camera is looking down on the subject; "low angle," that it is looking up, and so on. "Another angle" means simply that the camera continues to film a given action, but from a different position.

caper film. An adventure film centering on a major theft; generally presented from the thieves' point of view.

cast list. List (and, frequently, brief description) of the roles in a film.

character. A person in a film.

characterization. Any and all details of appearance and behavior devised by a scriptwriter to define a given story person as an individual.

chase. Use of pursuit of one character by another to build suspense in a film.

cheat. To shoot or edit film in a manner that simulates reality by falsifying the relationship between people and/or objects.

climax. The point in a screenplay at which the conflict between desire and danger reaches its ultimate peak.

close shot. A loose term that says only that the camera is close to the subject. Read it as somewhere in the neighborhood of a closeup or medium closeup.

closeup (CU). An emphasis shot that calls attention to some aspect of the subject—a facial expression, a fist-clenching, an inscription on an object.

commentary. Narration for a film, spoken by an off-screen voice in voice-over situations.

complication. A new and unanticipated story development that throws the central character/protagonist for a loss where the attaining of his ultimate objective is concerned. In effect, a confrontation, complete with goal, conflict, and disaster.

composition. The framing of a picture area to achieve a desired distribution and balancing of light, mass, shadow, color, and movement.

conflict. The interplay between forces seeking to attain mutually incompatible goals.

confrontation. A unit of conflict and the main structural component of plot. A time-unified clash between opposing forces in which one person or group attempts to attain an immediate goal and another person/group attempts to prevent attainment of said goal; its basic pattern is one of goal-conflict-disaster, with disaster representing an outcome which has consequences further endangering first person/group's desire.

continuity. 1. A detailed shooting script. 2. British term for story line.

continuity cutting. Editing film to present action in a smooth, logical flow that preserves the illusion of reality for the audience.

contrast. Comparison of one element (situation, object, person, emotion) with another markedly different.

contrived. A pejorative label which implies that some script phase, element, or device is unbelievable, artificial, and for author convenience. Since everything in a script actually is contrived, the label is meaningless and indicates only that someone doesn't like something about the story or presentation. The issue, for the writer, then becomes one of contriving more satisfactorily.

credit. Title acknowledging work done by some specialist (producer, director, writer, actor, technical staff member) on a film.

crisis. A peak in a screenplay's development, brought on by a major threat to the protagonist's chances of attaining his story goal.

cut. Instantaneous change from one shot to another by splicing the two pieces of film together.

cutaway. In continuity cutting, a shot which does not include any part of the preceding shot, as when a character glances out a window and the shot that follows shows what he sees.

cutback. The shot which follows a cutaway if it returns to the preceding action, as when a cutaway shot of what a character sees out a window is followed by a shot that includes the character as he turns away from the window and resumes the action in which he was previously engaged.

cut-in. A medium shot, closeup, or the like, filmed for cutting into a master scene.

cutter, cutting. Editor, editing. More narrowly, the person who actually cuts and splices the film, as differentiated from the editor, who selects the footage to be used and decides where it is to be cut/spliced.

day for night. Daylight exterior shots simulating night by means of filters.

denouement. The tying up of a film's loose ends following the climax and during or following the resolution. Here questions are answered, lingering tensions released, an ending given an emotionally satisfying twist, and so on.

Deus ex machina. When God or the scriptwriter intercedes to save a film from its logical conclusion.

director. The individual who interprets a script and supervises its filming.

dissolve (lap dissolve). An optical effect in which a fade in is superimposed over a fade out so that one shot replaces the other. Its most common use is as a transition through time and/or space between sequences.

documentary. A word with as many interpretations as there are people talking. In general, it refers to a film that avoids artifice and dramatization in favor of extreme realism, shooting in actual settings with non-professional actors who live the parts of the play.

dolly. A small, wheeled platform used to move a camera smoothly while it shoots.

dolly shot. A shot filmed from a moving dolly.

double system. A sound film system in which picture and sound are recorded on separate but precisely synchronized reels of film, thus, enhancing sound quality and simplifying editing.

down. Reduce volume of music or sound effects, as in such script instructions as "MUSIC: DOWN TO BG" or "MUSIC: DOWN & OUT."

dramatic scene. A confrontation.

dub. 1. Mix; re-record various sound tracks onto one composite track. 2. To record dialogue or other sound to match action in shots already filmed.

edit (editing, editor). To select, arrange, trim, and splice together film shots for optimum effectiveness.

effects (FX, SFX) track. Sound track on which a film's sound effects are recorded. These may range from footsteps to gunshots to the racing of a car's motor.

empathy. The tendency of viewers to share the experiences of filmed characters, as when they tense at some threat jeopardizing a person in a picture.

episodic. Script or film structure giving strong emphasis to incidents; less to continuity and the building of a sense of rising action. *Kiss of the Spider Woman* is an episodic film.

establish. To make clear any element important to understanding and appreciation of a sequence or film, and that element's relationship to the sequence or film's other elements.

exploitation film. A low-budget picture for a specialized audience—horror fans, bikers, or the like.

exposition. Introduction of information from the past necessary for understanding of a film story.

exterior (EXT.). Shots made out-of-doors.

extreme closeup (ECU). A strong emphasis shot, as when a shot of an eyeball fills the frame.

extreme long shot (ELS). A shot that reduces the size of the subject in relation to its background markedly more than a long shot.

fade. An optical effect used as a transitional device, in which the picture on the screen gradually goes to black (fade out) or takes form from black (fade in). Every film opens with FADE IN: and closes with FADE OUT. Between, fades may act as punctuation, separating major segments of a film. As punctuation, a fade is much stronger than—and not to be confused with—a dissolve.

fill light. A light used to fill in shadows cast by the key light and thus balance the picture.

flashback. The introduction into a film of a shot or sequence revealing something from the past, as when a character recalls a past event.

flat. A wooden framework supporting stretched and painted cloth used as a background for action.

follow action (follow shot). The camera moves horizontally or vertically on its tripod or on a dolly in such a manner as to keep attention centered on key action.

foreground. Action, objects, or setting closest to the camera in a given shot or shots.

frame. 1. One single picture on a piece of motion picture film. 2. To compose a shot to include, exclude, or emphasize certain things, as in "This shot is so framed that the narrowing distance between the two riders is immediately apparent."

freeze-frame. Repetition (via optical printing) of a single frame of a film so that its image is held on the screen for whatever time is desired.

French scene. A dramatic unit under a system of designation which decrees a new scene to begin with each non-incidental entrance or exit.

full shot. A shot that takes in all of a subject, be it an individual, a group, a car, or a house.

gimmick. A clever plot device, especially one that helps to resolve the film's problem.

head-on shot. Movement straight into the camera, as in the case of someone striding down a hall.

heavy. A villain-type character.

high-key lighting. Lighting in which light, highly illuminated areas predominate, as in most comedies.

hook. 1. A striking incident, unique action, or the like, used to capture audience attention at the beginning of a picture. 2. A linking device (question-answer, repetition, agreement-disagreement, etc.) used to render dialogue cohesive by tying each speech to the one ahead of it.

identification. The tendency of a screenplay's audience to take sides, in effect cheering the hero and booing the villain.

insert. A shot, frequently an extreme closeup, of some object or detail (a letter, a picture, a hand, a tattoo) which can be filmed in such a manner as to eliminate setting. Thus, it may easily be shot out of sequence and cut into the picture during editing.

interior (INT.). A shot filmed indoors.

jeopardy. Anything which endangers a character's chances of attaining his story goal and fulfilling his desire.

jump cut. Splicing together two shots taken from the same angle, especially if some element of the action is omitted. The effect is one of jerkiness and discontinuity.

key light. A shot's primary light source.

lead. The central character or main acting part in a film.

lighting set-up. The placing of lights to illuminate a given shot or shots. Since this task ordinarily takes at least an hour, it constitutes a major expense. Anything the writer can do in his script to limit the number of set-ups will count as a star in his crown.

limbo shot. In effect, a shot staged in space, with props but without a normal set. Often the action takes place in front of a large, blank fabric backdrop called a cyclorama.

lip sync. Dialogue recorded in precise synchronization with the filming, so that speech and lip movements match.

location. A natural setting for action, as differentiated from a sound stage.

long shot (LS). A shot that relates the subject to the background. Frequently, it constitutes an orientation or establishing shot.

loop. A strip of film with its ends spliced together so that it can be projected continuously as a guide for actors in dubbing lines to match lip movements or other action.

low-key lighting. Lighting in which dark, shadowy areas predominate, as in most horror pictures.

MacGuffin. The bone of contention in a film; the thing everyone is trying to save or steal.

mask. To block out a portion of a camera's field as it shoots, as in masking to simulate the view through binoculars or a keyhole.

master scene. An orientation shot (frequently a long shot) taking in all or a considerable part of the action in an entire sequence. Closer shots (cut-ins) of repetitions of the action then are filmed to build the sequence via emphasis on appropriate details.

master scene script. A script which details the action and dialogue of a film, but by and large does not include shooting instructions or camera angles or break down the action shot by shot.

medium closeup (MCU). A shot whose image size on the frame is between a medium shot and a closeup.

medium long shot (MLS). A shot whose image size on the frame is between a medium shot and a long shot.

medium shot (MS). A shot of the subject in and of itself, with only incidental background.

miniature. Small-scale model of an object or set, used to cut the cost of filming floods, train wrecks, airplane crashes, and the like.

mise-en-scene. A film's environment. The sum total of its setting.

mix (mixing, mixer). The combining of sound elements (voices, music, effects) from various tracks in desired proportions on a single rerecorded track.

montage. A combination of brief shots and optical effects, used for transition or to create emotional effects. It may condense months of searching into seconds or minutes, for example, or reveal the distortions of a character's thinking in insanity or a drug experience.

MOS. "Mit out sound." A gag-line reference to shots or sequences to be filmed silent.

motivation. The logical basis for a character's action.

moving shot (travel shot). A shot made from a moving vehicle.

Moviola. A sound/picture viewing device used in film editing.

music track. Sound track on which a film's music is recorded.

narration script. Commentary prepared for use of a film narrator in a voice-over recording situation.

narrator. A commentator (most often unseen) who voices appropriate interpretive remarks for a film's sound track.

nontheatrical film. Ordinarily, a film shown in schools, churches, clubs, and the like, and used to inform, influence, and inspire, rather than to entertain.

oater. Western film.

obligatory scene. A film's climactic confrontation, the elements for which have been planted. Unless these plants are paid off in an appropriate clash, the audience will be frustrated and disappointed.

one-shot (two-shot, three-shot, etc.). A shot that includes one or whatever people.

optical effects (opticals). Systematic progressive alteration of a motion picture shot by means of an optical printer, generally for transitional purposes. Common optical effects include fades, dissolves, wipes, superimpositions, and the like.

pan. To turn a camera from right to left or vice versa on its tripod while taking a shot. The vertical version of a pan is called a tilt.

parallel action. Footage in which action in different locations at the same time is shown as a series of successive sequences by cutting back and forth from one setting to the other.

pay off. To make significant use of something previously planted, as when at the climax of a film the protagonist faces down the villain with a previously planted pistol.

persistence of vision. The retention of an image of a viewed subject on the retina of the viewer for the fraction of a second after the subject has been removed. This phenomenon makes possible the motion picture, in which the audience sees a succession of still photos as a continuing flow of motion.

picaresque. A film—frequently episodic costume drama—which recounts the adventures of a rogue. Example: *Tom Jones.*

plant. Apparently offhand establishment of an idea, character, or property to be used more significantly later in the film. The fact that a gun is seen in a drawer when said drawer is opened to get a pad or pencil is an example.

plant, false. An apparent plant which is never paid off, as when Hero discovers a Yugoslav dinar in the change on Mysterious Stranger's nightstand—but no reference is ever made to it again. The audience has a right to irritation in such circumstances.

plot. A writer's dramatized plan of action for manipulating audience emotions.

plot line. 1. A line of dialogue essential to development/understanding of the plot. 2. A film's story line.

point of view (POV). 1. A shot in which the camera's position approximates that of a particular character and the audience sees what said character would have seen. 2. Attitude.

predicament. A situation so emotionally disturbing to the central character in a screenplay that he is impelled (that is, motivated) to take action directed at changing said situation.

premise. A hypothetical "What if—?" question that provides the basic idea for and springboard to a film story.

process shot. A shot in which foreground action is staged against a translucent screen on which a filmed background is projected.

producer. The individual who plans, coordinates, and supervises production of a film.

progression. Forward movement of a screenplay towards its climax through incorporation of new information and developments.

proportioning. The matching of emphasis to importance in a film script, building some segments large while holding others down.

proposal outline. A brief statement of purpose, target audience, concept, and specifications for a proposed fact film.

protagonist. A film's main character; the character in whose fate the audience is most interested.

quick save. Resolution of a film's problem in less time than seems believable, generally under circumstances that smack of author convenience.

rear projection. Projection of film onto a translucent screen from behind in order to provide background for live foreground action.

relief. A sequence or sequences designed to reduce audience tension (often through humor) after a period of high excitement.

resolution. The defeat of desire by danger or vice versa in consequence of the protagonist's behavior in the ultimate conflict that is the climax; the payoff for the hero's trauma; the method of solving the screenplay's main problem.

running gag. The building up of the humor of some incident or fragment of behavior by repetition as a film progresses.

rushes (dailies). Film processed overnight (or as soon as possible) for immediate viewing to check quality of photography and performances.

scenario. A largely obsolete term for a script form giving a general description of the action of a proposed film.

scene. A term today so loosely used as to be largely meaningless. Thus, it may refer to (1) a setting, (2) a shot, (3) a sequence, or (4) a confrontation.

script. A set of written specifications for the production of a motion picture.

seat-slammers. Throw-away lines at the beginning of a picture when, it is assumed, viewers will be more preoccupied with getting settled in their seats than with the film.

segue. Smooth transition from one sound (particularly, one musical number) to another.

sequence. 1. A related series of shots, unified by some element they hold in common—setting, concept, action, character, mood, or what have you. 2. A major segment of a film, on the order of a chapter in a novel.

sequence outline. A list and brief description of the sequences to be included in a film.

set (setting). An artificially constructed scene in which action to be photographed takes place.

set list. A list of all settings to be used in a film. If included (it isn't always), it ordinarily will follow the cast list and precede the script's text.

setting. The physical surroundings in which a given segment of a film's action is supposed to transpire—bedroom, ballroom, dairy, dock, or whatever.

sexploitation film. Film (probably X-rated) whose appeal is primarily based on explicit sexual activity.

shooting script. A detailed script which describes a film's action shot by shot and serves as a blueprint for production.

shot. The series of still pictures taken by a motion picture camera between the moment it starts and the moment it stops in a single run.

shot list. A shooting script.

situation. The fictional circumstances prevailing as a film opens.

skin flick. A sex film.

sound effects (SFX, FX). Any sound from any source other than voice over narration, lip-sync dialogue, or music.

sound stage. A building or portion of a building designed for the shooting of sound film.

space opera. A science fiction film.

special effects. Techniques for achieving unusual photographic effects unattainable by ordinary procedures.

speculation. Writing on a contingency fee basis; the writer doesn't get paid unless the producer or other person in charge likes the product. Forbidden under Writers Guild rules.

spine. A script's skeletal backbone; its basic plot.

splice. The joining of two pieces of film by any of various techniques.

split screen. Film so manipulated that different shots appear simultaneously in different sections of the screen when projected.

step outline. A sequence outline for a feature or TV film, specifying the action to take place in each sequence as the story develops.

sting. A striking sound (music, shout, etc.) which is used as emphasis or punctuation in a film.

stock shot. Footage of locales, action, or the like, drawn from film libraries to eliminate the need for shooting the sequences involved.

story. 1. In fiction films, the record of how somebody deals with danger. 2. Loosely, the plan of presentation of any film's contents.

story analyst. A studio story department employee who appraises and synopsizes potential screenplay material.

storyboard. A series of sketches, generally with comment, of proposed film action. It is designed to present the picture's line of development in visual terms.

story line. A screenplay's main line of development. Read the term as *story outline* and you won't go too far wrong.

story treatment. A semi-dramatized, present-tense, preliminary structuring of a screenplay or, more broadly, any script.

structure (structuring). A script's framework, its pattern of organization. The combining of story elements into such a pattern.

subjective camera. A technique sometimes used in instructional films in which the camera approximates the learner's point of view. It's also occasionally seen elsewhere, even in feature films; the outstanding example probably is *Lady in the Lake* (1946), in which the viewpoint character virtually never appears on screen.

subplot. A story-within-a-story, generally involving subordinate characters and developed in terms of action parallel to that of the main plot. A subplot's purpose ordinarily is to provide relief from main-plot tension.

superimposure. One or more shots in which one photographic image is printed on top of another, as in ghost effects, titles, etc.

suspense. Uncertainty of outcome; the fear something will or won't happen.

swish pan (blur pan, whip pan). A transitional device in which a pan so rapid that the images blur is used to change from one setting to another.

synchronization. Exact matching of a film's sound and action, as of speech to lip movements.

synopsis. A brief outline of a proposed film's content.

tag line (curtain line, punch line). The final speech in a confrontation, episode, or sequence; generally, one that tops those lines which have gone before.

tail-away shot. Movement directly away from the camera, as when a shot is of the back of a man departing.

take. One filming of a shot.

target audience. The group to which a film is designed to appeal.

teaser. Intriguing pre-title action used to capture audience attention, especially in a TV picture.

technical advisor. A person with detailed knowledge of a film's subject matter, assigned to assist the scriptwriter in preparation of his script.

tempo. The impression of pace in a film.

theme. A screenplay's implicit message.

tilt. Vertical movement of a camera on its tripod head while making a shot.

time-lapse photography. A technique by which filmed action is speeded up by allowing a greater length of time than usual to elapse between photography of successive frames. By this process, a plant may be made to appear to bloom in minutes, or the seasons to change before an audience's eyes.

titles. A film's listings of who did what in its production.

transition. 1. The bridge from one confrontation to another. 2. Anything that links together sequential units or elements in a film.

treatment outline. A third-person, present-tense summary of a proposed fact film script or, more broadly, any film.

trucking shot. Dolly shot. Shot from a moving vehicle, ordinarily a wheeled platform which in most cases moves with the subject at an approximation of set distance.

up. Increase volume of music or sound effects, as in such script instructions as "MUSIC: IN AND UP."

video. The side of a two-column script describing the action to be filmed. The visual (left) side.

videotaping. Electronic recording of images on a magnetically coated mylar tape.

viewer. A mechanical/optical enlarging unit used by editors to examine film.

voice-over. A narrator's commentary recorded for incorporation on a film's sound track.

weenie. An objectification of the hero's desire in simplistic films—and some not so simplistic. The thing sought: the jewels, the formula, the stolen money.

wild. Film shot or sound recorded with no synchronous relationship to each other.

wipe. A transitional optical effect in which one image appears to push another off the screen in any one of dozens of patterns.

workprint. A copy of film footage used in editing so that the original will not be damaged.

zoom. Simulation of camera movement toward or away from the subject, by means of a lens with variable focal length.

APPENDIX E

*Writers' Guild of America**

As mentioned in Chapter 16, the Writers' Guild of America is the scriptwriters' union, the organization that helps them establish working conditions and pay scales. The Guild's standards for admission are set forth in the information sheet reproduced here, along with a breakdown on the way credit for scripting employment is determined.

SCHEDULE OF UNITS OF CREDIT

Writers Guild of America Constitution and By-Laws
Article IV, Section 3, as amended 7/28-83

ONE UNIT
A series for which writer received "Created by" credit, **or**
Comedy-Variety Program: one unit per week of employment or one unit per show, whichever is more.

TWO UNITS
Story for theatrical motion picture short subject, **or**
Story for TV or radio program one-half hour or less.

THREE UNITS
Screenplay for theatrical motion picture short subject, **or**
Teleplay or radio play for program one-half hour or less, **or**
Television format or presentation for a new series.

FOUR UNITS
Story for one-hour TV or radio program.

*Courtesy of Writers Guild of America, west, Inc.

INFORMATION SHEET FOR ADMISSION TO THE WGA

The WGA represents writers primarily for the purpose of collective bargaining in its jurisdiction of screen, television and radio.

Membership entrance requirements are two (2) or more employments for writing services or sales of literary material or term or week-to-week employment; or a single employment for a theatrical screenplay, or two-hour teleplay, or two-hour radio play, or ninety (90) minute story and teleplay or ninety (90) minute story and radio play in the Guild's jurisdiction for an aggregate of twelve (12) Units of Credit as established by the WGA Constitution and Bylaws as amended July 28, 1983. A copy of the Units of Credit Schedule is on the reverse side of this information sheet. All employment or sales must have been during the two (2) years preceding application for membership and must be with a company or other entity that is signatory to the applicable WGA collective bargaining agreement. Options do not qualify as either employment or sales.

The initiation fee of $1,500.00 is payable only by Cashier's Check or by Money Order. All membership applications are to be supported by a copy of executed employment or sales contracts or other acceptable evidence of employment or sales.

We do not obtain employment or sales for writers nor do we refer or recommend members for writing assignments. We do not accept, evaluate or handle material for submission. Literary material should be submitted to a production company or through a literary agent.

Enclosed is a current list of our franchised agencies representing writers in fields under the Guild's jurisdiction. We regret that we cannot assist in finding, selecting or recommending an agent. We are also enclosing information on the Writers Guild Registration Service.

The Television Market List, featuring contact and submission information on current weekly prime-time television programs, is published monthly (except July and August) in the WGA Newsletter and is available to non-members at $2.50 (Two Dollars Fifty Cents) per issue or $20.00 (Twenty Dollars) for a yearly subscription. Please send your request with a check or money order to the WGA Newsletter, 8955 Beverly Blvd., Los Angeles, 90048.

We do not offer writing instruction or advice. For this information we suggest that you communicate with film schools, the state colleges, universities or with your local Board of Education.
Guild policy prevents us from disclosing the address or phone number of any Guild member. First Class correspondence may be addressed to a member in care of the Guild and will be promptly forwarded to members without a referral address such as an agent. Please contact the membership Department for further information.

FIVE UNITS

Story and teleplay or story and radio play one-half hour or less.

SIX UNITS

Story for 90-minute teleplay or radio play, **or**
One-hour teleplay or radio play, **or**
Comedy-variety special regardless of length.

EIGHT UNITS

Story for theatrical motion picture, **or**
Story for two-hour TV or radio program.

NINE UNITS

90-minute teleplay or radio play.

TEN UNITS

One-hour story and teleplay or story and radio play.

TWELVE UNITS

The following shall constitute two employments or sales and 12 units:
Screenplay for theatrical motion picture, **or**
Two-hour teleplay or two-hour radio play, **or**
90-minute story and teleplay or story and radio play.

Please note:

A rewrite is entitled to one-half the number of units allotted to its particular category.

A polish is entitled to one-quarter the number of units allotted to its particular category.

Where writers collaborate on the same project **each** shall be accorded the appropriate number of units for its category.

*   *   *

Since the Guild's pay scale changes with each new contract, the prices for theatrical/television scriptwriting given on page 401 are not necessarily those that will be in effect when this book appears. However, they'll give you an idea of the base rates prevailing from 1985 to 1988. It should be understood, of course, that these are base rates only. They set the minimum a writer may receive for a given type of script. In many cases the price negotiated for the individual writer by his agent will be markedly higher. Various modifications, too complex for discussion here, may also influence price in individual instances.

WGA 1985 THEATRICAL AND TELEVISION BASIC AGREEMENT
THEATRICAL COMPENSATION

EMPLOYMENT, FLAT DEALS	Effective 3/1/85 - 2/28/86		Effective 3/1/86 - 2/28/87		Effective 3/1/87 - 2/29/88	
	LOW	HIGH	LOW	HIGH	LOW	HIGH
A. Screenplay, Including Treatment	$22,801	$42,400	$24,169	$44,944	$25,740/25,619	$47,865/47,641
Installments:						
Delivery of Treatment	8,549	13,032	9,062	13,814	9,651/9,606	14,712/14,643
Delivery of First Draft Screenplay	10,259	19,549	10,875	20,722	11,582/11,528	22,069/21,965
Delivery of Final Draft Screenplay	3,993	9,819	4,232	10,408	4,507/4,485	11,084/11,033
B. Screenplay, Excluding Treatment	14,249	29,320	15,104	31,079	16,086/16,010	33,099/32,944
Installments:						
Delivery of First Draft Screenplay	10,259	19,549	10,875	20,722	11,582/11,528	22,069/21,965
Delivery of Final Draft Screenplay	3,990	9,771	4,229	10,357	4,504/4,482	11,030/10,979
C. Additional Compensation for Story Included in Screenplay	3,260	6,516	3,456	6,907	3,681/3,663	7,356/7,321
D. Story or Treatment	8,549	13,032	9,062	13,814	9,651/9,606	14,712/14,643
E. Original Treatment	11,806	19,549	12,514	20,722	13,327/13,265	22,069/21,965
F. First Draft Screenplay, With or Without Option For Final Draft Screenplay						
First Draft Screenplay	10,259	19,549	10,875	20,722	11,582/11,528	22,069/21,965
Final Draft Screenplay	6,839	13,032	7,249	13,814	7,720/7,684	14,712/14,643
G. Rewrite of Screenplay	8,549	13,032	9,062	13,814	9,651/9,606	14,712/14,643
H. Polish of Screenplay	4,276	6,516	4,533	6,907	4,828/4,805	7,356/7,321

LOW BUDGET - Photoplay costing less than $2,500,000
HIGH BUDGET - Photoplay costing $2,500,000 or more

WRITERS GUILD
REGISTRATION
SERVICE

WRITERS GUILD OF AMERICA, WEST, INC.
8955 BEVERLY BOULEVARD
LOS ANGELES, CA 90048-2456
PHONE: 213/205-2541

PURPOSE

The Guild's Registration Service has been set up to assist members and non-members in establishing the completion date and the identity of their literary property written for the fields of theatrical motion pictures, television and radio.

THE GUILD DOES NOT ACCEPT BOOK MANU-SCRIPTS, STAGE PLAYS, MUSIC, LYRICS, PHO-TOS, DRAWINGS OR ARTICLES OF PUBLIC RECORD FOR FILING.

VALUE

Registration does not confer any statutory protection, it merely provides evidence of the writer's claim to authorship of the literary material involved and of the date of its completion. A writer has certain rights under the law the moment the work is completed. It is therefore important that the date of completion be legally established. The Registration Office does not make comparisons of registration deposits to determine similarity between works, nor does it give legal opinions or advice.

COVERAGE

Since the value of registration is merely to supply evidence, it cannot protect what the law does not protect. Registration with the Guild does not protect titles (neither does registration with the United States Copyright Office).

PROCEDURE FOR DEPOSIT   One (1) 8½ × 11 unbound (no brads, staples, etc.) copy is required for deposit in the Guild files.

When it is received the property is sealed in a Guild Registration Envelope, timed and dated. A receipt is returned. Notice of registration shall consist of the following wording: REGISTERED WGAw NO. ___ and be applied upon the title page or the page immediately following. Scripts specifically intended for radio, television and theatrical motion pictures are registrable as are television series formats, step outlines and storylines. The specific field of writing and the proper writing credits should be noted on the title page. Each property must be registered separately (exception: three (3) episodes, skits or sketches for an existing series may be deposited as a single registration). Be sure that the name under which you register is your full legal name. The use of pseudonyms, pen names, initials or familiar forms of a proper name may require proof of identity if you want to recover the material left on deposit.

FEES $5.00 for members of WGAw and WGAe
$10.00 for non-members

THE FEE MUST ACCOMPANY THE MATERIAL THAT IS TO BE REGISTERED.

COPYRIGHT The Guild does not have a copyright service. For forms and instructions call: 202/287-9100.

DURATION Material deposited for registration after September 1, 1982 is valid for a term of five (5) years; material deposited for registration prior to September 1, 1982 is valid for a term of ten (10) years. You may renew the registration for an additional ten (10) year or five (5) year term, whichever is applicable, at the then current registration fee. You authorize the Guild to destroy the material without notice to you on the expiration of the term of registration if renewal is not made. The fee should accompany the request for renewal.

PROCEDURE FOR WITHDRAWAL The registration copy left on deposit cannot be returned to the writer without defeating the purpose of registration, the point being that evidence should be available, if necessary, that the material has been in the Guild's charge since the date of deposit.

However, if the writer finds it necessary to have the copy returned, at least forty-eight (48) hours notice of intended withdrawal must be given to the Guild. A manuscript will be given up only on the signature(s) of the writer(s). If the registration is in the names of more than one person, the written consent of all is required to authorize withdrawal. In case a registrant is deceased, proof of death and the consent of his representative or heirs must be presented. In no event, except under these provisions, shall any of the material be allowed to be taken from the Guild office unless a court order has been acquired.

If any person other than the writer named in the registration shall request confirmation of registration, the registration number and/or date of deposit, to see either the material deposited, the registration envelope or any other material, such request shall be denied unless authorization from the writer(s) or a court order is presented in connection therewith.

LOCATION OF REGISTRATION OFFICE

8955 BEVERLY BOULEVARD
LOS ANGELES, CA 90048

(corner of Almont Drive, one block east of Doheny Drive)

HOURS   10 A.M.–12 NOON
               2 P.M.–5 P.M.   MONDAY thru FRIDAY

APPENDIX F

*Writers' Guild of Great Britain**

Open to writers of motion picture and television scripts contracted by independent producers in the United Kingdom, the Writer's Guild of Great Britain (WGGB) acts as a collective bargainer for its members and maintains standard scriptwriting business procedures for the industry. It is affiliated with the Writer's Guild of America East and West, the English Canadian Guild ACTRA, the French Canadian Guild SARDEC, the Australian Guild, and the New Zealand Guild. The WGGB has established an agreement with The British Film and Television Producers Association (BFTPA) and The Independent Programme Producers Association (IPPA) for work in these areas. The agreement resolves such issues as minimum payment levels, contracts, the responsibilities of the contracted writer, the writer's rights, and screen credits.

For information on the Guild's activities or becoming a member, contact the Writer's Guild of Great Britain at 430 Edgware Road, London W2 1EH, England. Copies of the standard agreement and the standard contract based on this agreement may be purchased from the Guild.

The following schedule of minimum fees and use payments and accompanying definitions, drawn from the WGGB's agreement with producers, indicates what a scriptwriter working in Great Britain might expect. This schedule will periodically be renegotiated by the WGGB and BFTPA/IPPA.

DEFINITIONS

In this Agreement the following terms and expressions shall have the following meaning unless the context otherwise requires:

*Courtesy of Writers' Guild of Great Britain.

i) *Writer*
Subject to the provisions of Clauses 14, 15 and 16 hereof
Writer shall mean a Member of the Writers' Guild of Great
Britain and where the services of a writer are provided by a
company, Writer shall include where appropriate the company which provided those services. Where a joint writing
team is involved the payment shall be divided as agreed between them.

ii) *Treatment* (See also Notes to Schedule)
An outline or synopsis in narrative form of an entire story
indicating the fuller structure and development and char-
acterisation of the plot.

iii) *First Draft*
The first draft shall mean the full development of the treatment or in its absence a definition in terms of visual action
and dialogue suitable as a production for cinema and/or television exhibition.

iv) *Second Draft*
The second complete draft of the screenplay as requested by
the Associate, which, if accepted, shall become the script as
next defined.

v) *Principal Photography Script*
The approved and finally accepted version of a shooting
script for principal photography with individual scenes, camera shots and full dialogue incorporating all alterations and
amendments required by the Associate.

vi) *Television Series and Serials*
Two or more television productions made in succession each
either with a character or characters common to each all
having either a continuous theme and/or basic format or
situation.

vii) *Theatrical Distribution*
Release in any cinemas throughout the world.

viii) *Free Television*
Dissemination by any means through state or commercially
owned corporations or companies which does not require
payment by the viewer for the programme service or payment
only for a state or similar broadcasting licence.

ix) *Pay Television*
Pay television shall be deemed to mean those systems for
which the subscriber pays directly for each programme or

for a defined service. It shall not include basic cable where this is used for relay purposes in free television.

x) *Videogram*
A videogram shall be deemed to mean any form of videodisc or cassette offered for sale or rental to the general public for viewing in the home.

xi) *Non-theatric Use*
The initial payment for either cinema or television use shall cover non-theatric use throughout the world.

BFTPA/IPPA/AND WRITERS GUILD

SCHEDULE OF MINIMUM FEES AND USE PAYMENTS
to date from 11 March 1985

SECTION 1: HIGHER BUDGET FEATURE FILMS WITH A PRO-DUCTION BUDGET IN EXCESS OF £1,500,000

Treatment

Commencement Payment	£2,500
Acceptance Payment	£1,500

First Draft

Commencement Payment	£4,000
Delivery Payment	£4,000

Second Draft

Commencement Payment	£2,000
Delivery Payment	£2,000

Principal Photography Payment   £4,000
(to be made within seven days of start of
principal photography)

TOTAL MINIMUM PAYMENT   **£20,000**

Payments for Free Television Uses

UK Television (5 TX's over 7 years)	£6,666.66
US Network (Prime-time)	£10,000
US Network (Non Prime-time)	£1,666.66
US All other	£1,666.66
Rest of the World	£5,000

Payments for Pay Television Uses
HBO	£5,000
All Other World-wide	£1,666.66

Payments for Videogram Use   £2,500

NOTES:

1. **All the above use fees are at scale (i:e minimum always applies).**

2. *Treatment* should be delivered within the time agreed and the producer should have 30 days to consider and request any revisions. Such revisions should be completed within 14 days and the producer should signify acceptance or rejection within a similar period.

3. *Acceptance of treatment* means that the producer is satisfied that any necessary revisions have been completed to requirements.

4. *Rejection of treatment:*
   i) where the writer has supplied an original treatment rejection of it means that the rights therein revert to the writer in full. The only payment to be made is for commencement.

   ii) where the writer has supplied a treatment based on an idea or format provided by the producer all rights remain with and vest in the producer. The payments to be made are for both commencement and acceptance.

5. *If no treatment is required* the full appropriate payment including that for a treatment will be made in the following way. The commencement payment for the treatment shall be added to the first draft commencement payment and the treatment acceptance payment will be added to the first draft delivery payment.

6. *Payments* at all the stages from treatment to completion set out above are negotiable above the minimum and copyright only passes to the producer at each stage of payment as and when these occur.

7. *Cut-offs* apply at each stage from treatment to completion. If a writer has delivered at all stages then the principal photography payment apply as and when due.

8. *UK Television Use*
   Once UK television uses purchased over a period of seven years from the date of first transmission have elapsed each further transmission on UK television may be purchased by payment of 20 per cent of the current scale fee for that use.

9. *Disagreements* arising on the above would be dealt with through the disputes procedure.

SECTION 2:　A. LOWER BUDGET FEATURE FILMS
　　　　　　　B. ALL SINGLE TELEVISION MOVIES

A: LOWER BUDGET FEATURE FILMS
(having a production budget of £1,500,000 or less)

Treatment	
Commencement Payment	£1,000
Acceptance Payment	£1,000
First Draft	
Commencement Payment	£2,750
Delivery Payment	£2,750
Second Draft	
Commencement Payment	£1,000
Delivery Payment	£1,000
Principal Photography Payments	£2,500
(to be made within seven days of start of principal photography)	

TOTAL MINIMUM PAYMENT	**£12,000**

Payments for Free Television Uses	
UK Television (5 TX's over 7 years)	£4,000
US Network (Prime-time)	£7,500
US Network (Non Prime-time)	£1,500
US all other	£1,000
Rest of World	£2,000
Payments for Pay Television Uses	
HBO	£2,500
All Other World-wide	£1,000
Payment for Videogram Use	£1,000

NOTES:

1. **All the above use fees are at scale (i:e minimum always applies).**

2. *Treatment* should be delivered within the time agreed and the producer should have 30 days to consider and request any revisions. Such revisions should be completed within 14 days and the producer should signify acceptance or rejection within a similar period.

3. *Acceptance of treatment* means that the producer is satisfied that any necessary revisions have been completed to requirements.

4. *Rejection of treatment:*

   i) where the writer has supplied an original treatment rejection of it means that the rights therein revert to the writer in full. The only payment to be made is for commencement.

   ii) where the writer has supplied a treatment based on an idea or format provided by the producer all rights remain with and vest in the producer. The payments to be made are for both commencement and acceptance.

5. *If no treatment is required* the full appropriate payment including that for a treatment will be made in the following way. The commencement payment for the treatment shall be added to the first draft commencement payment and the treatment acceptance payment will be added to the first draft delivery payment.

6. *Payments* at all the stages from treatment to completion set out above are negotiable above the minimum and copyright only passes to the producer at each stage of payment as and when these occur.

7. *Cut-offs* apply at each stage from treatment to completion. If a writer has delivered at all stages then the principal photography payment shall apply as and when due.

8. *UK Television Use*
   Once a UK television uses purchased over a period of seven years from the date of first transmission have elapsed each further transmission on UK television may be purchased by payment of 20 per cent of the current scale fee for that use.

9. *Disagreements* arising on the above would be dealt with through the disputes procedure.

B: ALL SINGLE TELEVISION MOVIES SCREENED ON THE SAME DAY

Note: The figures set out below refer to productions on film or tape of 90 minutes duration. For productions of more or less than 90 minutes the script fee shall be pro-rated appropriately.

Treatment

Commencement Payment	£1,000
Acceptance Payment	£1,000

First Draft

Commencement Payment	£2,750
Delivery Payment	£2,750

Second Draft
Commencement Payment   £1,000
Delivery Payment   £1,000

Principal Photography Payment   £2,500
(to be made within seven days of start of
principal photography)

TOTAL MINIMUM PAYMENT   **£12,000**

Note: This minimum payment covers two free television transmissions
       in the UK and a theatrical release in the UK over a period of
       three months in not more than ten cinemas which shall not be
       all in the same circuit. This limited theatrical release shall take
       place within six months either side of the first television trans-
       mission in the UK.

Payments for Further Free Television Uses
UK Television 3rd and each showing thereafter   £2,000
US Network (Prime Time)   £7,500
US Network (Non Prime Time)   £1,500
US All other   £2,000
Rest of World   £2,000

Payments for Pay Television Uses
HBO   £2,500
All Other World-wide   £1,000

Payment for Videogram Use   £1,000

Theatrical
USA   Negotiable
Rest of the World   £1,000
UK (Full)   Negotiable

NOTES:

1. All the above use fees are at scale (**i:e minimum always applies**).

2. *Treatment* should be delivered within the time agreed and the producer should have 30 days to consider and request any revisions.
   Such revisions should be completed within 14 days and the producer
   should signify acceptance or rejection within a similar period.

3. *Acceptance of treatment* means that the producer is satisfied that any
   necessary revisions have been completed to requirements.

4. *Rejection of treatment:*
   i) where the writer has supplied an original treatment rejection of it means that the rights therein revert to the writer in full. The only payment to be made is for commencement.

   ii) where the writer has supplied a treatment based on an idea or format provided by the producer all rights remain with and vest in the producer. The payments to be made are for both commencement and acceptance.

5. *If no treatment is required* the full appropriate payment including that for a treatment will be made in the following way. The commencement payment for the treatment shall be added to the first draft commencement payment and the treatment acceptance payment will be added to the first draft delivery payment.

6. *Payments* at all the stages from treatment to completion set out above are negotiable above the minimum and copyright does not pass to the producer until all stage payments have been made as and when they occur.

7. *Cut-offs* apply at each stage from treatment to completion. If a writer has delivered at all stages then the principal photography payment shall apply as and when due.

8. *Disagreements* arising on the above would be dealt with through the disputes procedure.

SECTION 3:   TELEVISION SERIES AND SERIALS AS DEFINED
             WITH FORMAT PROVIDED BY THE PRODUCER

Note:
The figures set out below refer to productions on film or tape of 60 minute duration. For productions of more or less than one hour the script fee shall be pro-rated.

Treatment	25%	£1,062.50
First Draft when commissioned	25%	£1,062.50
First Draft when delivered	25%	£1,062.50
Final Draft when accepted	25%	£1,062.50
TOTAL MINIMUM PAYMENT		**£4,250**

Payments for Free Television Uses

United Kingdom:

First Repeat	75%
Second Repeat	50%
Third and each subsequent repeat	25%

United States:

US Network Prime Time	100%
US Network Non Prime Time	50%
US All Other	25%

*Rest of the World 100%

*For fiction on film or tape this use of the Rest of the World has to be purchased at the time of principal photography. For other programmes the 100% becomes payable as and when the first overseas sale has been made.

Payment for Pay Television Use
World-Wide 20%

Payment for Videogram Use 7½%

Notes:

1. *Disagreements* arising on the above would be dealt with through the disputes procedure.

2. *If no treatment is required* the full appropriate payment including that for a treatment will be made in two installments of 37½ per cent.

3. *Rest of the World Free Television Use Payment* includes theatrical and non-theatrical exploitation excluding the USA and the UK.

4. *Payments* at all the stages from treatment to completion set out above are negotiable above the minimum and copyright does not pass to the producer until all stage payments have been made as and when they occur.

5. *Cut-offs* apply at each stage from treatment to completion.

6. *Twice-Weekly serials* are not covered under the above proposals.

7. *Payment for Free UK Television Use after seven years from date of first transmission*

   Payment for each UK free television transmission which take place after the elapse of seven year from the date of the first UK transmission shall be made according to the following formula:

   25 per cent of *actual personal rate of script* × *current minimum rate.* ÷ *minimum rate at time of contract.*

8. The above payments are for established writers who shall be defined as those who have been commissioned to write screenplays of any type with an aggregate slot length transmission time of not less than two hours.

Index